D1707320

Canterbury, Christ Church Cathedral. *The Sower among Thorns and on Good Ground.* From the sixth typological window, last quarter of the twelfth century. Photograph: Victoria and Albert Museum, London, reproduced by kind permission of the Dean and Chapter of Canterbury.

Stained Glass before 1540
an annotated bibliography

A
Reference Publication in
ART HISTORY
Herbert L. Kessler, Editor

Stained Glass before 1540
an annotated bibliography

MADELINE HARRISON CAVINESS

with the assistance of
EVELYN RUTH STAUDINGER

REFERENCE PUBLICATIONS
IN
ART HISTORY
G. K. Hall & Co., 70 Lincoln Street, Boston, Massachusetts

Library of Congress Cataloging in Publication Data

Caviness, Madeline Harrison, 1938-
  Stained glass before 1540.

  (A Reference publication in art history)
  Bibliography: p.
  Includes index.
  1. Glass painting and staining, Medieval—Bibliography.
I. Staudinger, Evelyn Ruth. II. Title. III. Series.
Z5956.G5C38 1983 [NK5308]   016.74859′02   82-15629
ISBN 0-8161-8332-5

This publication is printed on permanent/durable acid-free paper
MANUFACTURED IN THE UNITED STATES OF AMERICA

To the memory of my father
ERIC VERNON HARRISON
1894-1982

Contents

The Author

Madeline Harrison Caviness is Professor in and Chairman of the Fine Arts Department of Tufts University in Medford, Massachusetts, where she has taught medieval art and architecture for ten years. She was born in London, England, in 1938 and has a B.A. from Cambridge University. At the Sorbonne she researched stained glass under the direction of the late Louis Grodecki and Jean Lafond, and later she enrolled in the doctoral program of Harvard University, where she received her Ph.D. degree in 1970. Her publications include many articles on medieval art; her first book, <u>The Early Stained Glass of Canterbury Cathedral, ca. 1175-1220</u>, written while she was a Fellow of the Radcliffe Institute, received the John Nicholas Brown Prize of the Medieval Academy in 1981. Her second book, the <u>Corpus Vitrearum</u> volume for Canterbury, was published later that year. Dr. Caviness is a Fellow of the Society of Antiquaries of London and currently serves on the Council of the Medieval Academy of America and the Board of Directors of the International Center of Medieval Art.

Preface

This bibliography was selected and annotated with several purposes in mind; it is intended as a useful research tool for those who may have an interest in the stained glass of a particular monument, and also as a guide for teachers selecting readings for advanced courses, such as seminars. It will also aid the general reader in finding basic works that provide an introduction to the field; these are designated as such and can be found most easily by looking in the more recent sections of the general bibliography, or under the country of interest.

In compiling such a work, many decisions have been made as to scope, organization, and selection. I decided to include the earliest painted glass fragments that may have been used in windows and to exclude painted glasses made for some other purpose, such as the Early Christian gold glasses that were either set in a wall or formed part of a vessel. I have also excluded colored glasses cut and set into decorative patterns, whether from the early period in the West or from the Islamic tradition.[1] In fact the number of published fragments of stained and painted window glass that have been dated before the twelfth century is quite small.[2]

The decision to extend the bibliography to include glass up to about 1540 needs explanation; evidently much of this glass is no longer medieval in style, since Italian Renaissance forms permeated even French glass painting by about 1530. It may be justified, on the one hand, by the fact that glass paintings of the fifteenth and sixteenth centuries have seldom been included in studies of painting; it is hoped that the entries appearing here will serve specialists in those periods. On the other hand, the glass painters of this later era were still working with essentially the same techniques as the glaziers of the Gothic cathedrals. In the middle decades of the sixteenth century, however, there was a decline in the production of monumental glass. Introduction of enamels as surface colorants, in the place of glasses that were colored through, transformed the appearance of small panels. I decided, therefore, not to include the extensive literature on these small enameled panels, most of which were produced in Switzerland from about 1540 on.

Preface

A bibliography covering the glass of all European countries and
Byzantium and dealing with such a long chronological span has to be
divided into manageable sections, most of which are geographical.
The modern political unit is used, and modern boundaries have decided
the position of works from a given monument; for instance, Strasbourg
is placed under France, not Germany. Countries in which there is
less glass preserved, such as Spain and Portugal, Belgium and Holland,
are grouped together under the Iberian peninsula and the Low Countries, respectively. A number of regions that have very little glass,
including Byzantium, are grouped together at the end.

Many studies of glass cut across geographical boundaries. An
introductory section includes general histories of stained glass.
Although most authors show some chauvinistic bias, there are a number
of general historical outlines that purport to deal with stained
glass in all regions. Some of these date from the nineteenth century; they tend to emphasize composition and ornament above figure
style, but are sometimes extremely useful for the relationships indicated between different regions across national boundaries. For
instance, N.H.J. Westlake, one of the outstanding pioneers of our
field, perceived important relationships between English and French
glass in the 1880s.[3] Indeed, many of the more detailed studies that
followed were too narrowly based; works such as Hans Wentzel's
Meisterwerke der Glasmalerei, or the superb collective publication
Le vitrail français, take too little account of foreign influences
and internationalism.[4] It is thus rather encouraging to see at least
one new work that attempts to deal with the main trends and currents
and regionalism of a single period, that is Louis Grodecki's Le
vitrail roman.[5] At the time of his death in March 1982, Grodecki was
preparing a similarly broad treatment of Gothic glass; it will be
carried to completion by Catherine Brisac.

The three following sections also treat glass that was produced
in a wide variety of sites. Section II deals with techniques used by
the medieval glazier, ranging from preparatory drawing, the making of
glass, cutting and leading, to painting and firing the glass, and
with technical studies that have revealed the ingredients of glass
and paint. Furthermore, such technical studies are often the concern
of the conservator, and a considerable recent bibliography on problems of conservation and restoration finds its place here. This section thus moves from the medieval technical treatises, through the
studies of medieval techniques by nineteenth-century glass painters,
to the twentieth-century analytic studies, with conservation in mind;
it would not have been possible to divide these three areas. In
selecting from the significant recent literature on technical aspects,
I have kept in mind the preeeminence of art historical interest for
our uses. This seems justified, particularly since there is an excellent annotated bibliography by Roy Newton which surveys the field
through 1973.[6] In 1972 the News Letter of the Technical Subcommittee
for the Corpus Vitrearum Medii Aevi, which presents up to date summaries of technical studies, began publication. Interested readers

are also referred to the "Checklist of Recently Published Articles
and Books on Glass" which appears annually in the Journal of Glass
Studies and to the German equivalent in Glastechnische Berichte. It
is worth noting in this connection, however, that the technical study
of painted glass has very much lagged behind the study of blown
glasses, especially those from antiquity, and the conservation problems are by no means identical.

The third section also cuts across national boundaries and deals
with stained glass in collections and sales. By presenting these
items together, we can gain an overview of the history of collecting
stained glass, which has some historical interest in itself. It is
notable that while the Protestant iconoclasm of the sixteenth century
resulted in great losses of medieval glass, the vandalism that oc-
curred during the secularization of French and German churches around
1800 caused some church windows to enter the collectors' market. In
fact this is an early date for appreciation of Gothic works in the
face of the neoclassical movement, and the activities of a dealer
such as Christopher Hampp, who operated between the Continent and
England very early in the nineteenth century, take on added poig-
nancy. Catalogs of collections have also been included in this section with sales catalogs; in fact there is some shading off between
the two categories, since a sales catalog may masquerade as the catalog of a collection (as in Maurice Drake's luxurious production on
the Costessey collection in 1920).[7] I have also included the modern
catalogs of museum collections, which begin remarkably early with the
important publication of the Berlin Museum's collections by Schmitz
in 1913. Related to these are review articles that deal with recent
acquisitions or with selected items from a collection. I have, however, eliminated many brief articles that deal only with the date and
provenance of a single piece, as these may be found through the
museum's files, but if a major contribution is made to the study of
German glass, for instance, the article may be included in that section, and the name of the museum will be found in the index.

Exhibitions of stained glass have been presented separately in
Section IV; included here are both specialized exhibits, which have
been few in number, and exhibitions of a general nature where an
important quantity of stained glass was included with objects such
as manuscripts, sculpture, and metal work. Some interesting statis-
tics emerge here that indicate the extent to which scholarly interest
in stained glass has lagged behind that in other media and perhaps
relate to the difficulty of shipping and installing glass in temporary
exhibitions. It is notable that the exhibition "Arts of the Middle
Ages" held at the Boston Museum of Fine Arts in 1940 contained no
stained glass at all, an oversight that scarcely seems possible when
one considers that every other medium was represented, including
monumental stone sculpture.[8] Even in France the first exhibition
that was devoted solely to medieval stained glass took place in Paris
in 1953; in America the first such exhibition was held in 1972.

During the past two decades it has been encouraging to see stained glass represented in the major medieval exhibitions, with the catalog entries and scholarly introductions written by specialists in the field.

The advantages of presenting the material within each of these sections chronologically are manifest. Not only is it easy to scan the most recent literature, but it is also possible to gain a general impression of the historiography of the field. I have purposely included most of the major early studies dating from the eighteenth and nineteenth centuries. These were often written by glass painters who, during the craft revival, interested themselves in the history of their own medium, in much the same way that Renaissance artists such as Ghiberti and Vasari studied the history of art.[9] Notable in this category are Charles Winston in England who, although a lawyer by profession, is said to have been a skilled glass painter; Pierre Le Vieil in France; and Josef Ludwig Fischer in Germany.[10] John Knowles continued the tradition in England in the first part of this century, and Gottfried Frenzel and J.-J. Gruber are living exponents of it in Germany and France.[11] In connection with the nineteenth-century revival of glass painting, specialized journals were created. Two were short-lived: the French Journal de la peinture sur verre was issued between 1896 and 1898, when it was renamed L'art sacré, and the German Zeitschrift für alte und neue Glasmalerei und verwandte Gebiete: Offizielles Organ des Verbandes deutscher Glasmalereien was produced in Munich and Leipzig between 1912 and 1915. Two other "trade journals" have continued to the present day: in England the Journal of the British Society of Master Glass-Painters has been published since 1924, and in the United States, Stained Glass: A Quarterly Devoted to the Craft of Painted and Stained Glass has been produced since 1907. These journals have generally been aimed at a reading public of practicing glass painters, and the extent of historical research presented is very limited. J.L. Fischer wrote extensively for the Zeitschrift, but a full version generally appeared elsewhere; articles of 1913, for instance, overlap with chapters in his Handbuch. The British journal has perhaps been the most serious of these four, particularly in its early years. Another journal that deserves mention alongside L'art sacré is Liturgical Arts; for instance, this contained a useful "Brief, Annotated Bibliography on Stained Glass" under the name of Theophilus in 1937; the author in fact was Orin E. Skinner, a glass painter in the Connick atelier in Boston.[12]

In the early period, learned societies such as the Société archéologique of France and the Archaeological Institute of Great Britain also interested themselves in stained glass and gave the field the archeological bias that it has to some extent continued to manifest. The nineteenth-century volumes of the Congrès archéologique, for example, contain brief presentations of windows in the context of church architecture, and questions of condition and restoration are raised. Similar studies appeared in Austria.

Monographic treatments also appeared early; the great volumes of the pères Cahier and Martin on the early glass of Bourges Cathedral were published in 1841, the same year as the first monograph on a medieval building.[13] These nineteenth-century volumes were usually illustrated with engravings from watercolors; the production of these drawings had gone along with the nineteenth-century craft revival and with the restoration of church windows. Drawings by glass painters both served the function of pre-restoration records and provided training for the neo-Gothic painters. Some albums of original drawings and tracings are preserved, and I have included a few of the more important collections under each country.[14] These are often invaluable to the present-day art historian because they accurately represent the state of the glass before nineteenth-century restorations and, sometimes, twentieth-century war damage. Photographic archives, which began to develop at the turn of the century, are also invaluable for this reason, but it has not been possible to include them here.

Stained glass is particularly vulnerable to breakage. Because broken glass was often replaced, specialists in our field have become more and more acutely concerned with problems of authenticity. It is for this reason that many of the early publications are extremely valuable; a parallel is found in the study of architecture, but such concerns are less pressing for the student of panel painting or manuscripts. This concern, and the vulnerability of medieval glass, led in the 1950s to the planning of a complete inventory of extant glass, to be published under the title Corpus Vitrearum Medii Aevi. These volumes, which have now been produced for at least a part of the glass preserved in most European countries, document as completely as possible the amount of restoration in each panel, and deal objectively with questions of date and iconography. Unfortunately such complete studies are extremely difficult to produce and require great expertise; ideally the glass is examined when it is down in ateliers for restoration.[15] Progress on these inventories, and the proceedings of biannual colloquia, have been reported from time to time in the periodical literature.[16] The existence of the Corpus volumes seems to be the only way to break away from the parochialism that has dominated the field. Unfortunately, whereas painting on glass should be included in the history of painting on an equal footing with painting on panels, walls, and parchment, it has tended to remain a separate study. One impediment to such integration, surely, has been the fear of non-specialists to select examples in glass, lest they turn out to be nineteenth-century reproductions. Only one modern survey of the history of painting has included stained glass as a major form of painting; it was coauthored by Florens Deuchler, whose doctoral dissertation dealt with the glass of Laon.[17] But history weighs heavily in a field such as this, and one has to note with regret that even the cataloging system devised by libraries since the nineteenth century has relegated stained glass to the category of decorative arts and crafts, and that works on this form of painting are mingled on the shelves with works on blown and molded glass vessels.

Beginning from the 1880s there have, however, been studies of glass that deal with the medium as one would treat any other in art history. It was from that period that the professional periodicals in Germany began to include important articles on stained glass, and it may be significant that the German term Glasmalerei (glass painting) places the medium on a level with panel painting or wall painting; it avoids the connotation of a decorative art implied by vitrail, and equally by stained glass.[18] Early studies in Germany addressed the standard art historical problems of attribution, provenance for pieces and collections, date, and iconography. At the turn of the century one encounters a high appreciation of the styles of the great artists of the early sixteenth century as manifested in various ways in glass.[19] This has naturally led to refinement of the observations and arguments used in making attributions; concerns which have continued to be prominent in the literature include the definition of the oeuvre of Peter Hemmel von Andlau and the relation between a designer such as Dürer and a workshop, such as the Hirsvogel atelier, that executed his windows.[20] More important for the field, since it goes beyond the minutiae of connoisseurship, was a pioneering article by Hans Wentzel in 1949 that addressed itself to the intimate relationship between the illumination of manuscripts, the decoration of walls, and the painting of windows in the Romanesque and Gothic periods.[21] In its breadth of scope it complements an equally important article of the previous year by Louis Grodecki that attempted to trace an atelier tradition across regional boundaries, from Poitiers and Bourges to Chartres.[22]

Connoisseurship was not the only art historical approach that was applied to the study of glass by German scholars. The Wölfflinian concepts of formal analysis influenced studies of composition published by August Schmarsow in 1916 and 1919, and Wölfflin's pupil Paul Frankl attempted in his last published work to solve the problem of the chronology of glazing at Chartres by applying terms that he had evolved to distinguish Romanesque and Gothic.[23] Alois Riegl was no doubt influential in a reevaluation of aesthetic judgments about early glass and the craft aspects of glass paintings;[24] both Heinrich Oidtmann in 1912 and Joseph Ludwig Fischer in 1914 wrote histories of glass painting from these broadened perspectives.[25] In 1937 Mathias Engels examined the reasons for separating glass studies from the history of painting and included among them the extent to which technique influences form in stained glass.[26] Louis Grodecki later reversed this argument by suggesting that the firm contours and brilliant non-naturalistic colors that are among the salient features of "Gothic" painting in all media resulted from the ascendency of glass in the thirteenth century.[27]

In France, where Grodecki trained under Henri Focillon, we have seen that there was also a strong archeological tradition. The other great French strength--going back to Cahier and Martin's work on Bourges--was the study of iconography. Émile Mâle acknowledged the importance of stained glass in his three-volume study of the iconography of French medieval art, published between 1898 and 1922; he also contributed chapters on glass painting to André Michel's general history of art. His student was Jean Lafond, one of the most prolific and far-sighted of the scholars who have specialized in the study of glass in this century; Lafond's work ranged over attribution problems in sixteenth-century glass, the history of techniques, the reconstruction of programs from fragments, and the reevaluation of the importance of glass painting in France in the fourteenth century.[28] He collaborated with Louis Grodecki on several major publications, including Le vitrail français and the first Corpus volume for France.

Despite the charge of historical chauvinism made earlier, Le vitrail français included chapters of general import that have given it a lasting place in twentieth-century glass studies. One of these, by Grodecki, reviewed theological attitudes to the material of glass and concluded that it was seen as an almost mystical substance through which the light of God passed in order to illuminate the interior of the church and the minds of men. This neo-Platonic function remained a belief until the end of the Middle Ages. There is very little doubt that in any medieval hierarchy of media, glass would be placed ahead of such base materials as plastered walls and sculptured stone. This seems to be borne out by the seriousness of subject matter one encounters; the borders of windows are scarcely ever filled with satirical or inconsequential subject matters, in contrast to those of manuscripts. It is thus not surprising that Jean Lafond could claim a place for the fourteenth-century windows of Saint-Ouen in Rouen at least alongside, and perhaps in advance of, the miniatures of Jean Pucelle.[29] Baltrušaitis has charmingly referred to some of the thirteenth-century manuscript pages, where geometric frames and decorative grounds so resemble stained glass windows, as "vitraux de poche."[30] Recent research has not only indicated important links between contemporary windows and manuscripts but has also shown the intimate connections between a great theologian who was an incumbent of the church and a window program he devised.[31]

Modern scholarship in glass painting is still in the hands of a relatively small number of specialists because of the expertise that is required to decide questions of authenticity. The methods and approaches scholars of glass use otherwise differ little from those of other medieval art historians. Our concerns include style, date, authorship, iconography, patronage, and the theological and social contexts for the work of art. The medieval field as a whole has always been so diversified that it is hard to perceive clear trends such as the movement away from formalism and toward contextual studies that has recently emerged in other fields.

In closing, something should be said of the methods used in collecting and selecting the bibliography. I would certainly not claim that the process of collection was exhaustive. In part I have relied on my own bibliography cards, amassed during twenty years or so of research, reading and teaching. The cards were supplemented by a very thorough screening of all the entries dealing with stained glass of the period that were included in the Chicago Art Index (1907-29), the Art Index since 1929, the Répertoire d'art et d'archéologie since 1910, and the Répertoire international de la litérature de l'art (RILA) since 1975. A general bibliography of glass by George Sang Duncan was also systematically searched for items dealing with stained glass;[32] both this and the lists of publications found in the Journal of the British Society of Master Glass-Painters in its early decades included a great deal of English material not represented in the Répertoire or the Art Index. For early French material the catalogs of the Forney and Duplessis Libraries in Paris are useful; the latter in particular, has a great many entries for the nineteenth century, only some of which are included here.[33] For the Germanic material the most useful source was the "Bibliographie zur deutschen Glasmalerei des Mittelalters" prepared by Rüdiger Becksmann for the Deutsche Verein für Kunstwissenschaft in Stuttgart in 1974, and his three-part supplement of 1975 on Alsace, Austria, and Switzerland.[34] In addition, Elisabeth Melczer combed the Kunsthistorisches Institut in Florence for some of the early German literature and for doctoral dissertations in German. I have also searched the Internationale Bibliographie der Kunstwissenschaft for the years 1902-1918, the Bibliographie zur Kunst und Kunstgeschichte for 1945-1957, the Bibliographie der Kunst in Bayern, 1973, and Bibliographie: Bildende Kunst, 1974 and 1975. The early sales catalogs might have been supplemented by a thorough search of the compendia by Frits Lugt and Algernon Graves; this would have been an extremely time-consuming project since the indexes do not aid in identifying sales of stained glass.[35] It has also been noted above that a systematic search was not made for nineteenth-century albums of watercolors. Entries for glass painters in standard biographical reference works, such as Thieme and Becker, Allgemeines Lexikon der bildenden Künstler, and the Neue deutsche Biographie, are not included in the bibliography, though they were searched for further references.

The most difficult task was the selection; a large amount of material was screened out, almost always on the basis of firsthand examination. The decision was not necessarily based on a uniform standard of quality, but on variables such as the rarity of the subject and the importance of the windows treated; the very large bibliography on Chartres windows has been rigorously screened, whereas the only publication on the fragmentary glass of some small parish church has been included even if it presents no more than a rudimentary description. If a Corpus volume or other thorough monograph has appeared on the windows of a given monument I have often excluded much of the earlier bibliography, in the expectation that the reader will begin with the monograph and take bibliography from that. In the same way, I exclude articles that are preliminary to publication in book form and theses that have been published in some other form, but include brief notices that provide additions or corrections to books. Book reviews have been included only when I happened to find one that seemed to make an important contribution to the subject; these have not been rigorously screened and more might have been found.[36] Students who lack a reading knowledge of the language of a book will generally find a reliable summary in a book review in their own language; these can easily be identified by searching the periodical indices for the two or three years following the book's date of publication.

Finally, the indexes require some explanation. I elected not to include an iconographic index, although this would be a valuable tool for research. One reason is that it would be so heavily weighted to common Christological scenes, such as the Nativity or Crucifixion, and compilation of an index of rare subjects only would be quite arbitrary. The other reason is that cycles that have been well published will have been included in the Index of Christian Art at Princeton in a much more complete way than is possible in this format. The topographical index includes both regions and sites; it provides cross-referencing when a technical study, for instance, deals largely with the glass of a single church, but it should be used with caution. It is advisable to look under the region as well as the town, since every site discussed in a regional study is not included in the index. Also, it is advisable to look through the sales and collections and exhibition catalog sections for mentions of, for example, Austrian glass, since the provenance of individual items is not listed in the index.

1. E.g., from late antiquity: Leila Ibrahim, Robert Scranton, and Robert Brill, <u>Kenchreai, Eastern Port of Corinth, II: The Panels of Opus Sectile in Glass</u> (Leiden: Brill, 1976); from seventh-century England: Rosemary Cramp, "Decorated Window-glass and Millefiori from Monkwearmouth," <u>Antiquaries Journal</u> 50 (1970):327-35. One exception is the glass from Studenica (Oth. 7, 8), where the design resembles painted glass.
2. See Ger. 91, 186, 201; It. 14, 18. For a review of the origins of glass painting, see the chapter "Die Ursprünge" in Frodl-Kraft (Gen. 65), pp. 13-28.
3. Gen. 16.
4. Ger. 97; Fr. 237.
5. Gen. 74.
6. Tech. 114, 120.
7. Coll. 34.
8. Museum of Fine Arts, Boston, <u>Arts of the Middle Ages: A Loan Exhibition, February 17 to March 24, 1940</u> (Boston, 1940).

9. R. Krautheimer, "The Beginnings of Art Historical Writing in Italy," in Studies in Early Christian, Medieval and Renaissance Art (New York, New York University Press, 1969), pp. 257-73.

10. E.J. Nash, "A Note on Charles Winston," Archaeologia cantiana 50 (1938):160. The list might be expanded to include E.-H. Langlois, Émile Thibaud, and J. Marchand in nineteenth-century France.

11. For additions to the works contained here, see "A Bibliography of Works by John Alder Knowles Relating to Ancient Stained and Painted Glass," Journal of the British Society of Master Glass-Painters 9, no. 1 (1943):26-29, which contains seventy-three items published between 1914 and 1943. Others could be added for the early part of this century, such as Day, D.M. Ross, "Lewis Foreman Day, Designer and Writer on Stained Glass," Journal of the British Society of Master Glass-Painters 3, no. 1 (1929):5-8; and also, Lucien Bégule.

12. Liturgical Arts 6 (1937):71-90.

13. Robert Willis, The Architectural History of Canterbury Cathedral (London: Longman, Pickering & Bell, 1841). Other early monographs on glass include Marchand & Bourassé on Tours, 1849 (Fr. 18), Lübke on Königsfelden, 1867 (Sw. 3), and Rahn on Lausanne, 1879 (Sw. 5).

14. There are substantial holdings in the Department of Prints, Victoria and Albert Museum, which I have not been able to inspect; nor were the collections of the Department of Manuscripts of the British Library and the Society of Antiquaries in London systematically searched. Continental collections were virtually untouched.

15. Unfortunately in most cases glass was reinstalled after storage during World War II before examination was possible; Lafond established the restoration charts for the roses of Notre Dame of Paris by using binoculars (Fr. 240). The glass of St.-Ouen of Rouen, however, was still in the restoration ateliers in the 1960s when the Corpus volume was prepared (Fr. 335). At Canterbury scaffolding was erected both inside and outside especially for the examination (Br. 244, 253).

16. Only reports with substantial summaries of papers given have been included here; others will be found in the Kunstchronik and Österreichische Zeitschrift für Kunst und Denkmalpflege. A review of publications in this series is given by Louis Grodecki, "Dix ans d'activité du Corpus Vitrearum," La revue de l'art 51 (1981):23-30.

17. Florens Deuchler, Marcel Roethlisberger, and Hans Lüthy, La peinture suisse du Moyen Âge à l'aube du XXe siècle (Geneva: Skira, 1975), pp. 28-33, 82-83.

18. Paul Robert, Dictionnaire de la langue française (Paris: Société du Nouveau Littré), 1973, p. 1912, defines vitrail as a decorative assemblage of pieces of colored glass.

Vetrata in Italian has the same meaning. "Stained glass" was abbreviated from stained and painted glass; the choice was unfortunate.

19. Ger. 5, 14, 27, 28.
20. A number of studies included in the technical section have served to clarify the role of drawings, most recently Wayment on the use of the term vidimus (Tech. 148).
21. Gen. 43.
22. Gen. 40.
23. Heinrich Wölfflin, a Swiss art historian (1864-1945), first published his Principles of Art History in German in 1915; in it he explored certain formal poles, such as linear vs. painterly, to distinguish between Renaissance and Baroque works. Similar terms were adapted by Frankl to define Gothic architectural style: Gothic Architecture (Baltimore: Penguin, 1962), pp. 11-12; these were also used in his article on Chartres (Fr. 272). For Schmarsow, see Gen. 23, 25.
24. For Riegl, whose Stilfragen appeared in 1893, followed by his Spätrömische Kunst-Industrie in 1901-23, see Otto Pächt, "Art Historians and Art Critics--vi: Alois Riegl," Burlington Magazine 105 (1963):188-193; Günter Metken, "Alois Riegl, 1858-1905," Revue de l'art 5 (1969):89-91; Henri Zerner, "Alois Riegl: Art, Value, and Historicism," Daedalus 105 (1976):177-88.
25. Ger. 40, 44.
26. Gen. 35; the question of Kunstwollen (will to form) as opposed to the technical limitations of design had been raised by Riegl.
27. Louis Grodecki, "Les problèmes de la peinture gothique," Critique 98 (July 1955):619-20. For Louis Grodecki's extensive bibliography see Claudine Lautier and Catherine Brisac, "Bibliographie de Louis Grodecki établie jusqu'en 1979," in Études d'art médiéval offertes à Louis Grodecki ed. Sumner McK. Crosby et al. (Paris: Éditions Ophrys, 1981), pp. 19-32.
28. Françoise Perrot, "Bibliographie des travaux scientifiques de Jean Lafond," La revue de l'art 10 (1970):95-96.
29. Corpus volume for St.-Ouen of Rouen (Fr. 335), pp. 39-40; Lafond compares Pucelle's works of ca. 1325 with the glass of the chapels, dated after 1318 and before 1339 (p. 14).
30. Jurgis Baltrušaitis, Réveils et prodiges: Le gothique fan-tastique (Paris: Armand Colin [1960]), p. 46.
31. Louis Grodecki, Sainte-Chapelle (Paris: Caisse nationale des monuments historiques, [1961]), p. 100; for the connection between the program for the windows in Bourges Cathedral and the canonized Archbishop William see Robert Gauchery and Catherine Gauchery-Grodecki, Saint-Étienne de Bourges (Paris: Éditions Huchettes, 1959), pp. 26-27; Linda Papanicolaou in her dissertation on the glass of Tours Cathedral (Fr. 395) has argued that an iconographic program

for that church was drawn up by Archbishop Pierre de
Lamballe and Canon Jacques de Guerande (pp. 234-40).
32. George Sang Duncan, <u>A Bibliography of Glass: From the Earliest
Records to 1940</u> (Sheffield: Society of Glass Technology,
1960). Conversely, Catherine D. Mack, <u>A Selected Bibliography of Books on Glass, Ceramics, and Refractories</u>
(Corning: Corning Glass Works, 1962) contains no entries
for stained glass.
33. <u>Catalog of Periodical Articles: Decorative and Fine Arts,
Bibliothèque Forney, Paris</u>, vol. 4, <u>Vitrail</u> (Boston: G.K.
Hall, 1972); Paris, Bibliothèque Forney, <u>Catalogue
matières: Arts-decoratifs, beaux-arts, métiers, techniques</u>,
vol. 4, <u>Vitrail</u> (Paris, 1974); <u>Catalogue de la Bibliothèque
d'art Georges Duplessis</u> (Lille: L. Danel; Paris:
G. Rapilly, 1900).
34. Typescripts available in the Arbeitstelle Corpus Vitrearum
Medii Aevi: "Erste Fassung," 1974; "Anhang I: Elsass,"
1975; "Anhang II: Österreich," 1975; "Bibliographie zur
schweizerischen Glasmalerei des Mittelalters," 1975.
35. Frits Lugt, <u>Répertoire des catalogues de ventes publiques
intéressant l'art ou la curiosité</u>, 3 vols. (La Haye:
Martinus Nijhoff, 1938-1964); Algernon Graves, <u>Art Sales
from Early in the Eighteenth Century to Early in the
Twentieth Century</u>, 3 vols. (London: A. Graves, 1918-1921).
36. An overview of works published from the 1940s to 1970s is provided by Hans Wentzel, "Neue Literatur zur Glasmalerei des
Mittelalters," <u>Kunstchronik</u> 4 (1951):123-29; A. van der
Boom, "Nieuwe publicaties over glasschilderkunst buiten
Nederland verschenen sedert 1945," <u>Bulletin van de Koninkijke Nederlandse Oudheidkundige Bond</u>, 6th ser. 6 (1953):
109-28; Eva Frodl-Kraft, "Mittelalterliche Glasmalerei
Erforschung," <u>Österreichische Zeitschrift für Kunst und
Denkmalpflege</u> 20 (1966):173-81, and frequent reviews in the
same journal; Louis Grodecki, "Chronique--Vitrail,"
<u>Bulletin monumental</u> 120 (1962):92-103, and many contribu-
tions in the same series, and also Louis Grodecki,
"Livres récents sur l'art du vitrail," <u>La revue de l'art</u>
10 (1970):97-98.

Acknowledgments

This bibliography had its beginnings in the files that I have kept over a period of twenty years. But it would not have been possible to expand these into a comprehensive listing and to select from that the items included here, without the help of a number of colleagues and institutions who have my gratitude. The fifteen hundred or so entries included here represent about fifty-five percent of the total that were searched and checked or scanned in the space of a year.

Very substantial contributions were made by Ms. Evelyn R. Staudinger, who was largely responsible for annotating items in English, French, and Italian that were not known to me; the final selection and editing of these entries, however, has been my own. A major contribution was also made by Ms. Jill Kerr of the British Academy, who undertook to search and summarize articles in the <u>Journal of the British Society of Master Glass-Painters</u> because it is unavailable in the Boston area; annotations for much of this material were prepared from her summaries.

Research on German bibliography was greatly aided by Dr. Rüdiger Becksmann and Dr. Fritz Herz of the Arbeitstelle Corpus Vitrearum Medii Aevi in Stuttgart, who permitted me to use materials in their library; assistance was also given by Ms. Elisabeth Melczer of Syracuse University, who had access to the libraries of the Corning Glass Center and the Kunsthistorisches Institut in Florence. In addition, a number of colleagues have responded to questions about specific items to which they had access, or about work in progress: Dr. Rüdiger Becksmann, M. Jean-Marie Bettembourg, Mme Catherine Brisac, Dr. Michael W. Cothren, Dr. Jane Hayward, Dr. Meredith P. Lillich, Dr. Ruth Mellinkoff, Mme Françoise Perrot, Dr. Virginia Raguin, and Dr. Hilary G. Wayment. Material in Polish, Swedish and Flemish was translated for me by Dr. Alex Kaczmarczyk, Ms. Fabia Bird and Dr. Philippe Evrard; Ms. Allyson E. Sheckler was of assistance with Spanish.

Preparation of the bibliography would not have been possible without access to a number of libraries; in addition to those

Acknowledgments

mentioned above, the Fine Arts Library of Harvard University deserves
special thanks. I am also grateful to Mr. Orin Skinner for the use
of materials belonging to Connick Associates. Travel to libraries in
London, Paris, and Stuttgart was made possible by a fellowship from
the American Council of Learned Societies in 1980.

Tufts University has supported this project in a number of ways.
I have depended a great deal on the interlibrary loan service provided by Wessell Library. A Faculty research award paid for some of
the copying and supplies, and in 1981 the cost of typing and the
service of research assistants was funded through the university,
with assistance from the Mellon Foundation. Mr. Fernando Menendez
and Ms. Corine Paulsen did much of the typing; Mr. Lasse B. Antonsen,
Ms. Deborah A. Fulton, and Ms. Norma Fishman Steinberg were responsible for much of the proofreading and final checking. I acknowledge
their help, as well as the university's support, with thanks.

Abbreviations and Symbols

Items not examined by the authors are followed by an abbreviated reference to the source if the items were listed in only one place. For manuscripts and some other rare items, the library where they may be consulted is given in abbreviated form. Following is a list of the abbreviations and symbols used in the text.

     *   Not examined by the authors.

   [ ]   Information not contained in the original source.

Becksmann   The appropriate section of Rüdiger Becksmann, "Bibliographie zur deutschen Glasmalerei des Mittelalters, Erste Fassung," 1974; "Anhang I: Elsass," 1975; "Anghang II: Österreich," 1975; "Bibliographie zur schweizerischen Glasmalerei des Mittelalters," 1975. All are available in typescript in the Arbeitstelle Corpus Vitrearum Medii Aevi, Lugostrasse 13, Freiburg-im-Breisgau.

Doucet   Library of the Institut d'art et d'archéologie, Université de Paris IV.

Duncan   George Sang Duncan, <u>A Bibliography of Glass: From the Earliest Records to 1940</u> (Sheffield, Society of Glass Technology, 1960).

N.U.C.   <u>National Union Catalog: Pre-1956 Imprints</u> (Chicago and London: Mansell Information/Publishing, 1968-1981).

Section I
General

1   *FÉLIBIEN des AVAUX, ANDRÉ. "De la vitrerie." In <u>Des principes de l'architecture, de la sculpture, de la peinture,
et des autres arts qui en dépendent</u>. Paris: J.B.
Coignard, 1st ed., 1675; 2d ed., 1690; 3d ed., 1699.
    Contains a history of glassmaking from Roman times and
technical information on painting glass, some of it from
an earlier anonymous treatise (see Gen. 45).

2   <u>L'origine de l'art de la peinture sur verre et la création des
verreries et communauté des maistres vitriers, faite par
les rois Philippe VI en 1320 et Louis XI en 1467, et depuis
confirmé par Henry III et Louis XIV, à present régnant</u>.
Paris, 1693, 51 pp. Reprinted in C. Leber, <u>Collection des
pièces relatives à l'histoire de France</u>, vol. 16 (Paris:
G.-A. Dentu, 1838), pp. 410-34.
    Follows the same late medieval source as Félibien
(Gen. 1).

3   *LENOIR, ALEXANDRE. <u>Notice historique sur l'ancienne peinture
sur verre, sus les moyens pratiques dans cet art depuis
l'époque de son invention jusqu'à nos jours; et par suite
sur Jean Cousin qui a excellé dans le même art</u>. Paris,
1824, 29 pp.
    "Historical note on ancient painting on glass, on the
methods used from the time of its invention to the present,
and on Jean Cousin who excelled in the art" [Duncan, 7813].

4   LANGLOIS, E.-H. <u>Essai historique et descriptif sur la peinture sur verre</u>. Librarie de la Bibliothèque de la ville.
Rouen: Édouard Frère, 1832, 301 pp., 8 pls.
    Discussion of the origin and progress of medieval glaz-
ing; deals with windows from major monuments in France and
neighboring countries; includes biographies of glass
painters and list of glaziers working in Rouen from 1384
to the 17th century.

Gen. 5

5   WILLEMENT, THOMAS. "Drawings of Ancient Stained Glass."
     London, British Library Add. MSS. 34,866-34,870. Ca. 1834.
     Examples from Great Britain and France.

6   *SHAW, T. History and Process of Stained Glass [London?]:
     1838. [Duncan, 12216(a)].

7   GESSERT, M.A. Geschichte der Glasmalerei in Deutschland und
     den Niederlanden, Frankreich, England, der Schweiz, Italien,
     und Spanien, von ihrem Ursprung bis auf die neueste Zeit.
     Stuttgart and Tübingen: J.G. Cottaschen, 1839, 312 pp.
     Partial English translation. William Pole, "The Art of
     Painting on Glass, or Glass Staining," in Quarterly Papers
     on Architecture, vol. 4 (London: J. Weale, 1845), 34 pp.
       Cursory review of documents, artists, and monuments
     divided into four periods: 999-1400, 1400-1600, 1600-1800,
     1800-1839.

8   GUILHERMY, FRANÇOIS de. "Notes sur diverses localités de la
     France. . . ." 18 vols. Paris, Bibliothèque nationale
     MSS. fr. 6094-6111. Ca. 1840-65.
       Valuable and often detailed notes, some made before or
     during restorations. Vol. 30 in the same series (MS. fr.
     6123) includes sites in Germany, Belgium, Holland, England,
     and Italy. An index is in the reading room of the Cabinet
     des manuscrits.

9   BUCKLER, C.A., and BUCKLER, J.C. "Notes and Drawings."
     London, British Library Add. MSS. 37,138; 37,139; 36,416.
     Ca. 1845-85.
       Chiefly English glass, including Dorset and Salisbury;
     also some French.

10   WARRINGTON, WILLIAM. History of Stained Glass from the
     Earliest Period of the Art to the Present Time: Illus-
     trated by Coloured Examples of Entire Windows in the
     Various Styles. London: The Author (42 Berkeley Street
     West), 1848, 93 pp., 26 color pls.
       General history spanning the 11th-19th centuries, with
     brief descriptions of major English and French monuments
     and accounts of some restorations by the author, who was a
     glass painter. Illustrations are from his own work.

11   *FRANKS, AUGUSTUS WOLLASTON. A Book of Ornamental Glazing
     Quarries, Collected and Arranged from Ancient Examples.
     London and Oxford, 1849, 112 color pls.

2

12 BOURASSÉ, JEAN JACQUES. "Vitrail." In <u>Dictionnaire d'archéo-</u>
<u>logie sacrée:</u> l'architecture . . . <u>les vitraux peints,</u>
<u>etc</u>. Vol. 2. Paris: J.-P. Migne, 1851. 2d ed., 1863,
cols. 680-96.
Corresponds to his introduction to <u>Les verrières du</u>
<u>choeur de l'église métropolitaine de Tours</u> (Fr. 18).

13 DIDRON, EDOUARD. "Histoire de la peinture sur verre."
<u>Annales archéologiques</u> 23 (1863):45-60, 201-24; 24 (1864):
211-25.
Introduction to the origins of glass, followed by eleven
chapters that deal with colored glass, grisaille, iconography, glass painters and their origins, monographs, techniques, and a bibliography of glass painting.

14 SCHÄFER, C. "Über die Glasmalerei." <u>Zeitschrift des Vereins</u>
<u>für Ausbildung der Gewerbe in München</u> 17 (1867):21 ff.
Reprinted in <u>Von deutscher Kunst: Gesammelte Aufsätze und</u>
<u>nachgelassene Schriften</u> (Berlin: Verlag von Wilhelm Ernst
& Sohn, 1910), pp. 16-33.
General outline of the period from the 9th century to
the present. Includes ornament and canopies. Illustrated
with drawings.

15 VIOLLET-le-DUC, EUGÈNE EMMANUEL. "Vitrail." In <u>Dictionnaire</u>
<u>raisonné de l'architecture française du XIe au XVIe siècle.</u>
Vol. 9. Paris: B. Bance, 1868. Reprint. Paris: Morel,
1870, pp. 373-462.
Overview of history, techniques, and principles of design; line drawings of examples of French glass, 12th-13th
centuries, many from tracings. His theories of color also
presented; cf. critique in Gen. 57.

16 WESTLAKE, NAT HUBERT JOHN. <u>A History of Design in Painted</u>
<u>Glass</u>. 4 vols. London and Oxford: James Parker, 1881-94.
Vol. 1, 1881, 145 pp., 89 figs. in text; Vol. 2, 1882,
112 pp., 95 figs. in text; Vol. 3, 1886, 154 pp., 118 figs.
in text; Vol. 4, 1894, 193 pp., 165 figs. in text.
Pioneering attempt to write a history of glass painting
in Europe up to the 17th century; composition, figure
styles and ornament of major sites, questions of influence
treated. Illustrated with drawings from various sources
which are useful but not always reliable prerestoration
records.

17 KOLB, HANS. Glasmalereien des Mittelalters und der Renais-
    sance. Stuttgart: Konrad Wittwer [1886-89], 61 pp.
    60 color pls. [Issued in ten parts, continuously num-
    bered].
        Annotated plates from watercolors. Contains chiefly
    German (including Strasbourg) material up to the 16th cen-
    tury and includes panels in German museums and details of
    ornament; also some Austrian and Swiss examples.

18 OTTIN, L. Le vitrail: son histoire, ses manifestations à
    travers les âges et les peuples. Paris: Librairie
    Renouard, [1896], 376 pp., 1 color pl., 34 b&w pls., figs.
    in text.
        General history up to the 19th century, focusing espe-
    cially on France. Includes an index of glass painters with
    their dates. Ornament is well illustrated.

19 DAY, LEWIS F. Windows: A Book about Stained and Painted
    Glass. London: B.T. Batsford, 1897. 3d rev. and enl.
    ed., 1909, 420 pp., 300 figs. in text.
        Broad survey illustrated with drawings. Especially
    useful for ornament.

20 "Zur Typologie der mittelalterlichen Glasmalerei." Zeit-
    schrift für alte und neue Glasmalerei 1, no. 5 (1912):
    56-58.
        Iconographic programs from St. Albans Cathedral (lost)
    and Ulm.

21 ARNOLD, HUGH, and SAINT, LAWRENCE B. Stained Glass of the
    Middle Ages in England & France. London: Adam and Charles
    Black, 1913. 2d ed., 1939, 283 pp., 50 color pls.
        Glass painting techniques and styles of the 12th-15th
    centuries. Some detailed observations are useful. Illus-
    trated with watercolors by Saint, whose originals are now
    in the Victoria and Albert Museum.

22 HEINERSDORFF, GOTTFRIED. Die Glasmalerei: Ihre Technik und
    ihre Geschichte, mit einer Einleitung und einem Anhang
    über moderne Glasmalerei von K. Scheffler. Berlin: Bruno
    Cassirer Verlag, 1914, 56 pp., 155 pls.
        Brief history of glass painting from the 12th century
    to the present; the outline of techniques compares medieval
    and modern practices. Well illustrated, with many details.

23   SCHMARSOW, AUGUST. Kompositionsgesetze romanischer Glasgemälde in frühgotischen Kirchenfenstern. Abhandlungen der
philologisch-historischen Klasse der Königl. sächsischen
Gesellschaft der Wissenschaften, vol. 33, pt. 2. Leipzig:
B.G. Teubner, 1916. 55 pp., 5 pls.
      Characterizes compositions in St.-Denis and in Chartres
west. See sequel, Gen. 25.

24   Vorbildliche Glasmalereien aus dem späten Mittelalter und der
Renaissancezeit, herausgegeben von der königlichen Akademie
des Bauwesens in Berlin. Berlin: Ernst Wasmuth, 1917,
14 pp., 16 pls.
      Loose album; large reproductions from watercolors,
chiefly of German and some Belgian works.

25   SCHMARSOW, AUGUST. Kompositionsgesetze frühgotischer Glasgemälde. Abhandlungen der philologisch-historischen Klasse
der sächsischen Gesellschaft der Wissenschaften, vol. 36,
pt. 3. Leipzig: B.G. Teubner, 1919, 122 pp.
      Presents a development in the composition (armature and
panel design, and color distribution) of Gothic windows
from Chartres west to Carcassonne and draws analogies between these and poetic structures and rhythms. Less concerned with chronology than with style divisions. See
Gen. 23.

26   WERCK, ALFRED. Stained Glass: A Handbook on the Art of
Stained and Painted Glass, Its Origin and Development from
the Time of Charlemagne to Its Decadence (850-1650 A.D.).
New York: N.L. Brown, 1922, 167 pp., 20 pls. (1 color).
      Origin and development of glass painting techniques here
divided into three periods--800-1350, 1350-1500, 1500-1650.
Part II deals with styles of ornamentation, followed by a
list of 14th-17th century European glaziers.

27   DAHMEN, WALTHER. Gotische Glasfenster: Rhythmus und
Strophenbau. Bonn and Leipzig: Kurt Schroeder, 1922,
63 pp., 6 figs.
      Application of Augustine's concepts of order and of
poetic structure in an analysis of the compositional organization of selected French and German windows.

28   SCHMITZ, HERMANN, ed. Deutsche Glasmalereien der Gotik und
Renaissance: Rund- und Kabinettscheiben. Sammelbände zur
Geschichte der Kunst und des Kunstgewerbes, 4. Munich:
Riehn & Reusch, 1923, 21 pp., 80 pls.
      Best general work on these small collector's pieces
(roundels and leaded panels); examples are chiefly German
and Swiss, from the late 15th century through the 16th.
Cf. Gen. 75.

29 SHERRILL, CHARLES HITCHCOCK. Stained Glass Tours in Spain and
    Flanders. New York: Dodd, Mead & Co., 1924, 245 pp.,
    17 figs.
        Superficial guide to major sites.

30 KNOWLES, J.A. "Imitation Stained Glass, Ancient and Modern."
    Journal of the British Society of Master Glass-Painters 1,
    no. 4 (April 1926):19-22.
        Documentary evidence for the use of oiled paper or linen
    to simulate glass in the 14th century and later.

31 SHERRILL, CHARLES HITCHCOCK. Stained Glass Tours in Germany,
    Austria, and the Rhinelands. London: John Lane, [1927],
    319 pp., 20 figs., maps.
        Superficial guide to major sites.

32 LEYRIS-BEAURY, [Mme]. "Rapports entre les vitraux et les
    miniatures de manuscrits de la fin du xie siècle au début
    du xive siècle: Influences reciproques." Bulletin des
    musées 1 (1929):203-4.
        Discussion of reciprocal influences between glaziers and
    miniaturists.

33 DRAKE, W. "Pedigrees of Families of Glass Painters." Journal
    of the British Society of Glass-Painters 5, no. 3 (Apr.
    1934):130-32.
        Geneologies for the Verrat family of Troyes, 1497-1548,
    and the Diependale family of Louvain, 1455-late 16th
    century.

34 CONNICK, CHARLES J. Adventures in Light and Color: An
    Introduction to the Stained Glass Craft. New York:
    Random House, 1937, 427 pp., 42 color pls., 47 b&w pls.,
    figs. in text.
        Criticism, not history. A stained glass artist's appre-
    ciation of light and color in medieval glass, illustrated
    with his impressionistic watercolors and with photographs
    and drawings. A useful guide to major European sites.

35 ENGELS, MATHIAS TH. Zur Problematik der mittelalterlichen
    Glasmalerei. Berlin: Triltsch & Huther, 1937, 72 pp.
        Publication of a doctoral dissertation (Bonn). Analyzes
    considerations that have separated the study of glass from
    that of other branches of painting: its relation to archi-
    tecture; its national character; and the relation of tech-
    nique to form.

36   HELBIG, J. "Circulation de modèles d'ateliers au XIVe
      siècle." Revue belge d'archéologie et d'histoire de l'art
      8 (1938):113-18.
           Examines the similarities between figures of ca. 1400 in
      Altenberg and Oxford and concludes that the models for
      their designs were miniatures which could easily circulate.

37   *MERSMANN, W. "Die Bedeutung des Rundfenster im Mittelalter."
      Ph.D. dissertation, University of Vienna, 1944.

38   WITZLEBEN, ELISABETH von. "Geträumte Architektur." Das
      Kunstwerk (Baden-Baden) 1, no. 12 (1946-47):4-17.
           Very general overview of architectural representations
      interpreted as the Heavenly Jerusalem, found in Germanic
      glass of the late 13th through the 14th centuries.

39   O'CONNOR, JOHN. "The Lawrence Saint Drawings of Stained Glass
      Windows." Carnegie Magazine (Pittsburgh) 21 (June 1947):
      3-6.
           Watercolors of French and English 12th-15th century
      windows. These drawings were exhibited at the Carnegie
      Institute and are now in the Victoria and Albert Museum,
      London.

40   GRODECKI, LOUIS. "A Stained Glass Atelier of the Thirteenth
      Century." Journal of the Warburg and Courtauld Institutes
      11 (1948):87-111.
           Provides a basic method for the complete visual analysis
      of windows. Attributes glass in Poitiers to the atelier of
      the Master of the Good Samaritan Window of Bourges and
      assigns the Lubin window in the Chartres nave to another
      shop of similar origin. Cf. Fr. 379.

41   _____. "Le vitrail et l'architecture au XIIe et au XIIIe
      siècle." Gazette des beaux-arts 36 (1949):5-24.
           Important study of developments in the design and color
      of windows ca. 1140-1260, especially in the region of Paris,
      seen in relation to trends in Gothic architecture.

42   WITZLEBEN, ELISABETH SCHÜRER von. Gotischer Farbfenster mit
      architektonischen Motiven. Baden-Baden: Woldemar Klein
      Verlag, 1949, 19 pp., 8 color pls., figs. in text.
           Picture book with examples of canopies in Austrian and
      German glass, 13th-15th centuries.

Gen. 43

43 WENTZEL, HANS. "Glasmaler und Maler im Mittelalter." Zeitschrift für Kunstwissenschaft 3 (1949):53-62.
Fundamental study of documents and original works from
the 12th to the 15th centuries that suggests painters
worked in a variety of materials--glass, manuscripts, and
murals.

44 The following papers on glass before 1540 were given at the
First International Congress on Stained Glass in Berne;
the congress, organized by Hans R. Hahnloser in 1953, was
a forerunner of the biennial colloquia of the Corpus
Vitrearum Medii Aevi.

44a Deuchler, Florens. "Die Chorscheiben der Kathedrale von
Laon: Scheidung von Helfern, Künstlern, und Ateliers, ihre
Beziehung zu Chartres."

44b Erffa, Hans Martin von. "Das Glasfenster im Abendland bis
zum Ende des 11. Jahrhunderts."

44c Frodl, Walter. "Die Aufnahme der Trecentomalerei in
Österreich."

44d Frodl-Kraft, Eva. "Ardagger (Niederösterreich), ein
Fenster der ersten Hälfte des 13. Jahrhunderts in seiner
Bezeihung zu den Vorlagen."

44e Grodecki, Louis. "Les vitraux de Saint-Denis: Le pro-
gramme iconographique et son exécution."

44f Hahnloser, Hans R. "Glazen uit het midden van de 15de eeuw
in het koor van de Münsterkerke te Bern." (on the Hans
Acker windows in Berne)

44g Meyer-Chagall, Franz. "Vorlage und Programm in den
Ateliers von Chartres."

44h Thiem, Gunther. "Hans Holbein der Ältere und die augsburger Malerei um 1500."

44i Wentzel, Hans. "Hans Acker und die ulmer Glasmalerei des
XV. Jahrhunderts."

Summaries of these papers appear in the following sources:

Boom, A. van der. "Het eerste internationale Congres voor glasschilderkunst gehouden te Bern." <u>Bulletin van de Koninkijke Nederlandse Oudheidkundige Bond</u>, 6th ser. 6 (1953):90–107.
    Dutch summaries, some of which are illustrated. English titles.

Erffa, Hans Martin von. "Die Berner Glasmalereitagung, 1953." <u>Kunstchronik</u> 6 (1953):113–20.
    German summaries.

Frodl-Kraft, Eva. "Mittelalterliche Glasmalerei: Organisation der Arbeit und Forschung, 1953." <u>Öster-reichischer Zeitschrift für Kunst und Denkmalpflege</u> 7 (1953):123–25.
    German summaries.

45   LAFOND, JEAN. "Félibien est-il notre premier historien du vitrail? Les 'Principes de l'architecture' et l' 'Origine de l'art de la peinture sur verre.'" <u>Bulletin de la Société de l'histoire de l'art français</u> (1954), pp. 45–60.
    Identifies some sources for Félibien (Gen. 1).

46   SOWERS, ROBERT. <u>The Lost Art: A Survey of One Thousand Years of Stained Glass</u>. Introduction by Herbert Read. New York: Wittenborn, 1954, 80 pp., 61 figs.
    The art of stained glass. Discusses its links with the past, as illustrated through French and English glass; its decline as a major art; its 19th century revival; and contemporary views on this art form.

47   DRAKE, W.J. <u>A Dictionary of Glass Painters and "Glasyers" of the Tenth to Eighteenth Centuries</u>. New York: Metropolitan Museum of Art, 1955, 224 pp.
    Alphabetical catalog of glass painters and designers, including their names, dates, places of origin, and notes on their known activities.

48   FRANZ, HEINRICH GERHARD. "Neue Funde zur Geschichte des Glasfensters." <u>Forschungen und Fortschritte</u> (Berlin) 29 (1955):306–12.
    Discusses recent finds of colored window glass in the Middle East (Byzantine, Islamic, and Syrian), including the painted fragments of 724–743 in Khirbat al-Mafjar near Jericho; and raises the problem of whether stained glass originated in the East or West.

General

General

49 FRODL-KRAFT, EVA. "Architektur im Abbild: Ihre Spiegelung in
    der Glasmalerei." Wiener Jahrbuch für Kunstgeschichte 17
    (1956):7-13.
       Relates canopies in French, German, and Austrian glass
    to architectural renderings in other media in the 12th-15th
    centuries. See also Gen. 38, 42, 61, 67; Fr. 355.

50 GRODECKI, LOUIS. "La couleur dans le vitrail du XIIe au XVIe
    siècle." In Entretiens sur la couleur (Colloque du Centre
    de recherches de psychologie comparative, Paris, 18-20 May
    1954). Paris, 1958, pp. 186-206.

51 ARMITAGE, EDWARD LIDDALL. Stained Glass: History, Technology,
    and Practice. London: Leonard Hill, 1959, 215 pp.,
    117 figs. (9 color), figs in text.
       Very clear explanations of technique. Short glossary
    and bibliography. An excellent introduction to the field.
    Brief historical chapters covering the 12th-19th centuries
    are largely illustrated with English examples.

52 BOOM, ANTON Van der. De Kunst der Glazeniers in Europa,
    1100-1600. Amsterdam and Antwerp: Wereld-Bibliotheek,
    1960, 261 pp., illus.
       General history with a bibliography.

53 FRENZEL, URSULA. Glasbilder aus gotischer Zeit. Munich:
    Berghaus Verlag, 1960, 71 pp., 29 color pls., 4 figs.
       General historical essay illustrated chiefly with exam-
    ples of 11th-16th century German and some Austrian and
    Swiss glass.

54 JOHNSON, JAMES ROSSER. "Art History and the Immediate Visual
    Experience." Journal of Aesthetics and Art Criticism 19
    (1961):401-6.
       Observations on the qualitative and quantitative percep-
    tion of light through stained glass in Chartres Cathedral.

55 BEYER, VICTOR. Offenbarung der Farbe, Kunst, und Technik der
    Glasmalerei. Das grosse Erbe. Ettal: Buch- und Kunst-
    verlag, 1963. 79 pp., 60 color pls. English translation.
    Stained Glass Windows. Edited by David Talbot Rice.
    Translated by M. von Herzefeld and R. Gaze. Realms of Art,
    3. Philadelphia: Dufour Editions, 1965 [1964], 72 pp.,
    60 color pls.
       Brief introduction to technical and historical develop-
    ments; annotated plates illustrating examples of French and
    Germanic glass from the 11th century to the present.

56 HUTTER, HERIBERT. Glasmalerei im Mittelalter. Vienna: Brüder Rosenbaum, 1963, 15 pp., 24 color pls.
Brief history followed by well chosen illustrations with informative captions.

57 JOHNSON, JAMES ROSSER. The Radiance of Chartres: Studies in the Early Stained Glass of the Cathedral. Columbia University Studies in Art History and Archeology, 4. London: Phaidon, 1964; New York: Random House, 1965, 96 pp., 14 color pls., figs. in text.
Chapters of general interest on the optics of light and color, Viollet-le-Duc's theories, and the character of medieval glasses, especially flashed red. Parts reprinted from the Art Bulletin 38 (1956):185-86; 39 (1957):221-24; and 45 (1963):121-34.

58 FRODL-KRAFT, EVA. "Das 'Flechtwerk' der frühen Zisterzienserfenster: Versuch einer Ableitung." Wiener Jahrbuch für Kunstgeschichte 20 (1965):7-20.
Basic work on woven design in French and Austrian Cistercian glass of the early 13th century and possible design sources in stonecarving, especially transennae. Cf. Fr. 375, 391, 407.

59 SOWERS, ROBERT. Stained Glass: An Architectural Art. New York: Universe, 1965, 128 pp., 111 figs. (8 color). German translation. Farbiges Glas als Element der Architektur. Tübingen: 1965.
Examples of medieval glass are integrated into a sensitive discussion, by a contemporary artist, of glass as an art form. Excellent introduction to the aesthetics of glass.

60 LAFOND, JEAN. Le vitrail. Je sais--je crois: Encyclopédie du catholique au XXe siècle, 12: Les arts chrétiens. Paris: Arthème Fayard, 1966. 2d ed., 1978, 246 pp., 28 figs. (20 color).
General history is followed by an extremely important section on iconoclasm and collecting ("Destinées"). Index and color illustrations added in second edition.

61 BECKSMANN, RÜDIGER. Die architektonische Rahmung der hochgotischen Bildfensters: Untersuchungen zur oberrheinischen Glasmalerei von 1250-1350. Forschungen zur Geschichte der Kunst am Oberrhein, 9-10. Berlin: Mann, 1967, 182 pp., 94 figs.
Architectural canopies in the Upper Rhine, including Freiburg, Strasbourg, and Königsfelden are related to

Gen. 61

French examples and to architectural drawings. Ph.D. dissertation, Freiburg, 1965.

62   FRODL-KRAFT, EVA. "Le vitrail médiéval: Technique et esthétique." Cahiers de civilisation médiévale 10 (1967): 1-13.
        Excellent brief essay; well-illustrated examples of design in iron, lead, and paint from the 12th to 14th centuries. Prelude to her book (see Gen. 65).

63   PIPER, JOHN. Stained Glass: Art or Anti-Art. London: Studio Vista, 1968, 95 pp., 58 figs. (4 color).
        The aesthetics of glass design by a prominent glass painter; contains a sensitive commentary on early glass and unusual illustrations, chiefly of English and French glass of the 12th and 13th centuries.

64   MORRISON, ELLEN. "Le vitrail médiéval: Le rôle de la soie." Cahiers de l'art médiévale 5, no. 3 (1969):5-18.
        Techniques used by glaziers during the 11th to 15th centuries as interpreted anew from Theophilus's Diversarum artium schedula. Controversial.

65   FRODL-KRAFT, EVA. Die Glasmalerei: Entwicklung, Technik, Eigenart. Vienna and Munich: Anton Schroll, 1970, 140 pp., 24 color pls., 48 figs. and drawings in text.
        The best general outline of history and techniques yet published; short bibliography and literature on the illustrations.

66   HAYWARD, JANE. "Stained Glass Windows." In The Year 1200. Vol. 2, A Background Survey, edited by F. Deuchler. New York: Metropolitan Museum of Art, 1970, pp. 67-84.
        Brief survey of formal developments and of the symbolic and iconographic content of glazing programs around 1200. Without bibliography or notes.

67   BACHER, ERNST. "Der Bildraum in der Glasmalerei des 14. Jahrhunderts." Wiener Jahrbuch für Kunstgeschichte (Festschrift fur O. Demus und O. Pächt) 25 (1972):87-95.
        Two- and three-dimensional composition of canopies, especially in Austrian glass; its relation to works in other media, including Italian painting. See also Gen. 49, etc.

68 GRODECKI, LOUIS. "Glasmaleréi." In Propyläen Kunstgeschichte. Vol. 7. Berlin: Propyläen Verlag, n.s. 7
(1972):239-46.
Glass painting throughout Europe in the 15th century.
Well-illustrated survey.

69 HAYWARD, JANE. "Glazed Cloisters and Their Development in the
Houses of the Cistercian Order." Gesta 12 (1973):93-109.
Survey includes examples from Heiligenkreuz, Wettingen,
and Altenberg, all dated ca. 1250-1500.

70 PERROT, FRANÇOISE. "L'art de la signature: La signature des
peintres-verriers." Revue de l'art 26 (1974):40-45.
The form and placement of signatures on medieval and
renaissance stained glass windows; includes a list of
examples from the 12th to 18th centuries in French, German,
Italian, Swiss, and Flemish glass.

71 BICKEL, WOLFGANG. "Zur Glasmalerei im Cistercienserorden."
In Die Cistercienser: Geschichte, Geist, Kunst. Edited by
Ambrosius Schneider. Cologne: Wienand, 1974, pp. 309-15.
Very general overview; discusses the response to the
proscription of colored glass in 1182; illustrated with
Austrian and German examples.

72 LEE, LAWRENCE; SEDDON, GEORGE; and STEPHENS, FRANCIS. Stained
Glass. London: Mitchell Beazley; New York: Crown
Publishers, 1976, 207 pp., approx. 525 color figs.
Good introduction to glass as an artist's medium. A
brief history of the period from the 11th century to the
present; also treats manufacture and restoration. Photo-
graphs of variable quality, by Sonia Halliday and Laura
Lushington.

73 BECKSMANN, RÜDIGER, ed. Akten des 10. Internationalen
Colloquiums des Corpus Vitrearum Medii Aevi. Stuttgart:
Akademie der Wissenschaften und der Literatur Mainz, 1971,
71 pp.
The Akten contain résumés of the following papers:

73a Becksmann, Rüdiger. "Architekturbedingte Wandlungen in der
deutschen Glasmalerei des 13. Jahrhunderts." pp. 19-20.

73b Beyer, Victor. "Le Zackenstil à Strasbourg." pp. 24-25.

73c Caviness, Madeline H. "New Observations on the Channel
School: A French Glass-Painter in Canterbury." pp. 30-31.

General

73d   Frodl-Kraft, Eva. "Zum Werden der 'gotischen' Farbsprache in der Glasmalerei." pp. 32-34.

73e   Grodecki, Louis. "Le style 'dur' de la peinture sur verre en France." pp. 26-28.

73f   Korn, Ulf-Dietrich. "Das Lohner Jesse-Fenster und die Soester Wandmalerei um 1200." pp. 22-23.

73g   Maercker, Karl-Joachim. "Frühe thüringisch-sächsische Glasmalereien und ihr Verhältnis zu Skulptur und Malerei." p. 21.

73h   Morgan, Nigel. "Early Grisaille Windows in England." p. 29.

These papers are also summarized more briefly in: Ferdinand Werner, "Zehntes Internationales Colloquium des Corpus Vitrearum Medii Aevi: Bericht über die vom 22. bis 28. Mai 1977 in Stuttgart und Freiburg veranstaltete Tagung." <u>Kunstchronik</u> 31, no. 2 (1978):55-59.

74   GRODECKI, LOUIS; BRISAC, CATHERINE; and LAUTIER, CLAUDINE. <u>Le vitrail roman</u>. Freiburg: Office du livre, 1977, 307 pp., 221 figs. (57 color).
    The first attempt since Westlake (Gen. 16) to present a history of western European Romanesque glass painting, including the retardetaire Germanic styles, in relation to other media. Annotated illustrations, bibliography, indexes.

75   WITZLEBEN, ELISABETH SCHÜRER von. <u>Bemalte Glasscheiben: Volkstümliches Leben auf Kabinett- und Bierschieben</u>. Munich: Georg D.W. Callwey, 1977, 218 pp., illus. (some color).
    Kabinettscheiben from the late 15th century on. General history, techniques, subjects (many 18th-19th century examples). Not as useful for the Middle Ages as Schmitz (Gen. 28).

76   COWEN, PAINTON. <u>Rose Windows</u>. London: Thames & Hudson, 1979, 144 pp., 85 color pls., more than 144 figs. German translation. <u>Die Rosenfenster der gotischen Kathedralen</u>. Freiburg-im-Breisgau, Basel, and Vienna: Herder, 1979, 144 pp., figs.
    General survey of subjects, interpretations, and geometries of rose windows of the 13th to 16th centuries, chiefly in France. Includes useful charts of programs.

Section II
Techniques of Glass Painting and Technical Studies, Including Conservation and Restoration

The reader is also referred to the following items in other sections: Exh. 43, 46; Br. 126, 238; Ger. 118.

1   "Compositiones variae." Lucca, Biblioteca capitolare MS. 490.
        Written between 787 and 816. Contains recipes for making colored glass, perhaps for mosaics.

   Burnam, John M., ed. A Classical Technology: Edited from Codex Lucensis, 490. Boston: Richard G. Badger, [1920], 170 pp.
        Transcription and English translation. Editor suggests the original was composed in Greek Alexandria.

   *Johnson, Rozelle Parker, ed. Compositiones variae: From Codex 490, Biblioteca Capitolare, Lucca, Italy, An Introductory Study. University of Illinois Studies in Language and Literature, vol. 23, pt. 3. Urbana: University of Illinois Press, 1939.

2   "Mappa clavicula."
        Technical treatise of which the earliest mention is in the Library of Reichenau, 821-22. A 9th century recension is in Sélestat, Bibliothèque municipale MS. 17, and a 12th century one, formerly Phillipps MS. 3715, is in the Corning Museum, N.Y. Like the "Compositiones variae" it contains information on colorants for glass, but nothing on painting and leading; may be connected with mosaics rather than stained glass.

   "Letter from Sir Thomas Phillipps, Bart, F.R.D., F.S.A., addressed to Albert Way, Esq., Director, communicating a transcript of a MS. Treatise on the preparation of pigments, and on various processes of the Decorative Arts practiced during the Middle Ages, written in the twelfth

Tech. 2

century, and entitled Mappae Clavicula." <u>Archaeologia</u> 32 (1847):183-244.
Phillipps's edition, of his own MS, done with the help of Way.

Smith, Cyril Stanley, and Hawthorne, John G., eds. <u>Mappae clavicula: A Little Key to the World of Medieval Techniques</u>. Transactions of the American Philosophical Society, n.s. 64, no. 4. Philadelphia, 1974, 128 pp. (39 pp. facsimile).
Facsimile reproduction and English translation of the 9th century treatise in Sélestat, collated with the Phillipps-Corning (12th century) recension.

3 THEOPHILUS, "De diversis artibus."
Book II deals with all the processes involved in making a stained glass window, including the production of colored glasses. 12th century MSS. are preserved in Wolfenbüttel (Herzog-August Bibliothek cod. Guelph Gudianus lat. 2069) and Vienna (Nationalbibliothek MS. 2527). There are various editions and translations:

<u>Zur Geschichte und Litteratur aus den Schätzen der Herzoglichen Bibliothek zu Wolfenbüttel</u>. 6 vols. in 3. Vol. 6, <u>Theophili presbyteri Diversarum artium schedula</u>, edited by Christian Leiste. Brunswick: Waysenhaus, 1773-1781.
Edition begun by G.F. Lessing from the Wolfenbüttel MS.

Raspe, R.E., ed. <u>A critical essay of Oil-Painting; proving that the art of painting in oil was known before the pretended discovery of John and Hubert van Eyck; to which are added, Theophilus De Arte Pingendi, Eraclius De Artibus Romanorum. And a review of Farinator's Lumen Animae</u>. London: H. Goldney, 1781, 153 pp.
Based on a MS in Cambridge; includes interpolated material.

Hendrie, Robert, ed. <u>An Essay upon Various Arts in three Books, by Theophilus, called also Rugerus, priest and monk, forming an Encyclopaedia of Christian art of the eleventh century</u>. London: J. Murray, 1847, 499 pp.
Based on London, British Library Harl. MS. 3915.

L'Escalopier, Charles de, ed. <u>Théophile, prêtre et moine: Essai sur divers arts</u>. Introduction by M. Marie Guichard. Paris: J.-A. Toulouse, 1843, 382 pp. Reprint. Nogent-le-Roi: Librairie des arts et métiers-Éditions, 1977.
Based on a MS in Cambridge.

Bourassé, Jean-Jacques, ed. "Essai sur divers arts . . .
par Théophile, prêtre et moine, formant une encyclopédie de
l'art chrétien au XII siècle." In Dictionnaire d'Archéologie sacrée, by J.P. Migne. Vol. 12. Paris: J.P. Migne,
1851, cols. 729-1014.
  Based on Hendrie.

Ilg, Albert, ed. Theophilus presbyter Schedula diversarum
artium. Quellenschriften für Kunstgeschichte, edited by
R. Eitelberger v. Edelberg, 7. Vienna: W. Braumüller,
1874, 447 pp.
  Used the early MS. in Vienna, collated with others
edited.

Theophili, presbyteri et monarchi, Diversarum artium
schedula liber secundus, translatore Georgio Bontemps.
Deuxième livre de l'essai sur divers arts . . . Entrait de
l'ouvrage d'Éraclius: De coloribus et artibus Romanorum
[translatore Georgio Bontemps]. Paris: Librairie du
dictionnaire des arts et manufactures, 1876, 60 pp.

*Traité des divers arts par Théophile, prêtre et moine.
Anonymous French translation. Paris: Émile Paul Frères,
1924, 128 pp. [National Union Catalog: Paris, Bibliothèque nationale, 131 pp.].

Theobald, Wilhelm, ed. Technik des Kunsthandwerks im
zehnten Jahrhundert, Des Theophilus presbyter, Diversarum
artium schedula. Berlin: VDI Verlag, GmbH, 1933, 584 pp.
  Based chiefly on the Wolfenbüttel MS., but omits parts
of Book I and includes extraneous material.

Dodwell, C.R., ed. and trans. Theophilus, De diversis
artibus: Theophilus, The Various Arts. London: Thomas
Nelson & Sons, 1961, approx. 177 pp.
  Critical edition and English translation, collating all
MSS but largely based on those in Wolfenbüttel, Vienna, and
London (British Library Harl. MS. 3915). Places the com-
position of the text in the first half of the 12th century
in northwestern Germany.

Hawthorne, John G., and Smith, Cyril Stanley, trans. On
Divers Arts: The Treatise of Theophilus. [Chicago]:
University Press, [1963], 251 pp., 16 pls., 27 figs. in
text. Reprint. New York: Dover, 1979.
  The translation and accompanying drawings offer a prac-
tical interpretation for even obscure parts of the text,
but these should be checked against Dodwell.

Tech. 4

4   HERACLIUS. "De coloribus et artibus Romanorum."
        Probably written in the 10th century in Italy; Book III,
    a later addition (12th-13th century), deals with making
    colored glasses.

    Merrifield, [Mary Philadelphia], ed. and trans. Original
    Treatises on the Arts of Painting. Vol. 1. London: J.
    Murray, 1849, pp. 204-57. Reprint. New York: Dover,
    1967.
        Latin text and English translation, collating several
    manuscripts, including B.L. Egerton MS. 840A and Le Bègue.

5   BRUCK, ROBERT, ed. and trans. "Der Tractat des Meisters
    Antonia von Pisa über die Glasmalerei." Repertorium für
    Kunstwissenschaft (Berlin) 25 (1902):240-69.
        Italian tract on glass painters of the last half of the
    14th century, edited from a MS in Assisi and translated
    into German. Includes instructions for silver stain and
    advice on the use of colors.

6   [MILANESI, GAETANO, ed.]. Dell'arte del vetro per musaico:
    tre trattatelli dei secoli xiv e xv. Scelta di curiosità
    letterarie inedite o rare, no. 51. Bologna: 1864, 197 pp.
    Reprint. Bologna: Commissione per i testi di lingua,
    1968.
        Edition of two Florentine texts and one by a Venetian,
    Baldassarre Ubriachi, dated 1443; these are concerned with
    making colored glasses and with the use of cartoons.

7   *De la practica di comporre finestre a vetri colorati, tratta-
    tello del secolo XV, edito per la prima volta. Siena:
    L. Lazzari, 1886, 32 pp. Reprinted in Alessandro Lisini,
    ed., La Diana: ressegna d'arte e vita senese 5 (1930):
    261-90.
        Attributed to Frater Francesco Formica, late 14th-early
    15th century. Entirely technical, primarily concerned with
    kilns for stained glass.

8   HAWKINS, JOHN SIDNEY. An History of the Origin and Establish-
    ment of Gothic Architecture; Comprehending an Account of
    Caesar Caesarianus, the First Commentator on Vitruvius and
    of his Translation of that Author, an Investigation of the
    Principles and Proportions of that Style of Architecture
    Called the Gothic: and an Inquiry into the Mode of Paint-
    ing upon and Staining Glass, as Practised in the Eccle-
    siastical Structures of the Middle Ages. London: J.
    Taylor, 1813, 259 pp., 21 figs.

Techniques and Technical Studies

Chapter XII (pp. 227-40) contains a brief section on the techniques of coloring glass and glass painting based on Félibien (Gen. 1).

9   BORDEAUX, R. "Principes d'archéologie pratique appliqués à l'entretien, la décoration, et l'ameublement artistique des églises: De la conservation et du retablissement des verrières peintes." Bulletin monumental 17 (1851):634-44.
    Extracts of Ministerial instructions to architects--they must protect ancient glass by an exterior grill, take a rubbing and trace the painted areas of every panel that is taken down, and permit cleaning only in pure water, without abrasion.

10 CHARLES, M. "De la conservation et de la restauration des anciens vitraux." Bulletin monumental 24 (1858):638-58.
    Observations on methods of conservation, principally for 15th and 16th century works and restoration techniques used on glass during the past ten years.

11 PETIT-GÉRARD. "Aspect général des vitraux d'Alsace." Congrès archéologique de France (Strasbourg, 1859) 26 (1860): 363-74.
    Discusses typical colors and restoration problems.

12 CHEVREUL, E. "Chimie appliquée aux beaux-arts: Mémoire sur les vitraux peints." Comptes rendus: Académie des sciences, Paris 57 (1863):655-66.
    Study of deposits on the outer surface of 17th century glass from St.-Gervais-et-Protais, Paris, one a glaziers' putty, the other containing calcium sulphate. Cleaning included soaking in a solution with sub-carbonate of soda, rinsing, and plunging into hydrochloric acid.

13 HASSLER, K.D. "Über Restauration mittelalterlicher Glasgemälde." Christliches Kunstblatt für Kirche, Schule, und Haus 8 (1871):120-26.
    Stresses the importance of understanding medieval glasswork in order to make faithful copies as replacements.

14 FOWLER, JAMES. "On the Process of Decay in Glass, and incidently, on the Composition and Texture of Glass at different periods, and the History of its manufacture." Archaeologia 46 (1880):65-162. Reprint. London: J.B. Nichols & Sons, 1879, 96 pp., 2 color pls., 18 figs.
    Good observation and illustration of structure and weathering.

Tech. 15

15   OIDTMANN, H. Die Glasmalerei: Allgemein verständlich dar-
     gestellt. Part 1, Die Technik der Glasmalerei. Cologne:
     J.P. Bachem [1892], 67 pp., 2 figs. and many in text.
     *Part 2, Die Geschichte der Glasmalerei, Vol. 1, Die Früh-
     zeit bis zum Jahre 1400. Cologne, [1898].
         Part 1 reviews medieval and modern techniques, including
     a discussion of Theophilus's text. Basic early treatment.

16   APPERT, LÉON ALFRED. Note sur les verres des vitraux anciens.
     Paris: Gauthier-Villars, 1896, 74 pp. New ed. 1924,
     71 pp.
         Composition and colorants found by analysis of 12th-16th
     century samples from Le Mans, Gisors, etc. Susceptibility
     to decomposition.

17   FRANCK, KARL. "Über die Technik eines frühgotischen Glasge-
     mäldes im Germanischen Museum." Nürnberg Germanisches
     Nationalmuseum: Anzeiger und Mitteilungen (1898):66-68.
         Observation of painting techniques in glass at St.
     Kunibert, Cologne are compared with the remarks of
     Theophilus; records stittckwork design in back-painting in
     15th century damask.

18   JAENNIKE, FRIEDRICH. Handbuch der Glas-Malerei. Stuttgart:
     Paul Neff, [1898], 299 pp., 31 figs. in text.
         Brief history, excellent bibliography, lengthy treatment
     of techniques.

19   JADART, HENRI. "Le vitrail de Puiseux et autres anciens
     vitraux des églises du départment des Ardennes." Revue
     historique ardennaise (Paris) 7 (1900):316-37. Reprint.
     Dole: Bernin, 1900 [50 copies].
         Cites many local examples of old glass taken out and
     replaced by modern windows; the 16th century fragments
     from the church at Puiseux to be put back.

20   WHALL, CHRISTOPHER W. Stained Glass Work: A Textbook for
     Students and Workers in Glass. Artistic Crafts Series of
     Technical Handbooks, edited by W.R. Letherby, 4. London:
     Pittman; New York: D. Appleton, 1905. 2d ed., 1920,
     380 pp., figs.
         Practical handbook with appendixes on the study of old
     glass with sites listed; and "on the restoring of ancient
     windows," with an ardent plea for care and conservation.

21 OIDTMANN, HEINRICH. "Über die Instandsetzung alter Glas-
    malereien." Zeitschrift für christlichen Kunst 19 (1906):
    258-75.
        Principles of conservation and restoration; the recovery
    of an iconographic program. Description of weathering
    crusts (patina) and methods of cleaning.

22 HEATON, NOEL. "Medieval Stained Glass: Its Production and
    Decay." Journal of the Royal Society of Arts 55 (1907):
    468-80.
        Chemical analysis of two English fragments reported; the
    process of crusting (patina) and the composition of paint
    discussed. Cf. Tech. 23, 142.

23 _____. "The Foundations of Stained Glass." Journal of the
    Royal Society of Arts 58 (1910):454-70.
        Reports some chemical analyses of English medieval
    glasses and speculates on the relation of composition
    to decay.

24 F[ISCHER], J[OSEF] L[UDWIG]. "Die Konservierung alter Glas-
    gemälde." Zeitschrift für alte und neue Glasmalerei 1,
    no. 1 (1912):6-8; no. 6:68-69; no. 7:72-73.
        Discusses the general problem of how to repair and con-
    serve stained glass and questions whether modern copies
    should replace glass in churches, with the original sent
    to a museum; concerned with moral and legal issues.

25 BIVER, PAUL. "Modes d'emploi des cartons par les peintres-
    verriers du XVIe siècle." Bulletin monumental 77 (1913):
    101-25. English translation. "French Glass Painters'
    Methods of Using Cartoons during the 16th Century."
    Journal of the British Society of Master Glass-Painters 3,
    no. 3 (Apr. 1930):112-17; 3, no. 4 (Oct. 1930):173-80; 4,
    no. 1 (Apr. 1931):24-31.
        Adaptation and reuse of 15th century cartoons in the
    16th century. Examples chiefly from the region of Troyes.

26 KNOWLES, JOHN A. "The Technique of Glass Painting in
    Mediaeval and Renaissance Times." Journal of the British
    Society of Arts 62 (1914):568-85; Antiquary 10 (Sept.
    1914).334-40, (Nov. 1914):419-22; Building News 106 (1914):
    702-5, 735-39. German translation. "Die Technik der
    Glasmalerei im Mittelalter und in der Renaissancezeit."
    Diamant 49, no. 22 (1 Aug. 1927):428-30; no. 24 (21 Aug.):
    464-68; no. 25 (1 Sept.):482-85; no. 26 (11 Sept.):508-9;
    no. 27 (21 Sept.):553-54; no. 28 (1 Oct.):549-50; no. 29

Tech. 26

(11 Oct.):576-78; no. 30 (21 Oct.):592-94; no. 32
(11 Nov.):632-35.
    Useful, though speculative, discussion of the components
of enamel or paint used on glass, of "geet" or black glass,
and of media or fixatives for the paint.

27   CHESNEAU, GABRIEL. "Contribution à l'étude chimique des
        vitraux du Moyen-Âge." Académie des sciences: Comptes
        rendus hebdomadaires des séances (Paris) 160 (1915):622-24.
        *Abstract in Journal of the Society of Glass Technology 2
        (1918): Abstract 10.
            Analysis of late 13th century glasses from Reims
        Cathedral (purple, green, red, and blue). Cf. Tech. 32.

28   SCHMITZ, JOSEF. "Die Erhaltung des Volkamerfensters in
        Nürnberg." Die Denkmalpflege 21 (1919):105-6.
            Documents the mid-19th century restorations and illus-
        trates the condition of the window, ca. 1900. Discusses
        problem of paint loss.

29   _____. "Die Instandsetzung alter Glasmalereien." Die Denk-
        malpflege 21 (1919):97-99.
            Technical and art historical aspects of conservation
        reviewed.

30   [KNOWLES, JOHN A.] "The Study of Ancient Painted Glass: Some
        Notes on a Lecture by John A. Knowles." Journal of the
        Society of Architects, n.s. 15 (1922):148-53.
            Observations on the 15th century's heterogeneous execu-
        tion of designs based on the same cartoon and on their
        further modification by restorers.

31   KNOWLES, JOHN A. "Forgeries of Ancient Stained Glass:
        Methods of Their Production and Detection." Journal of the
        Royal Society of Arts 72 (1923):38-55.
            The best study of techniques used in making forgeries.

32   CHESNEAU, GABRIEL. "Étude chimique des vitraux de l'église
        Saint-Remi de Reims." Académie des sciences: Comptes
        rendus hebdomadaires des séances (Paris) 178 (1924):852-54.
        *English translation. Journal of the Society of Glass
        Technology 9 (1925): Abstract 8.
            Chemical analysis of red and blue glasses from St.-Remi
        (late 12th century) compared with those of the west rose
        window of the cathedral (late 13th century); cobalt is
        notable in the earlier blue. Cf. Tech. 27.

33 HEATON, NOEL. "The Materials of the Medieval Glass-Painters."
    Journal of the British Society of Master Glass-Painters 1,
    no. 1 (Apr. 1924):16-27.
        Knowledge of methods of glass manufacture and the ef-
    fects of weathering help to detect forgeries.

34 KNOWLES, JOHN A. "Medieval Methods of Employing Cartoons for
    Stained Glass." Journal of the British Society of Master
    Glass-Painters 1, no. 3 (Oct. 1925):35-44. Reprinted as
    John A. Knowles, "Mediaeval Cartoons for Stained Glass:
    How Made and How Used," Journal of the American Institute
    of Architects 15 (1927):18-22. German translation.
    "Mittelalterliche Methoden für die Verwendung von Kartons:
    Anstalt farbigen Glases," Diamant 48, no. 5 (11 Feb. 1926):
    86-88; no. 6 (21 Feb. 1926):106-9.
        Based on Theophilus and 15th century practices in York;
    cites instances of the reuse of the same cartoon.

35 MELLOR, E. "Decay of Medieval Stained Glass from the Point of
    View of Lichenous Growths." Journal of the British Society
    of Master Glass-Painters 1, no. 2 (Apr. 1925):42.
        Very brief account of a slide lecture showing lichenous
    growths accelerating decay; an outdated theory.

36 NICHOLSON, Sir CHARLES. "Architecture and Stained Glass."
    Journal of the British Society of Master Glass-Painters 1,
    no. 2 (Apr. 1925):5-17.
        Changes in philosophy of restoration; outline of the
    role of various English artists, followed (pp. 44-46) by
    a debate on methods of protecting glass.

37 TOWER, W.E. "The 14th Century Glass at Tewkesbury and Its
    Recent Repair." Journal of the British Society of Master
    Glass-Painters 1, no. 2 (Apr. 1925):48-49.
        Describes corrosion and repairs.

38 KNOWLES, JOHN A. "The History of Copper Ruby Glass."
    Transactions of the Newcomen Society 6 (1925-26):66-74.
        First used in its translucent form during the Middle
    Ages, it gradually declines in use by the late 17th
    century.

39 *HEATON, NOEL. "The Technical Foundations of Stained Glass."
    Bulletin of the Stained Glass Association of America 21,
    no. 8 (Sept. 1926):7-11.

40   DENEUX, HENRI. "Un moule à plombs de vitraux du XIIIe
      siècle." Bulletin monumental 87 (1928):149-54. English
      translation. "A Thirteenth Century Mould for Making Calm
      Lead." Journal of the British Society of Master Glass-
      Painters 3, no. 2 (Oct. 1929):81-84.
           Unique find of a limestone mold for making lead cames.

41   DRAKE, MAURICE. "The Technique of Stained Glass." Archaeo-
      logical Journal (London and Manchester) 35 (1928):80-90.
           Various techniques used by glaziers from the 12th
      through the 19th centuries.

42   *GRUBER, JEAN-JACQUES. "Quelques aspects de l'art et de la
      technique du vitrail en France." Travaux des étudiants du
      Groupe d'histoire de l'art de la Faculté des lettres de
      Paris. Paris, 1918.
           Observations by a glass painter and restorer.

43   KNOWLES, JOHN A. "Ancient Leads for Windows and the Methods
      of Their Manufacture." Journal of the British Society of
      Master Glass-Painters 3, no. 3 (Apr. 1930):133-38.
           Discusses evidence for use of molds: Theophilus, pre-
      served ancient leads, and the chalk mold from Reims (see
      Tech. 40). Presence of professional camesmiths in York
      in the 15th century.

44   _____. "The Film on Ancient Stained Glass." Journal of the
      British Society of Master Glass-Painters 3, no. 4 (Oct.
      1930):181-88.
           Review of studies of decay in glass; raises the question
      of whether medieval glaziers fired on a "white skin" at
      Chartres, or whether this effect is the result of decompo-
      sition and corrosion. Cf. Tech. 47, 49.

45   EGLI, J. "Restoration von Glasgemälde in alter Zeit."
      Anzeiger für schweizerische Altertumskunde 33 (1931):265-66.
           Record of 17th century restorations to 16th century
      glass in the Rathaus at Rheinbeck.

46   HORNE, E.; KNOWLES, JOHN A.; and ROBINSON, J. ARMITAGE.
      "Marks on the Glass at Wells: A Discussion." Journal of
      the British Society of Master Glass-Painters 4, no. 2
      (Oct. 1931):71-80.
           Discussion of the function of the glaziers' marks found
      on 14th century glass.

47 SCOTT, A. "Apparent Decay of Ancient Glass at Wells Cathe-
    dral." Journal of the British Society of Master Glass-
    Painters 4, no. 4 (Oct. 1932):171.
        Identification of exterior scrapings from the choir
    clerestory glass as calcium sulphate, not a "flux." This
    crust is explained by the presence of sulphuric acid from
    the gas lighting and lime from the floor. Cf. Tech 44, 49.

48 CHESNAU, GABRIEL. "Contribution à l'étude de la technique des
    vitraux du Moyen Âge." Bulletin monumental 92 (1933):
    265-94.
        Results of chemical analyses of glass and leads from the
    12th and 13th centuries; samples from Reims, Châlons, and
    Amiens.

49 [KNOWLES, JOHN A.] "The Employment of Couverte on the Windows
    of Chartres Cathedral." Journal of the British Society of
    Master Glass-Painters 5, no. 1 (Apr. 1933):35-36.
        Reports a claim by Chevreul (translated from Mémoires de
    la Société archéologique d'Eure et Loir [1909]:459-62)
    that the original glaziers applied an oil-based paint to
    tone down their colors after installation [probably post-
    medieval]. Cf. Tech. 44, 47.

50 C., P.-E. "Le sauvetage des vitraux de Chartres." Illustra-
    tion 1 (1936):421-23.
        Discussion of work involved in taking down windows in
    case of an emergency.

51 PFISTER, RUDOLF. "Die Erhaltung des Konhoferfensters in St.
    Lorenz zu Nürnberg." Deutsche Kunst und Denkmalpflege
    (Munich) (1939):66-78.
        Documents the restoration carried out 1936-37 by Zettler
    of Munich, including his retouching of the paint. Contains
    an account of previous restorations (1722, 1836, etc.) and
    a chart showing the new glass. Illustrated with pre- and
    post-restoration photos.

52 JACOBI, RICHARD. "Kunststoffe als Grundlage für ein neues
    Verfahren zur Erhaltung alter Glasmalereien." Zeitschrift
    für angewandte Chemie 53 (1940):452-53.
        Explores the problem of preserving paint and rejects the
    older custom of repainting and refiring. Solutions for
    protection controversial. (See Tech. 122f).

Tech. 53

53   LAFOND, JEAN. Pratique de la peinture sur verre à l'usage des
        curieux: suivie d'un essai historique sur le jaune d'ar-
        gent; et d'une note sur les plus anciens verres gravés.
        Rouen: Lainé, 1943, 137 pp., 22 figs.
           Brief account of techniques, including an excellent sec-
        tion on painting and stitckwork; the second and third parts
        have been brought up to date by Lafond (Tech. 64, 82).

54   CHIGOT, PIERRE. "Note sur la restauration des verrières de la
        cathédrale de Moulins." Bulletin de la Société d'émulation
        du bourbonnais (1949):184-88.
           Summary of the restorations executed by the author, a
        glass painter, on the 15th and 16th century glass in the
        cathedral.

55   HEDWALL, J. ARVID; JAGITSCH, ROBERT; and OLSON, GILLIS.
        "Über die Belegung von Glasoberfläschen mit Schutzfilmen."
        Zeitschrift für physikalische Chemie 196 (1950):23-24.
           Suggests that the decay of glass attributed to the
        action of water and carbon dioxide might be inhibited by
        an organic coating and outlines the problem of finding the
        right lacquer and solvent.

56   MILNER-WHITE, E. "The Restoration of the East Window of York
        Minster." Antiquaries Journal 30 (1950):180-84.
           Condition and restoration of 117 panels executed by John
        Thornton of Coventry between 1405 and 1408.

57   UNWIN, MAX. "A Treatment for the Preservation of Glass."
        Museums Journal 51 (1951):10.
           Transparency can be restored to opaque ancient glasses
        by impregnating its crust with a medium with the same re-
        flective index, such as polyvinyl acetate in toluol.

58   MANSFELD, HEINZ, and OHLE, WALTER. "Die Instandsetzung der
        mittelalterlichen Glasmalereien in Neukloster." Denkmal-
        pflege in Mecklenburg: Jahrbuch (1951-52):173-89.
           Account of the recent cleaning and restoration of the
        13th century glass, with hydrochloric acid used to remove
        the "patina." Illustrations for before and after the
        cleaning include color plates, but neither the condition
        of the surface nor that of the paint is documented.

59   GEILMAN, WILHELM, and JENEMANN, HANS. "Der Phosphatgehalt
        alter Gläser und seine Bedeutung für die Geschichte der
        Schmelztechnik." Glastechnische Berichte 26 (1953):259-63.
           Phosphorus generally found in these analyses, but its
        presence in greater quantities in medieval stained glasses

was due to the use of sand and wood ash; the samples in Table 4 are French and German, 9th–19th centuries.

60 KNOWLES, JOHN A. "Early Nineteenth-century Ideals and Methods of Restoring Ancient Stained Glass." <u>Journal of the British Society of Master Glass-Painters</u> 11, no. 2 (1953):73–79.
Practice of removing original glass and replacing it by copies; examples from New College, Oxford; York; Durham; Winchester College; etc.

61 FRODL, WALTER. "Zur Wiederauffindung der Glasgemälde von Pichl bei Tragöss." <u>Österreiche Zeitschrift für Kunst und Denkmalpflege</u> 8 (1954):113–15.
Recovery of this late 13th century stolen glass and its restoration. Well illustrated.

62 GEILMANN, W., and BRUCKBAUER, T. "Beiträge zur Kenntnis alter Gläser, II: Der Mangangehalt Alter Gläser." <u>Glastechnische Berichte</u> 27 (1954):456–59.
The presence of small amounts of manganese in all the glasses that were analyzed may be accidental; larger quantities found in 9th–17th century French and German stained glass may be due to the use of wood ash (Table 4). Cf. Tech. 59.

63 JACOBI, RICHARD. "Zur Wiederherstellung der Obergadenfenster des Domchors (Köln)." <u>Kölner Domblatt</u> 8–9 (1954):173–78.
Condition of this window in Cologne Cathedral (see also Tech. 52, 68, 122f).

64 LAFOND, JEAN. "Un vitrail du Mesnil-Villeman (1313) et les origines du jaune d'argent." <u>Bulletin de la Société nationale des antiquaires de France</u> (1954):93–95.
The earliest dated use of silver stain (date inscribed), the work of an atelier from Rouen.

65 FRODL-KRAFT, EVA. "Mittelalterliche Glasmalerei: Restaurierung und Erforschung." <u>Österreichische Zeitschrift für Kunst und Denkmalpflege</u> 9 (1955):30–36.
Considers the aesthetic problems of restoration: the completion of a fragmentary window in Laxenburg with modern designs by Max Weiler, the elimination of mending leads (at Tamsweg, etc.).

66   GEILMANN, WILHELM. "Beiträge zur Kenntnis alter Gläser, III:
     Die Chemische Zusammensetzung einiger alter Gläser inbe-
     sondere deutscher Gläser des 10. bis 18. Jahrhunderts."
     Glastechnische Berichte 28 (1955):146-56.
        German medieval glasses distinguished from Roman and
     Middle Eastern by the use of beech ash instead of soda.
     Table 7 indicates the same trend in French stained glasses,
     12th-17th centuries.

67   *HETTEŠ, KAREL. "O ochrane sklenených pamatak pres odskel-
     novanim" [On the protection of old glass objects against
     "devitrification"]. Zpravy pamatkove pece 14 (1955):
     240-45.
        In Czech. Summarizes the history of conservation from
     Kunckel (1680) to Rathousky (1955). The latter has tried
     a silicone lacquer as a protective coating; conservation
     of a Gothic window in St. Bartholomew in Kolin is planned.
     (Newton, Critical Bibliography, Tech. 120, no. 68.)

68   JACOBI, RICHARD. "Das Konservierungsverfahren für die Ober-
     gadenfenster des kölner Domes." Kölner Domblatt 10 (1955):
     122-30.
        Records the removal of the mending leads, the cleaning,
     and the reassembly of the original glass between modern
     glasses that are molded to fit the uneven surface of the
     old glass (see 52, 63, 122f).

69   VERRIER, JEAN. "De la conservation et de la mise en valeur
     des vitraux anciens." Les monuments historiques de la
     France (1955):20-26.
        Complex problems of protection for stained glass con-
     front the Commission for Historical Monuments; discusses
     how these are being solved.

70   FRODL-KRAFT, EVA. "Mittelalterliche Glasmalerei: Restau-
     rierung und Erforschung, 1956." Österreichische Zeit-
     schrift für Kunst und Denkmalpflege 10 (1956):157-58.
        Restoration of lost paint on a backing glass.

71   MERTEN, HEINZ. "Die Glasmalereien der Münchner Frauenkirche."
     Deutsche Kunst und Denkmalpflege 14 (1956):113-27.
        Restorations to the 15th century windows necessitated by
     their deterioration since ca. 1914, and their recent in-
     stallation in the church.

72 JOHNSON, JAMES ROSSER. "Modern and Mediaeval Stained Glass:
    A Microscopic Comparison of Two Fragments." Art Bulletin
    38 (1956):185-86.
        Examination of possible methods used by medieval
    glaziers to produce multiple lamination in ruby glass;
    discusses theories of Jane Hayward, M. Chesneau, and Henry
    John Tress. See also Tech. 87.

73 RENTSCH, DIETRICH. "Über Erhaltungszustand und Technik der
    Sakristeifenster von St. Gereon in Köln." Jahrbuch der
    rheinischen Denkmalpflege 22 (1959):71-86.
        Condition and painting techniques of this early 14th
    century glass described; excellent photographs demonstrate
    paint loss, weathering, and back-painting.

74 FRENZEL, GOTTFRIED. "Schwarzloterhaltung und Schwarzlotres-
    taurierung bei mittelalterlichen Glasgemälden." Zeit-
    schrift für Kunstgeschichte 23 (1960):1-18.
        Problems of paint loss and the restoration of painted
    detail, especially in Nuremberg.

75 FRODL-KRAFT, EVA. "Beobachtungen zur Technik und Konser-
    vierung mittelalterlicher Glas-Malereien." Österreichische
    Zeitschrift für Kunst und Denkmalpflege 14 (1960)79-86.
        Medieval techniques of painting and the problems of
    deterioration of both glass and paint.

76 GEILMANN, WILHELM; BERTHOD, HANS J.; and TOG, GÜNTHER.
    "Beiträge zur Kenntnis alter Gläser, V: Die Verwitterungs-
    produkte auf Fensterscheiben." Glastechnische Berichte 33
    (1960):213-19.
        Analyses of the weathering products on stained glass
    (from German samples, 14th-15th centuries): silica with
    potassium and calcium sulphate, also syngenite, gorgeyite,
    and polyhalite found.

77 KÜHNE, KLAUS. "Beiträge zur Kenntnis mittelalterlicher
    Gläser." Silikatechnik 11 (1960):260-62.
        In 13th-15th century samples of German stained glass an
    earlier group with high lead and low soda content were
    shown to be more durable than the 15th century pieces with
    high potash and lime.

Tech. 78

78 LOWE, W. "The Conservation of Stained Glass." <u>Studies in</u>
    <u>Conservation</u> 5 (1960):139-49.
        Drastic methods of cleaning and restoration used on
    glass in the Victoria and Albert Museum [described to me
    by Jean Lafond as "une honte pour l'Angleterre"]. Cites
    opposing views on the replacement of missing pieces.

79 FRODL-KRAFT, EVA. "Ein Schreibenriss aus der Mitte des
    14. Jahrhunderts." In <u>Festschrift Hans R. Hahnloser</u>.
    Edited by Ellen J. Beer, Paul Hofer, and Luc Mojon. Basel
    and Stuttgart: Buchäuser Verlag, 1961, pp. 307-16.
        Drawing on parchment, ca. 1340-50, for a glass panel of
    St. Catherine found in the binding of a manuscript from
    Seitenstetten Abbey. Traces of drawing are found on both
    sides of the parchment, as are pricking marks (see Tech.
    100).

80 CHAMBRON, R. "L'évolution des procèdes de fabrication
    manuelle du verre à vitres du dixième siècle à nos jours."
    In <u>Advances in Glass Technology, II: History Papers and</u>
    <u>Discussions</u> (6th International Congress of Glass,
    Washington, D.C., 1962). New York: Plenum Press, 1963,
    pp. 165-78.
        Early distinction between the cylinder process in west-
    ern Europe and the crown process in the East; but crown
    glass appears in windows in the West by the 12th century
    and the size of the disk steadily increases.

81 GEILMANN, WILHELM. "Beiträge zur Kenntnis alter Gläser, VII:
    Kobalt als Färbungsmittel." <u>Glastechnische Berichte</u> 35
    (1962):186-92.
        Cobalt has been used continuously in glass since about
    1800 B.C. Table 2 compares the cobalt and copper content
    of stained glass fragments from various sites (chiefly
    German), 12th-19th centuries.

82 LAFOND, JEAN. "La technique du vitrail: Aperçus nouveaux."
    <u>Art de France</u> 2 (1962):246-49.
        13th-14th century examples of abrading colored layers to
    make white designs in red and blue flashed glasses; 14th
    century use of silver stain on colored glass; and glasses
    in striped colors, made ca. 1500, in the Roman manner.

83 TARALON, JEAN. "Le colloque international d'Erfurt et la
    sauvegarde des vitraux anciens." <u>Les monuments historiques</u>
    <u>de la France</u> 8 (1962):231-46.
        Discusses problems of weathering and paint loss in
    medieval glass and the conservation of original leads.

84   Corpus Vitrearum Medii Aevi. Reports on the 1962 colloquium, especially those presentations dealing with conservation problems:

Frodl-Kraft, Eva. "Die vierte Tagung des Corpus Vitrearum Medii Aevi 1962 in Erfurt." Österreichische Zeitschift für Kunst und Denkmalpflege 17 (1963):38-42.

Grodecki, Louis. "La quatrième réunion internationale du 'Corpus Vitrearum Medii Aevi' et ses enseignements." Bulletin monumental 121 (1963):73-82.

Hahnloser, Hans R. "Die vierte Arbeitstagung des 'Corpus Vitrearum Medii Aevi.'" Unsere Kunstdenkmaler 14 (1963): 35-36.

Wentzel, Hans. "Vierte Arbeitstagung zum 'Corpus Vitrearum Medii Aevi' in Erfurt." Kunstchronik 15 (1962): 311-15.

85   DERIX, HEINRICH. "Über die Restaurierung der xantener Domfenster 1872 bis 1962. Xantener Domblätter 6 (1963) 223-36. *Reprinted in 1600 Jahre xantener Dom (Cologne, 1964), pp. 223-36.
         Brief history of repairs, etc., in glass of ca. 1310 and of the early 16th century, documented with charts and photos.

86   FRENZEL, GOTTFRIED, and FRODL-KRAFT, EVA. "Referat auf der Tagung 'Corpus Vitrearum Medii Aevi,' Erfurt 1962." Österreichische Zeitschrift für Kunst und Denkmalpflege 17 (1963):93-99.
         Supersedes earlier observations on painting techniques, especially the methods of laying smear-shading, structural tone, and trace line and the use of exterior or back-painting.

87   JOHNSON, JAMES ROSSER. "The Internal Structure of Medieval Ruby Glass." Stained Glass 49, no. 2 (1964):17-22.
         Possible techniques used by medieval glaziers to produce the effects of multiple striations and uneven densities in ruby glass. See also Tech. 72.

88   FRODL-KRAFT, EVA. "Eine Glasgemälde-Restaurierung als
      methodisches Exempel." Österreichische Zeitschrift für
      Kunst und Denkmalpflege 19 (1965):54–57.
          Conservation and partial reconstruction of a 16th cen-
      tury representation of St. Michael damaged in World War II;
      some replacement glasses painted, some not.

89   *OEHL, J. "Restaurierung von verwitterten Kirchenfenstern mit
      Glasmalerei." Typescript. Strasbourg: Referat beim 5.
      Colloquium des Corpus Vitrearum Medii Aevi, 1965. [Orga-
      nized by the Comité international de l'histoire de l'art.]

90   FRODL-KRAFT, EVA. "Arbeitstagung Corpus Vitrearum Medii Aevi,
      Strassburg 1965." Österreichische Zeitschrift für Kunst
      und Denkmalpflege 20 (1966):47–49.
          Colloquium devoted to conservation problems; creation
      of a technical subcommittee; reports on research programs.

91   SOWERS, ROBERT. "On the Blues in Chartres." Art Bulletin 48
      (1966):218–22.
          Questions whether the unusual intensity of 12th century
      blues at Chartres results from a special technique of early
      glaziers or from the addition of 19th century glass; cf.
      the theories of Viollet-le-Duc and Johnson (Gen. 15, 57).

92   FRODL-KRAFT, EVA; BACHER, ERNST; BAUER, W.P.; and LÖTSCH, K.
      "Mittelalterliche Glasmalerei: Neufunde, Restaurierung,
      und Erforschung." Österreichische Zeitschrift für Kunst
      und Denkmalpflege 21 (1967):186–209.
          Restoration at several Austrian sites. Includes chemi-
      cal analyses of 14th century glass from Heiligenkreuz for
      corrosion products and colorants. Study of medieval leads.

93   BRILL, ROBERT. "The Scientific Investigation of Ancient
      Glasses." In VIII International Congress on Glass (London
      1–6 July 1968). Sheffield: Society of Glass Technology,
      1968, pp. 47–69.
          Summary of methods and instruments used in analyzing
      stained glass.

94   BRIVIO, ERNESTO. "Le vetrate del Duomo: Problemi di con-
      servazione e di riordinamento dell'intero 'Corpus.'" In
      Il Duomo di Milano (Congresso internazionale, Milano,
      1968). 2 vols. Milan: La Rete 1969, 2:153–66.
          19th and 20th century methods for the preservation of
      the 15th century windows in Milan.

95   FRODL-KRAFT, EVA. "6. Colloquium über das Corpus Vitrearum
     Medii Aevi, Ulm, 1968." <u>Österreichische Zeitschrift für
     Kunst und Denkmalpflege</u> 23 (1969):86-89.
          Summary of the discussion on approaches to restoration
     and conservation.

96   LAFOND, JEAN. "Le prétendue invention du 'Plat de verre' au
     XIVe siècle et les familles de 'grosse verrerie' en
     Normandie." <u>Revue de la Société savante de Haute-Normandie</u>
     49 (1968):25-40. Shorter English version. "Was Crown
     Glass Discovered in Normandy in 1330?" <u>Journal of Glass
     Studies</u> 11 (1969):37-38.
          Cites examples of crown glass of 13th century date from
     Rouen to refute the traditional attribution of its inven-
     tion to Philippe de Caqueray in 1330.

97   FRENZEL, GOTTFRIED. "Die Instandsetzung des Kaiserfensters
     und des Rieterfensters aus der St. Lorenzkirche zu
     Nürnberg." <u>Verein zur Wiederherstellung der St. Lorenz-
     kirche in Nürnberg, Mitteilungsblatter</u>, n.s. 9 (July 1968);
     also <u>Österreichische Zeitschrift für Kunst und Denkmal-
     pflege</u> 23 (1969):75-85.
          Documents previous restorations in these 15th century
     windows with charts; splintered glasses edgemended and
     backplated in recent restoration.

98   BRILL, ROBERT. "Scientific Studies of Stained Glass: A
     Progress Report." <u>Journal of Glass Studies</u> 12 (1970):
     185-212.
          Preliminary results of analyses for five ingredients in
     well-authenticated samples of the 12th-14th centuries sug-
     gest compositional classification will be possible. Many
     of these samples were damaged in a flood and further re-
     sults have not been published.

99   LAHANIER, CHARLES. "La radio-cristallographie et l'analyse
     par spectometrie de fluorescence X appliquées à la connais-
     sance des objets de musée." <u>Annales du Laboratoire de
     recherche des musées de France</u> (Paris) (1970):25-63.
          "Analyse de vitraux," pp. 44ff. Spectographic fluores-
     cence used for the analysis of four groups of glass frag-
     ments (Mt.-St.-Michel and St.-Pierre of Chartres, 12th
     century; Evreux Cathedral and St.-Ouen of Rouen, 14th
     century). The blue soda glasses of the early groups were
     not corroded. The type of potash used indicates whether
     glasses are from the same shop.

Tech. 100

100   WENTZEL, HANS. "Un projet de vitrail au XIVe siècle." Revue
de l'art 10 (1970):7-14. [English and German summaries.]
Parchment fragment with a drawing for a Throne of
Solomon preserved in the Stuttgart Museum, attributed to
Constance, ca. 1310-30; probably a sketch for a window.
Cf. other examples (Tech. 79).

101   FRENZEL, GOTTFRIED, and HINKES, GERDA. "Die Prophetenfenster
des Domes zu Augsburg: Vorbericht über den Erhaltungszustand und Vorschläge zur Konservierung." Jahrbuch der
bayerischen Denkmalpflege 28 (1970/71):83-100.
Close scrutiny of the condition of the 12th century
prophet figures during restoration in 1971, illustrated
with restoration charts and photos.

102   KORN, ULF-DIETRICH. "Ursachen und Symptome des Zerfalls
mittelalterlicher Glasgemälde." Deutsche Kunst und Denkmalpflege 29 (1971):58-74.
Documentation of severe cases of crusting (patina),
pitting, fracturing, and paint loss in 13th-15th century
German glass, especially as this deterioration progresses
in this century.

103   PARMENTIER-LIETAERT, MURIEL. "Apport du laboratoire pour
l'étude du verre médiéval: problèmes de méthode." Revue
des Archéologues et historiens d'art de Louvain 4 (1971):
274-75.
General résumé of a thesis (license, Louvain, 1970);
discusses the need for dated samples in the analysis of
medieval glass and the importance of soda-potassium ratios.

104   BACHER, ERNST. "Das Achte Colloquium des Corpus Vitrearum
Medii Aevi in York und Canterbury, 25. September-1. Oktober
1972." Österreichische Zeitschrift für Kunst und Denkmalpflege 27 (1973):76-77.
Summary of presentations dealing with conservation
problems.

105   BURMAN, P.A.T. "Corpus Vitrearum Medii Aevi, Canterbury
Meeting 30th September 1972: Canterbury Cathedral Glass."
Journal of the British Society of Master Glass-Painters 15
(1972-73):27-33.
Verbatim report of discussion of conservation problems.

106   Congrès international de verre: International Congress on
       Glass: Internationaler Glaskongress IX (Versailles
       27 Sept.-2 Oct. 1971), Communications artistiques et
       historiques: Artistic and Historical Communications:
       Kunstlerische und geschichtliche Vorträge. Paris:
       Institut du verre, 1972.
           Contains the following papers:

106a   Bettembourg, Jean-Marie. "Étude de verres bleus de
       vitraux. Analyse par spectométrie d'assorption atomique."
       pp. 225-39.
           Report of analyses of French 12th-17th century blue
       glasses by atomic absorption spectrometry; cobalt the
       colorant in most samples. Problems of analyzing for copper
       in red flashed or laminated glasses.

106b   Brill, Robert H. "Scientific Investigations of Early
       Stained Glass." pp. 307-16.
           Reports current methods of studying ancient glass. Sub-
       stantially the same as Tech. 98.

106c   Lahanier, Charles. "Analyse de verres de vitraux par
       spectométrie de fluorescence X." pp. 209-24.
           Results of analyses by x-ray fluorescence spectrometry
       of samples of 12th-14th century French glass.

106d   Vassas, C.D. "Étude chimique, thermographique, et physique
       de verre de vitraux de Moyen-Âge." pp. 241-66.
           Technical studies of French 12th-16th century samples;
       discusses the relation of chemical composition to decay.

106e   _____. "Étude colorimetrique de verres de vitraux du
       Moyen Âge." pp. 267-94.
           Colorimetric and chemical studies of glass samples from
       many French sites are related to medieval treatises. The
       limitations of this kind of study are described.

107   FRODL-KRAFT, EVA. "Konservierungsprobleme mittelalterlicher
       Glasmalereien." In Annales du 5e Congrès de l'Association
       internationale pour l'histoire du verre, Prague (6-11 July
       1970). Liège: Secrétariat Général, 1972, pp. 357-70.
           Special problems of conserving painted and leaded
       glasses; of returning corroded glass to transparency; of
       backplating and exterior glazing for protection; and of
       securing paint.

108   OLIN, JACQUELINE S.; THOMPSON, B.A.; and SAYRE, EDWARD V.
      "Characterization of Medieval Window Glass by Neutron
      Activation Analysis." In Developments in Applied Spec-
      troscopy. Edited by A.J. Perkins et al. Vol. 10. New
      York: Plenum Publishing, 1972, pp. 33-55.
         Analysis of trace elements in forty-five samples of
      different dates and provenance; groupings indicate a com-
      mon source.

109   BACHER, ERNST. "Aussenschutzverglasung." Österreichische
      Zeitschrift für Kunst und Denkmalpflege 27 (1973):66-68.
         Detailed explanation of the outer protective glazing
      installed at Graz (1971-72) and Leoben (1969-70).

110   _____. "Die Chorverglasung der grazer Leechkirche und ihre
      Restaurierung." Österreichische Zeitschrift für Kunst und
      Denkmalpflege 27 (1973):69-75.
         Documents the cleaning of this important collection of
      early 14th century windows.

111   CAVINESS, MADELINE HARRISON. "De convenientia et cohaerentia
      antiqui et novi operis: Medieval conservation, restora-
      tion, pastiche, and forgery." In Intuition und Kunstwis-
      senschaft: Festschrift für Hanns Swarzenski. Edited by
      Peter Bloch, Tilmann Buddensieg, Alfred Hentzen, and
      Theodor Muller. Berlin: Gebr. Mann Verlag, 1973,
      pp. 205-21.
         Medieval restorations in glass from Troyes Cathedral,
      the Ste.-Chapelle, etc.

112   FRODL-KRAFT, EVA. "Untersuchungen und praktische Erfahrungen
      in der Konservierung mittelalterlicher Glasgemälde, 1963-
      1972." Österreichische Zeitschrift für Kunst und Denkmal-
      pflege 42 (1973):55-65.
         Useful overview of conservation methods: analysis,
      cleaning, and consolidation. Well illustrated.

113   JACOBI, RICHARD. "Zur Frage der Erhaltung alter Glasmale-
      reien." Maltechnik Restauro: Internationale Zeitschrift
      für Farb- und Maltechniken, Restaurierung, und Museums-
      fragen 2 (1973):114-20.
         Methods of replacing mending leads with adhesives,
      cleaning, and casing the original glass in resin and new
      glass. Used in the windows of Cologne Cathedral and in
      those of St. Lorenz, Nuremberg.

114   NEWTON, ROY G. "Bibliography of Studies on the Deterioration
        and Conservation of Stained Glass." <u>Art and Archaeology:
        Technical Abstracts</u> (Supplement) 10 (1973):132–78.
            Brief interpretive introduction; 130 annotated items,
        1907–73, including technical literature not cited here.
        Cf. 120.

115   NOTMAN, JANET H. "The Restoration of a Stained Glass
        Roundel." <u>Scottish Art Review</u> 14, no. 2 (1973):10–13.
            Methods for restoration demonstrated on a 16th century
        Flemish panel representing St. Anne with the Virgin and
        Child in the Burrell collection.

116   PALLANT, R.J. <u>The Response of Some Leaded Windows to Simu-
        lated Sonic Bangs</u>. Royal Aircraft Establishment Report,
        73111. London: Her Majesty's Stationery Office, 1973.
            Tests to find the threshold at which damage occurs to
        leads or glass; slight damage at characteristic over-
        pressure of 2400 N/m^2; lead buckled and glass cracked at
        4900 N/m^2. Cf. findings at Cologne quoted by Grodecki,
        <u>Bulletin monumental</u> 127 (1969):49.

117   MARCHINI, GIUSEPPE. "Conservation of Stained Glass in Italy."
        <u>Journal of the British Society of Master Glass-Painters</u> 15
        (1973–74):11–15.
            Contrasts the current work of the Florentine Soprinten-
        denza alle Gallerie on the glass from Orsanmichele, etc. to
        the immediate postwar restoration of Assisi; recommends
        conserving earlier leading but replacing mending leads with
        adhesive; marking replacements of lost glass; and using
        outer protective glazing. Prefers to supply lost painted
        detail on a backing glass than to inpaint the original.

118   FRODL-KRAFT, EVA. "Mittelalterliche Glasmalerei: Erforschung,
        Restaurierung-Bermerkungen zu Verwittungsformen, und Kon-
        servierungsmassnahmen an mittelalterlichen Glasmalereien."
        <u>Österreichische Zeitschrift für Kunst und Denkmalpflege</u> 28
        (1974):200–209.
            Weathering crusts, back-painting, and the problems of
        cleaning. Documents conditions at the same sites
        1950/63–74. Well illustrated.

119   NEWTON, ROY C., and HEDGES, ROBERT E.M. "Analysis of Weather-
        ing Glass from York Minster." <u>Archaeometry</u> 16, no. 2
        (1974):244–45.
            Variations in the absolute amount of alkali (K_2O) and
        alkaline earth components (CaO) affects the degree of
        weathering.

Tech. 120

120   _____. The Deterioration and Conservation of Painted Glass:
       A Critical Bibliography and Three Research Papers. Corpus
       Vitrearum Medii Aevi: Great Britain--Occasional Papers, 1.
       London: British Academy, 1974, 93 pp., 8 figs.
          Annotated bibliography, essentially the same as
       Tech. 114 but alphabetically arranged and including foreign
       titles. Papers on "Recovery of Lost or Faded Decoration on
       Painted Glass," i.e., methods of detecting areas which had
       been painted; "A Study on Cleaning Painted and Enameled
       Glass in an Ultrasonic Bath," with Peter Gibson; and "Use
       of the 'Isoprobe' for Studying the Chemical Composition of
       Some 12th Century Glass from York Minster," with Robert
       Hedges.

121   OLIN, JACQUELINE S., and SAYRE, EDWARD V. "Neutron Activation
       Analytical Survey of Some Intact Medieval Glass Panels and
       Related Specimens." In Archaeological Chemistry. Edited
       by Curt W. Beck. Advances in Chemistry Series, 138.
       Washington: American Chemical Society, 1974, pp. 100-23.
          Comparison of oxides in 13th century panels from the
       Château de Rouen, Cartres, and elsewhere; similarities in
       composition may confirm provenance.

122   Conservation in Archaeology and the Applied Arts (Stockholm
       Congress, 2-6 June 1975). London: International Institute
       for Conservation of Historic and Artistic Works, 1975.
          The following papers are included:

122a   Ferrazzini, J.C. "Reaction Mechanisms of Corrosion of
       Medieval Glass." p. 135.
          Control of humidity an important factor in preventing
       corrosion (under 60% relative humidity recommended at
       0°C-30°C). Warns against radical cleaning.

122b   Frodl-Kraft, Eva. "Mediaeval Stained Glass Corrosion--
       Conservation--Restoration." pp. 105-10.
          33% relative humidity may be enough to initiate the
       process of weathering. Review of the problems of outer
       protective glazing and of silicone adhesives for mending
       and cleaning.

122c   Moncrieff, A. "Problems and Potentialities in the Conser-
       vation of Vitreous Materials." pp. 99-104.
          Review of the methods of mechanical cleaning (air
       abrasive, etc.), adhesives, outer protective glazing,
       protective coatings, and lamination.

122d   Bettembourg, Jean-Marie. "Étude de mastics elastomers--Le
         Masticage des panneaux de vitraux anciens." pp. 137-38.
             Tests of various putties reported; hazards of standard
         type.

122e   Newton, Roy G. "Conservation of Medieval Windows (Iso-
         thermal Glazing)." pp. 111-14.
             Review of the types of outer protective glazing; report
         on Lindena (East Germany) where this has been used since
         1897.

122f   Wolff, A. "The Conservation of Mediaevel Stained Glass
         According to the Jacobi Method of Lamination used at
         Cologne." pp. 115-20.
             Very clear description of the methods evolved by Richard
         Jacobi and a review of its advantages and disadvantages.
         Costly, but reversable.

123   FRODL-KRAFT, EVA. "Mittelalterliche Glasmalerei, Erforschung,
         Restaurierung: Das 9. Colloquium des Corpus Vitrearum
         Medii Aevi, Paris, September 1975." Österreichische Zeit-
         schrift für Kunst und Denkmalpflege 29 (1975):154-61.
             Summary of presentations and discussions dealing with
         conservation methods and the organization of the technical
         sub-committee.

124   HELBIG, JEAN. "Restoration et conservation des anciennes
         verrières de Belgique." Bulletin de l'Institut du
         patrimoine artistique 15 (1975):170-79.
             The activities of restorers of the 16th century windows
         in major Belgian churches.

125   MARCHINI, GIUSEPPE. "La vetrata ed il suo restauro."
         Mitteilungen des Kunsthistorischen Instituts in Florenz 19,
         no. 1 (1975):181-96.
             Restoration of a window representing the enthroned
         Madonna and Saints from Prato Cathedral, 1459; the design
         may be attributed to Filippo Lippi.

126   NEWTON, ROY G. "Cathedral Chemistry--Conserving Stained
         Glass." Stained Glass 70, no. 1 (Spring 1975):20-25.
             Describes the deterioration of glass and paint; the study
         of this process, and possible remedies.

127   _____. "The Weathering of Medieval Window Glass." Journal of
         Glass Studies 17 (1975):161-68.
              Publication of results of recent experiments concerning
         the weathering patterns of stained glass; outlines some
         future work to be undertaken in the field.

128   *SCHMIDT, CHRISTA. "Zur Restaurierung der Glasmalereien in
         Muhlhausen." Denkmalpflege in der Deutschen Demokratischen
         Republik 2 (1975):47-51.

129   "Actes du IXe colloque international du Corpus Vitrearum
         Medii Aevi." Verres et refractaires 30 (1976).
              The following papers are included with summaries in
         English, French, and German.

129a   Bauer, W.P. "Der Einfluss von Reinigungsmethoden auf die
         Glasoberfläche (Vorversuche und mikroskopische Untersuch-
         ungen)." pp. 62-64.
              Effect of different methods of cleaning on the glass
         surface, including abrasion and use of hydrofluoric acid,
         thiosulphate solution, and EDTA.

129b   Bettembourg, Jean-Marie. "Composition et alteration des
         verres de vitraux anciens." pp. 36-42.
              The weathering and solubility of ancient glass are a
         function of the ratio between the forming elements (Si,
         etc.) and the alkaline (K, Na).

129c   _____. "Protection des verres de vitraux contre les agents
         atmosphériques: Étude de films de résines synthétiques."
         pp. 87-91.
              Tests of protective synthetic coatings; polyurethane
         preferred over vinyl, acrylic, and epoxy.

129d   Ferrazzini, J.C. "L'influence de la corrosion sur la
         vitesse de décomposition des verres du Moyen Âge."
         pp. 26-29.
              The weathering of glass is an exponential function of
         time.

129e   Frodl-Kraft, Eva. "Einige Bermerkungen zu Wissenschaft
         und Handwerk in der Glasgemälde-Restaurierung." pp. 73-76.
              Reviews progress made in reliable techniques for clean-
         ing, mending, and double glazing and in the study of leads.

129f   Hayward, Jane. "Installation of St. Leonhard Glass at the Cloisters." pp. 77-79.
       New installation using double, thermal-sealed plexiglas outside.

129g   Husband, Timothy B. "A Stained Glass Tree of Jesse at the Metropolitan Museum of Art." pp. 69-72.
       Preservation and consolidation of ancient leading; post-medieval restoration replaced with dyed epoxy resin.

129h   Marchini, Giuseppe. "La restauration de la grisaille." pp. 65-68.
       Attempts to restore lost paint by putting graphite powder on the roughened area that had held the paint.

129i   Newton, Roy G. "Experimental Studies of the Protection of Medieval Windows Using External Glazing." pp. 80-86.
       Temperature variations in the interface between ancient glass and its external protective glazing, ventilated from the outside.

129j   Newton, Roy G., and Iliffe, C.J. "Using Triangular Diagrams to Understand the Behaviour of Medieval Glass." pp. 30-34.
       Chemical ingredients, expressed in molecular percentages and tabulated in a triangular diagram, give an indication of susceptability to weathering.

130   "La restauration des vitraux anciens." (Editorial) Revue de l'art 31 (1976):5-8.
       Report on the controversial removal, by chemical agents, of the exterior crusting on the 12th century glass of the west windows at Chartres and its replacement by a protective coating of artificial resin.

131   BECKSMANN, RÜDIGER. "Probleme der Restaurierung spätromanischer Glasmalereien." Kunstchronik 29 (1976):330-38, 343-44.
       Paper read at the Corpus Vitrearum Medii Aevi Colloquium in Linnich indicates severe conservation problems in German glass, especially the danger of paint loss; cites examples from Regensburg, Bücken-an-der-Weser, and Freiberg-im-Breisgau.

Tech. 132

132 GRODECKI, LOUIS. "Le chapitre XXVIII de la Schedula du moine
     Théophile: Technique et esthétique du vitrail roman." In
     Comptes rendus des séances de l'année 1976. Académie des
     inscriptions & belles-lettres. Paris: Éditions
     Klincksieck, 1976, pp. 345-47.
         A window of ca. 1230 at Ratisbon Cathedral is found to
     contain gemstones made by firing small colored glasses onto
     another instead of joining them with lead.

133 WOLFF, A. "Domfenster zu Köln: Konservierung und Restau-
     rierung." Arbeitsblätter für Restauratoren 9, no. 1
     (1976):29-41.
         Method currently in use for the lamination of old glass
     (of the 14th century from Cologne Cathedral) between
     polymer resin and modern glass. Discussion.

134 BECKSMANN, RÜDIGER, ed. Akten des 10. internationalen Col-
     loquiums des Corpus Vitrearum Medii Aevi. Stuttgart:
     Akademie der Wissenschaften und der Literatur Mainz, 1977,
     71 pp.
         Résumés of the following papers on conservation:

134a Bacher, Ernst. "Zu aktuellen Fragen der Konservierung
      mittelalterlichen Glasgemälde." pp. 52-53.

134b Bettembourg, Jean-Marie. "Les problèmes de la conservation
      des vitraux de la cathédrale de Bourges." p. 48.

134c Frenzel, Gottfried. "Bericht über die Erstellung eines
      Glasmalerei-Schedensatlas für Bundesrepublik Deutschland."
      p. 51.

134d King, Dennis. "Problems with the Ely Glass." p. 50.

134e Korn, Ulf-Dietrich. "Zur Restaurierung der Chorfenster der
      Stiftskirche zu Bücken." p. 49.

134f Mühlethaler, Bruno. "Kennen wir die Grenzen und Möglich-
      keiten für die Erhaltung mittelalterlicher Glasmalereien?"
      pp. 37-46.

134g Perez y Jorba, M., and Collongues, R. "Recherches récentes
      sur le processus de corrosion des vitraux." p. 47.

135   BETTEMBOURG, JEAN-MARIE. "La dégradation des vitraux." <u>Revue</u>
        <u>du palais de la découverte</u> 6, no. 53 (1977):41-50.
            Useful survey of the composition of medieval glasses and
        paint and the processes of decay; presents several tables
        with recent chemical analyses of French glasses compared
        with Middle Eastern examples.

136   FERRAZZINI, J.C. "Untersuchungen über eine neue in Chartres
        angewandte Methode zur Reinigung und Konservierung von
        mittelalterlichen Glasgemälden." <u>Maltechnik/Restauro:</u>
        <u>Internationale Zeitschrift für Farb- und Maltechniken,</u>
        <u>Restaurierung, und Museumsfragen</u> 83 (1977):145-54.
            Critical report on the applications of viacryl to pre-
        serve medieval glass in France; the hazards of removing
        paint in nonselective cleaning with EDTA, of accelerating
        decay by moisture seepage, and of further loss by removing
        the viacryl. English summary.

137   GOLDRICH, LOUIS MYRON. "An Examination of the Italian Glass
        Industry and Its Influence on Native Stained and Painted
        Glass." Master's thesis, University of Victoria, 1977.
        [Copy in Tufts University Library.]
            Very useful survey of medieval technical treatises and
        archeological evidence for glassmaking in Italy; mentions
        dated windows in Italy.

138   <u>Les monuments historiques de la France</u>, 1977.
            The following papers on conservation are included:

138a   Bettembourg, Jean-Marie. "Problèmes de la conservation des
        vitraux de la façade occidentale de la cathédrale de
        Chartres." pp. 7-14.

138b   Collongues, R. "La corrosion des vitraux." pp. 14-16.

138c   Grodecki, Louis. "Ésthetique ancienne et moderne du
        vitrail roman." pp. 17-30.

138d   Taralon, Jean. "Problématique de la restauration des
        vitraux." pp. 2-6.

139   BETTEMBOURG, JEAN-MARIE. "La conservation des vitraux
        anciens." <u>Revue du palais de la découverte</u> 6, no. 57
        (Apr. 1978):27-38.
            Methods used in the laboratories of the Commission for
        Historical Monuments, including cleaning with EDTA and the
        application of viacryl, demonstrated on the 12th century
        glass of Chartres.

Tech. 140

140   Les dossiers de l'archéologie 26 (Jan.-Feb. 1978).
           The following papers on technique and conservation are
       included:

140a   Bettembourg, Jean-Marie. "Dégradation et conservation des
       vitraux anciens." pp. 102-11.
           Cause and process of corrosion; methods of treatment.

140b   Grodecki, Louis. "Sauvons les vitraux anciens." pp. 12-25.
           Problems of preserving paint and old leads; also deals
       with 19th century overcleaning and decisions not to clean
       now.

140c   Lautier, Claudine. "La technique du vitrail." pp. 26-37.
           Medieval processes, from the making of the glass to the
       installation of the windows.

141   NEWTON, ROY G. "Colouring Agents Used by Medieval Glass-
       makers." Glass Technology 19 (1978):59-60.
           Argues, on the basis of a wide variety of analyzed
       glasses (7th-17th century), that the color often resulted
       from the presence of redox oxides, the furnace atmosphere,
       and the temperature; this control, rather than the addition
       of metal oxides, seems to be indicated by Theophilus.

142   COX, G.A.; HEAVENS, O.S.; NEWTON, R.G.; and POLLARD, A.M. "A
       Study of the Weathering Behaviour of Medieval Glass from
       York Minister." Journal of Glass Studies 21 (1979):54-75.
           Study and analysis of some 200 samples of 12th, 14th,
       and 15th century date. Concludes that silica content is
       high in glasses that are resistant to weathering. Early
       blue glass with 72% silica uniquely durable (Cf. Heaton's
       similar conclusions, Tech. 22, 23).

143   GOODALL, JOHN A. "Instructions for a Glazier by Thomas
       Froxmere, c. 1480." Antiquaries Journal 58 (1979):159-62.
           Pen sketch (London, British Library Landsdowne MS. 874 f.
       191) showing kneeling donors with the arms of Froxmere of
       Droitwich (Worcestershire) and describing the colors iden-
       tified as the design for a lost window.

144   HENCH, L.L.; NEWTON, R.G.; and BERNSTEIN, S. "Use of Infrared
       Reflection Spectroscopy in Analysis of Durability of
       Medieval Glasses, and Some Comments on Conservation Pro-
       cedures." Glass Technology 20 (1979):144-48.
           Proposes this technique as a means of studying corrosion
       of medieval glasses; experiment conducted on simulated
       glasses.

145   HREGLICH, S.; PROFILO, B.; and VERITA, M. "Studio della cor-
       rosione e colorazione dei vetri potassici della vetrata
       della chiesa dei S.S. Giovanni e Paolo a Venezia per mezzo
       della microsonda elettronica." <u>Rivista della Stazione
       sperimentale vetro</u> 9, no. 2 (Mar.-Apr. 1979):53-61.
       English translation. "Study on the Corrosion and Colour
       of Potassium Glass--Church of S.S. Giovanni and Paolo,
       Venice." <u>Corpus Vitrearum News Letter</u> 31-32 (Dec. 1980):
       16-23.
            Electron microscope study of the corrosion and colora-
       tion of the potassium glasses of a Venetian church window.

146   SPITZER-ARONSON, MARTHA. "Précisions sur les techniques mé-
       diévales des vitraux par des recherches en physique."
       <u>Verres et réfractaires</u> 33 (1979):26-34.
            Structure of red glasses, especially samples from York
       (12th-14th centuries), may indicate an origin in the
       region of the Meuse. Bibliography.

147   TENNENT, NORMAN H. "Clear and Pigmented Epoxy Resins for
       Stained Glass Conservation: Light Aging Studies." <u>Studies
       in Conservation</u> 24 (1979):153-64.
            Yellowing can be overcome by suitable room temperature
       curing systems and by the addition of coloring agents.
       Bibliography. French and German summaries.

148   WAYMENT, H.G. "The Great Windows of King's College Chapel and
       the Meaning of the Word 'Vidimus.'" <u>Proceedings of the
       Cambridge Antiquarian Society</u> 69 (1979):53-69.
            <u>Vidimus</u>, as used in contracts of the late Middle Ages,
       meant a preliminary sketch agreed on by a patron and
       glazier.

149   BECKSMANN, RÜDIGER. "Zur Sicherung und Restaurierung der
       mittelalterlichen Glasmalereien im Freiburg Münster."
       <u>Denkmalpflege in Baden-Württemburg</u> 9, no. 1 (1980):1-6.
            Cleaning of some of the nave windows that had received
       a false patina in an earlier 20th century restoration by
       Geiges.

150   BRISAC, CATHERINE. "La 'tête Gérente.'" <u>Revue de l'art</u> 47
       (1980):72-75.
            Suggests a provenance of Lyon and date of ca. 1180-1200
       for a famous head from the Gérente collection in Geneva,
       Musée de l'Ariana. The fine stitckwork in the beard is
       typical of the ateliers of the southeast.

Tech. 151

151   BETTEMBOURG, JEAN-MARIE. "Climatic Factors and Corrosion of
       Stained Glass Windows." In International Congress on Glass
       (Vienna, 7-13 September 1980), pp. 93-95.
          Study of the condition of the 16th century [sic]
       triforium glass of St.-Père at Chartres in relation to
       temperature and humidity damage; advocates external pro-
       tective glazing.

152   TENNENT, NORMAN H. "Fungal Growth on Medieval Stained Glass."
       Journal of the British Society of Master Glass-Painters 17
       (1980-81):64-68.
          Reports a rare case of fungus on a 15th century German
       panel in storage in the Burrell Collection, Glasgow.

153   KORN, ULF-DIETRICH. "Die Restaurierung der Heiligen-Geist-
       Kapelle in Uelzen." Corpus Vitrearum News Letter 33/34
       (Jan. 1982):20-27.
          Use of early photographs to copy the original design in
       replacing lost pieces in these panels dating from 1412. On
       old glass, the original paint was secured with Araldite but
       not retouched.

154   NEWTON, ROY G. "Why Does Condensation not Occur on Externally
       Protected Stained Glass Windows in English Cathedrals?
       Corpus Vitrearum News Letter 33/34 (Jan. 1982):12-19.
          Reports the results of experiments conducted at
       Canterbury and York using protective glazing ventilated to
       the exterior; the air space between the medieval glass and
       the modern protective glazing is always above the dew
       point. Cf. systems ventilated to the interior used on the
       continent, Tech. 109.

Section III
Collections and Sales

This section includes catalogues of collections and sales, and also articles on the history of individual collections and on glass in museums and private collections. Articles on panels originally from a single site and now preserved in museum and private collections may be included under the country of origin of the glass. The reader is also referred to the chapter entitled "Destinées" in Lafond, Le vitrail (Gen. 60) and to the following items: Br. 25, 171, 203; Fr. 119; Ger. 18, 50, 101; L.C. 61, 63; Sw. 41.

1 *A Particular of the Cloister. London:1773.
    Exhibition of 285 Flemish roundels from the Paterson collection held at Essex House, Essex St., the Strand. A copy is in the Victoria and Albert Museum, London.

2 LENOIR, MARIE ALEXANDRE. Histoire de la peinture sur verre et description des vitraux anciens et modernes, pour servir à l'histoire de l'art, relativement à la France, ornée de gravures et notamment des celles de la fable de Cupidon et Psyche d'après les dessins de Raphael. Musée de monuments français, 6. Paris: Guilleminet, 1803, 162 pp., 54 pls.
    Origin and technique of glass painting, followed by a description of panels in the Musée des monuments français, Paris.

3 *A Catalogue of the Ancient Stained Glass for Sale at the Warehouse in Norwich and no. 97, Pall Mall, London. London, 1804, 19 pp., 1 pl. Reprinted in the Journal of the British Society of Master Glass-Painters 12 (1955-59): 22-29.
    Continental glass being sold by Hampp and, probably, Christie. 284 items are listed with brief titles and dimensions.

Coll. 4

4 *A Catalogue of the most valuable and unique Collection of
Ancient Stained Glass, comprising noble Altar Pieces,
Windows for Churches, Collegiate Buildings, and Gothic
Country Residences; also many exquisite Cabinet Pieces,
of the finest Colouring and richest Enamel. The Whole
collected, at a very great Expense, by a Gentleman of enlarged Information and fine Taste, during the early Part of
the French Revolution, from the suppressed Churches and
Religious Houses, in Germany, France and the Netherlands,
which will be sold at auction, by Mr. Christie, At his
Great Room, in Pall Mall, on Thursday, June 16th, 1808,
and the following day. [London, 1808.]
    Eighty-nine lots, briefly titled. A copy of this cata-
log is in the Fitzwilliam Museum, Cambridge; see Coll. 48.
The remainder was sold July 17th, 1820.

5 *A Short Account of Lichfield Cathedral; more particularly of
the Painted Glass, etc. Lichfield: T.G. Lomax, 1811.
[Eight later editions; the 6th is attributed to Dean
Woodhouse.]
    Description of the 16th century glass from Herckenrode
(Belgium) installed in Lichfield Cathedral.

6 *[PAGET, RICHARD ARTHUR SURTEES.] A Catalogue of a Valuable
and Highly Curious Assemblage of Ancient Flemish Stained
Glass Collected on the Continent. Suited for Private
Chapels and Library Windows, which will be Sold by auction
by Mr. Christie at his Great Room, Pall Mall (London) on
Tuesday, May 7, 1816, at one o'clock. London: G. Smeeton,
[1816].
    "Original in London Victoria and Albert Museum is a
typewritten English script. A copy is thought to be in the
collection of Wilfred Drake." Duncan, 9658(a). See
Coll. 48.

7 *Verzeichnis einer Theils aus ganzen Kirchenfenstern, Theils
aus einzelhnen Scheiben bestehenden grossen Sammlung ge-
brannter Gläser aus verschiedenen auf einander folgenden
Zeitaltern der Glasmalerei, welcher am 3. Juni l.J. in dem
mit Nro. 12 bezeichneten, im Filzergraben dahier gelegenen
Hause zur öffentlichen Ansicht aufgestellt und am. 13.
September l.J. in demselben Lokale öffentlich versteigert
und gegen gleich baare [sic] Zahlung dem Meisbietenden
Zugeschlagen werden soll. Cologne: Du Mont-Schauberg,
1821.
    Johann Baptist Hirn collection, Cologne.

8 *Verzeichnis der seltenen Kunstsammlungen von Gemälden, ge-
   schmelzten Glasmalereye des dahier verstorbenen kgl.
   preuss. Hauptmanns Herrn Hans Albrecht von Derschau, welche
   zu Nürnberg . . . am 1. Aug. 1825 versteigert worden sollen.
   [Becksmann].

9 *Catalogue of Rare Prints and Illustrated Works Removed from
   Strawberry Hill. To be Sold by Auction, 13th June, 1842.
   Collected by H. Walpole. London: George Robins (Covent
   Garden), 1842.
       "Particulars of 58 items of glass windows for sale in-
   cluding glass by Abraham van Diepenbeke, Lucas van Leyden
   and others: pp. 238-247." Duncan, 14333.

10 *A Catalogue of the Highly Valuable and Interesting Collection
   of the Late E.B. Vigurs Esq., Comprising Ancient Stained
   Glass of Rare Beauty, Principally from the Archiepiscopal
   Palace of Lambeth. London, 1849.
       A copy in Lambeth Palace, London (Duncan, 14158).

11 *Katalog der Ende vor. Saecl. gesammelten Reichsfreiherr 1.v.
   Zwierleinischen Glasgemälde: Beginn der Versteigerung am
   19. Oktober 1872.
       Partial sale of a collection of German glass, 13th-17th
   centuries (see also Coll. 18, 22).

12 ENNEN, L. "Die Glasgemälde aus den jetzt zerstörten Kirchen
   Kölns." Zeitschrift für bildende Kunst: Kunst-Chronik 10
   (1875):705-9.
       The dispersal of glass from the churches of Cologne
   immediately following the French invasion; much bought by
   the English in 1802.

13 *EYE, A.v., and BÖRNER, P.E. Die Kunstsammlung von Eugen Felix
   in Leipzig: Katalog. Leipzig, 1880. [Becksmann].

14 MAYER von MAYERFELS, KARL. "Die Glasmalereien im ehemaligen
   Kloster Hofen jetzigem Sommern-Residenz-Schlosse St. Maj.
   des Königs Karl von Württemburg." Schriften des verein
   für Geschichte des Bodensees und seiner Ungebung 11 (1882):
   43-70.
       Description of 14th century glass panels installed in
   various rooms of the royal residence. Iconography not well
   identified; dated ca. 1350-70 on the basis of costume and
   compared to the windows in Ulm. Not illustrated.

15 ESSENWEIN, A. Katalog der im Germanischen Museum befindlichen
Glasgemälde aus älterer Zeit. Nuremberg: Verlag des
Germanischen Museums, 1884, 54 pp., 14 pls., 17 figs. in
text. 2d ed., 1898, 70 pp., 18 pls., 24 figs. in text.
Handlist of glass in this Nuremberg museum, now the most
important collection in Germany; illustrated chiefly with
drawings.

16 *Katalog der Kunstsammlungen des Fr. R. von Berthold. Cologne,
1885.
"Part 2 includes glass and glass painting," illustrated
(Duncan, 1108).

17 RAHN, J. RUDOLF. "Die Glasgemälde im gotischen Hause zu
Wörlitz." In Gesammelte Studien zur Kunstgeschichte: Eine
Festgabe zum 4. Mai 1885 für Anton Springer. Leipzig:
Seeman, [1885], pp. 176-225.
Collection of Johann Caspar Lavater (1741-1801) in
Wörliz near Dessau late 15th-17th century glass, largely
German (?) and Swiss. Catalog not illustrated.

18 *Die Freiherrlich von Zwierlein'schen Sammlungen von gebrannten
Glasfenstern, Kunstsachen, und Gemälden etc. zu Geisenheim:
Versteigerung des 12. bis 15. September 1887. Cologne,
1887, 12 pls.
Continues sale of 1872. German glass, 13th-17th cen-
turies (see Coll. 11,22).

19 RAHN, JOHANN RUDOLF. "Die schweizerischen Glasgemälde in der
Vincent'schen Sammlung in Constanz." Mitteilungen der
antiquarischen Gesellschaft in Zürich 20, no. 6 (1890):
179-263.
History of collections; inventory of 491 items, some
from the 14th-early 16th centuries, most after 1540.
Bibliography of Swiss glass. Not illustrated.

20 La collection Spitzer: Antiquité, Moyen-Âge, Renaissance.
Vol. 3. Paris: Quantin, 1891.
"Les vitraux," pp. 113-26, illus. engravings. Glass
from Boppard and French 16th century grisaille scenes installed in Spitzer's house, rue de Villejust, Paris. Sold
in 1893 (Coll. 21).

21 Catalogue des objets d'art, 33 rue de Villejust, . . . com-
posant l'importante et precieuse collection Spitzer
(17 Apr.-16 June). Vol. 2. Paris, 1893. Émile Molinier,
"Vitraux," pp. 65-67, nos. 1953-58; "Supplément,"
pp. 269-71, nos. 3349-69.
Glass from Boppard and French 16th century grisaille
scenes, previously cataloged (Coll. 20).

22 ROTH, F.W.E. "Die Freiherrlich von Zwierlein'sche Sammlung
    von Glasmalereien zu Geisenheim a. Rh." Jahrbücher des
    Vereins von Alterthumsfreunden im Rheinlande (Bonner Jahr-
    bücher) 96-97 (1895):293-303.
        Brief account of a large collection, begun in 1820 and
    dispersed in the 1870s, with information on sales in that
    period. 247 items of the 14th-17th centuries, including
    several panels from Altenberg (see Coll. 11, 18).

23 Katalog der gräfl. W. Douglas'schen Sammlung alter Glasgemälde
    auf Schloss Langenstein (Versteigerung). Cologne: J.M.
    Herberle, 1897, 38 pp., 59 entries.
        16th-17th, and 18th century glass from Germany and
    Switzerland.

24 *MESSIKOMMER. Auktion der Glasgemälde-Sammlung der Baronin de
    Trétaigne in Paris und von Glasgemälden aus der ehemaligen
    Vincent-Sammlung in Konstanz. Zurich: H. Messikommer,
    1904.

25 GALLERIE GEORGES PETIT. Catalogue des objets d'art et de
    haute curiosité, 11-16 mai. Paris, 1908.
        Important panels, chiefly French, from the collection of
    Octave Homberg. Illustrated.

26 SCHINNERER, JOHANNES. Katalog der Glasgemälde des Bayerischen
    National-museums. Kataloge des Bayerischen National-
    museums, 9. Munich: Verlag des Bayerischen National-
    museums, 1908, 103 pp., 40 pls.
        Scholarly catalog of the museum's holdings, ranging from
    13th century glass, perhaps from Tegernsee, to 16th century
    examples, largely south German.

27 BALET, LEO. Schwäbische Glasmalerei. Kataloge der kgl.
    Altertümersammlung in Stuttgart, 2. Stuttgart and Leipzig:
    Deutsche Verlag-Anstalt, 1912, 165 pp., 8 col. pls.,
    126 figs. in text.
        Brief entries for examples of 12th-16th century glass,
    chiefly German. Index and bibliography. Well illustrated.
    Still the most complete catalog of the Stuttgart Museums.

28 F., D. "Stained Glass Panels." Metropolitan Museum of Art
    Bulletin (Nov. 1912):212-14.
        Discusses the Evangelist symbols and the Three Righteous
    Men attributed to England, 13th century [these copies of
    glass at Canterbury have since been sold]; and a German
    14th century seated bishop.

Coll. 29

29 *FISCHER, JOSEF L. <u>Die Glasgemälde im Schloss Hohenschwangau:</u>
<u>Eine Sammlung König Maximilians II. von Bayern.</u> Munich,
1912.

30 GALERIE HELBING. <u>Katalog einer Kollektion von alten schweizer</u>
<u>und deutschen Glasgemälden aus dem Besitze des Herrn Hofrat</u>
<u>Eduard Kahlbau, Stuttgart, des Herrn Hauptmann a.D. Robert</u>
<u>Clemm, Burg Winzingen (Haardter Schloss genannt) sowie aus</u>
<u>schweizer Privatbesitz</u> (21 Nov.). Munich: Hugo Helbing,
1912, 65 pp., 80 figs.
    Important examples of German and Swiss glass from the
15th century on, many after 1550.

31 DAY, LEWIS F. <u>Stained Glass.</u> Victoria and Albert Museum
Handbooks. London: H.M. Stationery Office, 1913, 121 pp.,
66 figs.
    History of glass painting illustrated with examples in
the museum's collection and comparative material; inventory
of glass exhibited: English, French, German, Italian, and
Swiss, 12th-17th centuries.

32 LILL, GEORG. <u>Katalog einer Kollektion von alten schweizer und</u>
<u>süddeutschen Glasgemälden aus furstlichem suddeutschem</u>
<u>Schlossbesitz Galerie Helbing</u> (7 Oct. 1913). Munich: Hugo
Helbing, 1913, 36 pp., 60 figs.
    Sale of the collection of Lord Sudeley, Toddington
Castle (Gloucestershire), containing some 13th-14th century
French glass. The Swiss panels are after 1550. Some prices
are published in the <u>Zeitschrift für alte und neue Glas-</u>
<u>malerei</u> 1, no. 1 (1912):10-11; and 1, no. 2 (1912):18-19.

33 SCHMITZ, HERMANN. <u>Die Glasgemälde des königlichen Kunstge-</u>
<u>werbemuseums in Berlin mit einer Einführung in die Ge-</u>
<u>schichte der deutschen Glasmalerei.</u> 2 vols. Berlin:
Julius Bard, 1913. Vol. 1, <u>Text</u>, 275 pp., 406 figs. in
text. Vol. 2, <u>Katalog und Tafeln</u>, 29 pp., 70 pls.
    Vol. 1 is a history of German glass painting with brief
sections on Swiss glass, etc. Vol. 2 contains a checklist
of the collection, with dimensions and notes on restorations. Excellent photographs. Some of this important
glass was destroyed in World War II.

34 DRAKE, MAURICE. <u>The Costessey Collection of Stained Glass,</u>
<u>Formerly in the Possession of George William Jerningham,</u>
<u>8th Baron Stafford of Costessey in the County of Norfolk.</u>
Introduction by Aymer Vallance. Exeter: William Pollard &
Co., 1920, 49 pp., 25 pls.

Important collection of French and German glass bought
by Sir William Jerningham before 1909 and acquired by
Grosvenor Thomas in 1918.

35   "Stained Glass." Saint-Louis Bulletin of the City Art Museum
     6 (1921):2-6.
         Discusses a seated prophet, attributed to the school of
     Champagne, 12th-13th century; and three 15th century panels
     from Nuremberg.

36   AMERICAN ART ASSOCIATION. "Stained Glass Panels, Chiefly
     French, of the 13th, 14th, and 15th Centuries." In
     Illustrated Catalogue of the Noteworthy Gathering of Gothic
     and Other Ancient Art Collected by the Late Mr. Henry C.
     Lawrence of New York: January 28th. New York, 1921,
     Lots 338-89.
         Very important collection, largely acquired from Bacri,
     Heilbronner, Grosvenor Thomas, and French and Co. Includes
     glass from Soissons Cathedral and St.-Urbain of Troyes.
     Most examples illustrated. [Many lots are now in Ports-
     mouth Abbey, R.I.; see Exh. 49].

37   C., O.C. "Rearrangement of Stained Glass, Including Some
     Recent Acquisitions." Metropolitan Museum of Art Bulletin
     16 (1921):233-34.
         Records the installation of forty-six panels (13th-18th
     centuries); and the acquisitions of a French 14th century
     ornament fragment, a 15th century English panel represent-
     ing St. John the Evangelist, and two sashes bearing the
     date of 1620.

38   GALERIE GEORGES PETIT. Catalogue des objets d'art et de haute
     curiosité du Moyen-Âge et de la Renaissance . . . composant
     les collections de M. Raoul Heilbronner. Paris, 22-23 June
     1921.
         Lots 204-16 (pp. 62-64) are French 14th and 16th century
     glass. One example is illustrated.

39   HÔTEL DROUOT. Catalogue des vitraux anciens français, alle-
     mands, suisses, et divers des xiiie, xive, xve, & xvii^e
     siècles composant la collection [Frédéric] Engel-Gros
     (7 Dec. 1922). Paris, 39 pp.
         100 lots, chiefly 16th century, some French panels are
     earlier. Illustrated.

Coll. 40

40 S[WARZENSKI], H[ANNS]. "The Jesse Window." <u>Metropolitan</u>
    <u>Museum of Art Bulletin</u> 17 (1922):76-79.
       14th century Swabian glass.

41 THOMAS, ROY GROSVENOR. <u>Stained Glass: Its Origin and Appli-</u>
    <u>cation</u>. New York: privately printed, 1922, 18 pp., 4 pls.
       Summary of the history of glass from its origin in the
    10th century; discusses the construction of a window,
    forgeries, corrosion, and stylistic characteristics.
    Illustrated with panels in the author's collection (French
    and English, 13th-16th centuries).

42 DARMSTADT, HESSISCHES LANDESMUSEUM. <u>Kunst- und historische</u>
    <u>Sammlungen: Die Glasmalereien</u>. Darmstadt: Hessiches
    Landesmuseum, 1923, 12 pp., 5 woodcuts.
       Brief, lyrical notice; covers 13th century glass from
    Wimpfen.

43 LEGGE, THOMAS. "A Collection of the 15th Century Stained
    Glass." <u>Journal of the British Society of Master Glass-</u>
    <u>Painters</u> 1, no. 2 (Apr. 1925):40-42.
       Acquisition of glass in Norwich; local productions of
    ca. 1450-80.

44 PHILADELPHIA, PENNSYLVANIA MUSEUM. <u>Catalogue of the Collec-</u>
    <u>tion of Stained and Painted Glass in the Pennsylvania</u>
    <u>Museum</u>. Preface by Arthur Edwin Bye, contributions by
    Roy Grosvenor Thomas. Philadelphia: Pennsylvania Museum
    and School of Industrial Art, 1925, 96 pp.
       Seventy-two panels (14th-16th centuries) of English,
    French, Italian, Flemish, and German glass; a major por-
    tion are Swiss glass.

45 *<u>Sammlung Fr. O. Edler von Leber</u>. Vienna, 1925, 38 pls.
       "Auction catalogue for collection of von Leber (1803-
    1846)." Duncan, 7679.

46 OUVERLEAUX-LAGASSE, FÉLIX A. "Les vitraux de l'ancienne
    église abbatiale d'Herckenrode à la cathédrale de
    Lichfield." <u>Annales de la Société royale d'archéologie</u>
    (Bruxelles) 32 (1926):89-97.
       Seven windows executed in the Low Countries (1530-40)
    by Lambert Lombard and brought to England in the 19th cen-
    tury; two fragments from these abbey windows are now in the
    Victoria and Albert Museum (1624) and St. Mary's,
    Shrewsbury (16th century).

47 EDEN, F. SYDNEY. <u>The Collection of Heraldic Stained Glass at</u>
    <u>Ronaele Manor, Elkins Park, Pennsylvania</u>. London: Arden
    Press, 1927, 120 pp., 53 color pls. [106 copies only;
    available in the British Museum, the Victoria and Albert
    Museum, and the Fogg Museum].
        Important collection of English heraldic glass (14th-
    16th centuries) acquired through Roy Grosvenor Thomas and
    Thomas and Wilfrid Drake; many are from Cassiobury [now in
    the Philadelphia Museum of Art].

48 RACKHAM, BERNARD. "English Importations of Foreign Stained
    Glass in the Early Nineteenth Century." <u>Journal of the</u>
    <u>British Society of Master Glass-Painters</u> 2 (1927-28):86-94.
        Glass bought in France and the Low Countries by J.C.
    Hampp, 1802-8, some of which was sold by Christie in 1808;
    from Hampp's account book in the Fitzwilliam Museum,
    Cambridge.

49 "Sale of the 16th Century Glass from the Chapel of Ashridge
    Park, Hertfordshire." <u>Journal of the British Society of</u>
    <u>Master Glass-Painters</u> 2, no. 4 (Oct. 1928):210-11.
        16th century glass from Steinfeld installed in Ashridge
    in 1811. Bought for £27,000 and given to the Victoria and
    Albert Museum (see Coll. 50).

50 SOTHEBY AND CO. <u>Catalogue of the Magnificent Sixteenth Cen-</u>
    <u>tury Stained Glass Windows from the Chapel of Ashridge,</u>
    <u>Herts., to be Sold on the 12th of July</u>. London, 1928,
    20 pp., 7 collotype pls., 1 color frontispiece.
        Fifty-three lots; eleven windows originally from the
    abbey church of Steinfeld (see Coll. 49).

51 DEMOTTE, J. <u>Catalogue of an Exhibition of Stained Glass from</u>
    <u>the XIth to the XVIIIth Century</u>. New York, 1929.
        Fifty-five entries for sale, the majority early glass
    from France; also 13th-16th century glass from France,
    Austria, England, Germany, the Low Countries, and
    Switzerland. Includes photographic reproductions.

52 HAUG, HANS. "Le musée historique de la ville d'Obernai."
    <u>Archives alsaciennes d'histoire de l'art</u> 8 (1929):51-83.
        Fragments from SS. Peter and Paul from the end of the
    15th century; their style is compared with those of Walburg
    and St.-Guillaume. The dating of Niedermünster window
    formerly called 17th century, assigned to around 1514 on
    the basis of designs by Hans Baldung Grien.

Coll. 53

53   RACKHAM, BERNARD. "Stained Glass in the Collection of Mr.
       F.E. Sidney." Old Furniture 7 (May-Aug. 1929):223-30.
            Collection of Mr. F.E. Sydney of Hampstead (d. 1932).
       Discusses Swiss ecclesiastical heraldic glass from the
       15th, 16th, and 17th centuries and the evolution of glass
       painting in Switzerland (see Coll. 76).

54   EDEN, F. SYDNEY. "English Heraldic Glass in America."
       Connoisseur 85 (1930):363-64.
            Seventy-four panels of heraldic glass in Ronaele Manor;
       these date from the 14th and 15th centuries [and are now
       in the Philadelphia Museum of Art] (see Coll. 47, 55).

55   _____. "Heraldic Glass at Ronaele Manor." Connoisseur 86
       (1930):30-33.
            Innovative techniques, such as abrasion and various
       colors of flashed glass, were used in the 16th century.
       Anglo-Flemish and English shields are preserved in this
       collection.

56   RACKHAM, BERNARD. "Austrian Stained Glass at South
       Kensington." Burlington Magazine 59 (1930):291-92.
            Mid-14th century Mariological panels from Strassengel.

57   CHRISTIE, MANSON, AND WOODS. Catalogue of Fine Tapestry,
       Objects of Art and Furniture, and Early English and German
       Stained Glass, the Property of the Rt. Hon. Lord Manton.
       [Sale 30 July]. London: Christie & Co., 1931, pp. 18-29,
       Lot nos. 118-146.
            15th, 16th, and 17th century glass from England and
       Germany.

58   BRIGHT, HUGH. The Herckenrode Windows in Lichfield Cathedral.
       Lichfield: Lomax's Successors (F.H. Bull & E. Wiseman),
       1932, 21 pp., frontispiece, 9 figs.
            Glass, dated 1532-39, acquired from the Cistercian con-
       vent of Herckenrode (Belgium) by Sir Brooke Boothby in 1801
       and installed in the Lady Chapel and choir aisles in 1804-
       1814; subjects include Marianic and Christological cycles
       and donors.

59   EDEN, F. SYDNEY. "Vicissitudes of Ancient Stained Glass."
       Burlington Magazine 61 (1932):118-25.
            Examples of the migration of glass (12th-16th centuries)
       from its original location; emphasis on English collec-
       tions.

60 *GALERIE HELBING. <u>Versteigerungskatalog: Aus Schloss E. Sr.
    Erlaucht der Grafen K. zu E., Glasgemälde aus Fürstlichem
    Besitz</u>. Introduction by A. Feulner. Frankfurt-am-Main:
    Hugo Helbing, 1932. [Becksmann].

61 ROBINSON, J.A. "The Great West Window at Wells." <u>Journal of
    the British Society of Master Glass-Painters</u> 4, no. 3 (Apr.
    1932):109-22.
        Describes illustrations of the Life of St. John the
    Evangelist, a 16th century window obtained from Rouen via
    Hampp and Costessey.

62 SCHNEIDER, ARTHUR von. "Glasmalerei aus dem Münster im
    freiburger Augustinermuseum." <u>Pantheon</u> 9 (1932):185-87.
        14th-16th century examples from the Wrbna collection now
    in the Augustinermuseum in Freiburg-im-Brisgau; these in-
    clude panels designed by Hans Baldung Grien.

63 *WOODFORDE, CHRISTOPHER. <u>The Locksley Hall Collection of
    Stained and Painted Glass</u>. Privately printed, 1932,
    1 col. pl., 8 collotype pls.

64 KIESLINGER, FRANZ. "A Gothic Stained Glass Window."
    <u>Burlington Magazine</u> 62 (1933):87-88.
        Old Testament panels in the Malmedian Museum, Cologne
    and the Kunstgewerbemuseum, Vienna are attributed to 14th
    century Styria (Austria).

65 EDEN, F. SYDNEY. "Ancient Painted Glass at Old Hall,
    Highgate." <u>Connoisseur</u> 94 (1934):3-8.
        A description of the principal panels then in the col-
    lection of Lord Rochdale in London; English, French, Ger-
    man, and Swiss in origin, 13th-16th century in date [some
    are now in the Metropolitan Museum, New York].

66 F., v.O. "Luzern." <u>Pantheon</u> (1934):253-54.
        Sale of 15th and 16th century glass from the destroyed
    Deutsch-Ordenskirche of Wiener-Neustadt through Thomas
    Fischer of Lucerne.

67 *GALERIE HELBING. <u>Auktionskatalog: Gemälde neuerer und alter
    Meister, Keramik, Glasmalereien, Ostasiatica, Orienttep-
    piche, Möbel, Skulpturen, Graphik, Sammlung Architekt C.A.
    Meckel, Freiburg i. Br. u.a</u>. Munich: Hugo Helbing, 1934.
    [Becksmann].

Coll. 68

68   SKINNER, ORIN E.   "Stained Glass in the City Art Museum of
     Saint Louis."   Stained Glass 29, nos. 1-2 (Spring-Summer
     1934):7-20 and "Ancient Glass Acquired by the Saint Louis
     Museum," Stained Glass 30, no. 2 (Autumn 1935):59-63.
          Principally treats an early 13th century seated prophet
     from northern France.

69   DRAKE, WILFRED.   "Beatrix, Wife of Emperor Frederick
     Barbarossa."   Apollo 22 (July-Dec. 1935):80-81.
          A description of a small panel representing Empress
     Beatrix (1185) which came to England in the early 19th cen-
     tury [now in the Burrell collection, Glasgow].

70   KENT, ERNEST A: "John Christopher Hampp of Norwich."   Journal
     of the British Society of Master Glass-Painters 6 (1935-37):
     191-96.
          Publishes documents concerning this German-born weaver
     who dealt in stained glass ca. 1802-15.

71   GIESE, LEOPOLD.   "Die mittelalterlichen Glasgemälde in Goethes
     Nachlass."   Goethe: Vierteljahrsschrift der Goethe-
     Gesellschaft, n.s. 1 (1936):99-104.
          12th and 14th century German glass in the collection of
     the Goethe Museum in Weimar.

72   *LEPKE, R.   Antiquitäten, Glasgemälde alter und neuerer
     Meister: Auktionskatalog.   Bonn, 12-13 Feb. 1936
     (no. 2097).   [Becksmann].

73   RACKHAM, BERNARD.   Victoria and Albert Museum, Department of
     Ceramics: A Guide to the Collections of Stained Glass.
     London: Board of Education, 1936, 142 pp., 64 figs.
          The chapters on the historical development of glass
     painting from the 12th to the 19th century place examples
     from the museum's collection in their original context.

74   S[KINNER], O[RIN] E.   "Stained Glass in the Toledo Museum of
     Art."   Stained Glass 31, no. 2 (Autumn 1936):37-47.
          13th-16th century examples of variable quality, some of
     doubtful authenticity.

75   WOODFORDE, CHRISTOPHER.   "Foreign Stained and Painted Glass in
     Norfolk."   Original Papers of the Norfolk and Norwich
     Archaeological Society 26 (1936):73-84.
          Survey of 15th and 16th century glass now in churches
     and houses, such as Stradsett, Aylsham, Kimberley, and
     Spixworth Park, much of it collected on the continent by
     Hampp ca. 1800.

76 CHRISTIE, MANSON, AND WOODS. The Collection of English and Continental Furniture, Porcelain and Objects of Art, and Stained Glass Formed by F.E. Sidney, Esq. [Sale 9 Dec.] London: Christie's, 1937.
Nos. 52-91 are mainly German and Swiss panels from the 16th century (see Coll. 53).

77 STEINBERG, S.H. "The Nine Worthies and the Christian Kings." Connoisseur 104 (1939):146-49.
Reconstruction of a set of windows (ca. 1530) from which six panels remain; the designs are attributed to followers of Bernard Flower.

78 HAMMER GALLERIES, SAKS FIFTH AVENUE, and GIMBEL BROS. Art Objects and Furniture from the William Randolph Hearst Collection: Catalogue Raisonné [New York, 1941], pp. 130-48, 329-30.
About 150 lots of 12th-19th century glass, some of which are illustrated.

79 "Ancient Glass in Detroit Cathedral." Stained Glass 38, no. 3 (Autumn 1943):88-89.
14th-15th century French and Spanish glass to fill 20 windows. Not illustrated.

80 FRANKL, PAUL. "Four Pieces of Stained Glass." Record of the Museum of Historic Art, Princeton University 3, no. 1 (1944):8-15.
Acquisition of fragments of grisaille and canopy work; two are ascribed to Chartres ca. 1280, two to Germany ca. 1360 and 1515. For the former cf. Fr. 358, 364.

81 NORMILE, JAMES. "The William Randolph Hearst Collection of Mediaeval and Renaissance Stained and Painted Glass." Stained Glass 41, no. 2 (Summer 1946):39-44.
Panels given to the Los Angeles County Museum.

82 WITZLEBEN, ELISABETH SCHÜRER von. "Mittelalterliche Glasmalereien in Bayerischen Nationalmuseum." Zeitschrift für Kunst 2 (1948):141-44.
Overview of the riches of this collection, for the period 12th-16th centuries.

83 SCHNEIDER, ARTHUR von. Die Glasgemälde des Badischen Landesmuseum, Karlsruhe. Veröffentlichungen des Badischen Landesmuseums, 2. Freiburg-im-Breisgau: Urban-Verlag, 1950, 91 pp., 84 pls. (4 color).

Coll. 83

      Complete catalog, largely of south German and Swiss glass, chronologically arranged (13th-17th centuries) and fully illustrated. Introductory chapters on the history of the collection and the periods of glass painting represented.

84   SCHEYER, ERNST. "Henry Adams as a Collector of Art." <u>Art Quarterly</u> 15 (1952):221-33.
      Acquisition of the 13th century panels from Soissons Cathedral for the Gardner Museum, Boston.

85   WENTZEL, HANS. "A Late Gothic Window from Strassburg in Kansas City." <u>Art Quarterly</u> 16 (1953):328-30.
      A panel in the Nelson Museum attributed to Peter Hemmel von Andlau ca. 1470.

86   SCHUG-WILLE, CHRISTA. "Die figürlichen Glasmalereien des 14. Jahrhunderts in der Burgkapelle der Löwenburg in Kassel aus der Stadtkirche zu Hersfeld." <u>Zeitschrift des Vereins für hessische Geschichte und Landeskunde</u> 68 (1957):220-26.
      Christological and hagiographical cycles removed to Kassel ca. 1800.

87   <u>Das Schnütgen-Museum: Eine Auswahl</u>. Introduction by Hermann Schnitzler. Cologne: Das Schnütgen-Museum, 1958, 59 pp., 150 figs.
      Catalog of selected objects, including a dozen panels of high quality, dated 13th-16th centuries.

88   WELLS, WILLIAM. "Light into Art." <u>Scottish Art Review</u> 6, no. 2 (1957):32-33; 6, no. 4 (1958):7-10.
      550 panels of stained glass from the Burrell collection now in the Glasgow Museum; a 16th century Tree of Jesse fragment from Rouen, a 13th century window with patriarchs and saints, and two panels representing scenes from the Marriage at Cana (from the 13th and 15th centuries) are identified.

89   LAFOND, JEAN. "Vitraux français en Angleterre: Wilton (xiie et xiiie siècles)." <u>Bulletin de la Société nationale des antiquaires de France</u> (1959):241-43.
      Stained glass brought into England by Hampp in the 19th century and sold to Sidney Herbert; a panel in Wilton is attributed to the principal atelier of the Ste.-Chapelle. Not described in the Corpus volume (Fr. 240); see Caviness and Grodecki (Fr. 312), where this reference is also over-looked.

90 _____. "Le commerce des vitraux étrangers anciens en
Angleterre au XVIIIe et XIXe siècles." <u>Revue des Sociétés</u>
<u>savantes de Haute-Normandie: Histoire de l'art</u> 20 (1960):
5-15.
Some valuable documents on 18th century commerce in
glass, as well as material on Hampp.

91 VERDIER, PHILIPPE. "An Exhibition of Stained and Painted
Glass from the 13th to the 17th Century." <u>Bulletin of the</u>
<u>Walters Art Gallery</u> 12, no. 5 (1960): [2 pp.]
A brief account of the important French glass in this
collection and of a piece designed by Hans von Kulmbach.

92 GRIMME, ERNST GÜNTHER. "Mittelalterliche Scheiben in einer
Aachener Privatsammlung." <u>Aachener Kunstblätter</u> 19-20
(1960-61):25-44.
13th-16th century glass, chiefly from Austria and
Germany. Well illustrated.

93 WENTZEL, HANS. "Unbekannte mittelalterliche Glasmalereien der
Burrell Collection zu Glasgow." <u>Pantheon</u> 19 (1961):105-13,
178-86, 240-49.
Important study of the Austrian and German glass in this
collection, including panels from Erfurt, Strasbourg,
Wiener-Neustadt, and Boppard; and the discovery of a
prophet from the 12th century Jesse window [actually from
the Infancy window] of St.-Denis.

94 FRANKL, PAUL. "A Stained Glass Roundel in Boston (Mass.)."
<u>Gazette des beaux-arts</u> 60 (1962):521-28.
A Prodigal Son panel dated ca. 1210, cf. similar subjects at Sens, etc. [a fake; see Exh. 49].

95 BREMEN, WALTER. <u>Die alten Glasgemälde und Hohlgläser der</u>
<u>Sammlung Bremen in Krefeld: Katalog</u>. Beihefte Bonner
Jahrbücher, 13. Cologne and Graz: Böhlau Verlag, 1964,
173 pp., 257 figs.
Important examples of Austrian, German, and Swiss glass,
many of which were sold ca. 1969 to the Germanisches
Nationalmuseum. 14th-18th century in date, with many of
the items after 1550.

96 WENTZEL, HANS. "Neuerworbene Glasmalereien des Stuttgarter
Landesmuseums." <u>Pantheon</u> 22 (1964):211-19.
Recent acquisitions include a donor panel by Peter
Hemmel von Andlau (1492), three pieces from Passau ca.
1500, and Austrian glass of ca. 1440. English summary.

97 BEEH-LUSTENBERGER, SUZANNE. Glasgemälde aus frankfurter
Sammlungen. Frankfurt-am-Main: Waldemar Kramer, for the
Kuratorium kulturelles Frankfurt: Polytechnische Gesellschaft, 1965, 288 pp., 111 pls.
Fully illustrated catalog of over 100 panels in public
and private collections, about half of which are earlier
than 1500; most are German, and many are from Frankfort
churches. Indexes include donors and patrons.

98 BEYER, VICTOR. Les vitraux des musées de Strasbourg:
Catalogue. Introduction by Hans Haug. Strasbourg: Musée
de la ville, 1965, 43 pp., 5 color pls., 25 figs. 2d ed.,
revised and enlarged, 1966, 67 pp.
Brief catalog, with comments on technique and bibliography. Glass of the 13th-20th centuries arranged chronologically (cf. fasicule of glass from elsewhere in the 1965
exhibition, Exh. 29).

99 FRODL-KRAFT, EVA. "Die Geschichte eines Glasgemälde-Verkaufs."
Österreichische Zeitschrift für Kunst und Denkmalpflege 19
(1965):186-90.
Records sales of 14th century glass from St. Leonhard im
Lavantthale, 1929-35.

100 PERROT, FRANÇOISE. "Inventaire sommaire des vitraux déposés
dans les réserves du Musée de Cluny." Information d'histoire de l'art 2 (1966):132-33.
Glass in the Cluny Museum in Paris; about 150 windows
(French and Swiss), dated 11th-18th centuries; state of
research described (cf. Coll. 111).

101 BEEH-LUSTENBERGER, SUZANNE. Glasmalerei um 800-1900 im
Hessischen Landesmuseum in Darmstadt. Kataloge Hessischen
Landesmuseum, 2. Illustration volume. Frankfurt-am-Main:
Societäts-Verlag, 1967, 18 pp., 258 pls. (21 color); Text
volume. Hanau: Dr. Hans Peters Verlag, 1973, 336 pp.,
31 pls.
Complete scholarly catalog of this very large collec-
tion, chiefly of Germanic glass. Supplementary illustra-
tions include complete reproductions of the 9th century
Lorsch fragments.

102 RODE, HERBERT. "Ramboux' Plan einer Glasgemäldegalerie: Ein
Beitrag zur Frühgeschichte des Städtischen Museums Köln."
Wallraf-Richartz Jahrbuch 29 (1967):335-37.
History of glass collecting in Cologne after the secu-
larization of 1802; plans were made for a stained glass

gallery late in the 1840s, but instead the panels were installed in the cathedral.

103 HICKL-SZABO, H. "Seven Stained Glass Panels." Rotunda: Bulletin of the Royal Ontario Museum (Toronto) 1, no. 1 (1968):24-31.
     First publication and reproduction of a small collection of glass, including a St. Catherine (Austrian ca. 1385), a fragmentary donor (English ca. 1400), and south German and Swiss pieces of ca. 1490-1530.

104 HAUCK, MARIELUISE. "Mittelalterliche Glasmalereien im Historischen Museum der Pfalz, Speyer." Mitteilungen des historischen Vereins der Pfalz 67 (1969):242-51.
     Small collection of German and Swiss medieval glass, dated 15th-16th centuries. Superseded by the Corpus volume (Ger. 212).

105 HÔTEL DROUOT. Catalogue de la vente après décès de l'ancienne collection de vitraux anciens de M. Acezat (24-25 Nov.). Paris, 1969, 35 pp., 8 pls.
     163 lots of 13th-20th century French, Swiss, Flemish, and German glass from the collection of Michel Acezat, a glass painter.

106 HAYWARD, JANE. "Medieval Stained Glass from St. Leonhard im Lavanttal at the Cloisters." Metropolitan Museum of Art Bulletin, n.s. 28 (1969-70):291-92.
     Attributes these pieces to the atelier that worked at Judenburg ca. 1340.

107 SCHNEIDER, JENNY. Glasgemälde: Katalog der Sammlung des Schweizerischen Landesmuseums, Zürich. 2 vols. Stäfa: T. Gut & Co., [1907]. Vol. 1, 128 pp., 118 pls. Vol. 2, 130 pp., 120 pls.
     Analysis of style, technique, and iconography. Largely Swiss glass, from ca. 1200 on, arranged chronologically; the bulk of the collection is 16th-17th century armorial glass.

108 SEVERENS, KENNETH W: "A Stained Glass 'Flight into Egypt.'" Allen Memorial Art Museum Bulletin (Oberlin) 28 (1970-71): 124-32.
     Attributed to France and dated 13th century [a replica of a panel from the Hearst collection now in Canterbury Cathedral; both are fakes].

Coll. 109

109   LAFOND, JEAN. "Le château de Highcliffe, sculptures des
       Andelys et de Jumièges, vitraux de Rouen et de Saint-Denis."
       Bulletin de la Société nationale des antiquaires de France
       (1972):98-106.
              A Jesse Tree, ca. 1547, from St.-Vincent of Rouen, and a
       12th century St. Benedict and Shepherds from St.-Denis,
       both sold by Lenoir ca. 1801. Highcliffe Castle was built
       by Lord Smart of Rothesay ca. 1820.

110   WITZLEBEN, ELISABETH SCHÜRER von. "Kölner Bibelfenster des
       15. Jahrhunderts in Schottland, England, und Amerika."
       Aachener Kunstblätter 43 (1972):227-48.
              Traces some of the 15th century glass from Cologne that
       had passed through Hampp and the Costessey collection into
       British and American churches and museums; relates these
       pieces to glass in Cologne and to examples in German
       collections.

111   PERROT, FRANÇOISE. "Catalogue des vitraux religieux du Musée
       de Cluny à Paris." Thesis (3e cycle), University of Dijon,
       1973.
              Thorough catalog of the 12th-16th century religious
       glass in this collection.

112   COLE, WILLIAM C. "The Flemish Roundel in England." Journal
       of the British Society of Master Glass-Painters 15
       (1973-74):16-27.
              Describes work in progress on an inventory of over 700
       of these imported "Kabinettscheiben," including an investi-
       gation of their relation to prints.

113   GAMLEN, St. J.C. Ancient Window Glass at Chicksands Priory,
       Bedfordshire. London: John Roberts Press for the author,
       1974, 28 pp., 8 figs. (2 color).
              Collection of 13th-16th century glass, largely English,
       given by Sir George Osborn in the late 18th-early 19th
       century.

114   McCARTHY; LAURIE. "Two Gothic Stained Glass Roundels."
       Bulletin of the Krannert Art Museum 1, no. 1 (1975):6-23.
              The Prodigal Son panels in Champaign (Ill.) are
       attributed to Semur-en-Auxois [of dubious authenticity].

115   VILLINGER, CARL J.H. "Wo sind die Glasscheiben aus dem
       Kapitelsaal des konstanzer Münsters?" Freiburger Diözesan
       Archiv 96 (1976):361-64.
              Five panels of 16th century heraldic glass traced to the
       von Heyl collection in Worms; the others are still missing.

116   COLE, W. "Stained Glass at Auction." <u>Journal of the British</u>
       <u>Society of Master Glass-Painters</u> 16 (1979-80):65-68.
            English and foreign panels sold at Christie's and
       Sotheby's in London, Oct. 1978 to April 1979, with prices.
       Includes 15th century panels from Hampton Court,
       Herefordshire that were bought by the Burrell Collection
       in Glasgow.

117   SKEAT, FRANCIS. "A Survey of Stained Glass in Museums and Art
       Galleries: Part 2." <u>Journal of the British Society of</u>
       <u>Master Glass-Painters</u> 16 (1979-80):30-46.
            Checklist of medieval and modern glass; to be completed,
       and followed by an index.

118   COLE, WILLIAM. "Stained Glass at Auction." Journal of the
       <u>British Society of Master Glass-Painters</u> 17 (1980-81):
       57-63.
            Lots sold by Christie's and Sotheby's, May 1979 to
       March 1980, with prices.

Section IV
Exhibitions

Listed here are catalogs and a few selected notices of exhibitions that have included a significant quantity of stained glass. It is possible that certain of these catalogs were produced in conjunction with the sale of a collection (e.g., Exh. 2), but I have included in the previous section only those for which this is certain (e.g., Coll. 51). The reader is also referred to Ger. 194.

1   Paris, Musée des Arts Décoratifs. Catalogue illustré de l'Union centrale des arts décoratifs contenant environ 200 reproductions avec une étude sur l'art retrospectif publié sous la direction de F.-G. Dumas. Catalog by Victor Champier. Paris: Librairie d'art L. Barchet, 1884, 176 pp., line drawings.
     Brief description (pp. 142-47) of over 100 examples of French glass, dated 12th-16th centuries. These or, in some cases, photographs, were exhibited in the Musée des arts décoratifs. The complete catalog of L. Magne referred to in the text has not been found.

2   *RAHN, JOHANN RUDOLF. Ausstellung von Glasgemälden aus dem Nachlasse des Dichters J.M. Usteri (1763-1829). Zürich, 1899, 30 pp.
     "Exhibition of painted glass from the estate of the poet J.M. Usteri" (Duncan, 10894).

3   *KARLSRUHE, BADISCHER KUNSTGEWERBEVEREIN. Meisterwerke aus der deutschen Glasmalerei (Exhibition, 1901), 16 pp., 100 pls. [Becksmann].

4   *LONDON, FINE ART SOCIETY. Exhibition of Old Stained Glass, 13th-18th Centuries: Descriptive Catalogue. 1912, 36 pp. [Duncan, 4124].
     Reviewed in Zeitschrift für alte und neue Glasmalerei 1, no. 4 (1912):xiv. 144 pieces, including an English Crucifixion of ca. 1430 and later panels.

5   FRANKFURT-am-MAIN, STÄDELSCHES KUNSTINSTITUT. Ausstellung
    mittelalterlicher Glasmalereien aus Schloss Kappenberg,
    gesammelt von Freiherrn vom Stein. Catalog by G.
    S[warzenski] and O. G[ötz]. 1928, 4 pp., 9 figs.
        Brief introduction and entries for twenty 12th-16th cen-
    tury panels (see Exh. 30).

6   *DARMSTADT, HESSISCHES LANDESMUSEUM. Deutsches Glas zweitaus-
    end Jahre Glasveredelung. Catalog by H. Merten. 1935.

7   ZÜRICH, KUNSTGEWERBEMUSEUM. Ausstellung: Alte Glasmalerei
    der Schweiz (Wegleitung, 168), 11. Nov. 1945 bis 24. Feb.
    1946. Catalog by Fridtjof Zschokke, Alfred Scheidegger,
    and Walter Hugelshofer. 91 pp., 18 figs. (2 color).
        Thorough presentation of 327 examples of monumental
    glass, Kabinettscheiben, and drawings, 12th-16th century in
    date.

8   COLOGNE, UNIVERSITÄT. Kölner Glasmalerei vom 13. Jahrhundert
    bis zur Gegenwart: Ausstellung (Fall 1946) 20 pp.,
    28 figs.
        Checklist of thirty items from churches in Cologne.

9   *KREFELD (?). Niederrheinische Gläser und Glasmalereien
    (Ausstellung). Catalog by W. Bremen, A. Steeger, and
    M. Creutz. [Becksmann].

10 MUNICH, BAYERISCHES NATIONALMUSEUM. Meisterwerke alter
    deutscher Glasmalerei: Leihgaben des Hessischen Landes-
    museums Darmstadt: Ausstellung. 1947, 36 pp., 16 figs.
        Checklist of 185 panels of glass, 12th to 16th century,
    and related prints and drawings.

11 MÜNCHEN-GLADBACH, STÄDTISCHES MUSEUM. Kunstschätze der ehem.
    Benediktiner-Abtei St. Vitus: Ausstellung Mai-Juli 1948.
    Catalog by Franz Jansen. [München-Gladbach: Schagen &
    Eschen, 1948], 28 pp.
        Description of three 13th-century panels with New
    Testament and six Old Testament subjects (pp. 16 ff.,
    nos. 25-33).

12 *SÉLESTAT. Exposition des vitraux du Moyen-Âge de l'église
    Saint-Georges de Sélestat. Catalog by J. Walter. 1948.
    [Répertoire d'art et d'archéologie].

13   VIENNA, ÖSTERREICHISCHES MUSEUM FÜR ANGEWANDTEKUNST.
     Stephansdom: Geschichte, Denkmäler, Wiederaufbau: Aus-
     stellung September-November 1948.
         Richard Ernst, "Die Glasgemälde der Chorfenster von St.
     Stephan," pp. 21-29; Ignaz Schlosser, "Die Glasgemälde aus
     der 2. Hälfte des 14. Jahrhunderts," pp. 30-34. Brief
     essays and entries for two groups of 14th century panels,
     some now in museums. Selected illustrations.

14   *BASEL (?). Die mittelalterlichen Glasgemälde der Stephans-
     kirche in Mühlhausen: Ausstellungskatalog. Catalog by
     Fridtjof Zschokke. Basel: Öffentlicher Kunstsammlung,
     1948.

15   ROTTERDAM, BOYMANS MUSEUM. Kleurenpracht uit Franse
     Kathedralen, tentoonstelling. 1952, n.p., illus.
         Twenty-seven items, many of which were later in the
     Paris exhibition (Exh. 16).

16   PARIS, MUSÉE DES ARTS DÉCORATIFS. Vitraux de France, du xie
     au xvie siècle, Mai-Octobre 1953. Catalog by Louis
     Grodecki. 2d ed., corrected. Paris: Caisse nationale
     des monuments historiques, 1953, 109 pp., 40 figs.
         The first major exhibition, with a scholarly catalog,
     in France; sixty-three items, not all illustrated.

17   HÖRMANN, HANS. "Die Glasgemälde von St. Sebald in Nürnberg."
     Deutsche Kunst und Denkmalpflege (1955):140.
         Exhibition of restored glass in the Germanisches
     Nationalmuseum, Nuremberg.

18   KREMS (STEIN), MINORITENKIRCHE. Ausstellung: Die Gotik in
     Niederösterreich: Kunst und Kultur einer Landschaft im
     Spätmittelalter, 21 Mai bis 18 Oktober 1959. 2d enlarged
     edition. 144 pp., 40 figs.
         Eva Frodl-Kraft, "Glasgemälde"; essay and entries for
     twenty examples of 14th-15th century glass (pp. 55-62).

19   NUREMBERG, GERMANISCHES NATIONALMUSEUM. Meister um Albrecht
     Dürer: Ausstellung. 1961.
         Entries for glass painting by Gottfried Frenzel; attri-
     butions to Hans Baldung Grien, Hans von Kulmbach, Sebald
     Beham, and Dürer's workshop (pp. 47-51, 74, 112-19, 139,
     222).

20 LOWE, JOHN. "English Medieval Stained Glass and the York
'School of Glass Painting.'" Leeds Art Calendar 49 (1962):
39.
Seventeen English windows from the 14th-15th centuries
exhibited at Temple Newsam; stresses the importance of York
as a center of glass painting.

21 GLASGOW, ART GALLERY AND MUSEUM. Stained and Painted Heraldic
Glass, Burrell Collection: British and Select Foreign
Armorial Panels. Catalog by William Wells. Glasgow:
Corporation of the City, 1962, 73 pp., 4 color pls.,
303 figs.
Best publication of this important collection to date.
Chiefly British, 13th-16th century glass; some Flemish and
Dutch, 16th-17th century examples, etc. (see Exh. 28).

22 VIENNA, KUNSTHISTORISCHES MUSEUM. Europäische Kunst um 1400
(Achte Ausstellung unter den Auspizien des Europarates)
7 Mai bis 31 Juli 1962.
Contains an essay by Louis Grodecki, "Die Glasmalerei um
1400," pp. 221-28, and twenty-eight entries from Austria,
England, France, Germany, and Switzerland, pp. 229-39, some
of which are illustrated.

23 PARIS, MUSÉE DU LOUVRE. Cathédrales: Sculptures, vitraux,
objets d'art, manuscrits des XIIe et XIIIe siècles.
Preface by Marcel Aubert. 1962.
Brief introduction to 13th century glass with catalog
entries, by Louis Grodecki (pp. 143-63); selection of
French glass, some from storage. Poorly illustrated.

24 [KREMS (STEIN), MINORITENKIRCHE]. Die Gotik in Niederösterreich: Kunst, Kultur, und Geschichte eines Landes im
Spätmittelalter. Edited by F. Dworschak and H. Kühnel.
Vienna: Österreichischen Staatsbücherei, 1963, 246 pp.,
231 figs.
Includes "Die Glasmalerei," an essay by Eva Frodl-Kraft,
and entries for ten items, dated 13th-15th century. With
bibliography and illustrations (pp. 114-20).

25 BONN, RHEINISCHES LANDESMUSEUM. Glas, Form, und Farbe: Die
alten Gläser und Glasgemälde der Sammlung Bremen in Krefeld.
Ausstellung 17. Juli-4. Oktober 1964. Edited by H. v.
Petrikovits. Kunst und Altertum am Rhein, 10. Dusseldorf:
Rheinland-Verlag, 1964, 28 pp., 81 pls.
Exhibition of drinking glasses and stained glass from
the Bremen collection, more fully cataloged by W. Bremen,
Coll. 95 and Exh. 9.

26 KREMS, MINORITENKIRCHE. <u>Ausstellung: Romanische Kunst in</u>
    <u>Österreich</u>, (21 May-25 Oct. 1964), 366 pp., 72 figs.
        An essay on "Glasmalerei" and six entries by Eva Frodl-
    Kraft (pp. 105-15); 12th-13th century examples include
    Ardaggar and Weitensfeld glass.

27 SCHLOSS LENZBURG. <u>Glasmalerei des Aargaus I, mittelalterliche</u>
    <u>Bildfenster: Wettingen, Königsfelden, Zofingen, Staufberg</u>
    (Exhibition July-Oct. 1964). Catalog by Hans Dürst and
    Ellen Beer. 1964, 100 pp., 58 figs., 1 unbound plate.
        Historical introduction and checklist of works, dated
    13th-15th century. Swiss glass well illustrated with plans
    of window locations.

28 GLASGOW ART GALLERY AND MUSEUM. <u>Stained and Painted Glass,</u>
    <u>Burrell Collection: Figure and Ornamental Subjects</u>.
    Catalog by William Wells. Glasgow: Corporation of the
    City, 1965, 72 pp., 6 color pls., 225 figs.
        Complete publication of the collection; important 12th
    (St.-Denis)-17th century panels from all regions but Italy.

29 STRASBOURG, L'ANCIENNE DOUANE. <u>Exposition mille ans d'art du</u>
    <u>vitrail</u> (5 June-3 Aug. 1965). Catalog by Victor Beyer.
    Strasbourg: Musée de la Ville, 1965, 2 fascicles. Part 1,
    <u>Les vitraux des musées de Strasbourg</u>, 44 pp., 32 figs.
    (Coll. 98); Part 2, <u>Catalogue des vitraux empruntés</u>
    <u>d'ailleurs pour l'exposition</u>, 38 pp., 22 figs.
        Brief entries with dimensions and bibliography. In-
    cludes important pieces from Wissembourg, St.-Denis, Lyon,
    Gercy, etc. and also Alsatian glass.

30 HAMBURG, MUSEUM FÜR KUNST UND GEWERBE. <u>Meisterwerke mittel-</u>
    <u>alterlicher Glasmalerei aus der Sammlung des Reichsfrei-</u>
    <u>herrn vom Stein: Ausstellung</u>. Catalog by Peter Bloch and
    Rüdiger Becksmann. 1966, 75 pp., 25 pls.
        Thorough scholarly catalog of important examples of
    German glass, dated 12th-16th centuries, including the
    Gerlachus panels from Arnstein.

31 KREMS-an-der-DONAU, MINORITENKIRCHE. <u>Ausstellung: Gotik in</u>
    <u>Österreich</u>. 1967, 457 pp., 98 figs., folding plans.
        Introductory essay and entries for twenty-three items
    (13th-15th century) by Eva Frodl-Kraft (pp. 179-201).
    Illustrated.

Exh. 32

32   NEW YORK, CLOISTERS. <u>Medieval Art from Private Collections:</u>
     <u>A Special Exhibition</u>. Catalog by Carmen Gómez-Mereno. New
     York: Metropolitan Museum of Art, 1968, nos. 174-97.
          Entries by Jane Hayward. Important Austrian, English,
     and French glass of ca. 1150-1350, much of it from the
     Pitcairn collection.

33   PARIS, MUSÉE DU LOUVRE, PAVILLION DE FLORE. <u>L'Europe</u>
     <u>gothique: XIIe-XIVe siècles (Douzième exposition européene</u>
     <u>d'art organisée à l'initiative et sous les auspices du</u>
     <u>Conseil de l'Europe)</u> (2 Apr.-1 July 1968).
          Contains a note by Louis Grodecki, "Le vitrail gothique,"
     pp. 111-12, and thirty-four entries, ca. 1190-1330, from
     Austria, England, France, Germany, and Switzerland,
     pp. 113-35.

34   ULM, MUSEUM. Hans Acker: <u>Maler und Glasmaler von Ulm</u>
     (Exhibition 29 Sept.-3 Nov. 1968). Catalog by William
     Lehmbruck. 63 pp., 100 figs.
          Brief entries for glass from the Münster; panel paintings
     and frescoes. Review of problems of dating and attribution;
     activity placed ca. 1400-1461.

35   FREIBURG-im-BREISGAU, AUGUSTINERMUSEUM. <u>Kunstepochen der</u>
     <u>Stadt Freiburg: Ausstellung zur 800-Jahrfeien</u> (24 May-
     26 July 1970), 388 pp., color pls., 74 figs.
          Several items of glass, including 13th century panels
     from the cathedral and panels by Hemmel's workshop made for
     the Carthusian house ca. 1480. Entries by I. Krummer-
     Schroth.

36   NEW YORK, METROPOLITAN MUSEUM OF ART. <u>The Year 1200, A</u>
     <u>Centennial Exhibition</u>. Vol. 1, <u>Catalogue</u>, edited by Konrad
     Hoffmann. New York, 1970, pp. 193-233.
          Entries by Jane Hayward for thirty-seven examples of
     English, French, and German glass from American collections
     and from Europe.

37   NUREMBERG, GERMANISCHES NATIONALMUSEUM. <u>Albrecht Dürer,</u>
     <u>1471-1971</u> (Exhbition 21 May-1 Aug. 1971), pp. 712-32.
          Essay by Ursula Frenzel, "Dürer als Entwerfer für Glas-
     malerei"; and drawings for glass, including the Benedict
     cycle (nos. 712-31) and two panels from St. Sebald
     (no. 732). Cf. Ger. 151.

38 NEW YORK, CLOISTERS. "Stained Glass Windows: An Exhibition
    of Glass in the Metropolitan Museum's Collection."
    <u>Metropolitan Museum of Art Bulletin</u> 30, no. 3 (1971-72):
    97-101 and unnumbered pgs., 11 color pls., 57 figs.
       Catalog by Jane Hayward, bibliographic note by Dobrilla-
    Donya Schimansky. Brief entries for fifty items, including
    important pieces of German and Austrian glass; also English,
    French, and Dutch examples, 12th-17th centuries.

39 AMSTERDAM, RIJKSMUSEUM. <u>Franse kerkramen: Vitraux de France</u>
    (15 Dec. 1973-17 Mar. 1974). Catalog by Françoise Perrot,
    introduction by Louis Grodecki. 110 pp., 8 color pls.,
    26 figs.
       Twenty-six items, 12th-16th century in date, chiefly
    from storage; includes newly discovered panels of the 13th
    century from Amiens Cathedral.

40 COLOGNE, WALLRAF-RICHARTZ-MUSEUM. <u>Vor Stephan Lochner: Die
    Kölner Maler von 1300-1430</u> (Exhibition 29 Mar.-7 July
    1974).
       Herbert Rode,"Glasmalerei in Köln," pp. 55-58,
    118-26 (nos. 67-68) illustrated.

41 NUREMBERG, GERMANISCHES NATIONALMUSEUM. <u>Farbige Fenster aus
    deutschen Kirchen des Mittelalters</u>. Vol. 1, <u>Mainfränkische
    Glasmalerei um 1420: Fenster aus den Kirchen in Münner-
    stadt und Iphofen</u> (Exhibition 7 Dec. 1974-27 Jan. 1975).
    Catalog by Arno Schönberger, Rainer Kahsnitz, and Hermann
    Maué. 83 pp., 22 figs.
       Early 15th century glass recently restored by Gottfried
    Frenzel.

42 SYRACUSE, N.Y., EVERSON MUSEUM OF ART. <u>Medieval Art in Up-
    state New York</u> (Apr.-May 1974). Coordinated by Meredith
    Lillich, edited by Peg Weiss. 130 pp., 95 figs.
       Contains six entries for stained glass of the 12th-15th
    centuries from England and France.

43 FREIBURG-im-BREISGAU, AUGUSTINERMUSEUM. <u>Glasfenster aus dem
    freiburger Münster: Ihre Erhaltung und Sicherung</u> (Exhibi-
    tion 15 June-31 Aug. 1975). Catalog by Rüdiger Becksmann,
    essay by Gottfried Frenzel. 26 pp., 14 figs. (3 color).
       14th-16th century panels cleaned and conserved.

Exhibitions

44 GRAZ, ALTE GALERIE am LANDESMUSEUM JOANNEUM. Frühe Glasmalerei in der Steiermark: Sonderausstellung anlässich der
Restaurierung der Glasgemälde von St. Walpurgis (21 Feb.-
16 Mar. 1975). Catalog by Ernst Bacher. 32 pp., 6 pls.
(1 color).
13th–15th century glass in Austrian churches; its conservation and restoration.

45 LONDON, ARTS COUNCIL OF GREAT BRITAIN. Treasures from the
Burrell Collection (18 Mar.-4 May 1975). Catalog by
William Wells. 51 pp., 73 figs. [Also shown at the
Hayward Gallery.]
Catalog of selected 12th–17th century figured and orna-
mental glass.

46 MÜNSTER, WESTFÄLISCHES LANDESMUSEUM FÜR KUNST UND KULTURGE-
SCHICHTE. Konservieren, Restaurieren. 1975.
"Glasmalerei," pp. 89-108. Essay and entries by U.D.
Korn; photographs document the condition of the 13th cen-
tury Legden Jesse Tree, etc.

47 NÜREMBERG, GERMANISCHES NATIONALMUSEUM. Romanische Glasfenster aus der Marktkirche in Gloser (Exhibition 22 Mar.-
4 May 1975). Catalog by Rainer Kahsnitz. 89 pp., 20 figs.
The Cosmas and Damian window exhibited after restoration; contains a discussion of iconography, technique,
style, and date (ca. 1250).

48 STUTTGART, WÜRTTEMBERGISCHES LANDESMUSEUM. Die Zeit der
Staufer: Geschichte--Kunst--Kultur, Katalog der Ausstellung. Edited by Reiner Haussherr. Stuttgart, 1977,
vol. 1, pp. 276-97.
Brief introduction and full catalog entries by Rüdiger
Becksmann; twenty-one (12th-13th century) pieces include
the Gerlachus panels from Arnstein-an-der-Lahn.

49 CAMBRIDGE, MASS., BUSCH-REISINGER MUSEUM. Medieval and
Renaissance Stained Glass from New England Collections,
April 25-June 10. Catalog edited by Madeline H. Caviness.
Medford: Tufts University, 1978, 100 pp., 50 figs.,
1 color pl.
Full entries for forty-three items from public and
private collections; chiefly French and English, also
German, Flemish, and Dutch, 12th-17th century glass.
General introduction; bibliography.

50 COLOGNE, KUNSTHALLE. <u>Die Parler und der Schöne Stil, 1350-
1400: Europäische Kunst unter den Luxenburgern, Ein Handbuch zur Ausstellung des Schnütgen Museums in der Kunsthalle Köln</u>. 2 vols. 1978.
Stained glass entries from eleven sites (Altenberg,
Ebstorf, Mulhouse, Stendal, etc.), by Brigitte Lymant,
Karl-Joachim Maercker, and Christine Wild-Block.

51 GRAZ, STIFT ST. LAMBRECHT. <u>Landesausstellung: Gotik in der
Steiermark</u>. Graz: Universitäts-Buchdrückerei Styria,
1978.
Contains a section on Gothic glass by Ernst Bacher,
"Gotische Glasmalerei in Steiermark," pp. 151-71, figs.
54-59. 14th and 15th century panels.

52 BERNE, KUNSTMUSEUM. <u>Niklaus Manuel Deutsch: Maler, Dichter,
Staatsmann</u> (Exhibition 22 Sept.-2 Dec. 1979). Introduction
by Hugo Wagner.
Section by Heinz Matile, "Zum Thema Niklaus Manuel und
die Glasmalerei," (pp. 67-74) discusses the role of Deutsch
in designing windows. Forty-five entries for panels of
glass and drawings for glass include pieces executed by
Hans Funk and Lucas Zeiner early in the 16th century
(pp. 419-81).

53 DARMSTADT, HESSISCHES LANDESMUSEUM. <u>Das Bild in Glas: Von
der europäischen Kabinettscheibe zum New Glass</u>. [Catalog
by Suzanne Beeh-Lustenberger], 1979.
Catalog of an exhibition of small panels (Kabinettscheiben) includes twenty-eight brief entries for very high
quality German and Flemish glass, of ca. 1320-1540; three
pieces are from the circle of the Master of the Housebook,
and three are attributed to Hans Süss von Kulmbach.

54 NEW YORK, THE CLOISTERS. <u>The Royal Abbey of Saint-Denis in
the Time of Abbot Suger (1122-1151)</u>. Edited by Sumner M.
Crosby et al. New York: Metropolitan Museum of Art, 1981.
Jane Hayward, "Stained Glass at Saint-Denis," pp. 61-99.
General essay on date, styles, etc., followed by catalog
entries for panels from France and from American collections.

55 PARIS, GALERIES NATIONALES DU GRAND PALAIS. <u>Les fastes du
gothique: Le siècle de Charles V (9 octobre 1981-1 février
1982)</u>. Paris, 1981.
Françoise Perrot, "Vitraux," pp. 379-87. Brief note on
14th century glass in France, followed by illustrated catalog entries for panels from St.-Ouen at Rouen and from
Bourges.

56   NEW YORK, THE CLOISTERS. <u>Radiance and Reflection: Medieval
     Art from the Raymond Pitcairn Collection</u>. Catalog by Jane
     Hayward and Walter Cahn. New York: Metropolitan Museum
     of Art, 1982. 261 pp., 11 color pls., 99 figs.
        Many important examples of glass, chiefly French 12th-
     16th centuries, are cataloged by Hayward with contribu-
     tions by Michael Cothren, Charles Little et al., including
     panels from Angers, Braine, Lyons, St.-Denis, and Soissons.

Section V
Austria

The reader is also referred to the following entries that deal largely with Austrian glass: Gen. 31, 38, 42, 44c-d, 53, 67, 73d.

1   ZAPPERT, F.H.G. "Über einige Glasschildereien im Chorherren-stifte Klosterneuberg." Österreichische Zeitschrift für Geschichts- und Stattskunde 2 (1836):57-60, 63-64, 67-70.
    Attempts to record inscriptions and identify donors represented in the choir glass at Klosterneuberg.

2   CAMESINA, ALBERT. "Die ältesten Glasgemälde des Chorherren-Stiftes Klosterneuberg und die Bildnisse Babenberger in der Cistercienser-Abtei Heiligenkreuz." Jahrbuch der Zentral-Kommission zur Erforschung und Erhaltung der Kunst und historischen Denkmale 2 (1857):167-200.
    Description of some of the glass, which he dates to the 13th century. Cites documents referring to glass painters and providing material on their guild in Vienna (for the 15th-16th centuries). Illustrated with drawings.

3   CAMESINA, ALBERT. "Glasgemälde aus dem zwölften Jahrhunderts Kreuzgange des Cistercienser-stiftes Heiligenkreuz im Wiener Walde." Jahrbuch der Zentral-Kommission zur Er-forschung und Erhaltung der Kunst und historischen Denk-male 3 (1859):277-84.
    Brief description of the ornamental windows of the cloister, which he dates late 12th-early 13th century. Illustrated with drawings made from tracings.

4   LIND, KARL. "Inländische Glasgemälde mit Bildnissen von Mit-gliedern des Hauses Habsburg." Mitteilungen der K. K. Central-Commission zur Erforschung und Erhaltung der Baudenkmale (Vienna) 18 (1873):124-30.
    Discusses donor portraits in St. Florien and Wiener-Neustadt, 14th-15th century. Illustrations made after drawings.

Aus. 5

5   _____. "Glasgemälde mit dem Bildnisse Herzogs Rudolph IV."
      Berichte und Mitteilungen des Alterthums-Vereines zu Wien
      22 (1883):36-38.
        Donor portraits in glass; e.g., of 1347-49 in St.
      Florien and in Maria-am-Gestade in Vienna. Illustrations
      are from watercolors.

6   "Die alten Glasmalereien der Kirche des h. Laurentius zu St.
      Leonhard im Lavantthale." Mitteilungen der K. K. Zentral-
      kommission zur Erforschung und Erhaltung der Kunst- und
      historischen Denkmale, n.s. 14, no. 1 (1888):30-32.
        Brief account of the 14th century glass in situ before
      it was scattered in collections.

7   LIND, KARL. "Übersicht der noch in Kirchen Niederösterreichs
      erhaltenen Glasmalereien." Berichte und Mitteilungen des
      Alterthums-Vereines zu Wien 27 (1891):109-129.
        Listing of sites with medieval glass in upper Austria;
      illustrated with drawings. Supplemented by Aus. 8 and 9;
      cf. the Corpus volume (Aus. 39).

8   LÖW, ALOIS. "Alte Glasmalereien in Niederösterreich."
      Berichte und Mitteilungen des Alterthums-Vereines zu Wien
      31 (1895):9-28.
        Description of glass in Ebenfurth, Ebreichsdorf,
      Euratsfeld, Friedersbach, Kirchberg an der Pielach, and
      St. Stephen's, Vienna. Not illustrated.

9   FAHRNGRUBER, JOHANNES. "Unsere heimischen Glasgemälde."
      Berichte und Mitteilungen des Alterthums-Vereines zu Wien
      32 (1896):20-52.
        Checklist of sites with medieval glass, alphabetically
      arranged. Illustrated with drawings.

10 LIND, KARL. Meisterwerke der kirchlichen Glasmalerei.
      Edited by R. Geyling and A. Löw. Vienna: S. Czeiger,
      1897, 8 pp., 50 color pls.
        Large, accurate colored prints of glass, chiefly of the
      14th-15th centuries.

11 LÖW, ALOIS. "Die alten Glasgemälde bei Maria am Gestade in
      Wien." Berichte und Mitteilungen des Alterthums-Vereines
      zu Wien 34 (1899):109-18.
        Discusses problems of restoration, including the dis-
      rupted order of the glass; and donors and dates (early
      15th century).

12   _____. "Ein altes Glasgemälde im Stift Ardagger." Berichte
      und Mitteilungen des Alterthums-Vereines zu Wien 35 (1900):
      119-28.
            First detailed study of the St. Margaret window, dated
      in the early 13th century. Illustrated with drawings.

13   _____. "Die alten Glasfenster von St. Stephan in Wien."
      Berichte und Mitteilungen des Alterthums-Vereines zu Wien
      40 (1907):1-27.
            Pioneering work on the 14th century glass of St.
      Stephen's, now replaced by the Corpus volume (Aus. 27).

14   KIESLINGER, FRANZ. Die Glasmalerei in Österreich: Ein Abriss
      ihrer Geschichte. Vienna: Ed. Holzel & Co., [1920],
      115 pp., 23 color pls., 29 figs.
            First history of Austrian glass painting to the end of
      the 16th century. Relates it to other media and describes
      the principal collections. Cf. Aus. 17.

15   _____. "Die Glasmalereien des österreichischen Herzogshofes
      aus dem Ende des 14. Jahrhunderts." Belvedere: Illus-
      trierte Zeitschrift für Kunstsammler 1 (1922):147-54.
            Glass of ca. 1395 in St. Stephen's, Vienna, Ebreichsdorf
      Castle, etc., is related to the Court school and its de-
      pendence on French works of the 1370s is pointed out.
      English summary.

16   HEMPEL, EBERHARD. "Die Scheiben der Magdalenenkirche in
      Judenburg." Zeitschrift des historischen Vereines für
      Steiermark (Graz) 23 (1927):54-79.
            Discusses problems of custody and responsibility for
      conservation. The donors of the 14th century windows are
      identified and a late group is dated ca. 1420. Provides a
      checklist of panels which describe restoration of the win-
      dows in each period. Superseded by the Corpus volume
      (Aus. 39).

17   KIESLINGER, FRANZ. Gotische Glasmalerei in Österreich bis
      1450. Denkmäler deutscher Kunst, 3. Vienna: Amalthea
      Verlag, [1928-29], 93 pp., 109 pls.
            Excellent general history with a catalog of sites by
      region (12th-15th centuries) and a list of painters. Well
      illustrated.

18 _____. Glasmalerei in Österreich. Wolfrum Bücher, 9.
Vienna: Wolfrum, 1947, 31 pp., 48 pls. (16 color).
Very brief overview for the 12th-17th centuries. For a
fuller treatment see Aus. 17.

19 FRODL, WALTER. Glasmalerei in Kärnten, 1150-1500. Klagenfurt
and Vienna: Joh. Leon, 1950, 75 pp., 139 pls. (15 color).
Treats the development of composition, ornament, and
figure style in this region; his inventory of glass includes Judenburg, St. Leonhard im Lavantthale, Viktring,
Gurk, etc. Not yet replaced by the Corpus volume.

20 EGG, ERICH. "Die Haller Glasgemälde und ihre Meister."
Veröffentlichungen des Museum Ferdinandeum in Innsbruck
(Festschrift Otto Stolz) 31 (1951):85-94.
Documents concerning glass painted by Master Thoman the
Painter, who worked in Innsbruck (1460-91). Glass in the
parish church of Hall in part attributed to Thoman (ca.
1470), in part to Gumpolt Giltinger, who collaborated with
Holbein the Elder in Augsburg.

21 KORGER, FRANZ; HOLTER, KURT; and RAUKAMP, P. PETRUS. Die
Welser Glasfenster: Beschreibung ihrer Darstellungen,
Beiträge zu ihrer Geschichte. Wels: Stadtpfarre, 1951,
34 pp., 8 pls.
Description of the recently restored glass, dated after
1340. Christological cycles related to the Biblia
pauperum.

22 FRODL, WALTER. "Ein Glasgemäldefund in Bruck und seine
Zuordnung." Österreichische Zeitschrift für Kunst und
Denkmalpflege 7 (1953):10-14.
A Christ Blessing of ca. 1290 in the Joanneum Museum of
Graz is attributed to the master who worked at St.
Walpurgis bei St. Michael.

23 KIESLINGER, FRANZ. "Die Geschichte der mittelalterlichen
Glasmalerei in Wien." In Geschichte der bildenden Kunst in
Wien, by Richard Kurt Donin. Vol. 2, Gotik. Vienna:
Verlag für Jugend und Volk, 1955, pp. 201-16.
The development of glass painting in Austria from the
mid-13th century. Discusses extant and lost glass of
Vienna and provides a list of glass painters named in
documents of the late 13th century to 1666.

24 ALBENSBERG, ERIKA. "Glasmalerei in Steiermark von 1250 bis
    1400." Ph.D. dissertation, Graz, 1957, 285 pp., 42 figs.,
    116 pls. Résumé. Mitteilungen der Gesellschaft für Ver-
    gleichende Kunstforschung in Wien 16-17 (1963-64):59-62.
        Important developments of the late 13th-early 14th cen-
    tury, especially at St. Walpurgis, Graz, and Purgg; relates
    these examples to other media and to glass elsewhere. The
    provincial school of Kärnten, stemming from Klosterneuburg.

25 FRODL-KRAFT, EVA. "Ein Glasgemäldezyklus um 1300." Alte und
    moderne Kunst 4, no. 6 (1959):12-14.
        Panels from Steyr and Kreuzenstein Castle exhibited at
    Krems include a Resurrected Christ and a Duke Leopold;
    these should probably be associated with glass executed by
    Master Eberhard for Klosterneuburg as a gift from Leopold
    and Agnes, rather than with Lilienfeld.

26 HOLTER, KURT. "Die Biblia Pauperum und die Welser Glas-
    fenster." Christliche Kunstblätter 98 (1960):123-27.
        Christological and typological scenes in Wels (ca.
    1370-80) are compared with recensions of the Biblia
    pauperum; deals with the problem of dissemination of
    iconographic guides.

27 FRODL-KRAFT, EVA. Die mittelalterlichen Glasgemälde in Wien.
    Corpus Vitrearum Medii Aevi: Österreich, 1. Graz, Vienna,
    and Cologne: Böhlau, 1962, 192 pp., 8 color pls.,
    308 figs., plans in text.
        Rigorous and complete catalog of the medieval glass in
    Vienna (in the cathedral, Maria-am-Gestade, Ruprechtskirche,
    and the museums). Complete photographic reproductions,
    including restoration charts.

28 _____. "Die Kreuzgangverglasung und der Ambo des Nikolaus
    von Verdun." Österreichische Zeitschrift für Kunst und
    Denkmalpflege 19 (1965):28-30.
        The 14th century glass of the cloister includes free
    copies of scenes in the ambo by Nicholas of Verdun (1181).

29 _____. "Ein habsburgisches Bildfenster in Wiener-neustadt."
    Acta Historiae Artium: Academiae Scientiarum Hungaricae
    (Actes des journées internationales de l'histoire de l'art,
    1965) 13 (1967):227-33.
        A window with Maximilian and his family in St. George's
    Church, dated 1479, is reassigned to the mid-16th century
    and identified as a monument to the Emperor made when his
    tomb was erected in Innsbruck.

30   WERNER, NORBERT. "Ein Beitrag zur Struktur und Entwicklung
     der Glasmalerei im 1. Drittel des 15. Jahrhunderts. Aus-
     gewählte Beispiele Österreichs." Ph.D. dissertation,
     University of Giessen, 1965.
         Analysis of the compositional structure of windows in
     Viktring, Lavantthale, Maria Wörth, and Maria Höfl in
     relation to their treatment of pictorial space. Emphasizes
     traditions that separate glass painting from panel painting.

31   FRODL-KRAFT, EVA. "Die österreichischen Glasgemälde der
     Sammlung Bremen in Krefeld." Österreichische Zeitschrift
     für Kunst und Denkmalpflege 20 (1966):33–45.
         Attribution of a Virgin and Child to the atelier from
     Gaisberg ca. 1425; and of seven scenes from the Life of
     Christ to a shop that worked in Klosterneuberg, etc.
     Cf. Coll. 95.

32   BACHER, ERNST. "Studien zu den Bild- und Kompositionsformen
     der österreichischen Glasmalerei vom Ende des 13. bis zum
     Beginn des 15. Jh." Ph.D. dissertation, Vienna, 1967.
         Development of medallions, tall geometric panels
     (Langpassfenster), and canopied windows and their relation
     to architectural compositions.

33   FRODL-KRAFT, EVA. "Die 'Figur im Langpass' in der öster-
     reichischen Glasmalerei und die naumburger Westchor-
     Verglasung." In Kunst des Mittelalters in Sachsen:
     Festschrift Wolf Schubert. Weimar: Hermann Böhlaus
     Nachfl., 1967, pp. 309–14.
         The appearance of figures in elongated geometrically
     lobed frames at Ardagger ca. 1240 and the continued use of
     this form in Alpine glass into the 14th century.

34   _____. "Ein Glasgemälde aus der Werkstatt des Meisters von
     Pulkau." In Festschrift Karl Oettinger zum 60. Gerburts-
     tag. Edited by H. Sedlmayr and Wilhelm Messerer.
     Erlanger Forschungen, 20. Erlaufen: Universitätsband,
     1967, pp. 379–88.
         Panel of St. Stephen from Eggenburg now in the Diocesan
     Museum of St. Pölten is associated with the style of the
     Master of Pulkau and dated ca. 1520.

35   *BIEDERMANN, GOTTFRIED. "Studien zur österreichischen Glas-
     malerei des 14. Jh.: Zum Oeuvre des sogenannten 'Anna-
     berger Meisters.'" Ph.D. dissertation, Salzburg, 1970.

36 PERGER, RICHARD. "Wiener Bürger des 15. Jahrhunderts als
    Förderer der Leonhardskirche in Tamsweg." Jahrbuch des
    Vereines für Geschichte der Stadt Wien 26 (1970):76-102.
       Section on gifts of windows ca. 1430-50; Viennese donors
    with arms and inscriptions identified.

37 BRANDENSTEIN, HENRIETTE. "Die Stifter." Österreichische
    Zeitschrift für Kunst und Denkmalpflege 25 (1971):64-70.
       Identification of donors and their arms in the glass in
    the Waasenkirche, Leoben (see also Aus. 38).

38 FRODL-KRAFT, EVA. "Die Bildfenster der Waasenkirche in
    Leoben: Programm und Werkstatt." Österreichische Zeit-
    schrift für Kunst und Denkmalpflege 25 (1971):51-73.
       Early 15th century glass preserved in Leoben and else-
    where is identified as the product of two shops, one
    Viennese, one local; subjects include the infancy of
    Christ, his Passion, the Coronation of the Virgin, and
    representations of saints and founders. Discusses lost
    glass and copies.

39 FRODL-KRAFT, EVA; LIFSCHES HARTH, ERNA; KOCH, WALTER; and
    WEHDORN, MANFRED. Die mittelalterlichen Glasgemälde in
    Niederösterreich 1. Albrechtsberg bis Klosterneuburg.
    Corpus Vitrearum Medii Aevi: Österreich, vol. 2, pt. 1.
    Vienna, Cologne, and Graz: Böhlau Verlag, 1972, 240 pp.,
    8 color pls., 695 figs., plans in text.
       Exemplary presentation of all the medieval glass at
    these sites, which include Ardaggar and Heiligenkreuz.

40 RUKSCHCIO, BEATE. "Die Glasgemälde der St. Leonhardskirche ob
    Tamsweg/Lungau, Salzburg: Studien zur österreichischen
    Glasmalerei in der ersten Hälfte des fünfzehnten Jahr-
    hunderts." Das Münster: Zeitschrift für christliche
    Kunst und Kunstwissenschaft 27 (1974):411-13.
       Résumé of an unpublished Ph.D. dissertation, Vienna,
    1973. Dating and stylistic development of windows from
    the 1430s; relates these to manuscript and panel painting
    in Salzburg and to works from Vienna and elsewhere.

41 NIEMETZ, PAULUS. Die Babenberger-Scheiben im Heiligenkreuzer
    Brunnenhaus. Heiligenkreuz: Heiligenkreuzer Verlag, 1976,
    48 pp., 20 figs. (11 color).
       Late 13th century panels with Babenberger genealogy in
    the Washhouse of the cloister are related to family burials
    in the chapter house. Supplements the Corpus volume
    (Aus. 39).

Aus. 42

42   BACHER, ERNST. <u>Die mittelalterlichen Glasgemälde in der
      Steiermark, 1: Graz und Strassengel</u>. Corpus Vitrearum
      Medii Aevi: Österreich, vol. 3, pt. 1. Vienna: Böhlaus,
      1979, 256 pp., 8 color pls., 513 figs., figs. and plans in
      text.
         Definitive publication of the 14th-15th century glass
      preserved at these sites.

Section VI
British Isles

Two regional surveys, divided by country, are not included here although they cover most sites with stained glass in a cursory fashion; they are the volumes published by the Royal Commission on Historical Monuments and the guides in the Buildings of England series edited by Nikolaus Pevsner.

In addition to the entries in this section the reader is referred to the following items which include material on glass in Great Britain: Gen. 9, 16, 19, 39, 51, 63.

1   SELLARS, MAUD, ed. York Memorandum Book Lettered A/Y in the Guildhall Muniment Room. 2 vols. Publications of the Surtees Society, 120 and 125. Durham: Andrews & Co., 1912-15.
     Guild ordinances for 1376 to 1493. For glaziers, ca. 1380, see vol. I, pp. 50-52; and for 1463-4, see vol. II, pp. 208-10.

2   CULMER, RICHARD. Cathedrall Newes from Canterbury.
     [Canterbury]: John White, [?1643], 5 pp. Reprinted in G. S[mith], Chronological History of Canterbury Cathedral. Canterbury, 1883, pp. 309-13.
     Iconographic description of glass destroyed by this prelate during the Cromwellian Wars.

3   *HEARNE, THOMAS. Guilielmi Roperi vita D. Thomas Mori.
     Oxford: Edmund Hall, 1716, pp. 272-78. New ed. D.W. Rennie, ed., Remarks and Collections, vol. 5, Oxford Historical Society, 42, pp. 244-47, 258-59, 270.
     Prints an early MS description of the twenty-eight early 16th century windows in Fairford Church; the later edition contains information on glass taken down in the Civil War and never replaced.

Br. 4

4 GOSTLING, WILLIAM. <u>A Walk in and about the City of Canterbury</u>.
   Canterbury: Simons and Kirby, 1774, 134 pp. 2d ed., 1777,
   418 pp., illustrated. 3d ed., 1779, 335 pp. 4th ed., 1825,
   384 pp.
       Only account of the clerestory figures (the ancestors of
   Christ, 12th-13th century) in situ; important corrections
   appear in the second edition.

5 HUTCHINS, JOHN. <u>The History of Antiquities of the County of</u>
   <u>Dorset</u>. 1st ed., 2 vols. London: W. Bowyer and J.
   Nichols, 1774, 616 pp. 2d ed., 3 vols. London, 1796-1803.
   3d ed., corrected, augmented and improved by Richard Gough.
   1813-1815. 4th ed., improved by William Shipp and James W.
   Hodson. Vol. 1. **Westminster: John Bowyer and J. Nichols,**
   1861-70.
       Arranged by divisions. Useful early account of glass in
   churches and houses.

6 CARTER, J. <u>Specimens of the Ancient Sculpture and Painting</u>
   <u>now Remaining in England from the Earliest Period to the</u>
   <u>Reign of Henry VIII</u>. 2 vols. 1st ed. London: N.G. Bohn,
   1780-94, 120 pls. *New ed. by Dawson Turner, Sir Samuel
   Rush Meyrick, John Britton et al., 2 vols. London: 1938,
   120 pls.

7 COLLINSON, JOHN. <u>The History and Antiquities of the County of</u>
   <u>Somerset, Collected from Authentic Records and an Actual</u>
   <u>Survey made by the late E. Rack</u>. 3 vols. Bath:
   R. Cruttwell, 1791. [Index by F.W. Weaver and E.H. Bates.
   Taunton: Barnicott & Pierce, 1898.]
       Brief description of medieval glass, e.g., at Wells
   (p. 399).

8 *FOWLER, WILLIAM. <u>Coloured Engravings of Roman Pavements,</u>
   <u>Stained Glass, Monastic Buildings, Fonts, Brasses, etc.</u>
   3 vols. Atlas folio. Winterton, Yorkshire, 1796-1819,
   116 color pls. [Duncan, 4396].

9 _____. [<u>Coloured Engravings of Roman Mosaic pavements, also</u>
   <u>of the Stained Glass windows of the Cathedrals of York,</u>
   <u>Lincoln, etc</u>.]. Winterton, Yorkshire: Fowler, 1796-1829,
   89 pls. in 4 unbound vols., prospectus.
       Valuable records, though not well drawn; includes glass
   in many Lincolnshire churches, also Stamford, Ashton,
   Oxford, etc.

10 _____. To the Right Honourable Sir J. Banks, Bart., this Work
is Dedicated. 26 Representations of Mosaic Pavement, Discovered in Various Parts of Great Britain: Drawn and Engraved by W.F. Folio. Winterton, Yorkshire: Fowler, 1796.

11 HASTED, EDWARD, ed. The History and Topographical Survey of
the County of Kent. 12 vols. Canterbury: W. Bristow,
1732-1812. Vol. 11, Canterbury, 1800, pp. 377-82.
Brief description of the windows at Canterbury Cathedral
and other sites.

12 *FOWLER, WILLIAM. To the Right Honourable Sir J. Banks, Bart.,
this Work is Dedicated. "Eighteen Specimens of Ancient
Stained Glass. W.F. del. et fecit." Winterton, Yorkshire:
Fowler, 1802-12. [Duncan, 4399].

13 * _____. Collection of Engraved Coloured Plates Drawn from the
Originals by Wm. Fowler of Winterton, Yorkshire. Includes
Stained Glass Windows Particularly at York and Lincoln
Cathedrals: Selby Abbey; Oxford; Fairford; Durham; the
Seven Earls of Chester and Two Saxon Earls of Mercia from
the Windows at Aston Hall, near Birmingham, etc.; Roman
Pavements, etc.; with a Portrait of the Artist. Winterton,
Yorkshire: Fowler, 1804. [Duncan, 4400].

14 SMITH, JOHN THOMAS. Antiquities of Westminster: the Old
Palace: St. Stephen's Chapel. 2 vols. London:
T. Bensley for J.T. Smith, 1807, 276 pp., 64 pls. (some
color).
Publishes accounts for building and decoration of St.
Stephen's Chapel, 1329-ca. 1360 (glass mentioned on
pp. 157, 198-99, 232-34; color illustrations of fragments
of painted glass facing pp. 157 and 232).

15 HEDGELAND, J.P. Description and Etchings of the Painted Windows of the Church of St. Neot, in Cornwall, Restored in
the Year MDCCCXXIX. London: 2 Grove Place, 1831, 27 pp.,
16 color pls. *Identical material in Gilbert Davies,
Description of the Windows of St. Neots (Cornwall), 2 pts.
(London, 1830-31).
Description of the late 15th-early 16th century windows,
illustrated by prints from crude watercolor sketches.
Does not detail the restoration.

Br. 16

16   BALLANTINE, JAMES. <u>A Treatise on Painted Glass, shewing its</u>
      <u>applicability to every style of architecture</u>. London:
      Chapman and Hall, 1845, 51 pp., 8 pls.
          The principles of symmetrical proportions and harmonious
      coloring in ornamental glass in relation to Norman, Gothic,
      perpendicular, and Elizabethan architecture.

17   CARTER, OWEN B. <u>A series of the Ancient painted glass of</u>
      <u>Winchester Cathedral</u>. London: J. Weale, 1845, 8 pp.,
      28 pls.
          Introduction to the 16th century [<u>sic</u>] figural windows
      followed by twenty-eight colored drawings.

18   <u>Quarterly Papers on Architecture</u>. Vol. 4. London: J. Weale,
      1845.
          Contains the following fascicles, separately paginated:

18a   Bell and Gould. "Selections of Painted and Stained Glass
      from York." 4 pp., 5 color pls.
          Drawings of 14th–15th century figural and ornamental
      glass.

18b   Carter, Owen B., ed. "Painted or Stained Glass Selected
      from Winchester Cathedral, Traced from the windows and
      drawn. . . ." 4 pp., 24 color pls.
          Accurate scale reproduction of this 15th century glass
      before restoration.

18c   Waller, John G. "Painted or Stained Glass from West
      Wickham Church, Kent." 2 pp., 5 color pls.
          Valuable pre-restoration records from colored tracings
      (a 15th century saint).

19   WINSTON, CHARLES. "A Short Notice of the Painted Glass in
      Winchester and its Neighbourhood." <u>Proceedings at the</u>
      <u>Annual Meeting of the Archaeological Institute, at</u>
      <u>Winchester, 1845</u>. London: The Institute, 1846, separately
      paginated 1–8.
          Notes on the 13th–16th century glass in the cathedral,
      college, St. John's Church, St. Cross, etc. Cites Oxford
      connections of around 1400.

20   [WINSTON, CHARLES.] <u>An Inquiry into the Differences of Style</u>
      <u>observable in Ancient Glass Paintings, especially in</u>
      <u>England: with Hints on Glass Painting</u>. 2 vols. Oxford:
      John Henry Parker, 1847. Vol. 1, 384 pp. Vol. 2, 24 pp.,
      75 figs. (some color).

Early attempt to periodize stained glass; includes
appendices with the treatise of Theophilus, etc. Illustrations are from excellent watercolors (Br. 26).

21   HUDSON, O. Water-colors of stained glass, most from rubbings.
     London, Victoria and Albert Museum, Department of Prints
     and Drawings, Portfolio B 3a. Ca. 1848.

22   WINSTON, CHARLES. "Painted Glass at York." In <u>Memoirs
     Illustrative of the History and Antiquities of the County
     and City of York (Communicated to the Annual Meeting of
     the Archaeological Institute at York, 1846)</u>. London:
     Office of the Archeological Institute, 1848, pp. 18-23.
     [NB: pagination repeated.]
       Rudimentary, chronologically ordered list of glass from
     the 12th century fragments in the Minster (which he dates
     ca. 1200) to early 16th century examples. Not illustrated.

23   _____. "Painted Glass at Salisbury." In <u>Memoirs Illustrative
     of the History and Antiquities of Wiltshire and City of
     Salisbury (Communicated to the Annual Meeting of the
     Archaeololical Institute of Great Britain and Ireland at
     Salisbury, 1849)</u>. London: G. Bell, 1851, pp. 135-59.
       Notes on the damaging "restorations" of the cathedral
     by Wyatt and the repairs by William Ranger 1819-; and on
     13th century fragmentary figure panels and ornament. Some
     good colored engravings from drawings by Winston.

24   *BROWNE, JOHN. <u>A Description of the Representation and Arms on
     the Glass in the Windows of York Minster, also the Arms on
     Stone</u>. Edited with a biographical notice by Dean A.P.
     Purey-Cust. Leeds: R. Jackson, 1917, 290 pp., 475 figs.
     (many in color).
       Heraldic glass, chiefly of the 14th century, recorded in
     the middle of the 19th century. Rare. [Duncan, 1851].

25   WINSTON, CHARLES. "An Account of the Painted Glass in Lincoln
     Cathedral and Southwell Minster." In <u>Memoirs Illustrative
     of the History and Antiquities of the City and County of
     Lincoln (Communicated to the Annual Meeting of the Archaeo-
     logical Institute of Great Britain and Ireland, held at
     Lincoln, July 1848)</u>. London: Office of the Institute,
     1850, pp. 90-124, 1 diag.
       Chronological notation of 13th-15th century English
     glass at these two sites. 16th century French Christologi-
     cal cycle at Southwell given in 1818. Reprinted in Br. 38.

Br. 26

26 _____. "Watercolors of Stained Glass." London, British
     Library, Add. MSS. 35211 (4 vols. of drawings); 33846-33849
     (notes). Ca. 1850.
          Chiefly from rubbings. Very valuable and large collec-
     tion (see Br. 37).

27 WALLER, J. GREEN. "On Painted Glass in Morley Church."
     Journal of the British Archaeological Association 8 (1852):
     28-34.
          Description of the 15th century glass after restoration
     by Warringtcn in 1847; moved from Dale Abbey in 1539.

28 WINSTON, CHARLES. "On the Painted Glass at Bristol, Wells,
     Gloucester, and Exeter." In Memoirs Illustrative of the
     History and Antiquities of Bristol and the Western Counties
     of Great Britain; with some other communications made to
     the Annual Meeting of the Archaeological Institute of Great
     Britain and Ireland. Bristol, 1851. London: George Bell,
     1853, pp. 150-65.
          Probable date of the glass in the east window at Bristol
     given as ca. 1320, the remainder of a later date; contempo-
     rary glass at Wells; glass in Gloucester dated 1450-1500;
     early 14th century glass at Exeter. Reprinted in Br. 38.

29 CHESTER, GREVILLE J. "A Brief Account of the Painted Glass in
     Wells Cathedral." Transactions of the Somerset Archaeologi-
     cal and Natural History Society 6 (1855):125-30.
          Uses Wilson's stylistic divisions of glass painting as a
     reference for Wells glass (14th-19th centuries).

30 O'CONNOR, MICHAEL. "On Painted Glass in Lincoln Cathedral."
     Journal of the British Archaeological Association 11
     (1855):89-94.
          Based on style, the rose window is dated ca. the first
     quarter of the 13th century; the grisailles are of a
     slightly later date.

31 SCHARF, GEORGE. "Artistic Notes on the Windows of Kings
     College Chapel, Cambridge." Archaeological Journal 12
     (1855):356-69.
          General account of foreign influences in this late 15th-
     early 16th century glass. Gives plan with subjects; and
     notes general relation to Biblia pauperum.

32   WINSTON, CHARLES. "On the Glazing of the North Rose Window of
      Lincoln Cathedral." Archaeological Journal 14 (1857):
      211-20.
         Description of the window after close examination by the
      author during its restoration in 1848.

33   WINSTON, CHARLES, and WALFORD, WESTON STYLEMAN. "On the
      Heraldic Windows in the North Aisle of the Nave of York
      Cathedral." Archaeological Journal 17 (1860):22-34,
      132-48.
         Description of the glass and discussion of the life of
      Master Peter de Dene, whose name is inscribed on a window
      as the donor; dated ca. 1306-7 on the basis of the style
      and heraldic arms.

34   WINSTON, CHARLES. "An Account of the Painted Glass in the
      East Window of Gloucester Cathedral." Archaeological
      Journal 20 (1863):239-53.
         The late [sic] 14th century glass is discussed in rela-
      tion to the development of perpendicular architecture.

35   _____. "The Painted Glass in the Beauchamp Chapel at
      Warwick." Archaeological Journal 21 (1864):302-18.
         Description of the now fragmentary windows of mid-15th
      century date in the chapel, executed by John Prudde in
      foreign glass.

36   FAUSSETT, T.G. "On a Fragment of Glass in Nettlestead
      Church." Archaeologia Cantiana 6 (1864-65):129-34.
         Identification and date of the glass (1425-39) commemo-
      rating St. Thomas Becket, based on the research of the
      late Charles Winston.

37   *Catalogue of Drawings from Ancient Glass Paintings by the Late
      Charles Winston . . . Exhibited at the Rooms of the Arundel
      Society. 1865. 40 pp. [Duncan, 14906].
         See Br. 26.

38   WINSTON, CHARLES. Memoirs Illustrative of the Art of Glass-
      Painting. London: Murray, 1865, 362 pp., 37 illus.
         Survey of 13th-16th century glass in York, Lincoln,
      Southwell, Salisbury, New College Chapel and Hall, Oxford,
      Bristol, Wells, Gloucester, and Exeter with remarks on
      technique and style; includes a catalog of drawings by
      glass painters. Reprints papers on Lincoln and Gloucester
      (Br. 25, 28).

39 *CARTER, T.J.P. <u>King's College Chapel: Notes on Its History
and Present Condition</u>. London and Cambridge: Macmillan,
1867, 89 pp. [Duncan, 2164].
The earliest complete account of the 15th-16th century
windows.

40 JOYCE, J.G. <u>The Fairford Windows</u>. London: Arundel Society,
1871, 42 folio pls. (many color).
Useful pre-restoration record.

41 FOWLER, JAMES. "On Mediaeval Representations of the Months
and Seasons." <u>Archaeologia</u> 44 (1873):137-224.
Includes representations in 14th century glass from
Dewsbury Church, 15th century glass in St. Mary's Church,
Shrewsbury, and 13th century glass in Chartres and Notre-
Dame in Paris.

42 FERGUSON, S.F. "The East Window, Carlisle Cathedral: Its
Ancient Stained Glass." <u>Transactions of the Cumberland and
Westmorland Antiquarian and Archaeological Society</u> 2 (1875):
296-312.
Dates the Doom windows 1380-84 on the basis of a portrait
of John of Gaunt.

43 FOWLER, JAMES. "On a Window Representing the Life and Miracles
of St. William of York, at the North End of the Eastern
Transept, York Minster." <u>York Archaeological Journal,
1873/74</u> 3 (1875):198-348.
Description, iconography, and style of the 135 panels
dating from the first half of the 15th century; the largest
pictorial cycle of the saint's life in England.

44 LEES, THOMAS, and FERGUSON, R.S. "On the Remains of Ancient
Glass and Woodwork at St. Anthony's Chapel, Cartmel Fell."
<u>Transactions of the Cumberland and Westmorland Antiquarian
and Archaeological Society</u> 2 (1875):389-99.
Reconstruction of the glass from fragments that remain
in the five lights of the east window. These were probably
executed by an artist from the Low Countries; some are
after designs by van der Weyden.

45 LOFTIE, W.J. "Notes on Early Glass in Canterbury Cathedral."
<u>Archaeological Journal</u> 33 (1876):1-14.
Brief account of some of the extant glass, illustrated
with pre-restoration drawings.

46 FOWLER, J.T. "On the Saint Cuthbert Window in York Minster."
    <u>Yorkshire Archaeological Journal</u>, 1875-76 4 (1877):249-376.
        Detailed description of eighty-five panels and tracery
    lights dating from the middle of the 15th century. See
    also Br. 54.

47 FOWLER, JAMES. "The Great East Window, Selby Abbey."
    <u>Yorkshire Archaeological and Topographical Journal</u> 5
    (1877-78):331-49.
        Reconstruction of the original scheme of the window
    representing the Glory of the Messiah (1330-40).

48 NORTH, THOMAS. "Leicester Ancient Stained Glass." <u>Transac-</u>
    <u>tions of the Leicestershire Architectural and Archaeological</u>
    <u>Society</u> 4 (1878):134-45, 187-90, 199-202, 220-23, 232-42,
    250-52, 254-62.
        Roundels in ornamental surrounds acquired by the society
    from a house in Leicester; Marianic and Christological
    subjects. Sacraments, and Acts of Mercy; all early 16th
    century. Illustrated with line engravings.

49 HAMILTON, ANDREW. "Notes on Remains of Ancient Painted Glass
    in the Churches of Rivenhall, Witham, Faulkbourne, Cressing,
    White Notley, Bradwell, Little Braxted, and in the Original
    Windows of Faulkbourne Hall." <u>Transactions of the Essex</u>
    <u>Archaeological Society</u>, n.s. 2 (1879):71-90.
        12th-16th century glass.

50 FERGUSON, R.S. "Windermere (Bowness) Parish Church and Its
    Old Glass." <u>Transactions of the Cumberland and Westmorland</u>
    <u>Antiquarian and Archaeological Society</u> 4 (1880):44-75.
        Identifies six lights as those made for the Cartmel
    Priory around 1480; restoration of other fragments.

51 GRINLING, C.H. "Ancient Stained Glass in Oxford." <u>Proceed-</u>
    <u>ings of the Oxford Architectural and Historical Society</u>,
    n.s. 4 (1883):111-84.
        Chronological catalog of glass dating from the 13th-18th
    centuries.

52 PEREIRA, H.W. "Brief Notes on the Heraldry of the Glass and
    Other Memorials in Wells Cathedral." <u>Transactions of the</u>
    <u>Somerset Archaeological and Natural History</u> Society 34
    (1888):40-53.
        Identification of arms (14th-19th centuries).

53   CAMM, T.W.   "Some Notes on Old Stained Glass Windows."
      <u>Transactions of the Birmingham Midland Institute, 1888</u> 15
      (1890):95–106.
         Discussion of the Jesse Tree windows in St. Mary's,
      Shrewsbury (mid-14th century) and examples in York (one
      of the mid-14th century and another of later date) and Ulm
      (1480 by "Hans Wild"); description of the 15th century
      glass in Great Malvern Priory.

54   FOWLER, J.T.   "On the St. Cuthbert Window in York Minster."
      <u>Yorkshire Archaeological Journal</u> 11 (1891):486–501.
         Supplement to Br. 46; information gathered when the
      glass was taken down in 1887/8.

55   CLAYTON and BELL.   "Albums of Watercolors, 1895."   London:
      Victoria and Albert Museum, Department of Prints and
      Drawings, 94.J34.
         Very accurate studies, generally made from rubbings, of
      glass at Canterbury, Lincoln, etc.

56   [WILLIAMS, EMILY.]   <u>Notes on the Painted Glass in Canterbury</u>
      <u>Cathedral</u>.   Preface by F.W. Farrar.   Aberdeen: University
      Press, 1879, 74 pp., 27 figs.
         Important record of the state of the glass, illustrated
      from tracings made during the recent restoration.

57   KERRY, CHARLES.   "The Ancient Painted Window, Hault Hucknall
      Church." <u>Derbyshire Archaeological and Natural History</u>
      <u>Society</u> 20 (1898):40–51.
         Figural glass ca. 1527, now mounted in one window.

58   CHADWICK, S.J.   "The Old Painted Glass in Dewsbury Church."
      <u>Yorkshire Archaeological Society, 1898–99</u> 15 (1899):211–23.
         Original placement of glass (mostly 14th century) now
      arranged in three windows of the north transept; descrip-
      tion and style.

59   *CRESSWELL, BEATRIX.   <u>Notes on Ancient Glass in Devonshire</u>
      <u>Churches</u>.   N.d. [not before 1900], 107 pp., 18 photographs.
         "Single numbered typescript sheets, arranged in alpha-
      betical order of churches described, interleaved with blank
      sheets. Only few copies known to have been made. Copy in
      Exeter Public Library contains written notes by Maurice
      Drake." (Duncan, 2768).

60 KERRY, CHARLES. "The Painted Windows in the Chapel of St. Nicholas, Haddon Hall, Derbyshire." <u>Derbyshire Archaeological and Natural History Society</u> 22 (1900):30-39.
Heraldic and figured panels, including a Crucifixion with Saints (15th century).

61 JAMES, MONTAGUE RHODES. <u>The Verses Formerly Inscribed on Twelve Windows in the Choir of Canterbury Cathedral.</u> Cambridge Antiquarian Society Octavio Publications, 38. Cambridge: the Society, 1901, 48 pp.
Inscriptions from the extant and lost typological windows (late 12th century) as recorded in a 14th century MS in the Chapter Library; attempted reconstruction (see Br. 244, 255).

62 PUGH, GEORGE AUGUSTUS. "The Old Glass Windows of Ashton-under-Lyne Parish Church." <u>Lancashire Antiquarian Society</u> 20 (1902):130-38.
Identification of the Ashton family depicted in windows dating between 1460-70 and other subjects.

63 *WEYMAN, HENRY THOMAS. <u>The Glass in Ludlow Church: Also an Account of the Missing Ludlow Glass, Mentioned in the Ashmolean MS. of 1663 and Elsewhere (Illustrated from the Original Manuscript)</u>. Ludlow: G. Woolley, 1905, 32 pp. [British Library copy destroyed].
2d edition, 1925, omits the description of the lost glass.

64 DRAKE, FREDERICK MORRIS. "Heraldic Stained Glass in Ashton Church (Devon)." <u>Transactions of the Exeter Diocesan Architectural Society</u>, 3d ser. 2 (1907):167-74.
15th century shields in the east window of the Lady Chapel; six are from the same hand, possibly French, the other two of more inferior quality were executed at a later date.

65 HEATON, CLEMENT. "The Origin of the Early Stained Glass in Canterbury Cathedral." <u>Burlington Magazine</u> 11 (1907): 172-76.
Insists on the early appearance of the figures in the choir and notices affinities with Sens in the Trinity Chapel. Suggests that the glazing began by 1180 and that craftsmen were brought from Paris.

66   MACLAGAN, C.P.D. "The Old Stained Glass of All Saints, North
      St., York." In An Old York Church, All Hallows in North
      Street, Its Medieval Stained Glass, etc., by P.J. Shaw.
      York: Delittle, Fenwick & Co., 1908. Reprint. 1934,
      16 pp., figs. in text, 6 pls.
          Notes on the 14th and 15th century windows; illustra-
      tions are from very accurate watercolors; useful record.

67   BALL, W.E. "The Stained Glass Windows of Nettlestead Church."
      Archaeologia Cantiana 28 (1909):157-249.
          Of the 15th century glass only one window remains in
      situ; description and identification of twenty-two extant
      heraldic shields and ten shields formerly part of the
      church decoration.

68   DRAKE, FREDERICK. Two Papers Dealing with the Ancient Stained
      Glass of Exeter Cathedral and More Especially with the
      Restoration of the Great East Window. Exeter: William
      Pollard & Co., 1909, 29 pp., 17 pls.
          Restoration of the original composition of the 14th
      century glass in the choir clerestory and choir aisle;
      description of repairs made on the east window around 1320.

69   EDEN, FREDERICK SYDNEY. "Stained and Painted Glass in Essex
      Churches." Notes and Queries, 11th ser. 2 (1910):361-62,
      462-64; 11th ser. 3 (1911):41-42.
          Survey of churches which contain medieval and Renais-
      sance glass.

70   *KNOWLES, JOHN A. "Die Glasmaler von York." Diamant 50,
      nos. 8-10 (11 March-1 Apr. 1910).

71   DRAKE, MAURICE. A History of English Glass-Painting, with
      Some Remarks upon the Swiss Miniatures of the Sixteenth and
      Seventeenth Centuries. London: T. Werner Laurie, 1912,
      226 pp., 37 pls. (7 color).
          Three chapters cover the 12th-15th centuries; develop-
      ments in composition and technique; useful illustration of
      fragments.

72   DRAKE, FREDERICK MORRIS. "The Fourteenth Century Stained
      Glass of Exeter Cathedral." Transactions of the Devonshire
      Association for the Advancement of Science, Literature, and
      Art 44 (1912):231-51. Reprint. 21 pp., 4 illus.
          The evolution of 14th century glass; a progression is
      seen from the north clerestory windows, executed by a
      French atelier (early 14th century), to the great east
      window (end of the 14th century).

73 FOWLER, J.T. "On the Painted Glass at St. Anthony's Chapel."
    <u>Transactions of the Cumberland and Westmorland Antiquarian
    and Archaeologic Society</u>, n.s. 12 (1912):297.
        Seven Sacraments surrounding a central Crucifixion
    brought to the chapel in Cartmell Fell from Cartmell
    Priory around 1830; late 15th century in date.

74 DRAKE, F. MORRIS. "The Painted Glass of Exeter Cathedral and
    Other Devon Churches." Archaeological Journal 70 [n.s. 20]
    (1913):163-74.
        Four 14th century windows influenced by northern French
    glass and five others in Doddiscombleigh are all that have
    survived in Devonshire.

75 EDEN, F. SYDNEY. <u>Ancient Stained and Painted Glass</u>.
    Cambridge: University Press, 1913. 2d ed., enlarged,
    1933, 228 pp., 40 figs. (5 color).
        General history of glass painting in Great Britain up
    to the 17th century. Chapters on foreign influences and
    on heraldry. Many illustrations are from watercolors.

76 NELSON, PHILIP. <u>Ancient Painted Glass in England, 1170-1500</u>.
    London: Methuen & Co., 1913, 280 pp., 32 pls., 43 figs.
    in text.
        General history followed by very useful "County Lists
    of Ancient Glass." Well indexed.

77 _____. "The Fifteenth Century Glass in the Church of St.
    Michael, Ashton-under-Lyne." <u>Archaeological Journal</u> 70
    [n.s. 20] (1913):1-10.
        Iconography of the four windows representing the life of
    St. Helen; their textual sources; and reconstruction of the
    original order of the panels.

78 BENSON, G. <u>The Ancient Painted Glass Windows in the Minster
    and Churches of the City of York</u>. Yorkshire Philosophical
    Society, Annual Report, 1914. York: Coultas & Volans,
    1915.
        Description and identification of 14th, 15th, and 16th
    century glass in the cathedral and various parish churches.

79 FOWLER, J.T. "The Fifteen Last Days of the World in Medieval
    Art and Literature." <u>Yorkshire Archaeological Journal</u> 23
    (1915):313-37.
        Especially useful for the window in All Saints' North
    Street, York, which he dates ca. 1350, and a triptych in
    Oberwesel. Cf. Fr. 307.

Br. 80

80 _____. "Three Panels of Thirteenth Century Stained Glass from
Lanchester Church, Durham." Society of Antiquaries, Proceedings, 2d ser. 27 (1915):205-14.
13th century fragments in the central east lancet of
this parish church; the Shepherds, the Adoration of the
Magi, and the Flight into Egypt from an Infancy cycle, with
foliage as if they all formed part of a Jesse Tree.

81 GRIMKE-DRAYTON, T.D. "The East Window of Gloucester Cathedral." Transactions of the Bristol and Gloucestershire
Archaeological Society 38 (1915):69-97.
Identification of the shield and the dating (1347-49)
based on it; 15th century additions.

82 LETHABY, WILLIAM RICHARD. "Archbishop Roger's Cathedral at
York and Its Stained Glass." Archaeological Journal 72
(1915):37-48.
Reconstruction of a Jesse Tree and typological windows
from fragments which he dates ca. 1180; similarities to
glass at Angers.

83 RUSHFORTH, G. McN., and PITCHER, SYDNEY A. The Stained Glass
of Gt. Malvern Priory Church. 6 vols. Gloucester: S.A.
Pitcher, 1916-35. Vol. 1, 1916, 26 figs. Vol. 2, 1917,
56 figs. Vol. 3, 1935, 36 figs. Vol. 4, 1920, 56 figs.
*Vol. 5. Vol. 6, 1927, 42 figs.
Bound plates from superb black and white photographs by
Pitcher. Annotated by Rushforth. Very rare. Copy in the
Boston Museum of Fine Arts. (Cf. Br. 170).

84 BOUCHIER, E.S. Notes on the Stained Glass of the Oxford Dis-
trict. Oxford: B.H. Blackwell, 1918, 106 pp.
Guide to the 13th-mid-16th century glass in Berkshire,
Oxfordshire, and Buckinghamshire.

85 RUSHFORTH, GORDON McNEIL. "An Account of Some Painted Glass
from a House at Leicester." Archaeological Journal 75
(1918):47-68.
Description of figural windows with religious subjects
made in the first quarter of the 16th century and now
exhibited in the Leicester Museum.

86 ASHDOWN, C.H. History of the Worshipful Company of Glaziers
of the City of London, Otherwise the Glaziers and Painters
of Glass, AD 1328-1918. London: Blades, East and Blades,
[1919], 163 pp., 5 pls.
Account based on the Letter Books, etc. of the city of
London. Contains very important material about pricing,
foreigners in London, and guild regulations.

87 COUTEUR, J.D. Le. Ancient Glass in Winchester. Winchester:
    Warren & Son, 1920, 152 pp., 39 pls.
        Detailed record of the remains of the 14th-19th century
    glass in the cathedral; its iconography, style, and
    restoration.

88 *KNOWLES, J.A. "Stained Glass in the York Churches." 2 vols.,
    1920, 350 pp., 241 drawings (some color), photos, process
    illus.
        Manuscript in London, Victoria and Albert Museum Library,
    ref. nos. 86H. 15 and 16 [Duncan, 7229].

89 KNOWLES, JOHN ALDER. "The Periodic Plagues of the Second Half
    of the Fourteenth Century and their Effects on the Art of
    Glass-Painting." Archaeological Journal, 2d ser. 29 (1922):
    343-52. German translation. "Die periodischen Plagen in
    der zweiten Halfte des 14. Jahrhunderts und ihre Wirkungen
    auf die Glasmalerkunst." Diamant 49, no. 31 (1 Nov. 1926):
    606-9.
        Glaziers were impressed into the king's service ca. 1350,
    after the first plague; the author speculates that the east
    window at Gloucester and glazing in the York choir were
    delayed by the plague.

90 LONG, E.T. "Ancient Stained Glass in Dorset Churches."
    Proceedings of the Dorset Natural History and Antiquarian
    Field Club (Dorchester) 43 (1922):44-56.
        Checklist of the principal collections, chiefly 15th
    century in date, with brief descriptions.

91 RUSHFORTH, GORDON McNEIL. "The Great East Window of
    Gloucester Cathedral." Transactions of the Bristol and
    Gloucestershire Archaeological Society 44 (1922):293-304.
        Largely concerned with the identification of the saints,
    bishops, abbots, and kings represented in this window of
    ca. 1350.

92 EELES, FRANCIS C. "The 15th Century Stained Glass at
    Clavering." Transactions of the Essex Archaeological
    Society, n.s. 16 (1923):77-87.
        Description of the 15th century glass in St. Mary and
    St. Clement.

93 READ, HERBERT. "The Labours of the Months: A Series of
    Stained Glass Roundels." Burlington Magazine 43 (1923):
    167-68.
        Six roundels recently acquired by the Victoria and
    Albert Museum; English in origin and dated to the first
    half of the 15th century.

94 RUSHFORTH, GORDON McNEIL. "The Glass in the Quire Clerestory
of Tewkesbury Abbey." Bristol and Gloucester Archaeological Society Transactions 46 (1924):289-324.
Account of the 14th century glass from the choir after
the 1923 restoration supervised by the author. Includes
photographs.

95 COUTEUR, J.D. Le. "Ancient Glass in Timsbury Church, Hants."
Journal of the British Society of Master Glass-Painters 1,
no. 2 (Apr. 1925):36-37.
Fragments of before 1425 whose style is compared with
that of Thomas of Oxford.

96 EDEN, F.S. "Ancient Painted Glass in London." Journal of the
British Society of Master Glass-Painters 1, no. 2 (Apr.
1925):18-27.
Inventory of surviving glass in Westminster Abbey, St.
Margaret's, and elsewhere.

97 JONES, W. BELL. "Ancient Stained and Painted Glass in Flintshire." Flintshire Historical Society Journal 11 (1925):
69-78.
Inventory of 14th, 15th, and 16th century glass in
various churches.

98 KNOWLES, JOHN ALDER. "Disputes between English and Foreign
Glass Painters in the 16th Century." Antiquaries Journal
5 (1925):148-57. German translation. "Streitigkeiten
zwischen englischen und fremden Glasmalern im 16. Jahrhunderts." Diamant 48, no. 8 (11 Mar. 1926):143-46; 48,
no. 9 (21 Mar. 1926):169-70.
English opposition to Flemish immigrant glass painters
and their innovative techniques.

99 LETHABY, WILLIAM RICHARD. Westminster Abbey Re-examined.
London: Duckworth, 1925, 298 pp., illus.
Describes the remnants of the 13th century historiated
panels and grisaille windows and the glass dated ca. 1510
in Henry VIII's Chapel (pp. 234-53, 174-83).

100 MASON, ARTHUR JAMES. A Guide to the Ancient Glass in
Canterbury Cathedral. Canterbury: H.J. Goulden, 1925,
56 pp.
Complete description of the surviving glass, made during
the period of its restoration; useful to establish its
history.

101   PITCHER, SYDNEY. "Ancient Stained Glass in Gloucestershire
      Churches." <u>Bristol and Gloucester Archaeological Society</u>
      47 (1925):287-345.
          List of the medieval and Renaissance stained glass in
      the area's churches. Illustrated with sixty-two photo-
      graphs.

102   COUTEUR, JOHN DOLBEL Le. <u>English Mediaeval Painted Glass</u>.
      The Historic Monuments of England. London: SPCK, 1926,
      184 pp., 52 figs. 2d ed. London: SPCK, 1978, 200 pp.,
      pls. [Paperback edition].
          Cursory history illustrated with some little-known
      examples of glass; useful sections on techniques and
      iconoclasm.

103   KNOWLES, JOHN ALDER. "A History of the York School of Glass
      Painting, I." <u>Journal of the British Society of Master
      Glass-Painters</u> 1, no. 4 (Apr. 1926):25-41.
          Sections entitled "Introduction"; "Early History";
      "Variable quality of work." Continued: Br. 104, 112-13,
      117-18, 124-25, 133-34, 145-46, 149-50, 152-53, 160-61.
      Reprinted in his monograph of 1936 (Br. 169).

104   _____. "A History of the York School of Glass Painting, II."
      <u>Journal of the British Society of Master Glass-Painters</u> 1,
      no. 5 (Oct. 1925):16-28.
          Section entitled "The Extent to Which Ecclesiastics Were
      Responsible for the Making of Windows." See Br. 103. Re-
      printed in his monograph of 1936 (Br. 169).

105   LETHABY, W.R. "Early 13th Century Glass at Salisbury Cathe-
      dral." <u>Journal of the British Society of Master Glass-
      Painters</u> 1, no. 4 (Apr. 1926):17-18.
          Discusses rearrangement of the glass and suggests that
      the Jesse Tree fragments may be from the east or west wall.
      Some glass is also found at Grately. The Lady Chapel
      glazing is dated ca. 1240, the nave ca. 1275-1300.

106   RACKHAM, BERNARD. "The Glass of Winchester College Chapel."
      <u>Journal of the British Society of Master Glass-Painters</u> 1,
      no. 4 (Apr. 1926):23-24.
          Crowned initials, H and W, are associated with William
      of Wykeham and Henry IV and dated 1399-1404.

107   READ, HERBERT. <u>English Stained Glass</u>. London and New York:
      G.P. Putnam's, 1926, 260 pp., 70 pls. (5 color).
         General outline; the illustrations are more useful than
      the text; many excellent photographs by Sydney Pitcher.

108   SALZMAN, L.F. "The Glazing of St. Stephen's Chapel,
      Westminster, 1351-2." <u>Journal of the British Society of
      Master Glass-Painters</u> 1 (1926):14-41.
         Edition of the entries in the Exchequer Accounts for
      glazing with an analysis of cost and divisions of work.
      The windows are not extant.

109   EDEN, F. SYDNEY. "Ancient Painted Glass in the Conventual
      Buildings Other Than the Church, of Westminster Abbey."
      <u>Connoisseur</u> 77 (1927):81-88.
         Includes 13th century panels in the Jerusalem Chamber,
      two shields from Jericho's Parlour (dated ca. 1601 and
      1527), and a late 14th century shield inscribed with Abbot
      Littlington's initials.

110   HARRISON, F. <u>The Painted Glass of York: An Account of the
      Medieval Glass of the Minster and the Parish Churches</u>. The
      Historic Monuments of England. London: SPCK; New York and
      Toronto: MacMillan Co., 1927, 269 pp., 56 pls. (4 color).
         Brief, systematic catalog of 12th-16th century glass in
      the churches and museum. Complements Knowles (Br. 169).
      Color illustrations are from watercolors.

111   KNOWLES, JOHN ALDER. "Additional Notes on the History of the
      Worshipful Company of Glaziers." <u>Antiquaries Journal</u> 7
      (1927):282-93.
         The lives and works of the 14th-17th century glaziers
      who filled various positions in the company (cf. Ashdown,
      Br. 86).

112   _____. "A History of the York School of Glass Painting, III &
      IV." <u>Journal of the British Society of Master Glass-
      Painters</u> 2, pt. 1, no. 6 (Apr. 1927):31-37.
         Section entitled "The Continuance of Tradition and
      Accepted Treatment in Works of Art During the Middle Ages."
      See Br. 103. Reprinted in his monograph of 1936 (Br. 169).

113   _____. "A History of the York School of Glass Painting, V."
      <u>Journal of the British Society of Master Glass-Painters</u> 2,
      no. 2 (Oct. 1927):78-85.
         Section entitled "The Economics of York Stained Glass."
      See Br. 103. Reprinted in his monograph of 1936 (Br. 169).

114   COUTEUR, JOHN DOLBERL Le. "Long Medford Church, Suffolk and
       Its Portrait Glass." Journal of the British Society of
       Master Glass-Painters 2, no. 2 (Oct. 1927):74-77.
              Donor portraits identified and dated ca. 1470-90 on the
       basis of costume.

115   RUSHFORTH, GORDON McNEIL. "The Painted Windows in the Chapel
       of the Vyne in Hampshire." Archaeological Journal 34
       (1927):105-13.
              Description of glass dating from the first quarter of
       the 16th century, possibly executed in the Netherlands.

116   EDEN, F. SYDNEY. "Ancient Painted Glass at Colchester."
       Connoisseur Magazine 80 (Jan. 1928):13-19.
              Includes 16th century heraldic glass, 15th century heads
       of saints, small 14th century tracery lights, and 13th cen-
       tury border fragments.

117   KNOWLES, JOHN ALDER. "A History of the York School of Glass
       Painting, VI." Journal of the British Society of Master
       Glass-Painters 2, no. 3 (Apr. 1928):136-51.
              Section entitled "Secular Character of York Work." See
       Br. 103. Reprinted in his monograph of 1936 (Br. 169).

118   _____. "A History of the York School of Glass Painting, VII."
       Journal of the British Society of Master Glass-Painters 2,
       no. 4 (Apr. 1928):193-209.
              Section entitled "Characteristics of the York Type of
       Design." See Br. 103. Reprinted in his monograph of 1936
       (Br. 169).

119 * _____. "Die Glasmaler von York." Diamant 50, no. 8 (11 Mar.
       1928):168-70; 50, no. 9 (21 Mar. 1928):190-91; 50, no. 10,
       pp. 214-16.

120   MARSHALL, G. "Ancient Glass in the Churches of Eaton Bishop
       and Madley, Hertfordshire." Journal of the British Society
       of Master Glass-Painters 2, no. 4 (Oct. 1928):171-75.
              Largely 13th-14th century, west country styles.

121   SALZMAN, L.F. "Medieval Glazing Accounts." Journal of the
       British Society of Master Glass-Painters 2, no. 3 (Apr.
       1928):188-92.
              Extracts from Exchequer Accounts in the Public Record
       Office, 1351-97, for work at Windsor Castle, Dover Castle,
       Eltham Palace, etc.

122 _____. "Medieval Glazing Accounts." Journal of the British
Society of Master Glass-Painters 2, no. 4 (Oct. 1928):
116-20.
Extracts from Exchequer Accounts in the Public Record
Office, 1221-1351, for work at Windsor, Westminster, etc.

123 HIMSWORTH, J.B. "Some Fragments of Stained Glass in South
Yorkshire and Derbyshire." Journal of the British Society
of Master Glass-Painters 3, no. 2 (Oct. 1929):66-73.
Survey of surviving glass with references to antiquarian
sources; dates unreliable.

124 KNOWLES, JOHN ALDER. "A History of the York School of Glass
Painting, VII." Journal of the British Society of Master
Glass-Painters 3, no. 1 (Apr. 1929):31-42.
Section entitled "Characteristics of the York Type of
Design Continued." See Br. 103. Reprinted in his mono-
graph (Br. 169).

125 _____. "A History of the York School of Glass Painting, VII."
Journal of the British Society of Master Glass-Painters 3,
no. 2 (Oct. 1929):85-94.
Section entitled "Characteristics of the York type of
Design Continued." See Br. 103. Reprinted in his mono-
graph (Br. 169).

126 *_____. "The Practice of Ancient Glass Painting: A History of
Technique and Craftsmanship." 3 vols., 28 sections, and
21 appendices [1929].
Manuscript in London, Victoria and Albert Museum Library,
ref. nos. 86H. 17, 18, and 19 (Duncan, 7222).

127 RUSHFORTH, GORDON McNEIL. "Seven Sacraments Compositions in
English Medieval Art." Antiquaries Journal 9 (1929):83-100.
Unique iconography which may have originated in England
is exemplified in eight cycles from the 15th century [but
see van der Weyden's Seven Sacraments Altarpiece]. Cf.
Br. 140.

128 _____. "The Windows of the Church of St. Neots Cornwall."
Transaction of the Exeter Diocesan Architectural and
Archaeological Society 15 (1929):150-90. Reprint. Exeter:
Pollard, 1937, 43 pp.
Windows of ca. 1480 represent the Crucifixion and stories
of Adam, Noah and St. George; others executed between 1528
and 1530.

129 SALZMAN, L.F. "Medieval Glazing Accounts." Journal of the
British Society of Master Glass-Painters 3, no. 1 (Apr.
1929):25-30.
Continuation of extracts of accounts, 1399-1537, for
work at Westminster, Eltham, etc. (cf. Br. 121, 122).

130 EDEN, F. SYDNEY. "Ancient Painted Glass at Stamford-on-Avon."
Journal of the British Society of Master Glass-Painters 3,
no. 4 (Oct. 1930):156-65.
Complete descriptions of the 15th century donors in situ
in the church and of the domestic glass (14th-16th century)
from the Old Hall at Stamford.

131 FLETCHER, J.M.J. "The Stained Glass in Salisbury Cathedral."
Wiltshire Archaeological Magazine 45 (1930):235-53.
Description of the remains of the glass, mostly of the
13th century, none of which is in situ.

132 JAMES, MONTAGUE RHODES. Suffolk and Norfolk: A Perambulation
of the Two Counties with Notices of the History and Their
Adjacent Buildings. London and Toronto: Dent & Sons,
1930, 240 pp., illus. in text.
Useful, accurate notes on most of the glass surviving in
situ and on the foreign glass installed in the 19th century. Fully illustrated (1 drawing).

133 KNOWLES, JOHN ALDER. "A History of the York School of Glass
Painting, VIII." Journal of the British Society of Master
Glass-Painters 3, no. 3 (Apr. 1930):123-32.
Section entitled "Influence of Schools of Glass Painting
in Other Parts of England Upon York Design." See Br. 103.
Reprinted in his monograph of 1936 (Br. 169).

134 _____. "A History of the York School of Glass Painting,
VIII." Journal of the British Society of Master Glass-
Painters 3, no. 4 (Oct. 1930):189-99.
Section entitled "Influence of Schools of Glass Painting
in Other Parts of England Upon York Design Continued."
See Br. 103. Reprinted in his monograph (Br. 169).

135 *_____. "Historical Notes on (Early) Stained Glass in York
Cathedral, and Description of the Windows." 2 vols.,
drawings (some color), photographs, process illustrations.
Ca. 1930.
Manuscript in London, Victoria and Albert Museum Library,
ref. nos. 86H. 10 and 11 (Duncan, 7227).

136 *_____. "Stained Glass in St. Cuthbert's and St. William's
     Windows, York Cathedral." 3 vols., drawings, press cut-
     tings, illustrations.
          Manuscript in London, Victoria and Albert Museum Library,
     ref. nos. 86H. 12, 13, and 14 (Duncan, 7228).

137 PEATLING, A.V. Ancient Stained and Painted Glass in the
     Churches of Surrey. Guildford, Surrey Archaeological
     Society, 1930, 141 pp., 18 illus.
          Survey of 13th-19th century glass (of English and for-
     eign origin) based on selections from the late author's
     lectures.

138 RACKHAM, BERNARD. "The Ancient Stained Glass at Lindsell
     Church." Transactions of the Essex Archaeological Society
     n.s. 20, no. 1 (1930):73-77.
          Description of the 13th-16th century fragments, most of
     which are English.

139 RUSHFORTH, GORDON McNEIL. "Medieval Glass in Oriel College
     Chapel [Oxford]." Journal of the British Society of Master
     Glass-Painters 3, no. 3 (Apr. 1930):108-11.
          St. Margaret, dated ca. 1500.

140 _____. "The Sacraments Window in Crudwell Church." Wiltshire
     Archaeological Magazine 45 (June 1930):68-72.
          One of a group of 15th century windows with a central
     figure of Christ surrounded by and associated with repre-
     sentations of the sacraments (cf. Br. 127).

141 RACKHAM, BERNARD. "The Glass-Paintings of Coventry and Its
     Neighborhood." Walpole Society 19 (1930-31):89-110.
          Remnants from John Thornton's place of origin: the 14th
     century Jesse windows in Mancetter and Merevale; the window
     in St. Mary's Hall, Coventry, with Henry VI and other En-
     glish kings, dated to the late 15th century.

142 BINGLEY, A.G. "The Armorial Window at Cranleigh Church."
     Surrey Archaeological Collections 39 (1931):151-53.
          Brief description of the "Patron's Window" and identi-
     fication of its arms (15th century).

143 GARROD, H.W. Ancient Painted Glass in Merton College, Oxford.
     London: Oxford University Press, 1931, 51 pp., 2 illus.
          Dates the choir window to 1289-1311; identifies a figure
     repeated in the Twelve Apostles series as Henricus de
     Mamesfeld; discusses the 14th century arms in the east
     window.

144 HIMSWORTH, J.B. "Old Stained Glass in South Yorkshire and
     Derbyshire." <u>Journal of the British Society of Master
     Glass-Painters</u> 4, no. 2 (Oct. 1931):65-70.
         Especially useful for the musical instruments at
     Dronfield.

145 KNOWLES, JOHN ALDER. "A History of the York School of Glass
     Painting, IX." <u>Journal of the British Society of Master
     Glass-Painters</u> 4, no. 1 (Apr. 1931):32-41.
         Section entitled "Continental Influence on Design of
     Glass at York; the Influence of the Rhineland and Nether-
     lands." See Br. 103. Reprinted in his monograph of 1936
     (Br. 169).

146 _____. "A History of the York School of Glass Painting, IX."
     <u>Journal of the British Society of Master Glass-Painters</u> 4,
     no. 2 (Oct. 1931):81-93.
         Section entitled "Continental Influence on Design of
     Glass at York; the Influence of the Rhineland and Nether-
     lands Continued." See Br. 103. Reprinted in his mono-
     graph of 1936 (Br. 169).

147 ROBINSON, J. ARMITAGE. "The Fourteenth Century Glass at
     Wells." <u>Archaeologia</u> 81 (1931):85-118.
         Stylistic and technical characteristics date this glass
     to 1300-1334.

148 DOBLE, G.H. "Medieval Stained Glass in Cornwall and
     Brittany." <u>Journal of the British Society of Master Glass-
     Painters</u> 4, no. 4 (Oct. 1932):183-86.
         Lists only 15th-16th century glass in Cornwall; notes
     many sites in Brittany, including Dol (13th century) and
     Quimper.

149 KNOWLES, JOHN ALDER. "A History of the York School of Glass
     Painting, X." <u>Journal of the British Society of Master
     Glass-Painters</u> 4, no. 3 (Apr. 1932):146-55.
         Section entitled "Cistercian Influence on the Design of
     York Glass." See Br. 103. Reprinted in his monograph of
     1936 (Br. 169).

150 _____. "A History of the York School of Glass Painting, X."
     <u>Journal of the British Society of Master Glass-Painters</u> 4,
     no. 4 (Oct. 1932):189-202.
         Section entitled "Cistercian Influence on Design of York
     Glass Continued." See Br. 103. Reprinted in his mono-
     graph of 1936 (Br. 169).

Br. 151

151 CLAY, ERNEST C. "Ancient Glass in Buckland Church." Surrey
     Archaeological Collections 41 (1933):123.
          Rediscovery of a 15th century Virgin and Child, once
     described by Aubrey.

152 KNOWLES, JOHN ALDER. "A History of the York School of Glass
     Painting, XI." Journal of the British Society of Master
     Glass-Painters 5, no. 1 (Apr. 1933):37-48.
          Section entitled "Favorite Subjects in York Glass." See
     Br. 103. Reprinted in his monograph of 1936 (Br. 169).

153 _____. "A History of the York School of Glass Painting, XI."
     Journal of the British Society of Master Glass-Painters 5,
     no. 2 (Oct. 1933):82-92.
          Section entitled "Favorite Subjects in York Glass Con-
     tinued." See Br. 103. Reprinted in his monograph of 1936
     (Br. 169).

154 TOKE, N.E. "Painted Glass Windows at Stowting." Archaeologia
     Cantiana 45 (1933):31-36.
          A 14th century Virgin and Child set in grisaille quar-
     ries identified as originally from Selling Church; also
     cites three lights containing nimbed saints beneath cano-
     pies with donors (mid-15th century).

155 WOODFORDE, CHRISTOPHER. "Ancient Glass in Lincolnshire."
     Lincolnshire Magazine 1, no. 3 (1933):93-97; 1, no. 6
     (1933):197-99; 1, no. 11 (1934):363-67; 2, no. 9 (1936):
     265-67; 2, no. 12 (1936):346-48.
          Series of articles describing and dating the extant
     medieval and Renaissance glass, not including the cathedral.

156 *_____. Guide to the Medieval Glass in Lincoln Cathedral.
     London: Society for Promoting Christian Knowledge, 1933,
     44 pp., 12 illus.
          Provides a list of subjects; illustrated with drawings
     by Winston. Superseded by Lafond (Br. 191).

157 EELES, FRANCIS C. "Ancient Stained Glass at Farleigh
     Hungerford." Proceedings of the Somerset Archaeological
     and Natural History Society 80 (1934):57-62.
          Description of the east window which includes 15th cen-
     tury English glass and 16th century Flemish fragments,
     after its restoration.

158   HARDMAN, T.   "The Penancer's Window in the Nave of York
        Minster--A Discussion Between Mr. John T. Hardman and Mr.
        J.A. Knowles."   Journal of the British Society of Master
        Glass-Painters 5, no. 4 (Oct. 1934):177-84.
            Disputes Knowles's interpretation.

159   *KNOWLES, JOHN ALDER.   "Additional Notes on the St. William
        Window in York Minster, Part 1."   Proceedings of the
        Yorkshire Architecture and Yorkshire Archaeological Society
        1, no. 2 (1934).   Reprint.   55 pp., 7 illus.   [Cited in
        Journal of the British Society of Master Glass-Painters].
            Cf. Br. 197.

160   _____.   "A History of the York School of Glass Painting, XII."
        Journal of the British Society of Master Glass-Painters 5,
        no. 3 (Apr. 1934):133-41.
            Section entitled "Political Allusions in York Work."
        See Br. 103.   Reprinted in his monograph (Br. 169).

161   _____.   "A History of the York School of Glass Painting, XII."
        Journal of the British Society of Master Glass-Painters 5,
        no. 4 (Oct. 1934):187-95.
            Section entitled "Political Allusions in York Work Con-
        tinued."   See Br. 103.   Reprinted in his monograph (Br.
        169).

162   WOODFORDE, CHRISTOPHER.   "Essex Glass-Painters in the Middle
        Ages."   Journal of the British Society of Master Glass-
        Painters 5, no. 3 (Apr. 1934):110-15.
            13th-16th century glaziers identified by name only on
        the basis of miscellaneous accounts.

163   _____.   "Painted Glass in Saxlingham Nethergate Church,
        Norfolk."   Journal of the British Society of Master Glass-
        Painters 5, no. 4 (Oct. 1934):163-69.
            Discusses the 13th-15th century glass, including the
        late 13th century medallions of St. Edmund.

164   GREEN, MARY A.   Old Painted Glass in Worcestershire.
        Worcester: Ebenezer Baylis & Son, 1935, 251 pp., 18 pls.
        *Reprinted in nine parts in Worcestershire Archaeological
        Society Transactions, 1935-48.
            Catalog of extant 13th-19th century glass; condensed
        list of glass mentioned by previous authors but no longer
        extant.

Br. 165

165   GRIFFIN, R. "The Arms of Richard II as Shown in Windows at
      Westwell and Wateringbury." Archaeologia Cantiana 47
      (1935):170-76.
          Identification of two heraldic panels in Westwell which
      help to date the glass ca. 1396; two panels of a slightly
      later date found in Wateringbury (ca. 1405).

166   TOKE, N.E. "The Medieval Stained Glass Windows at Upper
      Hardres." Archaeologia Cantiana 47 (1935):153-65.
          Describes three 13th century medallions [severely damaged
      by fire in 1971] and the 14th century grisaille and lancets
      and identifies the arms.

167   COUNCER, C.R. "The Medieval Painted Glass at Mersham."
      Archaeologia Cantiana 48 (1936):81-90.
          Reconstructs the iconography of the west window (ca.
      1400) and identifies the arms.

168   EDEN, F.S. "The Heraldic Stained Glass at Grays Inn."
      Connoisseur Magazine 98 (July 1936):16-22.
          Description and restoration of the 16th century heraldic
      glass.

169   KNOWLES, JOHN ALDER. Essays in the History of the York School
      of Glass-Painting. London: SPCK; New York: MacMillan
      Co., 1936, 283 pp., 53 pls. (2 color), 79 figs. Also
      serialized in the Journal of the British Society of Master
      Glass-Painters, 1926-1934 (Br. 103-4, 112-13, 117-18,
      124-25, 133-34, 145-46, 149-50, 152-53, 160-61).
          Still the best work on glass produced in York in the
      12th-16th centuries. Sections on patronage, iconography,
      economics, and the glass painters' guild; also contains
      discussions of styles and the relationship of glass to
      other media.

170   RUSHFORTH, GORDON McNEIL. Medieval Christian Imagery as
      Illustrated by the Painted Windows of Great Malvern Priory
      Church Worcestershire, Together with a Description and
      Explanation of All the Ancient Glass in the Church.
      Oxford: Clarendon, 1936, 456 pp., 189 figs. (11 color
      from watercolors), plan and figs. in text.
          Scholarly examination of this program, dated ca. 1430-
      1501. Notes losses, restorations, donors, style, and
      especially iconography and provides sources for the Old
      Testament cycle.

171   WOODFORDE, CHRISTOPHER. "Foreign Stained and Painted Glass in
        Norfolk." Norfolk and Norwich Archaeological Society 26
        (1936):73-84.
            German, Flemish, French, and Swiss glass from the mid-
        15th to 16th centuries brought to England, particularly
        through Hampp.

172   RUSHFORTH, GORDON McNEIL. "Additional Notes to the Painted
        Windows in the Chapel of the Vyne." Walpole Society
        Publications 25 (1936-37):167-69.
            David Joris of Delft, one of the craftsmen engaged in
        Calais, ca. 1520-21, and taken to Basingstoke to work on
        these windows, has left a biographical account of his
        journey.

173   HARRISON, FREDERICK. Stained Glass of York Minster. Trea-
        sures of Art. London: Studio; New York: Studio Publica-
        tions, [1937], 32 pp., 8 color pls.
            Annotated illustrations of details of the 13th-15th
        century windows; the brief introduction contains extracts
        from medieval account books. Good photographs.

174   WOODFORDE, CHRISTOPHER. "A Group of Fourteenth-Century
        Windows, Showing the Tree of Jesse." Journal of the
        British Society of Master Glass-Painters 6, no. 4 (Apr.
        1937):184-90.
            Attributes eight windows in the west country, dated ca.
        1330-50, to one atelier on the basis of overall design and
        decorative motifs. Overlooks differences of execution.
        The group includes Madley, Ludlow, St. Mary's in
        Shrewsbury, Tewkesbury, and Bristol Cathedral.

175   COUNCER, C.R. "The Medieval Painted Glass of Boughton Aluph."
        Archaeologia Cantiana 50 (1938):131-39.
            Reconstruction of the original 14th century glass based
        on four 17th and 18th century sources; identification of
        the arms.

176   JONES, K.H. "The Thirteenth-Century Glass at Nackington
        Church, near Canterbury." Archaeologia Cantiana 50
        (1938):161-62.
            Two windows ca. 1220, supposedly from Canterbury
        Cathedral, have been recently restored. This provenance
        is not accepted by Caviness, Br. 255.

Br. 177

177 WOODFORDE, CHRISTOPHER. "The Fourteenth-Century Glass in
     North Luffenham Church, Rutland." Journal of the British
     Society of Master Glass-Painters 7, no. 2 (Apr. 1938):
     69-73.
          Discussion of earlier accounts of the glass and problems
     arising from the 19th century restoration. Figures of
     saints dated by donor and style ca. 1300-1310, heraldry
     ca. 1330-50.

178 COLVIN, H.M. "Medieval Glass from Dale Abbey." Derbyshire
     Archaeological and Natural History Society's Journal 13
     (1939):129-41.
          Description of five lights transferred to Morley Church
     in 1538 by Sir Henry Sacheverell; these are dated to the
     second half of the 14th century and to the 15th century.

179 *EDEN, FREDERICK SYDNEY. Ancient Stained and Painted Glass in
     London. London: SPCK, 1939, 48 pp., 4 pls., 4 figs. in
     text.

180 WOODFORDE, CHRISTOPHER. "English Stained Glass and Glass-
     Painters in the Fourteenth-Century." Proceedings of the
     British Academy (1939):29-49.
          Concentrates on records of glass-painters, or of men
     named "LeVerrour" or "LeGlasier." No supporting references.

181 _____. "The Painted Glass in Withcote Church." Burlington
     Magazine 75 (1939):17-22.
          Description of the figural windows and their inscrip-
     tions, which date from ca. 1536-37; these are tentatively
     attributed to Gaylon Hone, the king's glazier, who was
     Flemish by birth.

182 EVETTS, L.C. "Genealogical Windows at Canterbury Cathedral."
     Burlington Magazine 78 (1941):95-98, 112-18.
          Suggests that most of the Ancestors of Christ were made
     for the clerestory ca. 1200; the typological windows in the
     aisles are dated slightly later (cf. Br. 183).

183 RACKHAM, BERNARD. "Genealogical Windows at Canterbury
     Cathedral." Burlington Magazine 78 (1941):165-66.
          Argues for an earlier dating of the clerestory than that
     given by Evetts (cf. Br. 182).

184   EDEN, FREDERICK SYDNEY. "Ancient Heraldic Glass at
       Winchester." Connoisseur Magazine 110 (March 1942):49-53.
       Few examples of 15th-17th century heraldry in the
       cathedral, close, and Westgate.

185   EVETTS, L.C. "Medieval Painted Glass in Northumberland."
       Archeologia Aeliana, 4th ser. 20 (1942):91-109.
       Provides a list of churches containing 13th, 14th, and
       15th century fragments and a brief description of their
       glass.

186   RACKHAM, BERNARD, and BATY, C.W. "The Jesse Window at
       Llanrhaiadr, Denbighshire." Burlington Magazine 80 (1942):
       62-66, 121-24.
       Part 1 identifies the source as a French woodcut from
       the Book of Hours by Jean Pigouchet done for Simon Vostre
       (1498) and used by the glazier at Thornhill, York. Part 2
       describes the window (1533), its site, and condition.

187   GODDARD, E.H. "A List of Wiltshire Churches Containing Old
       Glass." Wiltshire Archaeological and Natural History
       Magazine 50 (1943):205-13. Includes 13th-19th century
       glass.

188   WOODFORDE, CHRISTOPHER. "Some Medieval English Glazing
       Quarries Painted with Birds." Journal of the British
       Archaeological Association, 3d ser. 9 (1944):1-11.
       Numerous 13th-15th century examples from collections in
       England; their form, placement, and identification of the
       species are discussed.

189   COUNCER, C.R. "The Medieval Painted Glass of Chilham."
       Archaeologia Cantiana 58 (1945):8-13.
       Remains of medieval glass in three 15th century windows.

190   _____. "The Medieval and Renaissance Painted Glass of
       Eastwell." Archaeologia Cantiana 59 (1946):109-13.
       Numerous fragments of 14th century heraldic glass.

191   LAFOND, JEAN. "The Stained Glass Decoration of Lincoln
       Cathedral in the Thirteenth Century." Archaeological
       Journal 103 (1946):119-56.
       Still the most thorough critique of this heavily re-
       stored glass; to be replaced eventually by Nigel Morgan.

192 WOODFORDE, CHRISTOPHER. <u>Stained Glass in Somerset, 1250-1830</u>.
     London: Oxford University Press, 1946, 314 pp., 52 pls.
     (12 color), 7 figs.
         Describes glass at the major sites, beginning with Wells
     Cathedral (14th century); discusses the variety of styles
     in the 15th century; cites documentary evidence for
     glaziers and possible centers for their work. Argues that
     there is no cohesive school. Color illustrations are from
     watercolors.

193 RIDGEWAY, MAURICE H. "Coloured Window Glass in Cheshire,
     Part 1: 14th century." <u>Transactions of the Lancashire and
     Cheshire Antiquarian Society</u> 59 (1947):41-84.
         Introduction to the history of stained glass concentrat-
     ing on 14th century developments in England as seen in the
     Cheshire windows; the appendix includes an index of 14th
     century glass, extant and destroyed, and a glossary (con-
     tinued in Br. 195).

194 TRUMAN, N. "Ancient Glass in Nottinghamshire." <u>Transactions
     of the Thoroton Society</u> 51 (1947):50-65; 52 (1948):58-68.
         Incomplete survey of 14th-16th century glass arranged
     alphabetically by location; ends with L's.

195 RIDGEWAY, MAURICE H. "Coloured Window Glass in Cheshire,
     Part II: 1400-1550." <u>Transactions of the Lancashire and
     Cheshire Antiquarian Society</u> 60 (1948):58-85.
         Continuation of the 1947 article, dealing with 15th-16th
     century glass, much of which is today destroyed (see
     Br. 193).

196 KNOWLES, JOHN ALDER. "An Attempt to Determine the Original
     Arrangement and Contents of the Windows in the Western
     Portion of the Choir of York Minster." <u>Yorkshire Archaeo-
     logical Journal</u> 37 (1948-51):442-55.
         The lower, 15th century windows are a complete series
     representing a group of martyrs, while the clerestory glass
     represents kings and ecclesiastics. All of these histori-
     cal figures contributed to the establishment of Christian-
     ity in Northumbria.

197 _____. "Technical Notes on the St. William Window in York
     Minster." <u>Yorkshire Archaeological Journal</u> 37 (1948-51):
     148-61.
         Discusses adjustments resulting from a change in window
     design in the course of glazing, ca. 1421; the varied exe-
     cution of panels made from the same cartoons indicates a
     number of painters in the workshop, perhaps that of John
     Thornton.

198   MOORE, D.G. "Memoirs Concerning Sir Richard York (of York)
       Knight (obit. A.D. 1498) and the Ancient Stained Glass of
       a Memorial Window Formerly in the Church of St. John, the
       Evangelist, Ousebridge End, in the City of York (Lately
       Removed into the North Transept of York Minster)."
       Yorkshire Archaeological Journal 37 (1948-51):213-30.
            Biographical information concerning Sir Richard York
       verifies the tradition that the window (end of 15th cen-
       tury) was a memorial to him.

199   HUTCHINSON, F.E. Medieval Glass at All Souls College: A
       History and Description, Based upon the Notes of the Late
       G.M. Rushforth. London: Faber & Faber, 1949, 67 pp.,
       2 color pls., 31 figs.
            Brief, useful account of this important collection of
       Oxford glass, of which some is attributed on documentary
       evidence to John of Oxford, 1441.

200   LAMBORN, E.A. GREENING. The Armorial Glass of the Oxford
       Diocese, 1250-1850. London: Oxford University Press,
       1949, 179 pp., 64 pls.
            Introduction to the art of heraldry followed by a cata-
       log of armorial glass.

201   RACKHAM, BERNARD. The Ancient Glass of Canterbury Cathedral.
       London: L. Humphries for the Friends of Canterbury
       Cathedral, 1949, 209 pp., 21 color pls., 80 b&w pls.
            Description of the glass preserved in the cathedral,
       with chapters on chronology, French influences, etc. Out-
       dated (cf. Br. 244, 255).

202   OAKESHOTT, WALTER. "The Ancient Glass of Canterbury."
       Antiquaries Journal 31 (1951):86-89.
            Review of Rackham, Br. 201. Raises important questions
       about the restorations and the authenticity of the glass
       (cf. also Caviness, Br. 244, 255).

203   BRIGHT, HUGH. The Lady Chapel Windows, Lichfield Cathedral.
       New and rev. ed. with an additional note by Sir Eric
       Maclagan. Lichfield: Lichfield Cathedral, 1950, 25 pp.,
       7 pls., 1 fig.
            Perhaps the same as *Hugh Bright, The Herckenrode
       Windows in Lichfield Cathedral, 1st ed. (Lichfield: 1932,
       20 pp., 9 pls.; 2nd ed., 1934). Seven windows probably de-
       signed by Lambert Lombard in the first half of the 16th
       century and originally located in the Cistercian Abbey
       Church of Herckenrode were brought to Lichfield in the
       early 19th century.

Br. 204

204   GRODECKI, LOUIS, and RACKHAM, BERNARD. "The Ancient Glass of
        Canterbury Cathedral." Burlington Magazine 92 (1950):
        294-97, 357.
            Grodecki disputes Rackham's dating (Br. 201) of some of
        the choir clerestory figures to the 12th century and cites
        comparisons from manuscripts. Continued in Br. 206.

205   WOODFORDE, CHRISTOPHER. The Norwich School of Glass-Painting
        in the Fifteenth Century. London: Oxford University
        Press, 1950, 233 pp., 44 pls.
            Town records reveal the names of about sixty glass
        painters who lived in the 13th-16th centuries but no extant
        glass can be attributed to any of them. The glass in sev-
        eral Norfolk and Suffolk churches is described, with a
        useful chapter on Labors of the Months.

206   GRODECKI, LOUIS, and RACKHAM, BERNARD. "The Ancient Glass of
        Canterbury Cathedral." Burlington Magazine 93 (1951):
        94-95.
            See Br. 204.

207   HUDLESTON F., and HUDLESTON, C.R. "Medieval Glass in Penrith
        Church." Transactions of the Cumberland and Westmorland
        Antiquarian and Archaeological Society, n.s. 51 (1951):
        96-102.
            Argues that the portraits represent Joan Beaufort and
        Ralph Nevill, first earl of Westmorland, and therefore the
        glass is earlier than the late 14th-early 15th century.

208   WOODFORDE, CHRISTOPHER. The Stained Glass of New College,
        Oxford. London: Oxford University Press, 1951, 111 pp.,
        1 color pl., 20 figs.
            Examines the accounts, including those which mention
        Thomas Glasyer of Oxford (1386-1416), and the earlier de-
        scriptions of the glass; describes briefly the extant
        windows.

209   JEAVONS, S.A. "Medieval Painted Glass in Staffordshire
        Churches." Transactions of the Birmingham Archaeological
        Society 68 [1951-52]:25-73.
            Survey of the 14th century glass; includes an appendix
        with a checklist of sites and dates of glass.

210   HARRISON, KENNETH PRITCHARD. The Windows of King's College
        Chapel, Cambridge. Cambridge: University Press, 1952,
        100 pp., 2 figs. in text.

Discusses the dates and authorship of the windows,
according to the documents. Brief list of subjects. Useful, but now outdated by the Corpus volume (Br. 239).

211   MILNER-WHITE, ERIC. "The Resurrection of a Fourteenth-Century
      Window." Burlington Magazine 94 (1952):108-12.
         Discovery and repositioning of a lost glass from the
      nave of York Cathedral (1328-38) representing the Virgin's
      parentage and history.

212   OSWALD, ARTHUR. "Barnard Flower, the King's Glazier."
      Journal of the British Society of Master Glass-Painters 11,
      no. 1 (1952):8-21.
         Documented his activities, 1496-1517, especially at
      Cambridge and Westminster; cites other glaziers mentioned
      in the accounts.

213   RACKHAM, BERNARD. "The Ancient Windows of Christ's College
      Chapel, Cambridge." Archaeological Journal 109 (1952):
      132-42.
         Description, reconstruction, and identification of the
      royal portraits for four windows executed for Godshouse
      (now Christ's College) in 1505-10; their style influenced
      by the royal atelier in London before Bernard Flower.

214   SALZMAN, L.F. Building in England down to 1540: A Documen-
      tary History. Oxford: Clarendon, 1952, 629 pp., 21 figs.
         Section on "Glazing" (pp. 173-86) provides a well-
      documented survey of the facture and use of glass in
      religious and secular buildings and the economics of the
      stained glass trade.

215   KNOWLES, JOHN ALDER. "The West Window, St. Martin-Le-Grand,
      Coney Street, York." Yorkshire Archaeological Journal 38
      (1952-55):148-84.
         Description of canopies, tracery lights, and panels
      representing the Life of St. Martin, donated by Robert
      Semer between 1432 and 1437 and attributed to J. Chamber
      the Elder and Younger, who worked on the St. Cuthbert win-
      dow in York Cathedral.

216   HARRISON, KENNETH PRITCHARD. "Designs from Dürer in the Win-
      dows of King's College Chapel, Cambridge." Burlington
      Magazine 96 (1954):349.
         The windows, depicting the Fall of the Rebel Angels
      (1515-17) and Christ being Nailed to the Cross (1526-31),
      were influenced by Dürer's designs; Dirk Vellert probably
      executed the latter window.

117

Br. 217

217 WOODFORDE, CHRISTOPHER. English Stained and Painted Glass.
     Oxford: Clarendon Press, 1954, 101 pp., 80 pls.
          Brief survey illustrated with photographs of representa-
     tive panels, beginning with the early glass of York Minster,
     which he dates mid-12th century.

218 KNOWLES, JOHN ALDER. "Notes on Some Windows in the Choir and
     Lady Chapel of York Minster." Yorkshire Archaeological
     Journal 39 (1956-58):91-118.
          Study of the late 14th century glass from the south
     clerestory; its subject, history, original placement, and
     style; attributed to an atelier from London.

219 KIRBY, H.T. "The Baptism of St. Christopher: A Unique Piece
     of Stained Glass." Apollo 66 (1957):156.
          Small panel from Birtsmorton Church (14th-15th century
     glass) surrounded by unrelated architectural and ornamental
     fragments; the only other known representation of this sub-
     ject is in Italy.

220 RACKHAM, BERNARD. The Stained Glass Windows of Canterbury
     Cathedral. Canterbury: SPCK, 1957, 96 pp., 8 figs.
     (4 color), plans.
          The best small guide to date, with a checklist of glass
     of all periods; includes the early Jesse Tree panels that
     were returned after his 1949 publication (Br. 201).

221 SABIN, ARTHUR. "The Fourteenth Century Heraldic Glass in the
     Eastern Lady Chapel of Bristol Cathedral." Antiquaries
     Journal 37 (1957):54-70.
          East window dated mid-14th century on the basis of its
     heraldry (cf. Winston's date of ca. 1320).

222 WAYMENT, HILARY G. "The Use of Engravings in the Design of
     the Renaissance Windows of King's College Chapel,
     Cambridge." Burlington Magazine 100 (1958):378-88.
          Identification of the sources for the 16th century win-
     dows of the first period is found in engravings from the
     Biblia pauperum and the Speculum humanae salvationis; glass
     of the second period is related to Lucas van Leyden, Dürer,
     and the school of Raphael.

223 KIRBY, H.T. "The 'Jesse Tree' Motif in Stained Glass: A
     Comparative Study of Some English Examples." Connoisseur
     Year Book (1959):85-90.
          Examples in 14th and 15th century glass.

224 KNOWLES, JOHN ALDER. "The East Window of St. Michael-Le-
Belfrey Church." Yorkshire Archaeological Journal 40
(1959-62):145-59.
14th century panels from at least three different sites
have been installed in this 16th century church, the last
in York to be constructed in the Gothic style.

225 _____. "John Thornton of Coventry and the East Window of
Great Malvern Priory." Antiquaries Journal 39 (1959):
274-82.
Argues that the Great Malvern Priory window (ca. 1450)
could not have been the work of John Thornton, who died in
1435; similarities in the design to his glass suggest that
the cartoons had been passed on to his son.

226 BAKER, JOHN. English Stained Glass. London: Thames &
Hudson; New York: Harry N. Abrams, [1960], 224 pp.,
103 figs., 33 color pls. French translation. L'art du
vitrail en Angleterre. Paris: Arthaud, 1961. Italian
translation. Le vetrate inglesi. Milan: Electra, 1961.
Paperback edition. English Stained Glass of the Medieval
Period. London: Thames & Hudson, 1979, 96 pp., 41 pls.
(some color).
Introduction by Herbert Read, photographs by Alfred
Lammer. Brief historical outline for the 12th-16th centuries, with annotated plates and a bibliography. Text by
a Canterbury-trained glass painter. Well illustrated.

227 MILNER-WHITE, ERIC. Sixteenth Century Glass in York Minster
and in the Church of St. Michael-le-Belfrey. York: St.
Anthony's Press, 1960, 20 pp., 10 pls.
Attributes the cathedral's south transept windows
(1504-10) and its thirteen Tudor panels, originally from
St. Wilfred's (ca. 1535), and the St. Michael-le-Belfrey
glass (1530-37) to John Almayn, a German working in York;
also deals with other 16th century panels.

228 RANSOME, DAVID R. "The Struggle of the Glaziers' Company with
the Foreign Glaziers, 1500-1550." Guildhall Miscellany 2
(1960-68):12-20.
William Neve, the last English-born King's Glazier, was
succeeded by Barnard Flower ca. 1502-3. Cites resistance
to foreign glaziers.

Br. 229

229 GANDERTON, EDWIN WILLIAM, and LAFOND, JEAN. Ludlow Stained
and Painted Glass. Ludlow: Friends of the Church of St.
Lawrence, 1961, 109 pp., 40 pls., plan.
Tree of Jesse and other subjects dated to the first half
of the 14th century; Creed, Palmers, and Ten Commandments
windows, ca. 1445.

230 *NEWTON, PETER A. "Schools of Glass Painting in the Midlands,
1275-1430." Ph.D. dissertation, University of London,
1961.

231 HILL, DEREK INGRAM. The Stained Glass of Canterbury Cathedral.
Canterbury: Friends of Canterbury Cathedral, [1962],
36 pp., 8 figs., plan.
Very brief guide to the glass of all periods.

232 KIRBY, H.T. "Clerical Portraits in Stained Glass: Two Famous
Oxfordshire Rectors." Antiquaries Journal 42 (1962):
251-52.
Identification of the figures in a Horley Church window
as Henry Rumworthe, alias Cirencester (died 1420), and
Robert Gilbert (died 1448).

233 KNOWLES, JOHN ALDER. "An Inquiry into the Date of the Stained
Glass in the Chapter House at York." Yorkshire Archaeological Journal 40 (1959-62):451-61.
Argues that the subject medallions, which show similarities in design to the Merton College glass (1283), were
executed in the 13th century for an earlier building; the
backgrounds, borders, and grisailles which now surround
them are dated to the 14th century.

234 STROHM, PAUL. "The Imagery of a Missing Window at Great
Malvern Priory Church." Transactions of the Worcestershire
Archaeological Society, 3d ser. 1 (1965-67):65-68.
Supports Gordon Rushforth's identification (Br. 170) of
a Joshua scene to end the Old Testament cycle.

235 CAVINESS, MADELINE H. "Fifteenth-Century Stained Glass from
the Chapel of Hampton Court, Herefordshire: The Apostles'
Creed and Other Subjects." The Walpole Society Publications 42 (1968-70):35-60.
Extensive remains of this high quality glass have been
scattered in collections since 1923. Installed in Hampton
Court sometime between 1434 and 1683, it had probably been
made ca. 1420 for another building (Hereford Cathedral?).

236 GEE, E.A. "The Painted Glass of All Saints' Church, North
      Street, York." Archaeologia 102 (1969):151-202.
          Publishes documents relating to the glass and divides it
      into two stylistic groups: two windows are dated ca.
      1310-40; the others, ca. 1410-40, were executed by John
      Thornton or his school.

237 FRENCH, T.W. "Observations on Some Medieval Glass in York
      Minster." Antiquaries Journal 51 (1971):86-93.
          Argues for a date ca. 1175-1200 for glass that was re-
      used in the nave and elsewhere and ascribes some of the
      glass in the choir to ca. 1335 on the basis of stylistic
      comparisons with the west window (1339), manuscripts, and
      glass in Rouen.

238 HARVEY, JOHN H., and KING, DENNIS S. "Winchester College
      Stained Glass: I, History of the Glass, Its Dispersal and
      Recovery; II, Technical Report on the Restoration of the
      Glass." Archaeologia 103 (1971):149-77.
          Thorough, well-illustrated account of the glass that had
      been dispersed, written after its return and restoration in
      1951. Includes the Tree of Jesse usually attributed to
      Thomas of Oxford, ca. 1387-94, and questions whether the
      London painter Herebright of Cologne was involved in the
      design.

239 WAYMENT, HILARY G. The Windows of King's College Chapel,
      Cambridge. Corpus Vitrearum Medii Aevi: Great Britain,
      supp. vol. 1. London: Oxford University Press for the
      British Academy, 1972, 140 pp., 154 pls. (36 color).
          Clear and thorough presentation, completely illustrated.

240 MARKS, RICHARD. "The Stained Glass Patronage of Sir Reginald
      Bray." Report of the Society of the Friends of St.
      George's [Windsor Castle] and the Descendants of the
      Knights of the Garter 5 (1973-74):199-202.
          Donations of glass to Peterborough Cathedral (ca. 1480),
      Great Malvern Priory (1501-1502), and Shere (Surrey), as
      well as St. George's Chapel.

241 KING, DAVID J. Stained Glass Tours Around Norfolk Churches.
      [Norwich]: Norfolk Society, 1974, 40 pp., 1 color pl.,
      14 figs.
          Guide to major sites with 13th-16th century glass (some
      of which is German and Flemish). Useful supplement to
      Woodforde's book (Br. 205).

Br. 242

242   MARKS, RICHARD. "Henry Williams and His 'Ymage of Deth'
      Roundel at Stamford on Avon, Northamptonshire." Antiquaries
      Journal 54 (1974):272-74.
           Votive panel with a kneeling donor and a skeleton hold-
      ing a bow and arrow provided for in the will of the vicar
      (1501) and preserved in the parish church.

243 *MARKS, RICHARD C. "The Stained Glass of the Collegiate Church
      of the Holy Trinity, Tattershall (Lincs.)." Ph.D. disser-
      tation, University of London, 1975.
           Discusses the iconography, date, and style of this im-
      portant glass from the second half of the 15th century.

244   CAVINESS, MADELINE H. The Early Stained Glass of Canterbury
      Cathedral, circa 1175-1220. Princeton: University Press,
      1977, 190 pp., 4 color pls., 219 figs., folding plan, figs.
      in text.
           Analysis of the problems of dating, stylistic develop-
      ment, and the relation of these windows to French glass and
      works in other media; reconstruction of the programs and
      iconographic sources. Complements the Corpus volume
      (Br. 255).

245   HASELOCK, JEREMY, and O'CONNOR, DAVID E. "The Stained and
      Painted Glass." In A History of York Minster, by G.E.
      Aylmer and Reginald Cant. Oxford: Clarendon, 1977,
      pp. 370-72.
           The most recent synopsis, including dates for the vari-
      ous 14th and 15th century campaigns.

246   BAKER, MALCOLM, and FARMER, D.H. "Medieval Illustrations of
      Bede's Life of St. Cuthbert." Journal of the Warburg and
      Cortauld Institutes 41 (1978):16-49.
           Compares the cycles in 12th to 13th-century manuscripts
      (Oxford, University College MS. 165 and British Library
      Add. MS. 39943) with the scenes in the 15th-century window
      in York Minster, concluding they are related in iconography.
      A date as late as the 1430s is questioned for the window.

247   DAVIDSON, CLIFFORD, and O'CONNOR, DAVID E. York Art: A Sub-
      ject List of Extant and Lost Art, Including Items Relevant
      to Early Drama. Early Drama, Art, and Music References
      Series, 1. Kalamazoo: Medieval Institute, Western Michigan
      University, 1978, 209 pp., 44 pls.
           Provides an iconographic index to the glass in York
      churches.

248 MARKS, RICHARD. "The Glazing of Fotheringhay Church and
      College." Journal of the British Archaeological Associa-
      tion 131 (1978):79-109.
          Reconstruction of the lost 15th century glazing program
      for the Yorkist College of All Saints on the basis of
      antiquarian sources.

249 EELES, FRANCIS C. "The Ancient Stained Glass of Westminster
      Abbey, from a Manuscript Dated 1938." Journal of the
      British Society of Master Glass-Painters 17 [16], no. 2
      (1978-79):17-30.
          Complete checklist of 13th-16th century remnants,
      without documentation or adequate illustrations. Con-
      tinued: Br. 251, 253.

250 NEWTON, PETER A., and KERR, JILL. The County of Oxford: A
      Catalogue of Medieval Stained Glass. Corpus Vitrearum
      Medii Aevi: Great Britain, 1. London: Oxford University
      Press for the British Academy, 1979, 248 pp., 34 color
      illus., 159 figs.
          First thorough publication of all the glass in the
      county, including the well-known 13th century panels at
      Dorchester and Stanton Harcourt, the important 14th cen-
      tury remnants at Beckley and Chinnor, and very diverse
      examples of 15th century glazing. Excellent analyses of
      iconography. City of Oxford in preparation.

251 EELES, FRANCIS C. "The Ancient Stained Glass of Westminster
      Abbey: Part 2." Journal of the British Society of Master
      Glass-Painters 16 (1979-80):47-53.
          Fragments of the 13th-15th centuries, including canopies
      of the "Westminster School." Continues Br. 249.

252 WAYMENT, HILARY G. "The Stained Glass in the Chapel of the
      Vyne." In National Trust Studies, 1980. Sotheby Parke
      Bernet Publications. London: Philip Wilson, 1980,
      pp. 35-47.
          Glass near Basingstoke (the Vyne and the Chapel of the
      Holy Ghost) made ca. 1522 by artists from the Low Countries;
      cites documentary and stylistic associations with David
      Joris, Pieter Coeck, and Bernard van Orley.

253 EELES, FRANCIS C. "The Ancient Glass of Westminster Abbey:
      part 3." Journal of the British Society of Master-Glass
      Painters 17 (1980-81):10-17.
          Continues Br. 249, 251.

Br. 254

254   WAYMENT, HILARY G. "Echo Answers 'Where': The Victorian
        'Restoration' of the Great West Window at Fairford."
        <u>Journal of the British Society of Master Glass-Painters</u> 17
        (1980-81):18-27.
            Provides evidence that the original, early 16th century
        glass in the upper register of the Last Judgment window was
        removed by Chance Brothers of Smethwick ca. 1861 and may
        survive in collections.

255   CAVINESS, MADELINE H. <u>The Windows of Christ Cathedral,</u>
        <u>Canterbury</u>. Index by Jill Kerr. Corpus Vitrearum Medii
        Aevi: Great Britain, vol. 2. London: Oxford University
        Press for the British Academy, 1981, 372 pp., 18 color pls.,
        912 figs.
            Complete publication of the medieval glass, including
        the program of lost typological windows and extant panels
        of the 12th-16th centuries.

256   WAYMENT, HILARY G. "The East Window of St. Margaret's,
        Westminster." <u>Antiquaries Journal</u> 61 (1981):292-301.
            The style of the crucifixion window with royal donors
        and patron saints is associated with Leiden and is dated
        ca. 1515-27. It may have been made for Waltham Abbey and
        was moved twice in the eighteenth century; drawings made in
        1737 show it was significantly altered by William Price the
        younger a few years later.

257   _____. "The Stained Glass of the Chapel of the Vyne, and the
        Chapel of the Holy Ghost Basingstoke." <u>Archaeologia</u> 107
        (1981):141-52.
            Argues that a Christological Cycle, with donor portraits,
        was made ca. 1522-24/25 for the Basingstoke Chapel and
        later moved to the Vyne; attributes the designs to Bernard
        van Orley and Pieter Coeck.

Section VII
France

The reader is also referred to the following items in other sections: Gen. 15, 31; Ger. 201.

1   SUGERIUS [Suger], [Abbot]. "De administratione; de consecratione."
       Composed at St.-Denis ca. 1140-53; includes material on the glass of the choir.

    Panofsky, Erwin. Abbot Suger on the Abbey Church of St.-Denis and Its Art Treasures. Princeton: University Press, 1946; 2d ed., 1979, 285 pp., 31 figs.
       Edition and translation with commentary; contains a survey of earlier editions and a bibliography.

2   Le VIEIL, PIERRE. L'art de la peinture sur verre et de la vitrerie. Paris: L.-F. Delatour, 1774, 259 pp., 13 figs. Geneva: Minkoff Reprint, 1973.
       Brief history of glass painting, especially useful for the revival in the 17th-18th centuries and for restorations such as that of Notre-Dame in Paris. Techniques described include glassmaking and enamelling, as well as painting.

3   MURR, CHRISTOPH GOTTLIEB von. Journal zur Kunstgeschichte und zur allgemeinen Litterature 3 (1776):37-43.
       Review of Le Vieil, Fr. 2. Synopsizes historical section.

4   LANGLOIS, E.-H. Mémoire sur la peinture sur verre et sur quelques vitraux remarquables des églises de Rouen. Rouen: F. Baudry, 1823, 52 pp., 5 pls.
       Treats most of the 13th-16th century glass in Rouen; useful descriptions of St.-Patrice and St.-Vincent. References to other glass in Normandy. Illustrations are from drawings by Espérence Langlois.

5   ARNAUD, ANNE-FRANÇOIS. Voyage archéologique et pittoresque
    dans le département de l'Aube et dans l'ancien diocèse de
    Troyes. Troyes: Imp. de L.-C. Cardon, 1837, 244 pp.,
    119 illus.
        Discusses 16th century glass in Bar-sur-Seine, Martin-
    ès-Vignes, Ricey-Haut, Rumilly-les-Vauds, and Sefonds; and
    13th century glass in Troyes.

6   RENOUVIER, JULES. "Notice sur la peinture sur verre et sur
    mur, dans le Midi de la France." Bulletin monumental 5
    (1839):416-24.
        Brief summary of 14th-16th century glass.

7   MARTIN, ARTHUR, and CAHIER, CHARLES. Monographie de la cathé-
    drale de Bourges. 2 vols. Paris: Poussielgue-Rusand,
    1841-44. Vol. 1, Vitraux du 13e siècle, 303 pp. Vol. 2,
    72 colored plates (folio size), engraved from tracings.
        Vol. 1 contains description and iconographic analysis.
    Vol. 2 is still the most complete publication of this im-
    portant collection and includes a great deal of comparative
    material from other French sites.

8   SICOTIÈRE, LÉON de la. "Notice sur les vitraux de l'église
    Notre-Dame d'Alençon." Bulletin monumental 8 (1842):
    105-15.
        Iconography and description of eleven windows dated
    1511-43.

9   THIBAUD, ÉMILE. Considérations historiques et critiques sur
    les vitraux anciens et modernes et sur la peinture sur
    verre. Clermont-Ferrand: Thibaud-Landriot, 1842, 143 pp.,
    3 pls.
        Deals with the making of and use of glass in windows;
    chapter 4, "Histoire de la peinture sur verre" (pp. 33-93),
    extends up to the 18th century and includes a treatment of
    Bourges and Clermont-Ferrand and a section on signatures in
    glass and documents concerning glass painters (pp. 77-93).
    Illustrated with drawings after Lasteyrie.

10 LASSUS, J.B. Monographie de la cathédrale de Chartres.
    Vol. 1. Paris: Imp. royale, 1842, 72 pls. (bound, folio
    size). Vol. 2, Explication de planches, by Paul Durand.
    Paris: Imp. nationale, 1881, 178 pp.
        Vol. 1 contains engravings, many colored, of 12th-15th
    century glass. The text volume (vol. 2) provides a de-
    scription of the plates.

11 FILLON, B. "Notice sur les vitraux de Ste. Radegonde."
Mémoires de la Société des antiquaires de l'ouest 11
(1844):483-95.
Dates the Last Judgment and the Life of Ste. Radegonde
windows to the early 14th century; the Life of St. Blaise
is dated to the end of the 14th century.

12 BATISSIER, L. "Traité de la peinture sur verre." In
Histoire de l'art monumental. Paris: Furne et Cie,
Libraires-Éditeurs, 1845, pp. 647-64.
Origin of stained glass in France during the reign of
Charles le Chauve and its progress from the 12th-16th
centuries.

13 TEXIER, J. "Histoire de la peinture sur verre en Limousin."
Bulletin archéologique et historique du Limousin 1 (1846):
20-29, 94-148.
Pre-restoration account of glass at Banlieu, etc.

14 BARTHÉLEMY, A. de. "Lettre à M. Henri Gérente sur les anciens
peintres sur verre de Tréguier." Bulletin monumental 13
(1847):577-85.
Information gathered from church documents pertaining
to 15th-17th century glaziers.

15 *BARRAUD, [Abbé]. "Description des deux grandes rosaces de la
cathédrale de Beauvais (XVIe s.)." Mémoires de la Société
académique d'archéologie, sciences, et arts du département
de l'Oise 1 (1847):225-46. Reprint. Beauvais: Imp. A.
Desjardins, [1850].
Chiefly iconographic description.

16 GUERBER, V. Essai sur les vitraux de la cathédrale de
Strasbourg. Strasbourg: L.F. Roux, 1848, 124 pp., 4 color
pls.
Iconographic program and chronology of the glazing, with
a section on ornament.

17 AUBER, [Abbé]. Histoire de la cathédrale de Poitiers, contenant la théorie de ses vitraux peints. 2 vols. Poitiers
and Paris: A. Dupré, 1849.
Vol. I, chapters 16-20 (pp. 522-95) include discussion
of the history and style of the stained glass and description of the 12th and 13th century windows. Illustrated
with drawings of window schemata.

18 MARCHAND, J.; BOURASSÉ, [CHANOINE]; and MANCEAU, [CHANOINE].
    Les verrières du choeur de l'église métropolitaine de
    Tours. Paris: V. Didron, 1849, 75 pp., plan, 18 pls.
        Outline drawings are a useful record made during
    Guérin's restorations.

19 *CHARLES, L. Atelier de verriers à la Ferté-Bernard, à la fin
        du quinzième siècle et au seizième. Le Mans: Galienne,
        1891, 40 pp.

20 Congrès archéologique de France (Laon, Nevers, Gisors, 1851)
        18 (1852):368-69.
            Description of the glass in the Lady Chapel of St.-
        Germer-de-Fly: the Life of St. Germer, construction of the
        chapel, and the Lives of Christ and the Virgin are all said
        to be of 13th century type.

21 SCHNEEGANS, L. "Vitrail du XIIe siècle à la cathédrale de
        Strasbourg, représentant Saint-Candide, martyr." Revue
        d'Alsace 4 (1853):1-16.
            The iconography of three windows representing SS.
        Maurice, Victor, and Candide.

22 LASTEYRIE, F. FERDINAND de. Histoire de la peinture sur verre
        d'après ses monuments en France. 2 vols. Paris: Type de
        Firmin Didot Frères, Fils, et Cie, 1853-57, 314 pp.,
        110 pls.
            Glass from the 12th-19th centuries, beginning with
        Angers as the most ancient; colored drawings by the author
        are often important pre-restoration records.

23 AMÉ, ÉMILE. Recherches sur les anciens vitraux incolores du
        département de l'Yonne. Paris: V. Didron, 1854, 12 pp.,
        6 pls.
            Tracings of blank glazed windows made in 1842 include
        examples at Pontigny and Sens (the Abbey of St.-Jean and
        the hospital).

24 TROCHE, N.M. La Sainte-Chapelle de Paris: Notice historique,
        archéologique, et descriptive. Paris: Boucquin, 1853,
        107 pp., 1 fig.
            Includes (pp. 40-50) a description of the 13th century
        windows and their restorations.

25 *BARRAUD, [Abbé]. "Description des vitraux des chapelles de la
      cathédrale de Beauvais"; and "Description des vitraux des
      hautes fenêtres du choeur de la cathédrale de Beauvais."
      Mémoires de la Société académique d'archéologie, sciences,
      et arts du département de l'Oise 3 (1856):50-86, 277-313,
      respectively.
         Chiefly iconographic.

26 LENOIR, ALEXANDRE. Historique de la peinture sur verre et
      description de vitraux anciens et modernes, pour servir à
      l'histoire de l'art en France. Paris: J.B. Dumoulin,
      1856, 158 pp., 45 pls. [Reprinted from Musée des monuments
      français 6, first published 1803; subsequently supplemented
      by plates and a section on technique].
         General history through the 18th century; most illustra-
      tions are of 16th century works. Description of glass in
      the Musée des monuments français includes some St.-Denis
      panels.

27 TOURNEUR, VICTOR. "Quelles sont les verrières les plus re-
      marquables du départment de la Marne?" Congrès archéolo-
      gique de France (Châlons-sur-Marne, 1885) 22 (1856):88-90.
         One of the few 19th century accounts of the glass in
      St.-Remi at Reims; see also Fr. 39.

28 STRAUB, A. "Notice sur les verrières de l'église, aujourd'hui
      paroissiale, de l'ancien couvent de Sainte-Marie-Magdeleine
      à Strasbourg." Bulletin de la Société pour la conservation
      des monuments historiques d'Alsace 1 (1856-57):100-116.
         Detailed description of the six choir windows dating
      from the end of the 15th century.

29 TOURNEUR, VICTOR. Histoire et description des vitraux et des
      statues de l'intérieur de la cathédrale de Reims. Reims:
      P. Regnier, 1857, 77 pp., 2 engraved figs.
         Most complete description before the World War I
      damage (pp. 7-62).

30 STRAUB, A. "Notice sur deux verrières de l'église de Saint-
      George à Schlestadt." Bulletin de la Société pour la con-
      servation des monuments historiques d'Alsace 2 (1857-58):
      215-18.
         Representing the legends of SS. Catherine and Agnes
      (first half of the 15th century and mid-16th century).

31 COFFINET, [Abbé]. "Peintres-verriers de Troyes." <u>Annales</u>
<u>archéologiques</u> 18 (1858):212-24.
Lists the names of 14th-17th century glaziers and includes an index of their monograms.

32 PETIT-GÉRARD, B. "Note sur les vitraux d'Alsace et sur un
ancien vitrail de l'église abbatiale de Wissembourg."
<u>Bulletin de la Société pour la conservation des monuments</u>
<u>historiques d'Alsace</u> 3 (1858-59):81-86.
Focuses on the early 14th century ornamental grisaille
window donated by Abbé Edelinus.

33 STRAUB, A. "Analyse des vitraux de l'ancienne collégiale de
Haslach." <u>Congrès archéologique de France</u> 26 (1859):
296-363.
Description and iconography of the apse windows from the
end of the 13th century and the nave windows dated 1380-
1420.

34 PETIT-GÉRARD, B. "Aspect général des vitraux d'Alsace dans
leurs rapports avec ceux du centre de la France." <u>Congrès</u>
<u>archéologique de France</u> 26 (1860):363-74.
12th-15th century glass in Strasbourg and elsewhere;
remarks on the yellows and green characteristic of the
region and on the heavy painting.

35 SCHAUENBOURG, P.R. de. "Mémoire: Enumération des verrières
les plus importantes conservées dans les églises d'Alsace."
<u>Congrès archéologique de France (Strasbourg, 1859)</u> 26
(1860):211-67, 297-363.
Description of the glass in Strasbourg Cathedral and of
restorations to be carried out; also notes other glass in
the region (Rosenwiller, Schlestadt, Lautenbach, etc.).

36 STRAUB, A. "Analyse des vitraux de l'église de Walbourg."
<u>Congrès archéologique de France (Strasbourg, 1859)</u> 26
(1860):344-63.
Description of the glass remaining (15th century).

37 PETIT-GÉRARD, B. "Quelques remarques sur les artistes-
verriers strasbourgeois du XVe siècle, à propos de la
réparation d'un vitrail de l'église de Sainte-Madeleine."
<u>Bulletin de la Société pour la conservation des monuments</u>
<u>historiques d'Alsace</u> 4 (1860-61):1-10.
Documents pertaining to the glaziers active in the city;
description of the Ste. Madeleine window of 1481 after its
restoration.

38 BRULÉE, [Abbé]. "Description des verrières de la cathédrale de Sens." <u>Bulletin de la Société archéologique de Sens</u> 7 (1861):161-216.
    Complete iconographic description. Not illustrated. Includes "Note sur les restes de vitraux de Saint-Pierre-le-Rond" (pp. 213-16).

39 TOURNEUR, VICTOR. "Les verrières de l'église Saint-Rémi de Reims." <u>Congrès archéologique de France (Reims, 1861)</u> 28 (1861):87-102.
    Reaffirms an 11th century date for some of the glass; other figures are 12th-13th century (see Fr. 27).

40 HUCHER, EUGÈNE. <u>Calques des vitraux peints de la cathédrale du Mans</u>. 2 vols. Paris: Didron; Le Mans: Monnoyeur Frères, 1864, Vol. 1, unpaginated text. Vol. 2, portfolio of 100 color pls.
    Many full-size prints made from tracings, some of which show the pre-restoration state of the works (1860). 12th-15th century glass is reproduced with brief annotations.

41 *_____. <u>Vitraux peints de la cathédrale du Mans, ouvrage renfermant les réductions des plus belles verrières et la description complète de tous les vitraux de cette cathédrale</u>. Paris: Didron, 1865, 82 pp., 20 pls.

42 GUILHERMY, FRANÇOIS de. <u>Description de la Sainte Chapelle</u>. 1st ed. Paris: à la Sainte-Chapelle, 1867. 3d ed., Paris: Imp. E. Capiomont et V. Renault, 1878.
    Description of the glass by the man who helped in the restoration (pp. 50-63).

43 DIDOT, A. <u>Receuil des oeuvres choisies de Jean Cousin, reproduits en facsimiles</u>. Paris: Librairie de Firmin Didot, Frères, Fils et Cie, 1873, 20 pp.
    Discussion of the life of the 16th century artist, Jean Cousin, and his contributions in painting, sculpture, stained glass, miniatures, and engravings.

44 *PURDAY, C.-H. "Croquis, 1873-1874." 10 vols. Paris, Bibliothèque de la Direction du Patrimoine MS. 4º, 1844.
    Drawings of glass at various sites. Lost.

45 LECOCQ, GEORGES. <u>Étude sur les vitraux de la collégiale de Saint-Quentin</u>. St.-Quentin: Imp. Ch. Poette, 1874, 53 pp.
    Documents pertaining to the corporation of tailors; consideration of stained glass as it enlightens local history.

46 SÉGANGE, L. du BROC de. "Les vitraux de la cathédrale de
    Moulins." Bulletin monumental 42 (1876):142-60; 211-46.
       Description and iconography of the 15th and 16th century
    windows; comments on Flemish influence.

47 CHARLES, ROBERT. "Un atelier de peintres verriers à Montoire
    au XVIᵉ siècle." Bulletin de la Société d'archéologie et
    des sciences vendômois 16 (1877):297-300.
       16th century documents pertaining to the activities of
    an atelier which executed windows in St.-Gervais (1534-37).

48 ANDRÉ, A. De la verrerie et des vitraux peints dans l'an-
    cienne province de Bretagne. Reims: J. Plihon; Rennes:
    Imp. de Charles Catel et Cie, 1878, 281 pp.
       Summary of extant medieval and Renaissance glass.

49 BÉGULE, LUCIEN. Monographie de la cathédrale de Lyon. Lyon:
    Imp. Mougin-Rusand, 1880, 224 pp., 34 pls.
       "Les vitraux" (pp. 99-156): a description of glass from
    the 12th/13th-16th centuries; the early glass was executed
    in a Lyon atelier.

50 JANITSCH, JULIUS. "Die älteren Glasgemälde des strassburger
    Münsters." Reportorium für Kunstwissenschaft 3 (1880):
    156-72, 252-75, 361-76; 4 (1881):46-72.
       Divides the glass into Romanesque, transitional, and
    Gothic and suggests that some is reused from the earlier
    building. Illustrated with engravings.

51 MULLER, E. "Le vitrail de Saint Pantaléon à la cathédrale de
    Noyon." Revue de l'art chrétien 14, no. 2 (1881):429-34.
       Iconography of the 13th century windows and their
    Byzantine stylistic influences [sic].

52 SCHAUENBOURG, P.R. de. "Les vitraux peints de l'ancienne
    église Saint-Étienne de Mulhouse." Bulletin du Musée
    historique de Mulhouse 6 (1881):95-101.
       Brief description of the 14th century windows.

53 FLORIVAL, ADRIEN de, and MIDOUX, ÉTIENNE. Les vitraux de la
    cathédrale de Laon. 4 fascicules. Paris: Librairie
    archéologique de Didron, 1882-91. Fascicle 1, 126 pp.,
    17 engraved pls., Fascicle 2, 62 pp., 8 engraved pls.,
    Fascicle 3, 51 pp., 8 engraved pls., Fascicle 4, 93 pp.,
    1 engraved pl.
       Valuable description of the late 12th-early 13th century
    roses and lancets; illustrations are from drawings made
    during the restoration by Denis.

54 LUCOT, CH. <u>Les verrières de la cathédrale de Châlons en général et plus particulièrement les verrières des collatéraux.</u> Châlons-sur-Marne: Imp. Thoulle, 1884, 16 pp., 2 pls. Description of the 15th and 16th century windows.

55 BARBIER de MONTAULT, X. "Le vitrail de la Crucifixion à la cathédrale de Poitiers." <u>Bulletin monumental</u> 51 (1885): 17-45, 141-68.
   Argues that the glass was a gift of Theobald V, Count of Blazon (ca. 1228) [not so, cf. Fr. 157].

56 BONNEAU, [Abbé]. "Description des verrières de la cathédrale d'Auxerre." <u>Bulletin de la Société des sciences historiques et naturelles de l'Yonne</u> 39 (1885):296-348.
   Thorough iconographic study of the 13th century windows after restorations by the Vessière brothers and Leprévost, but before those of Steinheil; detailed description but few illustrations.

57 MAGNE, LUCIEN. <u>L'oeuvre des peintres-verriers français: Verrières des monuments élevés par les Montmorency: Montmorency-Écouen-Chantilly.</u> Paris: Firmin-Didot, 1885. Text vol., 210 pp., figs. in text, 48 figs. at end. Album, 7 [8?] unbound pls.
   Introduction has a general history of glass painting in France; describes late glass (dated to the second half of the 16th century). Illustrated by photos.

58 _____. "Le vitrail." <u>Gazette des beaux-arts</u>, 2d ser. 31 (1885):138-63, 417-24; 32 (1885):53-60.
   Brief history of French glass painting from the earliest records to the 17th century. Some useful pre-restoration notes and illustrations.

59 PROST, BERNARD. <u>Notice sur les anciens vitraux de l'église de Saint-Julien (Jura) et incidemment sur ceux de Notre-Dame de Brou (Ain)</u>. Lons-le-Saulnier: Declume Frères, 1885, 24 pp., 6 pls.
   The Life of Christ and Annunciation windows in St.-Julien (ca. 1510) are inscribed with the initials of the donors, Guillaume and Pierre Darlay, and are similar in style to those in Brou executed ca. 1525. Illustrations are from drawings.

60   VERHAEGEN, N. "L'art de la peinture sur verre au Moyen Âge."
      Revue de l'art chrétien, n.s. 4, no. 3 (1886):297-305,
      437-42.
          Artistic role of stained glass in France from the 12th-
      16th centuries and the principal characteristics of each
      age.

61   MAGNE, LUCIEN. "Les vitraux de l'ancienne abbaye de Garcy
      [sic], département de Seine-et-Oise." Commission des
      antiquités et des arts 7 (1887):75-98.
          Important early notation of glass now in the Musée de
      Cluny, originally from the abbey of Gercy. Many photo-
      graphs.

62   RONDOT, NATALIS. Les peintres verriers de Troyes du XIVe
      siècle et XVe siècle. Paris: Archives de l'art français,
      1887, 24 pp. [Reprinted from Revue de l'art français 8].
          Lists eighty-two glass painters and includes information
      on their activities from 14th-16th century documents.

63   BOUILLET, A. "L'église Sainte-Foy de Conches (Eure) et ses
      vitraux." Bulletin monumental 54 (1888):131-53, 253-312.
          Useful and complete description of these important early
      16th century windows; emphasizes iconography and heraldry.
      Illustrated with photographs.

64   MÉLY, F. de. "Étude iconographique sur les vitraux du XIIIe
      siècle de la cathédrale de Chartres." Revue de l'art
      chrétien, n.s. 6 (1888):413-29.
          Alphabetical list of saints represented in the 13th
      century glass.

65   DESPIERRES, G. Portail et vitraux de l'église Notre Dame
      d'Alençon: Nomenclature des peintres, peintres-vitriers
      aux quinzième et seizième siècles à Alençon. Paris:
      E. Plon, Nourrit, et Cie, 1891, 24 pp.
          Brief description of eleven windows (1511-43) with Old
      and New Testament subjects, executed by several hands;
      notes donors and inscriptions, documentation, and local
      glass painters in the 15th-17th centuries.

66   MÉLOISES, ALBERT des. Les vitraux de la cathédrale de Bourges
      postérieurs au XIIIme siècle. 8 fascicules. Paris:
      Desclée, de Brouwer, 1891-97, 91 pp., 29 color pls.
      (numbered I-XXI & A-H).
          Introduction by Eugène de Beaurepaire. Annotated
      lithographs, some to scale, reproducing 15th-16th century
      glass in the chapels, with details of ornament. Includes

glass from the Ste.-Chapelle. Useful pre-restoration record. Very rare.

67 DEMANGE, M. "Les vitraux de l'église de Blénod-les-Toul." *Mémoire de la Société d'archéologie de Lorraine*, 3d ser. 21 (1893):311-39.
   16th century windows in the choir and transept.

68 GOSSART, M., and BLANQUET, [Abbé]. *Vitraux du choeur de la cathédrale d'Évreux.* Album de la Société des amis des arts du département de l'Eure. Évreux: the Society, 1893, 13 pls.
   Illustrations are from drawings of 14th and 15th century glass; coats of arms identified.

69 RÉGNIER, LOUIS. *Monographie de l'église de Nonancourt et de ses vitraux.* Mesnil-sur-Estrée: Typographie Firmin-Didot et Cie, 1894, 69 pp., 1 fig., 1 plan.
   Description of twelve windows in the nave, eight in the aisles, and fragments of two windows from the chapel of the Virgin, all dated to the first quarter of the 16th century.

70 MERSON, OLIVIER. *Les vitraux.* Bibliothèque de l'enseignement des beaux-arts. Paris: Librairie d'éducation nationale, Alcide Picard et Kaan, 1895, 315 pp., 125 figs. in text.
   Historical chapters, arranged by glass designer, discuss glass from its origin up to the 19th century. Very useful pre-restoration drawings.

71 ROTHIER, F. *Souvenir de l'église St.-Remi de Reims.* Reims: Rothier, 1896.
   Photographs of the 12th century glass before the World War I damage.

72 BONNEAU, [Abbé]. "Les verrières de l'église de Saint-Bris." *Bulletin de la Société des sciences et d'histoire naturelle de l'Yonne* 52 (1898):359-70.
   Description of the 15th century windows, which also contain 16th century glass; most were executed 1520-50, probably by an Auxerre glazier.

73 MÉTAIS, [L.]. "Un vitrail du XVIe siècle à Courville." *Bulletin archéologique du Comité des travaux historiques et scientifiques* (1900):26-33.
   Identification of the window dated 1526 as representing the Life of St. James of Compostella; comparison with other known depictions of this legend.

Fr. 74

74   DURAND, G. <u>Monographie de l'église Notre-Dame, cathédrale d'Amiens</u>. 2 vols. Paris: A. Picard et Fils, 1901-3, 664 pp.
        Description and reconstruction of the badly damaged 13th century windows in the cathedral (pp. 543-93).

75   BRUCK, ROBERT. <u>Die elsässische Glasmalerei vom Beginn des XII. bis zum Ende des XVII. Jahrhunderts</u>. 2 vols. Strasbourg: W. Heinrich, 1902. Vol. 1, 154 pp., 6 pls., figs. in text. Vol. 2, 81 unbound pls.
        Outlines technical developments; discusses ornament; and describes the glass at major sites (Strasbourg Cathedral and St.-Guillaume, Wissembourg, Mulhouse, Walbourg, Thann, etc.). Superb photographs; captions in German and French.

76   BAVEUX, [Abbé]. "Les vitraux de l'église de Brienne-le-Château." <u>Congrès archéologique de France (Troyes and Provins, 1902)</u>. 69 (1903):350-75.
        Subjects and inscriptions in the 16th century windows. Some photographs.

77   CANÉTO, FRANÇOIS. <u>Sainte-Marie d'Auch: Son histoire, ses vitraux, son choeur, son avant-choeur, et sa crypte</u>. 6th ed. Auch: Imp. Centrale, 1903, 44 pp., 8 pls.
        16th century historiated windows.

78   ADAMS, HENRY. <u>Mont-Saint-Michel and Chartres</u>. Washington, 1904. Reprinted with an introduction by Ralph Adams Cram. Boston and New York: Houghton Mifflin, 1913.
        Chapters 8-10 (pp. 128-97) provide a poetic appreciation and broad historical introduction to the glass of Chartres; probably the most famous treatment of this subject in English.
        Parts also reprinted in Robert Branner, <u>Chartres Cathedral</u> (New York: Norton, 1969), pp. 234-74.

79   OTTIN, L. "Essai de repertoire général des vitraux anciens." <u>Art sacré: Revue mensuelle illustrée de l'art chrétien</u>, 4th ser. 6, no. 32 (Nov. 1904):7-11.
        Checklist of medieval glass; introduction and discussion of the earlier use of glass at Île-de-France sites. Not illustrated.

80 HURAULT, E. Les vitraux anciens de l'église Saint-Alpin à
Châlons-sur-Marne. Paris: Édition de la revue l'art
sacré, [1905?], 19 pp., 6 illus.
   Description and restoration of the 16th century windows
executed by Châlons' glaziers; notes Italian influence in
the grisaille windows. See also Fr. 84.

81 MÂLE, ÉMILE. "La peinture sur verre en France [de l'époque
romane]." In Histoire de l'Art, by André Michel. Vol. 1,
pt. 2. Paris: A. Colin, 1905, pp. 782-95.
   Classic statement of his views on the importance of St.-
Denis and its influence on Chartres, Le Mans, Angers, and
Poitiers; notes the existence of another school in the east
(Châlons and Reims). Describes the general character and
technique of 12th century glass.

82 OTTIN, L. "Essai de répertoire général des vitraux anciens."
Art sacré: Revue mensuelle illustrée de l'art chrétien,
4th ser. 7, no. 34 (Jan. 1905):15-19; no. 35 (Feb.):12-15;
no. 37 (Apr.):8-12; no. 38 (May):11-13; no. 39 (June):9-10;
no. 40 (July):7-9; no. 41 (Aug.):3-7; nos. 42-43 (Sept.-
Oct.):4-14; no. 44 (Nov.):9-17; no. 45 (Dec.):4-13.
   Checklist of glass; nos. 34-39 complete the Île-de-
France, the rest deal with Champagne.

83 MÂLE, ÉMILE. "La peinture sur verre en France [à l'époque
gothique]." In Histoire de l'Art, by André Michel.
Vol. 2, pt. 1. Paris: A. Colin, 1906, pp. 372-96.
   Pioneering attempt to see relationships among sites
such as Chartres, Auxerre, Laon, and Le Mans in the 13th
century and to claim an autonomous French development in
the 13th-14th centuries. Illustrated with drawings.

84 OTTIN, L., and HURAULT, E. "Essai de répertoire général des
vitraux anciens." Art sacré: Revue mensuelle illustrée
de l'art chrétien, 4th ser. 8, no. 46 (Jan. 1906):7-13;
no. 47 (Feb.):22-27; no. 48 (Mar.):41-43; no. 49 (Apr.):
55-59; no. 50 (May):71-80; no. 51 (June):81-87; no. 52
(July):96-105; no. 53 (Aug.-Sept.):113-22; no. 54 (Oct.):
136-41; no. 55 (Nov.):151-58; no. 56 (Dec.):1-12.
   Continuing checklist: Champagne, Châlons-sur-Marne,
Brittany. In part a reprint of Fr. 80.

85 LUCOT, CH. Les verrières de la cathédrale de Châlons (église
Saint-Étienne). Paris and Brussels: Édition de la revue
l'art sacré, 1907, 39 pp., 9 illus.
   Description of the 12th-17th century windows in the
transepts, choir, nave, and apse chapels.

86   OTTIN, L. "Essai de répertoire général des vitraux anciens."
      Art sacré: Revue mensuelle illustrée de l'art chrétien,
      4th ser. 9, no. 57 (Jan.-Feb. 1907):13-24; no. 58 (Mar.-
      Apr.):25-36; no. 59 (May-June):37-43.
         Checklist of glass in Châlons-sur-Marne.

87   SHERRILL, CHARLES HITCHCOCK. Stained Glass Tours in France.
      New York: John Lane, 1908, 298 pp., 16 illus.
         Very general introduction to the development of French
      glass from the 12th-16th centuries, followed by a tour
      guide.

88   LUTZ, S., and PERDRIZET, P.F.E. Die elsässichen typologischen
      Glasmalereien von Mülhausen. Mulhouse, Colmar, and
      Wissembourg: Buchdr. E. Meiniger, 1909.
         Style and iconography of glass in SS. Peter and Paul,
      Wissembourg (ca. 1288), St. Stephen, Mulhouse (1314-40),
      and St. Martin, Colmar (ca. 1325); influence of the
      Speculum humanae salvationis and Biblia pauperum.

89   RAYON; E: "Les vitraux des églises de Seine-et-Marne."
      Paris: Bibliothèque de la Direction du Patrimoine 4°
      Doc. 11. 1909.
         Manuscript provides descriptions which include the
      iconography and condition of the glass, and illustrate
      church plans and window schemata.

90   FARCY, LOUIS de. Monographie de la cathédrale d'Angers.
      3 vols. Vol. 1, Les immeubles. [Angers: Josselin],
      1910, 286 pp., 52 pls.
         Chapter 14 includes a description of the 12th-13th cen-
      tury windows in the nave, transepts, and choir, with photo-
      graphic reproductions; and a list of 14th-20th century
      repairs to the glass.

91   HACKSPILL. "Fragment d'un vitrail du XVIᵉ siècle provenant
      de l'église Saint-Denis d'Airaines." Bulletin tri-
      mestrielle de la société des antiquaires de Picardie 24,
      nos. 2-3 (1910):378-80.
         A fragment of a scene from the life of St. John the
      Evangelist; the only remaining figure is Aristodème, who
      gave the saint poison to drink.

92   PILLION, LOUISE. "Le vitrail de la fontaine de vie et de la
      nativité de Saint Étienne à l'église Saint-Étienne de
      Beauvais." Revue de l'art chrétien 60 (1910):367-78.
         Identification of the 16th century St. Stephen window
      based on Sienese panel paintings; attribution of the
      Fountain of Life window to Engrand le Prince.

93 RAYON, E. "Les vitraux du département des Côtes-du-Nord:
    Inventaire." Paris, Bibliothèque de la Direction du
    Patrimoine 4o Doc 13. 1910.
        Manuscript describes the iconography and condition of
    the windows and includes window plans, etc.

94 BÉGULE, LUCIEN. Les vitraux du Moyen Âge et de la Renaissance
    dans la région lyonnaise et spécialement dans l'ancien
    diocèse de Lyon. Lyons: A. Rey et Cie, 1911, 254 pp.,
    32 pls., 273 figs.
        Survey of the major sites with glass, ranging from the
    12th century church of Le Champ-près-Froges to such 16th
    century sites as Chambéry, topographically arranged. Early
    glass of Lyon Cathedral is illustrated in drawings, but
    the remaining monuments are illustrated by good photo-
    graphs.

95 FARCY, L. de. "Les vitraux de la nef de la cathédrale
    d'Angers." Mémoires de la Société nationale d'agriculture,
    science, et arts d'Angers, 5th ser. 14 (1911):363-73.
        Description of all the windows dating from the second
    half of the 12th century.

96 MÂLE, ÉMILE. "Le vitrail français au XVe et au XVIe siècle."
    In Histoire de l'Art, by André Michel. Vol. 4, pt. 2.
    Paris: A. Colin, 1911, pp. 773-814.
        An early attempt to give an overview of historical
    developments; raises the problems of lost Parisian monu-
    ments, regional styles, and major artists.

97 OURSEL, CHARLES. L'église Notre-Dame de Dijon. Petites
    monographies. Paris: Henri Laurens, 1911, 104 pp.,
    42 figs.
        Discusses two 13th century windows representing the
    Legends of SS. Benignus and Bartholomew and a 16th century
    Crucifixion window.

98 SIMON, PAUL. La grande rose de la cathédrale de Reims: Étude
    historique et descriptive. Sa reconstruction à l'aide des
    documents certains. Sa restauration. Reims: L. Michaud,
    1911, 87 pp., figs.
        Valuable account of the late 13th century west rose
    prior to its damage in World War I.

France

Fr. 99

99   JOSSIER, O.-F. <u>Monographie des vitraux de Saint-Urbain de
     Troyes</u>. Troyes: P. Novel, 1912, 280 pp., figs.
         Useful pre-restoration account of the late 13th century
     glass in situ.

100 KUNZE, HANS. "Die Königsbilder im strassburger Münster:
     Nebst einem Abriss der Baugeschichte des Münsters bis zum
     Tode Erwins." <u>Zeitschrift für die Geschichte des Ober-
     rheins</u>, n.s. 27 (1912):612-39.
         Critiques the earlier literature on the iconography of
     the German Emperors series in the north aisle of the nave;
     dates the program ca. 1275 and justifies its presence in
     the church.

101 SIMON, PAUL. "Notes sur les vitraux de la cathédrale de
     Reims." <u>Congrès archéologique de France (Reims, 1911)</u> 2
     (1912):288-304.
         Comments on the styles of the 13th century glass in the
     clerestory and west rose, valuable because they were made
     before the World War I damage; illustrations are from
     tracings.

102 BIVER, PAUL, and SOCARD, EDMOND. "Le vitrail civil au XIVe
     siècle." <u>Bulletin monumental</u> 77 (1913):258-64.
         Remnants of secular glass, especially important frag-
     ments of 14th century date that had been used to fill gaps
     in St.-Père of Chartres: a centaur, birds, monkeys, etc.
     (see Fr. 224).

103 BOSSEBOEUF, L. "Un portrait de Jacques Hurault, seigneur de
     Cheverny." <u>Réunion des Sociétés des beaux-arts des dé-
     partements</u> (1913):79-82.
         Identification of a kneeling figure with a patron saint
     (dated 1514) from the chapel at Cheverny.

104 CHABEUF, HENRI. "Un vitrail du XVIe siècle à Notre-Dame de
     Dijon." <u>Revue de l'art chrétien</u> 63 (1913):37-39.
         Description of the Assumption of the Virgin window [now
     in the sacristy].

105 CHAPPÉE, J. "Le vitrail de Vernantes." <u>Revue de l'art chré-
     tien</u> 63 (1913):254-55.
         15th century window now in the Museum St.-Jean in
     Angers represents the Virgin flanked by two kneeling
     donors, King René and Jean de Laval.

140

106   CLÉMENT, JOSEPH. "Les tissus dans les verrières de la cathé-
      drale de Moulins." <u>Bulletin de la Société d'émulation du
      bourbonnais</u> 21 (1913):435-37.
         Study of the ornamental grounds in the 14th and 15th
      century windows; the St. Catherine panel may have been
      influenced by Italian glass.

107   GAUCHERY, P. "Riom: Monuments religieux." <u>Congrès archéo-
      logique de France, 1913</u> 80 (1916):154-64.
         Description of 15th century windows in Ste.-Chapelle de
      Riom, which are contemporary with the reign of the duc de
      Berry.

108   LEFÈVRE-PONTALIS, D.-EUGÈNE. "Note biographique sur maître
      Jean Huë, d'Étampes (XVe siècle)." <u>Annales de la Société
      historique et archéologique du gâtinais</u> 31 (1913):44-60.
         Identification of the donor of a 15th century window in
      Notre-Dame d'Étampes as Jean Huë; notes this figure's his-
      torical importance.

109   _____. "La verrière de maître Jean Huë dans l'église Notre-
      Dame d'Étampes et la nudité traditionelle du Christ dans la
      scène du baptême." <u>Revue de l'art chrétien</u> 63 (1913):
      237-42.
         Examines the non-traditional iconography of this scene
      (before 1489) in which Christ is clothed, citing Flemish
      influence and including comparative examples from other
      media.

110   MAGNE, LUCIEN. <u>Décor du verre: Gobeleterie, mosaïque,
      vitrail</u>. L'Art appliqué aux métiers, 3. Paris: Renouard,
      1913. 2d edition, enlarged by Henri-Marcel Magne, 1927,
      228 pp., 144 figs.
         Section on glass painting in the 12th-16th centuries
      (pp. 110-72) by a designer and restorer; illustrated with
      photographs.

111   ROUSSEL, JULES. <u>Vitraux du XIIe au XVe siècle d'après les
      clichés des Archives de la commission des monuments histo-
      riques</u>. Paris: A. Guérinet, [1913], 105 unbound pls.
      issued in 3 albums.
         Photographs of 12th-16th century glass and recent work
      by Leprévost selected from the archives of the Commission
      for Historical Monuments.

112   BUSHNELL, A.J. de HAVILLAND. <u>Storied Windows: A Traveller's</u>
      <u>Introduction to the Study of Old Church Glass from the 12th</u>
      <u>Century to the Renaissance, Especially in France</u>. Edinburgh
      and London: W. Blackwood, 1914, 338 pp., 2 maps, 38 figs.
         Brief sections on most of the major French collections;
      very inaccurate in historical details and iconography.
      Poorly illustrated.

113   JAHN, JOHANNES. <u>Der Stil den Westfenster der Kathedrale zu</u>
      <u>Chartres</u>. Inaugural Dissertation, University of Leipzig,
      Weida in Thüringen, 1917, 76 pp.
         Describes and formally analyzes the three west windows
      (mid-12th century); discusses the relation of form to con-
      tent. Raises the question of the primacy of Chartres or
      St.-Denis (cf. Mâle, Fr. 81, and Westlake, Gen. 16).

114   CHARTRAIRE, EUGÈNE. <u>La cathédrale de Sens</u>. Petites mono-
      graphies des grandes édifices de la France. Paris: Henri
      Laurens, [1921], 124 pp., illus.
         Brief account of the glass (pp. 85-93). Dates the early
      windows (depicting Thomas Becket, St. Eustace, the Prodigal
      Son, and the Good Samaritan) soon after 1184. Also groups
      the 13th, 14th, and 16th century glass.

115   RAYON, E. "Les vitraux du département de la Vienne:
      Inventaire." Paris, Bibliothèque de la Direction du
      Patrimoine 4° Doc 12, 140 pls. 1922.
         Manuscript illustrated with plans and window schemata
      covers Poitiers Cathedral, the church of Ste.-Radegonde,
      etc.

116   _____. "Les vitraux du département de l'Orne: Inventaire."
      Paris, Bibliothèque de la Direction du Patrimoine 4°
      Doc 10, 140 pls. 1922.
         Manuscript descriptions include plans, window schemata,
      etc.

117   _____. "Les vitraux de l'Indre-et-Loire: Inventaire."
      2 vols. Paris, Bibliothèque de la Direction du Patrimoine
      4° Doc 7, 525 pls. 1923-24.
         Manuscript descriptions include plans, window schemata,
      etc. Vol. 1 covers Champigny-sur-Vende and Tours Cathe-
      dral. Vol. 2 deals with other churches.

118 DUBOIS, PIERRE. Les vitraux de la cathédrale d'Amiens.
Amiens: Imp. Yvert et Tellier, 1924, 23 pp., no illus.
[Reprinted from Journal d'Amiens, 28, 29, and 30 August
1924].
    Description of the late 13th century glass executed by a
local atelier and still in situ; the original glazing program, its partial destruction, and its restoration are also
discussed.

119 FLETCHER, RORY, and KNOWLES, JOHN ALDER. "Exhibition of
French Painted Glass in London, about A.D. 1802." Notes &
Queries 146, no. 40 (5 Apr. 1924):243-44; 146, no. 42
(19 Apr. 1924):293.
    Questions the location of a 16th century window from
Rouen that had been in the collection of glass taken by
Stevenson and Van Hampp from France in the 19th century
and that had been exhibited to facilitate resale.

120 CHÊNE, A. "Les vitraux anciens de Saint-Germain l'Auxerrois."
Le centre de Paris: Bulletin de la Société historique et
archéologique des 1re & 2e arrondissements de Paris 2
(1924-32):167-81.
    Iconographic study of extant 15th-16th century windows,
without identification of donors.

121 EDEN, FREDERICK SYDNEY. "The 12th Century Medallions at
Rivenhall, Essex." Journal of the British Society of
Master Glass-Painters 1, no. 3 (Oct. 1925):20-23.
    12th century panels from Chenu-sur-Sarthe (Maine),
acquired by the vicar in 1840.

122 MAYER, G., and RABIER, J. "La merveille d'Issoudun: La
vieille vitre de l'église Saint-Cyr." Revue du Berry et
du Centre (Académie du Centre, Châteauroux) (Apr. 1925):
33-38.
    Large window with three lancets executed ca. 1480;
identification of arms.

123 *COUFFON, R. "Quelques notes sur les seigneurs de Coëtman."
Société d'émulation Côtes-du-Nord 58 (1926):41-125.
[Répertoire d'art et d'archéologie.]
    Illustrates a window of 1467-70 in Tonquédec, made in
the atelier of Olivier le Coq and Jehan le Levenan of
Lantreguer; subjects depicted include Christ's Passion
and the Last Judgment.

124   DELAPORTE, YVES, and HOUVET, ÉTIENNE. Les vitraux de la
       cathédrale de Chartres. 4 vols. Chartres: E. Houvet,
       1926. Histoire et Description, by Delaporte, 532 pp.,
       1 color pl., 67 figs. in text. Vols. 1-3, Reproductions,
       by Houvet, 10 color pls., 284 pls. unbound.
           Still the definitive work; explores the problems of
       dating and restorations; provides complete descriptions and
       the only complete photographic record.

125   ECHIVARD, A. "La grande rose de la cathédrale du Mans." La
       province du Maine, 2d ser. 6 (1926):205-11.
           Description of the window, which dates after 1430, and
       its 16th-20th century restorations.

126   RITTER, GEORGES. Les vitraux de la cathédrale de Rouen:
       XIIIe, XIVe, XVe, et XVIe siècles, reproductions en hélio-
       typie publiées avec une introduction historique et des
       notices iconographiques. . . . Cognac (Charente):
       Impression d'art des établissements FAC, 1926, 106 pp.,
       100 pls.
           Analysis of the 13th-16th century glass in the cathe-
       dral; all windows are described in depth and are illus-
       trated panel by panel with photographs.

127   RAYON, E. "Les vitraux du département de l'Oise: Inventaire."
       2 vols. Paris, Bibliothèque de la Direction du Patrimoine
       4º Doc 9. 1926-27.
           Manuscript descriptions include plans and window
       schemata; vol. 1 covers Beauvais. With bibliography and
       iconographic index.

128   BRANET, A. "La chapelle Sainte-Anne de la cathédrale d'Auch."
       Bulletin du Gers 28 (1927):20-25.
           Identifies the subjects of the portraits in the 15th and
       16th century medallion windows as Jean V, Pierre de Beaujeu,
       Charles d'Armagnac, and Charles d'Alençon.

129   DUPORTAL, J. "Le psautier de la reine Ingeburge du Musée
       Condé et les vitraux de Chartres." Revue de l'art 52
       (1927):193-208.
           Claims similarities between the psalter and the 12th
       century windows at Chartres and concludes that the MS.
       dates from the mid-12th century (cf. Deuchler, Fr. 219,
       306).

130 GERMAIN de MAIDY, L. "Sur les anciens vitraux de Flavigny."
Bulletin mensuel de la Société archéologique de la Lorraine
et du Musée historique lorrain: Revue historique de la
Lorraine, 2d ser. 22 (1927):57-60, 73-78.
Description of three windows from a cycle executed in
1530 by Valentin Busch which originally contained seven
windows; includes identification of heraldry.

131 GAUDIN, FÉLIX. Le vitrail du XIIe au XVIIIe siècle en France.
Les arts décoratifs depuis l'antiquité jusqu'au XIXe
siècle. Paris: Flammarion, 1928, 64 pp., 57 figs.
Reprints. 1944, 1961.
Very general history by a glass painter and restorer.

132 GRUBER, JEAN-JACQUES. "Quelques aspects de l'art et de la
technique du vitrail en France (dernier tiers du XIIIe
siècle, premier tiers du XIVe). In Travaux des étudiants
du Groupe d'histoire de l'art de la faculté des lettres de
Paris. Paris: Institut d'art et d'archéologie, 1928,
pp. 71-94.
Characteristics of glass executed between 1270 and 1328
include its color, its technique, and its relation to
architecture; particular emphasis is placed on Évreux
Cathedral glass.

133 *MARTIN, HENRI. Les vitraux de la cathédrale d'Auch.
Toulouse: Éditions L. Bars Feuilles au Vent, 1928.

134 RANQUET, HENRY du. La Cathédrale de Clermont-Ferrand. 1st
ed. Paris: Henri Laurens, [1913]; 2d ed., 1928, 115 pp.,
40 illus.
Mid-13th century windows attributed to a Parisian
atelier on the basis of stylistic similarities with Ste.-
Chapelle; cites 14th century windows in the nave. Not as
thorough as Fr. 151.

135 WALTER, JACQUES. "Les deux roses du transept sud de la
cathédrale de Strasbourg." Archives alsaciennes d'histoire
de l'art (Paris and Strasbourg) 7 (1928):13-33.
Iconography of the 14th century rose window with scenes
from the New and Old Testaments that were inspired by the
miniatures in the Hortus deliciarum (end of the 12th
century).

Fr. 136

136 BOISSONNADE, P. "Le vitrail de la Crucifixion à la cathédrale de Poitiers." Bulletin de la Société des antiquaires de l'ouest 8 (1928-30):803-15.
Repeats Barbier de Montault's erroneous statement (Fr. 55) that the window was probably donated by Thibaud de Blason after the crusade against Spain in 1212. See also Fr. 157.

137 BÉGULE, LUCIEN. La cathédrale de Sens--Son architecture, son décor. Lyons: Société anonyme de l'imprimerie A. Rey, 1929.
Chapter (pp. 43-75) on the 13th-16th century glass; the description of each window includes fragments reused in the axial chapel. Well illustrated, in part with drawings.

138 EAGLE, W.H. "La date du vitrail du chevet de la cathédrale de Dol." Bulletin monumental 88 (1929):508-13.
Reconsideration of the 13th century date for the eight lancets, concluding from technical and stylistic details that the window was executed between 1330-50.

139 ERNST-WEIS, JOSEF. "Valentin Busch: Ein biographischer Versuch." Elsass-lothringisches Jahrbuch (Festschrift zu Ehren des 70. Geburtstages von Georg Wolfram mit Beiträgen seiner Freunde und Fachgenossen) 8 (1929):122-33.
Cites a monogram in a window in Metz Cathedral with a date of 1521 and documents concerning other works. Gives his date of death as 1541.

140 FOURREY, R. "Les verrières historiées de la cathédrale d'Auxerre, XIIIe siècle." Bulletin de la Société des sciences historiques et naturelles de l'Yonne 83 (1929): 5-101.
Complete description of all the 13th century windows in the ambulatory of the cathedral.

141 LAFOND, JEAN. "Les vitraux." In L'église Saint-Étienne de Beauvais, by V. Leblond. Paris: Henri Laurens, 1929, pp. 64-115.
Description and analysis of the unified style of the early 16th century glass by Engrand le Prince and his family; mentions early glass in the west façade.

142 RAYON, E. "Les vitraux du Loir-et-Cher: Inventaire." Paris, Bibliothèque de la Direction du Patrimoine 4º Doc 8. 1929.
Manuscript description includes plans and window schemata for all the glass in the region.

143   JUSSELIN, MAURICE. "Un donateur pour les verrières de Saint-Père de Chartres au début du XIVe siècle." Bulletin monumental 89 (1930):540-41.
        Legacy of 300 pounds (Chartain) for windows in the nave, made ca. 1308.

144   SVAHN, A. "Un vitrail de l'église des Iffs." Bulletin de l'Ille-et-Vilaine 56 (1930):193-98.
        Identification of the subject of the 16th century window as the Vision of St. Paul (contrary to Ch. Brune's suggestion that it is the Battle of Duguesclin under the walls of Mantes).

145   GAUDIN, FÉLIX. "Les vitraux du Saint-Suaire à la chapelle du château de Chambéry." Mémoires de l'Académie des sciences, belles-lettres, et arts de Savoie 7 (1931):93-108.
        Description of the three principal 16th century windows depicting scenes from Christ's Passion.

146   GOSSET, POL. "Un vitrail du sacre de Charles VIII dans la collection Arconati Visconti." Bulletin des Musées de France 3 (1931):249-51.
        17th century text describes the glass, now in the Louvre, and names as donor the Coquillant family of Reims; it was inspired by a verse written for the coronation of Charles VIII (1494) and executed soon after.

147   TOUBA, J. "Die alten Fenster der Kirche von Zettingen." Jahrbuch der elsass-lothringischen wissenschaftlichen Gesellschaft zu Strassburg 4 (1931):58-89.
        Description of three 15th century windows in the choir; replaced by Hauck (Fr. 332).

148   BELL, J.C. "Ancient Stained Glass of Alsace." Journal of the British Society of Master Glass-Painters 4, no. 4 (Oct. 1932):163-70.
        Useful survey of glass in and around Strasbourg.

149   BOISSONNOT, HENRI. Les verrières de la cathédrale de Tours. Paris: Imp. Frazier-Soye, 1932, 59 pp., 19 pls.
        Iconography and description of windows completed ca. 1260; includes colored drawings.

Fr. 150

150 LAUGARDIÈRE, [M.] de. "Les vitraux de Saint-Bonnet de
Bourges." Bulletin monumental 91 (1932):247-85.
Descriptions of the 15th century fragments from the
earlier church (damaged by fire in 1487), including donors
from the Lallemant family, and of windows from ca. 1535 by
Jean Lécuyer and a follower.

151 RANQUET, HENRY du. Les vitraux de la cathédrale de Clermont-
Ferrand (XIIe, XIIIe, XIVe, XVe siècles). Clermont-Ferrand,
1932, 290 pp., 11 pls. (9 color), figs. in text. [Very
rare--only 400 copies printed.]
Detailed iconographic description of the glass; dates
the 13th century campaign in the 1270s-1280s. Style judgments unreliable.

152 TROYON, PIERRE. "Les verrières de Clermont-Ferrand." Revue
des deux mondes, 8th ser. 22 (1934):932-36.
Synopsis and review of the rare volume by Ranquet
(Fr. 151).

153 RAYON, E. "Les vitraux du Finistère: Inventaire." Paris,
Bibliothèque de la Direction du Patrimoine 4⁰ Doc 6. 1932.
Manuscript descriptions include plans and window
schemata for all the glass in the region.

154 SPENCER, JEANNETTE DYER. "Les vitraux de la Sainte-Chapelle
de Paris." Bulletin monumental 91 (1932):333-407.
Important early study of the state of the glass from a
scaffold; established from documents that the glass was
completed by 1248 (Thèse de l'école du Louvre, 1925).

155 SVAHN, A. "Le vitrail de la Passion, église des Iffs."
Bulletin de l'Ille-et-Vilaine 58 (1932):93-103.
Description of the twenty New Testament panels from the
first quarter of the 16th century and their scriptural
sources.

156 LAFOND, JEAN. "Les Vitraux." In La cathédrale de Coutances,
by P. Colmet Daage. Petites monographies des grands édi-
fices de la France. Paris: Henri Laurens, 1933, pp. 82-99,
illus.
Description of the 13th century windows (ca. 1215-20
and later); and a 15th century Last Judgment window
donated by Geoffrey Herbert.

157 CROZET, RENÉ. "Le vitrail de la Crucifixion à la cathédrale de Poitiers." Gazette des beaux-arts, 6th ser. 11 (1934): 218-31.

Based on a study of technique and style, demonstrates that the window was executed in the 12th century and donated by Henry II and Eleanor of Aquitaine (cf. Auber, Fr. 17); refutes the conclusions of Barbier de Montault regarding a 13th century date for the glass and the identification of its donor (Fr. 55).

158 GAUCHERY, ROBERT. "Les vitraux de la chapelle d'Étampes à la cathédrale de Bourges." Mémoires de la Société des antiquaires du Centre (Bourges, 1931-33) 45 (1934):155-78.

Glass executed 1452-65 (now destroyed) represented members of the d'Étampes family with donors; biography of figures and identification of their coat of arms provided.

159 HEUDUIN, A. "Une verrière du XVIe siècle récupérée de l'église Saint-Pierre de Roye." Bulletin de la Société des antiquaires de Picardie 35 (1934):491-95.

Panels representing the Death of the Virgin, rearranged during a 1914 restoration; includes donor portraits of Antoine Cardon and his wife, Marguerite Gilles.

160 B[IEBEL], F[RANKLIN] M. "12th century French window." Bulletin of the City Art Museum of St. Louis 20, no. 4 (1935):48-52.

Recent acquisition of four panels from the region of La Flèche; cites their stylistic relationship to the early windows at Chartres and St.-Denis; dates them in the 12th century. Cf. correct identification by Hayward (Fr. 231).

161 BIVER, PAUL. L'école troyenne de peinture sur verre. pt. 1, vol. 1. Paris: Librairie Gabriel Enault, 1935, 223 pp., 222 figs. [Rare (Doucet). Only one volume published.]

Glass painting in and near Troyes in the late 15th-16th centuries. Focuses on iconographic cycles. Poor black and white plates, but the windows reproduced are not available from other sources.

162 THIRIA. "Les vitraux de Metz au XVe siècle." Cahiers lorrains 15 (1936):91-92.

Based on a study of technique, description, color, and costume an approximate date of 1440 is given the glass; notes similarity in style to work in St.-Ségolène.

163   TRINICK, JOHN. "The 'Ascension' Window of Le Mans." Apollo
       23 (Jan.-June 1936):65-66.
           Places it immediately after the oldest Augsburg panels,
       which he dates ca. 1050. Style has its origins in manu-
       scripts of the 11th century.

164   URSEAU, [CH.]. "Un vitrail angevin du XVIᵉ siècle: La
       Crucifixion de Soulaire." Bulletin monumental 95 (1936):
       223-32.
           Early 16th century Crucifixion scene with donor por-
       traits, one believed to be Étienne Gragnet, curé of
       Soulaire Church; acquired by the Musée St.-Jean in Angers.

165   AUBERT, MARCEL, and CLAUDEL, PAUL. Vitraux des cathédrales de
       France aux XIIᵉ et XIIIᵉ siècles. Paris: Plon, 1937,
       18 pp., 19 color pls. English translation. Coulton, G.G.
       and Aubert, Marcel. Stained Glass of the XIIth and XIIIth
       Centuries from French Cathedrals. Art and Nature in Colour.
       London: B.T. Batsford, 1938, 12 pp., 19 color pls. German
       translation. [Aubert, Marcel], and Huch, Ricarda. Farben-
       fenster grosser Kathedralen des 12. und 13. Jahrhunderts.
       Leipzig: Iris Druck Curt Weller & Co. Verlag, 1937, 18 pp.,
       19 pls.
           Picture book, not of very high quality.

166   COHN, WERNER. "A Glass Painting by the Master E.S."
       Burlington Magazine 70 (1937):71-77.
           Attribution of a panel with a naked man, identified
       here as Adam, to the Master E.S.; the quality of the glass
       painting is close to that of the artist's drawings and is
       higher than that of glass executed under his influence.
       Glass is now in the Musée de la ville, Strasbourg.

167   URSEAU, [CH.]. "Hugue de Chamblancé et les vitraux de la nef
       de la cathédrale d'Angers." Bulletin monumental 96 (1937):
       327-33.
           Three windows (depicting the Legends of St. Catherine of
       Alexandria, of the Death and Burial of the Virgin, and of
       St. Vincent of Spain) donated at the end of the 12th cen-
       tury by Hugue.

168   DELAPORTE, YVES. "Vitraux anciens récemment découverts dans
       l'église Saint-Pierre de Dreux." Bulletin monumental 97
       (1938):425-31.
           Description of 13th century fragments possibly made
       originally for the Collegiate Church of St.-Étienne.

169   BERTRAND, LAZARE. "Note sur un vitrail de la cathédrale de
       Sens conservé au Musée de Baltimore." Bulletin de la
       Société archéologique de Sens 43 (1939-43):535-38.
            Identification of a heavily restored 13th century fig-
       ure as a bishop (formerly called St. Savinien). [Proven-
       ance questionable; Soissons is more likely than Sens.]

170   LAFOND, JEAN. "Romain Buron et les vitraux de Conches."
       Annuaire de la Normandie (1940-41):8-51.
            Attribution of some of the early 16th century windows in
       the choir to this artist from Gisors.

171   SIVADE, HENRY. "L'héraldique dans les verrières de la basi-
       lique des SS. Nazaire et Celse à la cité de Carcassonne."
       Mémoires de la Société des arts et des sciences de
       Carcassonne, 3d ser. 6 (1941-43):249-50.
            Description of heraldry and attempt to identify donors.

172   HONORÉ-DUVERGE, SUZANNE. "Le prétendu vitrail de Charles le
       Mauvais à la cathédrale d'Évreux." Bulletin monumental 101
       (1942):57-68.
            Identification of a 14th century window portrait as the
       Count of Mortain, Pierre de Navarre.

173   LAFOND, JEAN. La résurrection d'un maître d'autrefois: Le
       peintre-verrier Arnoult de Nimèque (Aert van Cort ou van
       Hort, Aert Ortkens, Arnoult de la Pointe). Rouen: Imp.
       Lainé, 1942, 102 pp., 24 pls.
            The culmination of thirty years of study of the oeuvre
       of this painter, a foreigner active around Rouen, ca. 1490-
       1530.

174   _____. "Les vitraux royaux du XIVe siècle à la cathédrale
       d'Évreux." Bulletin monumental 101 (1942):67-93.
            Identifies the king as Charles VI, "Jeanne de France"
       as Blanche de Navarre; glass executed 1390-98.

175   MOT, GUSTAVE-J. "Le vitrail du bois de vie à Saint-Nazaire de
       Carcassonne." Bulletin de la Société archéologique du Midi
       de la France, 3d ser. 5 (1942):176-87.
            Iconography of the window based on St. Bonaventure's
       mystical treatise, the Lignum vitae, available since 1275;
       comparison with miniatures dates the glass to the 14th cen-
       tury; executed by a local atelier.

176 QUIÉVREUX, FRANÇOIS. "Les vitraux du XIIIe siècle de l'abside de la cathédrale de Bourges." Bulletin monumental 101 (1942):255-75.
　　Dating of three groups of windows to 1215-20 based on stylistic similarities to Chartres; iconographic unity of the program.

177 VERRIER, JEAN. Die Kathedrale von Bourges und ihre Fenster. [Paris]: Bücher der Eiche, [1942], 20 pp., 79 pls. (24 color). French version. La cathédrale de Bourges et ses vitraux. Paris: Éditions du Chêne, 1943, 20 pp., 79 pls. (24 color).
　　Introduction to the architecture, sculpture, and stained glass (13th, 15th, and 16th centuries) of the cathedral, followed by large color photographs by F. Quiévreux.

178 ZSCHOKKE, FRIDTJOF. Die romanischen Glasgemälde des strassburger Münsters. Basel: B. Schwabe & Co., 1942, 222 pp., 4 pls., 53 figs.
　　Attempted dating and reconstruction of the program of glass in the earlier building; assigns a date of ca. 1200 on the basis of surviving fragments and 19th century drawings (see Fr. 281).

179 WENTZEL, HANS. "Die romanischen Glasgemälde des strassburger Münsters et Mittelalterliche Bildfenster der Schweiz." Phoebus 2 (1948-49):91-95.
　　Review of Fridtjof Zschokke (Fr. 178). Questions the methods of dating; raises the problems of deciding the French or German origin of this glass; underlines the aspects of early Gothic character.

180 DUPIEUX, PAUL. "Peintres verriers du XVIe siècle à Moulins." Bulletin de la Société d'émulation bourbonnais (1945): 287-91.
　　Documents pertaining to Pierre and Jean Goupy, who worked in Moulins 1510-60 and may have designed windows in the collegiate church (1484-1560).

181 AUBERT, MARCEL. Le vitrail en France. Arts, styles et techniques. Paris: Larousse, 1946, 163 pp., 64 color pls.
　　General account of 12th-15th century glass painting. Poor color illustrations.

182 GRINNELL, ROBERT. "Iconography and Philosophy in the Crucifixion Window at Poitiers." Art Bulletin 28 (1946):171-96.
Postulates that the east window is made up of different
elements, some dated ca. 1150, some 1163-72. Claims there
are eastern elements in the iconography. (Based on a Yale
doctoral dissertation.)

183 *QUIÉVREUX, FRANÇOIS. "Le mystère du Christ et de l'église
dans les vitraux de déambulatoire de Bourges." Dieu
vivant 5 (1946):101-17. [Répertoire d'art et d'archéologie, 1945-47.]
Iconographic study of ten 13th century ambulatory windows.

184 GRODECKI, LOUIS. Vitraux des églises de France. Paris:
Édition du Chêne, 1947, 31 pp., 32 color pls., 10 figs.
2d ed., 1948. English translation. The Stained Glass of
French Churches. Translated by Rosemary Edmunds and A.D.B.
Sylvester. London: Lindsay Drummond, 1948.
Very useful introduction; emphasizes the 12th-13th
centuries.

185 *LEVÊQUE, JANINE. "Les métiers en France au XIIIe siècle
d'après les signatures de vitraux." Diplôme d'état
supérieure d'histoire et géographie, University of Paris,
1947.

186 ROFFIGNAC, BERTRAND de. "Les représentations du monde dans
les vitraux de la cathédrale de Bourges." Mémoires de
l'union de la Société savante de Bourges 1 (1947-48):45-64.
Two manners in which glass painters represented the
cosmos as exemplified in four 13th century windows at
Bourges.

187 CANTON, G.R., and HAINSSELIN, P. "Étude sur les vitraux de
Picardie." Bulletin trimestriel de la Société des antiquaires de Picardie 42-53 (1947-70).
A series of articles on 13th-16th century glass, topographically arranged, covering iconography, style, restorations, and the dating of windows, as follows:
1. Mareuil (Somme). 42 (1947-48):117-26.
2. Liercourt (Somme). 42 (1947-48):161-67.
3. Bray-les-Mareuil (Somme). 42 (1947-48):406-14.
4. La Fresnoye (Somme). 43 (1949-50):177-89.
5. With F. Vasselle, Villers-Campsart (Somme). 43
(1949-50):269-84, 322-36, 375-82. 44 (1951-52):38-50.
6. Chépy (Somme). 44 (1951-52):101-14.
7. Vieulaines (Somme). 44 (1951-52):174-83.

8. Ercourt (Somme). 44 (1951-52):232-44.
9. Bouillancourt-en-Séry (Somme). 45 (1953-54):66-79, 149-58.
10. Biencourt (Somme). 46 (1955-56):210-24, 249-56, 295-300.
11. Hymmeville (Somme). 47 (1957-58):80-89.
12. Folleville (Somme). 49 (1961):36-52, 70-76, 112-24; (1962):14-29, 254-60.
13. Pont-Remy (Somme). 50 (1963-64):99-116, 148-64, 177-84, 243-52.
14. Frémont (Somme). 50 (1963-64):268-75.
15. Saveuse (Somme). 50 (1963-64):316-36.
16. Thoix (Somme). 51 (1965-66):68-79.
17. Éramecourt (Somme). 51 (1965-66):119-32.
18. Conty (Somme). 51 (1965-66):195-215.
19. Argoules (Somme). 51 (1965-66):284-302.
20. Paillart (Oise). 52 (1967-68):59-92.
21. Fluy (Somme). 52 (1967-68):234-41.
22. Souplicourt (Somme). 53 (1969-70):20-26.
23. Villers-sur-Authie (Somme). 53 (1969-70):103-28, 161-80, 236-60.

188 LAFOND, JEAN. "Les vitraux français du Musée Ariana et l'ancienne vitrerie de Saint-Fargeau (Yonne)." Genava 26 (1948):115-32.
  Catalog of twenty panels, chiefly from St.-Fargeau, dated just before 1250. See Tech. 150; Exh. 49; Fr. 373.

189 GRODECKI, LOUIS. "The Jacques Coeur Window at Bourges." Magazine of Art 42 (1949):64-67.
  Represents the Annunciation begun in 1447 for a chapel built by Jacques Coeur; the window was executed by an artist from the same milieu as Jean Fouquet; shows Flemish influence.

190 SABLAYROLLES, J. "Rétrospective sur les verrières de Saint-Nazaire." Bulletin de la Société d'étude scientifique de l'Aude 50 (1949):28-34.
  Documents concerning repairs to the 14th century glass of Carcassonne Cathedral between 1690 and 1840; iconographic program examined.

191 VERRIER, JEAN. Vitraux de France aux douzième et treizième siècles. Histoire des arts plastiques. Paris: Triquet, [1949], 47 pp., 10 pls., 4 figs. in text.
  Annotated illustrations of 12th and 13th century glass in Ste.-Chapelle, in the cathedrals of Chartres, Sens, and Bourges, and in St.-Denis.

192 COUFFON, RENÉ. "Vitraux anciens de l'église Saint-Mathurin de Moncontour." Congrès archéologique de France (1949) 107 (1950):63-69.
       Six windows executed between 1520 and 1540 are remarkable examples of Breton glass; four others appear to be from the Flemish school.

193 SAUVEL, TONY. "Les manuscripts limousins: Essai sur les liens qui les unissent à la sculpture monumentale, aux émaux, et aux vitraux." Bulletin monumental 108 (1950): 117-44.
       Iconographic and stylistic comparison of manuscripts with works in sculpture, enamel, and stained glass. The Sacramentary of Limoges compared with the work of the earliest glaziers at St.-Denis.

194 GRODECKI, LOUIS. "Les vitraux de la cathédrale de Châlons-sur-Marne." Bulletin de la Société nationale des Antiquaires de France (1950-51):196-203.
       Glass dated between 1145 and 1155 because of its iconographic and stylistic affinities with Mosan enamels and the altar of Stavelot; therefore contemporary with St.-Denis glass.

195 _____. "Quelques observations sur le vitrail au XIIe siècle en Rhénanie et en France." Mémorial d'un voyage d'études de la Société nationale des antiquaires de France en Rhénanie (1951):241-48.
       12th century glass in Châlons derived from a Mosan source; cites close relationship between French and Rhenish art.

196 _____. "Suger et l'architecture monastique." Bulletin des relations artistiques France-Allemagne. Special issue (May 1951), 4 pp. [no pagination].
       Theological disagreement between Suger and St. Bernard over the spiritual function of art, especially glass; comparison of Cistercian grisaille (at Obazine) with the griffin windows of St.-Denis.

197 _____. "Un panneau français au Musée de Princeton et les vitraux de Riom." La revue des arts 4 (1951):209-21.
       Scenes from the life of St. Louis from the chapel of the Palais de Justice in Riom; discusses problems of restoration, style, and date (ca. 1460-80) and the relation of this work to glass in Bourges.

198 BIDAUT, JACQUES. "Église Sainte-Radegonde de Poitiers."
 Congrès archéologique de France (Poitiers, 1951) 109
 (1952):113-14.
   Describes 13th-14th century glass.

199 FISCHEL, LILLI. Die karlsruher Passion und ihr Meister.
 Karlsruhe: G. Braun, 1952, 65 pp., 67 pls.
   Gives a chapter to "Werke der Glasmalerei" (pp. 25-33);
 attributes the Life of Christ at St. Walburg and the windows in the church of St. Wilhelm, Strasbourg to this
 master (1461 and later).

200 GRODECKI, LOUIS. "À propos des vitraux de Châlons-sur-Marne:
 Deux points d'iconographie mosane." In Art mosan: Jour-
 nées d'études, Paris, 1952. Edited by Pierre Francastel.
 Paris: A. Colin, 1953, pp. 161-70.
   Discusses themes relating to the Synagogue and Job; and
 connections with the Stavelot altar and Rupert of Deutz.

201 _____. "Les vitraux de la cathédrale de Poitiers." Congrès
 archéologique de France (1951) 109 (1952):138-63.
   Discussion of the restoration and iconography, with
 particular emphasis on problems of dating and attribution.
 Groups the windows into three series: the 12th century,
 the early years of the 13th century, and the early 14th
 century.

202 _____. "Vitraux exécutés par ordre de Suger pour l'abbatiale
 de Saint-Denis entre 1140 et 1146 environ." Bulletin de la
 Société nationale des antiquaires de France (1952-53):
 48-52.
   The iconography of the first program at St. Denis, completed as early as 1148-50.

203 ARNHOLD, H. "Parties anciennes et parties récentes des
 vitraux à l'église des Dominicains." Annuaire de la
 Société historique et littéraire de Colmar 3 (1953):43-46.
   List of medieval panels which includes about half the
 remaining glass.

204 GRODECKI, LOUIS. "Un vitrail démembré de la cathédrale de
 Soissons." Gazette des beaux-arts, 6th ser. 42 (1953):
 169-76.
   Important panels from the Tree of Jesse of ca. 1220 in
 the apse clerestory, formerly in Berlin and in Bryn Athyn
 (Pa.). See also Fr. 247, 414.

205   LAFOND, JEAN. "Le vitrail en Normandie de 1250 à 1300."
       Bulletin monumental 111 (1953):317-58.
           Glass in Rouen, Coutances, Sées, Fécamp, Évreux, etc.,
       seen largely as a reflection of Parisian developments.

206   WENTZEL, HANS. "Das mutziger Kreuzigungsfenster und verwandte
       Glasmalereien der 1. Hälfte des 14. Jahrhunderts aus dem
       Elsass, der Schweiz, und Süddeutschland." Zeitschrift für
       Schweizerische Archäologie und Kunstgeschichte 14 (1953):
       159-79.
           Relates a window with a Crucifixion and Saints, now in
       the Strasbourg Museum, to manuscript illumination, and to
       glass from the upper Rhine; discusses the problem of
       localizing painters in this period.

207   GRODECKI, LOUIS. "La restauration des vitraux du XIIe siècle
       provenant de la cathédrale de Châlons-sur-Marne." Mémoires
       de la Société d'agriculture, commerce, science, et arts de
       la Marne, 2d ser. 28 (1953-54):323-52.
           Panels to be returned to the treasury of the cathedral;
       reconstruction of three cycles depicting the Infancy, the
       Redemption, and the Relics of St. Stephen.

208   DAVIS, FRANK. "A Page for Collectors: From Rouen to York."
       Illustrated London News 225, no. 2 (1954):706.
           A 16th century window originating from St.-Vincent of
       Rouen and representing the Seven Deadly Sins was acquired
       by York Cathedral in 1947.

209   LAFOND, JEAN. "Les vitraux de la cathédrale de Sées."
       Congrès archéologique de France (Orne, 1953) 111 (1954):
       59-83.
           Description of glass of ca. 1270-80 and ca. 1375; re-
       lates the first group to Rouen.

210   _____. "Le vitrail anglais de Caudebec-en-Caux." La revue
       des arts 4 (1954):201-6.
           Window in the church of Notre-Dame inscribed as a gift
       of Foulques Eyton, Captain of Caudebec under Henry V,
       1435-47.

211   _____. "Le vitrail du XIVe siècle en France: Étude histo-
       rique et descriptive." In L'art du XVIe siècle en France,
       by Louise Lefrançois-Pillion. Paris: Albin Michel, 1954,
       pp. 185-238.
           Still the best overview of this period.

212 *OHRESSER, X. "Hans Baldung Grien et les vitraux de l'Hotel de Ville d'Obernai." Revue d'alsace 93 (1954):116-20. [Becksmann].

213 BAILLARGEAT, RENÉ. "Les vitraux de la collégiale Saint-Martin de Montmorency (description)." Mémoires fédérales de la Société historique et archéologique de Paris, Ile-de-France 7 (1955):149-92.
Description of medieval and modern windows in the collegiate church, including twelve dated 1524-45; one window was executed by Engrand le Prince. Continued in Fr. 216.

214 LAFOND, JEAN. "La peinture sur verre à Jumièges." In Jumièges: Congrès scientifique du XIIIe centenaire. Vol. 2. Rouen: Lecerf, 1955, pp. 529-36.
Suggests a strong relationship among the 14th century glass at Jumièges, Rouen, and Évreux; description of the 15th and 16th century glass. Updated in 1960 (Fr. 248).

215 _____. "Les vitraux d'Argentan." Bulletin monumental 113 (1955):259-75.
Describes glass of ca. 1450-1550 in two churches; most of it destroyed in 1944.

216 BAILLARGEAT, RENÉ. "Les vitraux de l'église collégiale Saint-Martin de Montmorency (étude technique)." Mémoires fédérales de la Société historique et archéologique de Paris, Ile-de-France 8 (1956):157-85.
Evolution of design in glass painting which marks the transition from the Middle Ages to the Renaissance, as exemplified in the 16th century Montmorency glass. Sequel to Fr. 213.

217 BEYER, VICTOR. "Eine strassburger Glasmaler-Werkstätte des 13. Jahrhunderts und ihre Beziehungen zu den Rheinlanden: Werke in Münster, in der Dominikaner-und-Thomaskirche." Saarbrücker Hefte 4 (1956):49-62.
Stylistically homogeneous group of windows from the second half of the 13th century; their relation to Rhenish manuscripts and to glass in Assisi.

218 DELAPORTE, YVES. "Le vitrail de la 'Parenté de Notre-Dame' à Martigny." Art de Basse-Normandie 4 (1956):6-11.
Description and iconography of the 16th century window, possibly based on an engraving by Jean-Bertrand of Périgueux.

219   DEUCHLER, FLORENS. "Die Chorfenster der Kathedrale in Laon:
      Ein ikonographischer und stilgeschichtlicher Beitrag zur
      Kenntnis nordfranzösischer Glasmalerei des 13. Jahrhun-
      derts." Ph.D. dissertation, Bonn University, 1956,
      2 vols., text and pls.
          Most thorough study to date; dates the glass in the east
      lancets before 1205, when it was reinstalled in the new
      choir wall. Some of the conclusions were published in 1967
      (Fr. 306).

220   *GRODECKI, LOUIS. "Les vitraux de la cathédrale de Rouen."
      Les monuments historiques de la France 2 (1956):101-10.

221   _____. "Vitraux de Saint-Germain-des-Prés." Bulletin de la
      Société nationale des antiquaires de France (1956):82-83.
          Glass from the Lady Chapel, now dispersed, is divided
      into three style groups; notes the diversity of Parisian
      ateliers working during the years immediately before the
      decoration of Ste.-Chapelle. Cf. Verdier (Fr. 269), who
      argues the Life of St. Vincent is from the refectory.

222   *GRODECKI, LOUIS, and GRUBER, JEAN-JACQUES. "La restitution
      des vitraux 'royaux' de la cathédrale d'Évreux." Les monu-
      ments historiques de la France 2 (1956):201-16.
          New arrangement of the 14th century glass in Évreux,
      especially the windows with the donors now identified as
      Pierre de Mortain and Charles VI.

223   LAFOND, JEAN. "À propos des vitraux de XVe siècle provenant
      de l'église Saint-Vincent et transférés à la cathédrale de
      Rouen." Revue des Sociétés savantes de Haute Normandie 4
      (1956):37-45.
          Two styles of glass: windows in the baptismal chapel,
      post-1470 were executed by Arnold of Nijmegen atelier,
      and windows in the choir, dated 1511-28, were made by
      Engrand and Jean Le Prince.

224   _____. "Le vitrail civil français à l'église et au musée."
      Médicine de France 77 (1956):17-32.
          Some chance survivals of glass from secular buildings,
      14th-17th centuries, some with religious subjects (see
      Fr. 102).

Fr. 225

225   BEYER, VICTOR. "La dépose des vitraux de l'église des
      Dominicains [Strasbourg] et la verrière de la vie de Saint
      Barthélmy." Cahiers alsaciens d'archéologie, d'art, et
      d'histoire 1 (1957):143-62.
           Description and iconography of the eighteen panels from
      the Bartholomew window executed ca. 1260; 13th and 14th
      century glass now in the cathedral and the Musée de
      l'oeuvre.

226   FRANKL, PAUL. "Unnoticed Fragments of Old Stained Glass in
      Notre-Dame de Paris." Art Bulletin 39 (1957):299-300.
           Claims that a panel with two sibyls in the axial chapel
      is Alsatian work of ca. 1320.
           A critique by Louis Grodecki, "Chronique: Vitrail,"
      Bulletin monumental 116 (1958):150-52, indicates that they
      were copied by Coffetier (?) in 1855 from fragments now in
      Portsmouth Priory, Rhode Island; subsequent examination has
      revealed little original glass in the Rhode Island panels.

227   _____. "Der Glasmaler Theobald von Lixheim." Zeitschrift für
      Kunstwissenschaft 11 (1957):55-90.
           The signed and dated (1504) window in Metz Cathedral was
      very heavily restored by Geiges in 1907-12. Reconstructs
      the original style from the restorer's drawings. Attrib-
      utes windows in Walburg (St. Clara, etc.) and Obernai to
      von Lixheim and claims he collaborated with Peter Hemmel.

228   GRODECKI, LOUIS. "Les verrières d'Évreux." L'Oeil 29 (1957):
      18-25.
           Evolution of the styles in 14th century glass based on a
      study of the windows in Évreux, which show influence from
      Paris and Rouen. Compares glass painting with miniature
      and panel paintings.

229   _____. "Les vitraux de Saint-Urbain de Troyes." Congrès
      archéologique de France (Troyes, 1955) 113 (1957):123-38.
           Brief but complete description of the glass remaining
      in situ, with attention to problems of restoration and
      attrition, as well as style and dating (before 1277 for the
      choir).

230   _____. "Stained Glass Windows of St. Germain-des-Prés."
      Connoisseur 140 (1957):33-37.
           13th century fragments now in the chapel of Ste.-
      Geneviève were from a lost building of the period 1234-50,
      probably from the hemicycle of the Lady Chapel. Others in
      museums overseas.

231   HAYWARD, JANE. "Identification of the 'Crucifixion' Window."
      Bulletin of the City Art Museum of St. Louis 42, no. 1
      (1957):19-22.
           The Saint Louis panels (ca. 1200) originally occupied an
      east window in the parish church of Montreuil-sur-Loire
      where a modern copy is now positioned (cf. Fr. 160).

232   LAFOND, JEAN. "Les vitraux de la cathédrale Saint-Pierre de
      Troyes." Congrès archéologique de France (Troyes, 1955)
      113 (1957):29-62.
           Still the only complete description of the 13th-14th
      century glass in situ. Poorly illustrated.

233   VERDIER, PHILIPPE. "La verrière de Saint Vincent à Saint-
      Germain-des-Prés." Mémoires fédérales de la Société
      historique et archéologique de Paris, Ile-de-France 9
      (1957-58):69-87.
           Argues from engravings in the Commission for Historical
      Monuments and from the iconographic program in St. Germain-
      des-Prés that the eight panels representing St. Vincent,
      now in the Walters Art Gallery, Baltimore, originated from
      the Lady Chapel, while the two remaining windows were from
      the abbey church; both are mid-13th century in style.

234   FRITZ, ROLF. "Die Aldegrever-Inschrift von Conches."
      Westfalen 36 (1958):159-66.
           Reinterprets the inscription on the hem of St. Louis's
      robe; the date of 1520 cannot be correct, but the putti
      below are copied from an engraving by H. Aldegrever of
      1535; the glass painter is probably Romain Buron. Cf.
      Lafond (Fr. 170).

235   GRODECKI, LOUIS. "Les vitraux de Châlons-sur-Marne et l'art
      mosan." In Actes du XIXe Congrès internationale d'histoire
      de l'art (Paris, 1958). Paris: UNESCO, pp. 183-90.
           Existence of a strong relationship between Mosan art and
      three late 12th century windows (depicting the Crucifixion,
      the Legend of the Relics of St. Étienne, and the Infancy of
      Christ).

236   HAYWARD, JANE. "The Angevine Style of Glass Painting."
      2 vols. Ph.D. dissertation, Yale University, 1958,
      310 pp., 153 figs., 8 pls.
           Establishes the development of this local style within
      the school of the West and independent of the Ile-de-France,
      on the basis of examples of 12th century glass in various
      Angevin churches.

237 PARIS, MUSÉE des ARTS DÉCORATIFS. Le vitrail français. Text
     by Marcel Aubert, André Chastel, Louis Grodecki, Jean-
     Jacques Gruber, Jean Lafond, François Mathey, Jean Taralon,
     and Jean Verrier. Paris: Édition des deux mondes, 1958,
     336 pp., 32 color pls., 310 figs. [Rare].
        The best treatment to date of glass painting in France;
     includes chapters on spiritual functions, techniques, and
     restoration; bibliography and indexes.

238 SALVINI, JOSEPH. "Vitraux peu connus du département de la
     Vienne." Bulletin de la Société des antiquaires de
     l'ouest, 4th ser. 4 (1958):627-30.
        Description of glass dating from the 15th-18th centuries.

239 AHNNE, PAUL, and BEYER, VICTOR. Les vitraux de la cathédrale
     de Strasbourg. Strasbourg: Édition des Dernières Nou-
     velles, 1959, 19 pp., 16 color pls. German translation.
     Die Glasmalereien des Strassburger Münsters. 1960.
        Guide to the 13th-14th century windows, with a selection
     of plates annotated to include transcribed inscriptions.
     Useful.

240 AUBERT, MARCEL; GRODECKI, LOUIS; LAFOND, JEAN; and VERRIER,
     JEAN. Les vitraux de Notre-Dame et de la Sainte-Chapelle
     de Paris. Corpus Vitrearum Medii Aevi: France, Vol. 1,
     Département de la Seine, pt. 1. Paris: Caisse nationale
     des monuments historiques and C.N.R.S., 1959, 359 pp.,
     8 color pls., 101 pls., plans in text.
        Rather cursory but complete publication of these impor-
     tant 13th century windows, including some examples now in
     collections.

241 GAUCHERY, ROBERT, and GAUCHERY-GRODECKI, [CATHERINE]. Saint-
     Étienne de Bourges. Grandes cathédrales de France. Paris:
     Éditions Huchettes, 1959, 109 pp., 65 pls.
        Discusses the architecture, sculpture, and stained glass
     of the cathedral; and the exceptionally high quality 13th
     century windows, whose iconographic program was probably
     dictated by Saint Guillaume.

242 LAFOND, JEAN. "Les vitraux de la cathédrale Saint-Étienne
     d'Auxerre"; "Les vitraux [de Cravant, église Saint-Pierre-
     et-Saint-Paul]"; "Les vitraux [de Saint-Julien-du-Sault]";
     and "Les vitraux de l'église Notre-Dame de Ville-neuve-sur-
     Yonne." Congrès archéologique de France (Auxerre-Sens,
     1958) 116 (1959):60-75, 289-93, 365-69, 378-82, respec-
     tively.

Brief descriptions of 13th-16th century glass at these sites.

243 SIMON, JACQUES. "Restauration des vitraux de Saint-Remi de Reims." <u>Les monuments historiques de la France</u>, n.s. 5 (1959):14-25.
Restorer's account of the recently completed restoration, following damage in World War I.

244 BEYER, VICTOR. "Les roses de réseau des bas-côtés de la cathédrale et l'oeuvre d'un atelier strasbourgois du XIIIe siècle." <u>Bulletin de la Société des amis de la cathédrale de Strasbourg</u>, 2d ser. 7 (1960):63-96.
Examines the style of the tracery lights in the nave aisles and that of the glass from the Dominican church and St. Thomas; discusses the influence of the atelier in Assisi and the relation of this glass to manuscript painting (e.g., Aschaffenburg Gospels).

245 FRANKL, PAUL. <u>Die Glasmalereien der Wilhelmerkirche in Strassburg</u>. Studien zur deutschen Kunstgeschichte, 320. Baden-Baden and Strasbourg: Heitz, 1960, 85 pp., 18 figs.
Reconstruction of 14th, 15th, and 16th century windows in this parish church; detailed study of the middle group, with an attribution to Peter Hemmel and a synopsis of previous opinions.

246 GRIMME, ERNST GÜNTHER. "Das Karlsfenster in der Kathedrale von Chartres." <u>Aachener Kunstblätter</u> 19-20 (1960-61): 11-24.
The 13th century Charlemagne window in Chartres Cathedral is compared to drawings of a lost window in St.-Denis; iconographic sources cited (cf. Fr. 395).

247 GRODECKI, LOUIS. "Les vitraux soissonais du Louvre, du Musée Marmottan et des collections américaines." <u>La revue des arts</u> 10 (1960):163-78.
Early 13th century glass dispersed from Soissons Cathedral: panels from the Lives of SS. Nicaise and Eutropie, now in the Gardner Museum, Boston; the Virgin from the Tree of Jesse, previously in Berlin (destroyed); panels from the Lives of SS. Crépin and Crépinien, etc., now in the Corcoran Art Gallery, Washington; and a St. Blaise in the Marmottan, Paris. Cites their stylistic relation to Laon glass of ca. 1205-15.

248 LAFOND, JEAN. <u>Les vitraux de l'ancienne abbaye de Jumièges:</u>
<u>Chapelle de la Mailleraye-sur-Seine, église paroissiale de</u>
<u>Jumièges</u>. Rouen: Lecerf, [1954]. 3d ed., corrected and
enlarged, ca. 1960, 41 pp., 34 figs.
14th century glass now in La Mailleraye includes an
Apostle's Creed, secular subjects, and some later fragments.

249 GRODECKI, LOUIS. "Les vitraux allégoriques de Saint-Denis."
<u>Art de France</u> 1 (1961):19-46.
Reconsideration of the sources and influence of some of
these esoteric subjects.

250 _____. "Les vitraux de la cathédrale du Mans." <u>Congrès</u>
<u>archéologique de France (Maine, 1961)</u> 119 (1961):59-99.
Brief description and critique of the authenticity of
these 12th-15th century windows.

251 _____. "Les vitraux de Saint-Denis: L'enfance du Christ."
<u>De Artibus Opuscula</u> (Essays in Honor of Erwin Panofsky) 40
(1961):170-86.
Attempted reconstruction of the Infancy window, including those panels in Twycross and in storage. See also
Fr. 386, 398.

252 _____. "Un groupe de vitraux français du XIIe siècle." In
<u>Festschrift Hans R. Hahnloser zum 60. Geburtstag, 1959</u>.
Edited by Ellen J. Beer, Paul Hofer, and Luc Mojon.
Basel: Birkhäuser, 1961, pp. 289-98.
A group of windows in a Byzantinizing style from Lyon,
Clermond-Ferrand, and Le Champ-près-Froges, dated to the
latter part of the 12th century.

253 _____. "Vitraux de la fin du XIIe siècle ou du début du XIIIe
siècle à la cathédrale de Troyes." <u>Bulletin de la Société</u>
<u>nationale des antiquaires de la France</u> (1961):57-58.
Fragments in London, New York, and Paris show analogies
with Champenois miniatures and Mosan art. Cf. Tech. 111,
and Fr. 362.

254 HUILLET d'ISTRIA, MADELEINE. <u>La peinture française de la fin</u>
<u>du Moyen Âge: Le maître de Moulins</u> (Thèse pour le doctorat
des lettres). Paris: Presse universitaires de France,
1961, 113 pp., 6 color pls., 142 figs.
Recognizes several artists, of different regions who
have conflated as one "Master of Moulins." Suggests an
attribution to Étienne Saulnier and a date of ca. 1485-90
for the Bourbon windows in Moulins.

164

255   JOHNSON, JAMES R. "The Tree of Jesse Window of Chartres: 'Laudes Regiae.'" <u>Speculum</u> 36 (1961):1-22.
      Suggests a connection between the iconography of this mid-12th century window and historical events concerning the royal house of France, 1146-50.

256   LAFOND, JEAN. "Jean Lécuyer, un grand peintre-verrier de la Renaissance." <u>Médecine de France</u> 123 (1961):17-32.
      Windows in Bourges, ca. 1530-40.

257   _____. "L'église de Moulineaux et le vitrail dit de Saint Louis." In <u>Festschrift Hans R. Hahnloser zum 60. Geburtstag, 1959</u>. Edited by Ellen J. Beer, Paul Hofer, and Luc Mojon. Basel: Birkhäuser, 1961, pp. 299-306.
      Critiques its authenticity and questions the significance of the emblems of France and Castille: important for historical method.

258   _____. "Les vitraux de Châlons-sur-Marne et de Saint-Quentin et l'oeuvre de Mathieu Bléville." <u>Bulletin de la Société de l'histoire de l'art</u> (1961):21-28.
      The only study of this master's signed and dated work in Châlons (1525-26); attributes a window in St.-Quentin to him. Poorly illustrated.

259   _____. "Les vitraux de l'abbaye de la Trinité de Fécamp." In <u>L'abbaye bénédictine de Fécamp: Ouvrage scientifique du XIIIᵉ centenaire, 658-1958</u>. Edited by Jehan Le Povremoyne, vol. 3. Fécamp: L. Durand et Fils, 1961, pp. 97-264.
      Late 13th and early 14th century glass, including rarely illustrated cycles of St. Margaret, St. Louis, Edward the Confessor, and the Desert Fathers; important windows by Arnold of Nijmagen, dated ca. 1515.

260   _____. "Notre-Dame-des-Marais et les vitraux de La Ferté-Bernard." <u>Congrès archéologique de France (Maine, 1961)</u> 119 (1961):224-45.
      Catalog of 16th century glass attributed to Robert Courtois, Jean Courtois, and François Delalande.

261   SWOBODA, KARL M. "Zur Frage nach dem Anteil des führenden Meisters am Gesamtkunstwerk der Kathedrale von Chartres." In <u>Festschrift Hans R. Hahnloser zum 60. Geburtstag, 1959</u>. Edited by Ellen J. Beer, Paul Hofer, and Luc Mojon. Basel: Birkhäuser, 1961, pp. 37-46.
      Groups the windows by style and discusses them in relation to the transept sculpture.

262   WILL, ROBERT. "Deux abbés de Murbach: Protecteurs des arts
       au XVIe siècle." Cahiers alsaciens d'archéologie, d'art,
       et d'histoire 5 (1961):125-40.
           Three designs for stained glass and two heraldic windows
       (1520, 1528) with the arms of Georges de Masevaux, abbot of
       Murbach; some of these are by Hans Holbein the Younger and
       his school.

263   LAFOND, JEAN. "Une victime de la guerre: La vitrerie de
       l'église Saint-Michel de Pont-l'Évêque." Bulletin de la
       Société des antiquaires de Normandie 56 (1961-62):569-86.
           Compares 15th century glass from Lisieux, mid-16th cen-
       tury glass from Rouen, and decorative panels (ca. 1619)
       from Bernay; notes the importance of episcopal cities as
       centers for glass painting.

264   GRAHAM, HENRY B. "A Reappraisal of the Princeton Window from
       Chartres." Record of the Art Museum of Princeton Univer-
       sity 21 (1962):30-45.
           Analysis of the condition and painting style of the 13th
       century Martyrdom of St. George panel reveals that most of
       it is 19th century restoration work.

265   HAUCK, MARIE-LUISE. "Die spätmittelalterlichen Glasmalereien
       in Settingen/Lothringen." Saarbrücker Hefte 15 (1962):
       20-30.
           Examines stylistic problems: relations to Ulm and
       Berne (Hans Acker) and Strasbourg (Peter Hemmel von
       Andlau).

266   LAFOND, JEAN. "Christ en croix de la cathédrale de Quimper."
       Bulletin de la Société nationale des antiquaires de France
       (1962):36-38.
           Glass from ca. 1417, influenced by Netherlandish minia-
       tures, is now replaced with a copy; the original is in the
       Château of Castelnau-de-Bretonoux.

267   _____. "Un évêque breton parmi les vitraux du choeur de la
       cathédrale d'Évreux." Bulletin de la Société nationale
       des antiquaires de France (1962):144-51.
           Identifies the arms as those of Thibaut of Malestroit,
       bishop of Tréguier in 1378, who died in 1408 (not those of
       Bernard Cariti, bishop ca. 1376-83).

268   VERDIER, PHILIPPE. "The Window of Saint Vincent from the
       Refectory of the Abbey of Saint-Germain-des-Prés (1239-
       1244)." Journal of the Walters Art Gallery 25-26
       (1962-63):38-99.
          Important Parisian glass in the Walters Art Gallery and
       the Metropolitan Museum; the suggested provenance of the
       refectory and the closeness of style to the Ste.-Chapelle
       and St.-Julian-du-Sault would now be questioned.

269   [CAVINESS], MADELINE HARRISON. "A Life of St. Edward the
       Confessor in Early Fourteenth-Century Stained Glass at
       Fécamp, in Normandy." Journal of the Warburg and Courtauld
       Institutes 26 (1963):22-37.
          Iconographic study of glass, made for the Lady Chapel,
       ca. 1307, in relation to its English manuscript sources.

270   DELAPORTE, YVES. L'art du vitrail aux XIIe et XIIIe siècles:
       technique, inspiration. Chartres: Houvet, 1963, 63 pp.,
       16 color pls., 30 figs.
          General chapters on techniques and iconographic pro-
       grams; well illustrated with examples from Chartres
       Cathedral.

271   FRANKL, PAUL. "The Chronology of the Stained Glass in
       Chartres Cathedral." Art Bulletin 45 (1963):301-22.
          Proposes a chronology of glazing on the basis of arma-
       ture and panel design: choir (begun 1203), nave (1214-27),
       transepts (completed 1240), in line with his theory of
       east-to-west construction.

272   GRODECKI, LOUIS. Chartres. Paris: Draeger & Verve, 1963,
       206 pp., 141 illus.
          Discussion of the subjects and style groups of the 13th
       century windows (pp. 139-96). Numerous color pls.

273   _____. "Problèmes de la peinture en Champagne pendant la
       seconde moitié du douzième siècle." In Romanesque and
       Gothic Art: Studies in Western Art. Acts of the Twentieth
       International Congress of the History of Art, edited by
       Millard Meiss et al. Princeton: University Press, 1963,
       pp. 129-41.
          Panels from Troyes Cathedral attributed to the "Mosan"
       painter of the Capucins Bible; discusses problems of dating
       this glass and that of St.-Remi of Reims. Cf. Fr. 362.

274 LAFOND, JEAN. "Guillaume de Marcillat et la France." In
     Scritti di storia dell'arte in onore di Mario Salmi.
     Vol. 3. Roma: De Luca Editore, 1963, pp. 147-61.
         Documents concerning this French glass painter, who was
     called to Rome in 1506.

275 _____. "L'arbre de Jessé d'Engrand Le Prince à Saint-Étienne
     de Beauvais." Cahiers de la céramique, du verre, et des
     arts du feu 30 (1963):117-27.
         Description and style of this window of ca. 1520; some
     figures are identified as portraits (Charles V and a self-
     portrait of Engrand).

276 MAILLARD, ELISA. "Structure géométrique du vitrail de la
     Crucifixion de la cathédrale Saint-Pierre de Poitiers."
     In Actes du 87e Congrès nationale des sociétés savantes
     (archéologie) Poitiers: 1962. Paris: Imp. nationale,
     1963, pp. 329-37.
         Proposes that the composition of this 12th century win-
     dow was based on the golden ratio.

277 REINHARDT, HANS. La cathédrale de Reims: Son histoire, son
     architecture, sa sculpture, ses vitraux. Paris: Presses
     universitaires de France, 1963, 253 pp., 48 figs. Reprint.
     Marseille: Laffite Reprints, 1979.
         Book 4, "Les vitraux" (pp. 181-94) deals with the pro-
     gram, styles, and chronology; argues that some of the glass
     in the choir was reused from an earlier program, but the
     colored hemicycle windows were supplied between 1227 and
     1240.

278 ROQUES, [Mlle]. "Vitraux du XVIe siècle en Savoie et en
     Dauphiné." Actes du 87e Congrès nationale des sociétés
     savantes (archéologie) Poitiers: 1962. Paris: Imp.
     nationale, 1963, pp. 339-47.
         Chambéry and Vienne related to Brou and close to
     Flemish works; Le Bourget, St.-Chef, and Dingy-St.-Clair
     belong to another group inspired by prints.

279 VILLETTE, JEAN. Les vitraux de Chartres. Paris: Hachette,
     1963, 144 pp., 9 color pls., 21 figs.
         Very general treatment of the cathedral's 13th-15th
     century glass, illustrated with new but not very good
     photographs by Michon.

280 MUSSET, L. "Une description inédite des vitraux de l'église des Jacobins de Caen." Bulletin de la Société des antiquaires de Normandie 57 (1963-64):686-93.
Description of destroyed windows from the mid-13th century based on texts by Hermant and Peiresc.

281 CAMES, G. "Les plus anciens vitraux de la cathédrale de Strasbourg." Cahiers alsaciens d'archéologie, d'art, et d'histoire 8 (1964):101-26.
Among the examples of early glass (ca. 1200), the enthroned ruler now in the Musée de l'oeuvre Notre-Dame is identified as Charlemagne and compared with the smaller figures of German kings in the north aisle; emphasizes Byzantine affinities.

282 FOURNÉE, JEAN. Le Jugement Dernier: Essai d'exégèse d'une oeuvre d'art, le vitrail de la cathédrale de Coutances. Paris: J. Fournée, 1964, 176 pp., 60 pls.
Mid-15th century window, heavily restored after World War I. Cites textual and pictorial sources for the theme; very general overview. Poorly illustrated.

283 GAUTHIER, MARIE-MADELEINE, and MARCHEIX, MADELEINE. "Le vitrail de Saint Jean-Baptiste à l'église Saint-Michel-des-Lions de Limoges." Cahiers de la céramique, du verre, et des arts du feu 35 (1964):173-87.
Glass from the 15th century—its restoration, iconography, and style; and its connection with Limousin enamelers, who referred to the same manuscript source.

284 GRODECKI, LOUIS. "Chronologie des vitraux de Chartres." Bulletin monumental 122 (1964):99-103.
Criticism of Frankl's method of dating (Fr. 272).

285 SULKIS, ELLEN L. "The Four Stained Glass Windows in the North Ambulatory of Saint Étienne of Sens: Dating Dispute." Master's thesis, Columbia University, 1964.
Survey of opinions. Concludes that the same atelier worked in Canterbury in 1200-1208, Sens 1209-10, Canterbury 1214-18/19, and Sens 1218/19-1220.

286 VAIVRE, JEAN-BERNARD de. "Les verrières de Viry." Mémoires de la société d'histoire et archéologie Châlons-sur-Saône 38 (1964-65):89-92.
Iconography of the Passion of Christ window and the donor panels executed before 1520, probably by the Master of Moulins.

Fr. 287

287   CASTELNUOVO, ENRICO. <u>Le vetrate della Cathedrale di Chartres</u>.
       Milan: Fratelli Fabbie, 1965, 22 illus.
            Introduction to the glass in Chartres, its quality and
       function, followed by colored reproductions.

288   GRODECKI, LOUIS. "Le Maître de Saint Eustache de la cathé-
       drale de Chartres." In <u>Gedenkschrift Ernst Gall</u>. Edited
       by Margarete Kühn and Louis Grodecki. Berlin: Deutscher
       Kunstverlag, 1965, pp. 171-94.
            Classicizing glass painter who provided a window in the
       nave of Chartres was probably trained in the region of
       Laon/Soissons and later (?) worked in St.-Quentin.

289   _____. "Les vitraux de XIIe siècle de Saint-Germer-de-Fly."
       In <u>Miscellanea pro arte: Hermann Schnitzler zur Vollendung
       des 60. Lebensjahres am 13. Januar, 1965</u>. Dusseldorf:
       Schwann, [1965], pp. 149-57.
            Panels of ca. 1170-80 from the ambulatory reused in the
       13th century Lady Chapel; partial reconstruction of three
       Christological cycles: the Infancy, Ascension, and sym-
       bolic Crucifixion.

290   AUZAS, PIERRE-MARIE. "Les médaillons de la chapelle Saint-
       Guillaume de Notre-Dame de Paris: Vitraux du XIIIe
       siècle." <u>Cahiers de la céramique, du verre, et des arts du
       feu</u> 37 (1966):30-33.
            Installation of two panels (of Adam and Eve and an un-
       identified fragment) formerly in the Musée de l'oeuvre.
       Summaries in English and German.

291   BAUDOT, M., and DUBUC, RENÉ. "Les verrières de la cathédrale
       d'Évreux: Cinq siècles d'histoire." <u>Nouvelles d'Eure</u> 27
       (1966):26-55.
            History of restorations; identification of subjects, in-
       cluding donors, in the surviving late 13th-early 16th cen-
       tury glass. Well illustrated. Bibliography.

292   BECKSMANN, RÜDIGER. "Bemerkungen zu einer gotischen Orna-
       mentsscheibe aus der Colmarer Franziskanerkirche in der
       Sammlung Bremen." <u>Bonner Jahrbücher: Jahrbücher des
       Vereins von Altertumsfreunden im Rheinlande</u> 166 (1966):
       287-92.
            14th century ornament from the Franciscan church in
       Colmar. Cf. Coll. 95.

293 BLOCK, CHRISTIANE. "Les vitraux de Rosenwiller." L'information de l'histoire de l'art 11 (1966):214-16.
The composition and iconography of the windows (1340-
1355) were inspired by glass in the choir of Königsfelden
and Niederhaslach. Summary of a thesis (Diplôme d'Études
supérieures, Strasbourg, 1966).

294 GAUCHERY, ROBERT. "Un vitrail du XVe siècle à l'église de
Vierzon." Cahiers d'archéologie et d'histoire du Berry 5
(1966):33.
Panel with Christ on the Cross restored in the 17th century when a heraldic shield was added.

295 GRODECKI, LOUIS. "Le vitrail roman de Gargilesse (Indre)."
In Mélanges offerts à René Crozet, professeur à l'Université de Poitiers . . . à l'occasion de son soixante-
dixième anniversaire. Edited by Pierre Gallais and
Yves-Jean Riou. Poitiers: Société d'études médiévales,
1966, pp. 953-57.
Christ in Majesty window from the end of the 12th century was probably executed in an atelier of Poitou.

296 HAUCK, MARIE-LUISE. "Die 'Geburt Christi' von Martin
Schongauer auf einem Gemälde in der metzer Kathedrale."
Saarheimat 10 (1966):346-47.
Window dated 1484-1505 is dependent on an engraving by
Schongauer; its style is compared with that of Peter Hemmel
von Andlau.

297 _____. "Le cycle de la passion de Saint-Martin de Metz:
Vitraux du XVe siècle d'après des gravures du Maître E.S."
Cahiers alsaciens d'archéologie, d'art, et d'histoire 10
(1966):77-88.
Comparison of the cycle (before 1452) with engravings
by Master E.S. shows a collaboration among artists and a
connection with Strasbourg ateliers.

298 _____. "Unbekannte spätgotische Glasmalereien in der Kirche
zu Finstingen (Fénétrange)." Zeitschrift des deutschen
Vereins für Kunstwissenschaft 20 (1966):121-34.
Crucifixion and other subjects, ca. 1480, attributed to
a Metz workshop.

299 HAYWARD, JANE, and GRODECKI, LOUIS. "Les vitraux de la cathédrale d'Angers." Bulletin monumental 124 (1966):7-67.
The most complete modern description of the 12th-13th
century and 15th-16th century glass, with consideration
given to questions of dating.

300 KRAUS, HENRY. "Notre-Dame's Vanished Medieval Glass, I: The
     Iconography." Gazette des beaux-arts, 6th ser. 68 (1966):
     131-48.
          The contents and appearance of some of the chapel win-
     dows, based on drawings by Gaignières, etc. (continued,
     Fr. 308).

301 MEULEN, JAN Van der. "A Logos Creator at Chartres and Its
     Copy." Journal of the Warburg and Courtauld Institutes 29
     (1966):82-100.
          Examines the different iconographic content of the same
     scene in two clerestory rosettes and concludes that one is
     by a post-medieval artist.

302 POPESCO, PAUL. "Verrière du bon samaritain de la cathédrale
     de Chartres." Cahiers de la céramique, du verre, et des
     arts du feu 38 (1966):119-37.
          Establishes a connection between the structure and ma-
     terial of the window and the religious significance of its
     theme; discusses its state of conservation, and its compo-
     sition, color, technique, and style. English and German
     summaries.

303 CAVINESS, MADELINE H. "Three Medallions of Stained Glass
     from the Sainte-Chapelle of Paris." Bulletin of the
     Philadelphia Museum of Art 62 (1966-67):245-59.
          Panels identified as scenes of Holofernes' army from
     the bottom of the Judith window; restoration charts (cf.
     the shorter French version, Fr. 312).

304 *BANNIER, I. "Die Glasmalereien des 15. Jahrhunderts im Chor
     von St. Georg in Schlettstadt." Ph.D. dissertation,
     University of Basel, 1967.

305 BEYER, VICTOR. "La verrière du Jugement Dernier à l'ancienne
     église des Dominicains de Strasbourg." Cahiers alsaciens
     d'archéologie, d'art, et d'histoire (Hommage H. Haug) 11
     (1967):33-44.
          Reconstruction of a window with twenty-five panels exe-
     cuted around 1417, with stylistic analysis.

306 DEUCHLER, FLORENS. Der Ingeborgpsalter. Berlin: Walter de
     Gruyter, 1967.
          Pp. 149-161 compare the glass in the east lancets of
     Laon Cathedral (dated before 1205) with the Psalter of
     Queen Ingeborg (Chantilly, Musée Condé MS. 1695). Cf.
     Fr. 219.

307 GRODECKI, LOUIS. "Les quinze signes précurseurs de la fin du
     monde dans les vitraux allemands, français, et alsaciens."
     In Kunst des Mittelalters in Sachsen: Festschrift Wolf
     Schubert dargebracht zum 60. Geburtstag. Weimar: Hermann
     Böhlaus Nachf., 1967, pp. 292-99.
          Textual and pictorial traditions; the earliest extant
     cycle found at Nuremberg (14th century) and independent
     inventions at Walburg and Angers (15th century).

308 KRAUS, HENRY. "Notre-Dame's Vanished Medieval Glass, II:
     The donors." Gazette des beaux-arts, 6th ser. 69 (1967):
     65-78, 364.
          Concludes that the ecclesiastics, not burghers, gave
     most of the windows, in contrast with the glazing of
     Chartres, etc.; poorly documented (part I, Fr. 300).

309 MINARD, LOUIS. "Vitrail de la dormition de la Vierge."
     Bulletin de la Société d'émulation bourbonnais 53 (1967):
     448-54.
          Glass in the collegiate church at Moulins inspired by a
     bas-relief in the same church; dates from the beginning of
     the 16th century.

310 WITZLEBEN, ELISABETH SCHÜRER von. Licht und Farbe aus Frank-
     reichs Kathedralen. Augsburg: Hannesschläger, 1967,
     259 pp., 46 color pls., 96 figs. French translation. Les
     vitraux des cathédrales de France. Fribourg: Office du
     livre; Paris: Bibliothèque des arts, 1968, 260 pp. En-
     glish translation. Stained Glass in French Cathedrals.
     New York: Reynal, 1968, 264 pp.
          General history of French glass painting, 9th-16th cen-
     turies with well-chosen illustrations. Not as thorough as
     Le vitrail français (Fr. 237), but the translations are
     useful.

311 BERGER, R. "Les vitraux de la cathédrale Notre-Dame de
     Clermont." L'Auvergne littéraire, artistique, et histo-
     rique 45 (1968):2-40.
          Description and iconography of the ambulatory, clere-
     story, and rose windows from the late 12th-15th centuries.

312 CAVINESS, MADELINE HARRISON, and GRODECKI, LOUIS. "Les
     vitraux de la Sainte-Chapelle." La revue de l'art 1-2
     (1968):8-16.
          Six panels recognized in collections since 1959 (cf.
     Fr. 240).

313   GRODECKI, LOUIS; BAUDOT, MARCEL; and DUBUC, RENÉ. "Les
       vitraux de la cathédrale d'Évreux." Bulletin monumental
       126 (1968):55-73.
          Grodecki's critique of some dates proposed by Baudot
       and his identification of the donors represented, espe-
       cially Charles le Mauvais of Navarre, whom Grodecki would
       prefer to identify as Pierre de Mortain; responses by
       Baudot and Dubuc.

314   HOFFMANN, KONRAD. "Sugers 'anagogisches Fenster' in St.
       Denis." Wallraf-Richartz-Jahrbuch 30 (1968):57-88.
          Study of pictorial iconographic sources in other media
       and of the spiritual function of these five windows.

315   KRAUS, HENRY. "Christian-Jewish Disputation in a 13th-Century
       Lancet at the Cathedral of Troyes." Gazette des beaux-arts,
       6th ser. 72 (1968):151-58.
          A pendant to the Marriage at Cana, this Disputation
       scene is placed in the historical context of heresies and
       controversies surrounding the Eucharist. Summary in
       French.

316   SOWERS, ROBERT. "The 12th-Century Windows in Chartres: Some
       Wayward Lessons from the 'Poor Man's Bible.'" Art Journal
       28 (1968-69):166-73.
          Discussion of the way in which the three early windows
       of the façade were modified by their changed setting after
       the fire of 1194.

317   BEYER, VICTOR. Glasmalereien einer bedeutenden Kirche: Das
       strassburger Münster. Beruhmte Glasmalereien in Europa.
       Augsburg: Josef Hannesschläger, 1969, 127 pp., 20 color
       pls., 25 figs., plan. French translation. *La cathédrale
       de Strasbourg. Chefs-d'oeuvre du vitrail européen. Paris:
       Bibliothèque des arts, 1970.
          Same format as Ger. 170.

318   HAUCK, MARIE-LUISE. "Die Gefangennahme Christi oder der
       Judaskuss, eine unbeachtete Glasmalerei Peter Hemmels in
       Museum zu Hagenau (Elsass) und die Fenster der strassburger
       Wilhelmerkirche." Archives de l'église d'Alsace, n.s. 17
       (1969):243-65.
          Discusses a Betrayal of Christ in the Hagenau Museum,
       identical in design to one in Walburg dated 1461, and
       other fragments from a Passion cycle; argues for a prov-
       enance of St. Wilhelm, Strasbourg, and an attribution to
       Peter Hemmel, who worked there.

319 KRAUS, HENRY. "New Documents for Notre-Dame's Early Chapels."
Gazette des beaux-arts, 6th ser. 74 (1969):121-34.
Document of 1243 refers to an Assumption in glass, for
which the author suggests a date of ca. 1182. French
summary.

320 LAFOND, JEAN. "Les Courtois (Robert, Pierre, et Jean) et les
peintres verriers de La Ferté-Bernard." Mémoires de la
Société nationale des antiquaires de France, 9th ser. 4
(1969):195-241.
Attribution of the 15th century glass in Notre-Dame-des-
Marais to Robert Courtois; the 16th century glass attributed
to Jean Courtois and François Delalande; its diversity in
style argues against Leopold Charles's theory that the
glass was of local origin.

321 * ____. "Les vitraux de l'arrondissement de Pont-Audemer."
Nouvelles d'Eure 36 (1969):22-48. [Issued with 60 slides].
Glass of the 13th-16th centuries, illustrating the Lives
of Christ, the Virgin, and various saints.

322 LILLICH, MEREDITH PARSONS. "The Stained Glass of Saint-Père
de Chartres." Ph.D. dissertation, Columbia University,
1969.
Discusses the chronology of the glazing, ca. 1240-1315;
the iconographic program; and its stylistic relation to
the western school. Published in part (Fr. 393, 403).

323 POPESCO, PAUL. Glasmalereien einer bedeutenden Kathedrale:
Die Kathedrale von Chartres. Berühmte Glasmalereien in
Europa. Augsburg: Josef Hannesschläger, 1969, 144 pp.,
50 figs. (20 color), plan. French translation. La cathédrale de Chartres. Chefs-d'oeuvre du vitrail européen.
Paris: Bibliothèque des arts, 1970.
Same format as Ger. 170, but with notes on the illustrations. Presents the idea that some of the glass in the
mid-12th century west windows is the result of restoration
after the fire of 1194.

324 SALVINI, JOSEPH. "Le vitrail de la chapelle de Baudiment."
Bulletin de la Société des antiquaires de l'ouest 10
(1969):240.
Heraldic glass from the 16th century with arms of the
Nuchèze family.

Fr. 325

325 SCHAAF, A. "Vitrail roman de l'église Saints Pierre et Paul de Wissembourg." Cahiers de l'art médiéval 5, no. 3 (1969-70):27.
Rose window in the north transept represents the enthroned Virgin and Child; dated to the middle of the 12th century (cf. Fr. 344).

326 PÉRÉ, ANDRÉ. "Arnaut de Moles, artiste gascon." Bulletin de la Société archéologique, historique, littéraire, et scientifique du Gers 70 (1969):456-79; 71 (1970):54-73.
His life and work; examines influences on his work and characterizes his style as exemplified in the glass at Auch Cathedral (ca. 1513).

327 BEYER, VICTOR. "Un vitrail du 16e siècle à la cathédrale de Strasbourg." La revue de l'art 10 (1970):73-76.
Design of a head used as a stopgap replacement is attributed to Hans Baldung Grien, its execution to Louis de Marmoutier. English and German summaries.

328 BEYER, VICTOR; CHOUX, JACQUES; and LEDEUR, LUCIEN. Vitraux de France du Moyen Âge à la Renaissance. Vol. 1, Alsace, Lorraine, Franche-Comté. Colmar-Ingersheim: Ed. SAEP., 1970, 256 pp., 75 pls. (some color), 3 maps.
Survey of glass painting in each of these regions, from the 11th (Wissembourg) to 16th centuries, with a checklist of sites and selected bibliography.

329 BLOCK, CHRISTIANE. "Le vitrail de la vie de la Vierge de Vieux-Thann et sa place dans la peinture du Rhin supérieur au XVe siècle." La revue de l'art 10 (1970):15-29.
The Life of the Virgin in a Tree of Jesse (1466) is of a regional type. Its stylistic relations to panel painting and to glass at Bourguillon are presented. English and German summaries.

330 FIOT, ROBERT. "Jean Fouquet à Notre-Dame-la-Riche de Tours." La revue de l'art 10 (1970):30-46.
Attribution of a group of windows of ca. 1440-60 is made on the basis of style and in accordance with a reference in Francesco Florio.

331 GRODECKI, LOUIS. "Saint Louis et le vitrail." Monuments historiques de la France 16 (1970):5-21.
The existence of a court style which emerged from the Île-de-France ca. 1230-70 and conformed to the aspirations of St. Louis; iconography of the saint in 13th, 14th, and 15th century glass.

176

332 HAUCK, MARIE-LUISE. "Die Glasgemälde der Kirche von Zettingen
(Lothringen)." Bericht der Staatlichen Denkmalpflege in
Saarland 17 (1970):117-234.
Full publication of an important cycle in the choir (ca.
1434-50) that includes a typological creed window. Examines iconographic connections with the Upper Rhine (Strasbourg, Thann) and Boppard and makes comparisons with manuscript painting. Bibliography and indexes.

333 LAFOND, JEAN. "La Cananéenne de la cathédrale de Bayonne et
le vitrail parisien aux environs de 1530. La revue de
l'art 10 (1970):77-84.
Attribution to Jean Chastellain of a window dated 1531
depicting the Canaanite; the artist worked at St.-Germain
l'Auxerrois, Paris, in 1533. English and German summaries.

334 _____. "Un panneau du 13e siècle provenant d'un vitrail des
Septs Dormants d'Éphèse." Bulletin de la Société nationale
des antiquaires de France (1970):262-64.
The Worcester Art Museum panels made by a Rouen atelier
(cf. Grodecki); notes the discovery of other fragments from
this window.

335 LAFOND, JEAN; PERROT, FRANÇOISE; and POPESCO, PAUL. Les
vitraux de l'église Saint-Ouen de Rouen. Vol. 1. Corpus
Vitrearum Medii Aevi: France, Vol. 4, pt. 2, Département
de la Seine-Maritime, 2. Paris: Caisse nationale des
monuments historiques and C.N.R.S., 1970, 260 pp., 6 color
pls., 76 pls., plans in text.
Definitive publication of the 14th century glass in the
choir. The second part is not yet published.

336 LILLICH, MEREDITH PARSONS. "An Early Image of Saint Louis."
Gazette des beaux-arts, 6th ser. 75 (1970):251-56, 4 figs.
Identification and dating (soon after 1297) of a figure
in the apse clerestory of St.-Père of Chartres.

337 _____. "The Band Window: A Theory of Origin and Development."
Gesta 9 (1970):26-33.
Designs involving horizontal rows of figures set in
grisaille at Auxerre, Tours, etc. The suggested derivation
from St.-Remi of Reims is improbable.

338 MURATOVA, XENIA. "Deux panneaux inconnus de vitraux français
du 13e siècle au musée de Kiev." La revue de l'art 10
(1970):63-65.
Discussion of two early thirteenth century heads (depicting St. Paul and Ezekiel) in relation to glass in the north-
east of France. English and German summaries.

339   PERROT, FRANÇOISE. "La rose de l'église de Donnemarie-en-
      Montois." Bulletin de la Société d'histoire et d'archéo-
      logie de Provins 124 (1970):53-69.
          Eight medallions with subjects from the Last Judgment
      (the Resurrection; the Saved) in the rose of the east wall
      of the choir. Related to Laon and dated the first half of
      the 13th century.

340   _____. "Le vitrail au temps de Saint Louis." In Le siècle de
      Saint Louis. Paris: Hachette, 1970, pp. 160-69.
          Development of the St. Louis style of glass painting
      which originated in Paris and is best exemplified by the
      Ste.-Chapelle windows (1241-48); and its influence in sur-
      rounding churches.

341   _____. "Un panneau de la vitrerie de la chapelle de l'Hôtel
      de Cluny." La revue de l'art 10 (1970):61-72.
          A Christ Carrying the Cross in the Cluny Museum is
      traced to the Parisian Hôtel de Cluny and dated soon after
      1496 through comparison with engravings. English and
      German summaries.

342   POLGE, HENRI. "L'iconographie des attitudes à la cathédrale
      Sainte-Marie d'Auch: Étude de statesthésie rétrospective."
      Bulletin de la Société archéologique, historique, litté-
      raire, et scientifique du Gers 71 (1970):7-32; 189-250;
      323-51; 447-65.
          Study of the variety of attitudes and poses found in the
      glass at Auch (ca. 1513).

343   POPESCO, PAUL. "Les panneaux de vitrail du XIIe siècle de
      l'église Saint-Pierre de Chartres, ancienne abbatiale."
      La revue de l'art 10 (1970):47-56.
          A panel with the Ascension in storage at the Château de
      Champs is assigned to a lower window in St-Père and dated
      ca. 1175. English and German summaries.

344   SCHULTZ-FOYARD, SIMONE. "Un vitrail roman alsacien: La
      Vierge de Wissembourg." L'information de l'histoire de
      l'art 15 (1970):16-21.
          Rose window representing the Virgin and Child; compares
      it with Strasbourg Cathedral glass and with manuscripts and
      dates it ca. 1200 (cf. Fr. 325).

345 BARNES, CARL F., Jr. "The Location of the 'Sainte-Chapelle' Stained Glass in the Cathedral of Soissons." Art Bulletin 53 (1971):459-60.
Documentary evidence for the transfer of these panels of ca. 1250 from the west end of the nave into the choir ca. 1770.

346 BEYER, VICTOR. "Les vitraux du collatéral sud de la cathédrale de Strasbourg." Cahiers alsaciens d'archéologie, d'art, et d'histoire 15 (1971):123-34.
Dates glass in the south nave aisle (New Testament history) ca. 1332-40 on the basis of the building's history and stylistic comparisons with Königsfelden (cf. Wentzel, Ger. 97, ca. 1300-1310).

347 CAVINESS, MADELINE HARRISON. "French Thirteenth Century Stained Glass at Canterbury: A Fragment from the Sainte Chapelle of Paris in St. Gabriel's Chapel." Canterbury Cathedral Chronicle 66 (1971):35-41.
Fragment of an Annointing recognized since 1959 (cf. also Fr. 240, 312).

348 *KEBERLE, B. "Die Glasmalereien in den Langhausfenstern der Florentiuskirche zu Niederhaslach." Société d'histoire et d'archéologie de Molsheim et environs (1971):15-36.
Summary of a doctoral dissertation, Basel, 1964.

349 PASCAUD-GRANDBOULAN, ANNE. "Le vitrail de la Vierge à la Trinité de Vendôme." L'information d'histoire de l'art 16 (1971):128-32.
Summary of a Master's thesis, University of Paris IV. 12th century window is similar to the early glass in Angers but is of a unique iconographic type.

350 BLOCK, CHRISTIANE. "Les vitraux du choeur de l'église de Rosenwiller: Un tournant dans l'art du 14e siècle en Alsace." Cahiers alsaciens d'archéologie, d'art, et d'histoire 16 (1972):119-50.
This glass, influenced by Königsfelden and Niederhaslach, contributed to the formation of a new style characteristic of the second half of the 14th century. Based on the author's thesis (1966).

351 BRISAC, CATHERINE. "La verrière du Champ-près-Froges (Isère)." L'information d'histoire de l'art 17 (1972): 158-62.
Summary of a Master's thesis, University of Paris IV. A Christological window of ca. 1160 that probably

originated in the Cluniac Priory of Domène demonstrates
Germanic and Byzantinizing traits.

352   CAREL, JACQUES. "Les restes de vitraux de l'église de
      Rustroff." Pays lorrain 53, no. 1 (1972):49-53.
          Scenes from the Life of the Virgin, executed 1431-35 by
      a glass painter from Lorraine, show middle Rhenish
      influence.

353   _____. "Un fragment de vitrail du 16ᵉ siècle dans la chapelle
      du cimetière de Faulquemont." Pays lorrain 53, no. 4
      (1972):185-87.
          Represents a kneeling bishop; probably the work of
      Valentin Busch, 1540-50, or a follower.

354   DUFOURCQ, MARTINE. "Les vitraux de la chapelle Saint-Thomas
      en l'église Notre-Dame de Saint-Lô (Manche)." L'informa-
      tion d'histoire de l'art 17 (1972):49-53.
          Summary of a Master's thesis, University of Paris IV,
      1971. Windows probably executed ca. 1430-35 by two local
      artists.

355   FRODL-KRAFT, EVA. "Zu den Kirchenschaubildern in den Hoch-
      chorfenstern von Reims--Abbildung und Abstraktion." Wiener
      Jahrbuch für Kunstgeschichte 25 (1972):53-86.
          Extent to which the representations of the cathedrals in
      the archdiocese of Reims, made for the windows of the
      choir, are based on real Romanesque or Gothic buildings.
      Examines relation of 'statuary' in them to Reims sculpture;
      concludes that some must be as late as the mid-13th century.

356   GAIL, LAURENCE de. "Le vitrail dit de la Création à l'église
      de Ceffonds (Haute-Marne)." L'information d'histoire de
      l'art 17 (1972):88-92.
          Summary of a Master's thesis, University of Paris IV,
      1971. Iconography of the 16th century glass and the in-
      fluence of Troyes.

357   LEDIT, CHARLES JEAN. Cathédrale de Troyes: Les vitraux.
      Troyes and Paris: Tetraktys, [1972], 108 pp., 50 figs.
      (2 color).
          Guide to 13th and 15th century glass, with plans of the
      windows. Illustrations complement those of Lafond's arti-
      cle by showing the later glass (cf. Fr. 232).

358 LILLICH, MEREDITH PARSONS. "A Redating of the Thirteenth
     Century Grisaille Windows of Chartres Cathedral." Gesta
     11, no. 1 (1972):11-18.
          On the basis of comparisons with dated examples from
     other sites, contests the dates provided by Frankl and
     Delaporte (Fr. 124, 272).

359 PERROT, FRANÇOISE. Le vitrail à Rouen. Connaître Rouen.
     Rouen: Lecerf, 1972, 62 pp., 5 color pls., 24 figs.
          Survey of important examples of the 13th-16th centuries
     in the churches of Rouen.

360 CHOUX, JACQUES. "Valentin Bousch à Saint-Nicolas-de-Port et
     à Flavigny." Pays lorrain 54 (1973):157-70.
          Based on documentary sources, attributes the glass at
     St.-Nicolas-de-Port (1514-20) and Flavigny (1531-33) to
     the German glazier, Valentin Busch, who worked almost ex-
     clusively in Lorraine.

361 CONTAMINE, PHILIPPE. "L'oriflamme de Saint-Denis aux 14e et
     15e siècles." Annales de l'est 25, no. 3 (1973):179-244.
          Study of the religious and royal symbol and its inclu-
     sion in stained glass and miniatures.

362 GRODECKI, LOUIS. "Nouvelles découvertes sur les vitraux de
     la cathédrale de Troyes." In Intuition und Kunstwissen-
     schaft: Festschrift für Hanns Swarzenski. Edited by Peter
     Bloch, Tillmann Buddensieg, Alfred Hentzen, and Theodor
     Müller. Berlin: Gebr. Mann Verlag, 1973, pp. 191-203.
          Revises his previous opinion on dating (cf. Fr. 253 and
     274), allowing for the possibility that these panels origi-
     nated in the building that burned in 1188 (as also in
     Tech. 111).

363 LAFOND, JEAN. "Un chef-d'oeuvre: Le vitrail d'Arnoult de
     Nimègue à l'église Saint-Foy de Conches." Cahiers de la
     céramique, du verre, et des arts du feu 2 (1973):50-65.
          Window in the north aisle depicting the Virgin, St.
     Adrian, St. Romanus, and donors is dated ca. 1510 and
     compared with other works by Arnold of Nijmegen.

364 LILLICH, MEREDITH PARSONS. "Three Essays on French Thirteenth
     Century Grisaille Glass." Journal of Glass Studies 15
     (1973):69-78.
          Identifies fragments in the Corning Museum as from
     Bourges Cathedral, St.-Urbain of Troyes, and the Château
     of Rouen [?].

Fr. 365

365   LOUIS, THOMAS. "L'oeuvre de Valentin Bousch, peintre verrier
       à la cathédrale de Metz (1520-1539)." Archeologia 56
       (1973):32-38.
           The life and work of the 16th century glazier who intro-
       duced Renaissance style in the windows at Metz (dated
       1520); discusses their relation to the late 15th century
       program by Thiebault of Lixheim.

366   SCHER, STEPHEN K. "Note sur les vitraux de la Sainte-Chapelle
       de Bourges." Cahiers d'archéologie et d'histoire du Berry
       35 (1973):23-44.
           Suggests that Beauneveu participated directly in the
       execution of the head of St. Joseph now in the museum at
       Bourges.

367   SUAU, JEAN-PIERRE. "Les vitraux du 14e siècle de la cathé-
       drale de Narbonne." Narbonne: archéologie et histoire
       (Congrès organisé par la Fédération historique du Languedoc
       méditerranéen et du Roussillon 1972) 2 (1973):237-69.
           Identification and description of the stained glass in
       the apsidal chapels; the chronology of the windows, which
       were executed by two ateliers (1295-1300, 1330-35); and
       their stylistic relation to Normandy.

368   VAIVRE, JEAN BERNARD de. "Les armoiries de Pierre de
       Mortain." Bulletin monumental 131 (1973):29-40; 161-62.
           Examination of various arms and portraits of Pierre de
       Navarre (d. 1412) confirms the identity of the figure in
       the glass of Évreux (cf. Fr. 313).

369   BLOCK, CHRISTIANE. "La vie de la Vierge et l'enfance du
       Christ dans les vitraux de la cathédrale de Strasbourg:
       Une oeuvre executée avant 1331 pour le bas-côté sud."
       Bulletin de la Société des amis de la cathédrale de
       Strasbourg 11 (1974):43-56.
           Reconstruction of a window made for one of the eastern-
       most bays and reinstalled in 1331 in a more westerly loca-
       tion when the chapel of St. Catherine was planned.

370   BOUZY, ALAIN. "Une réalisation exemplaire à Chartres: Un
       cellier du XIIe siècle pour le centre international du
       vitrail." Sites et monuments 68 (Oct.-Dec. 1974):11-13.
           Announcement of the site for the Centre international
       du vitrail: the 12th century storehouse of Loëns, to the
       north of the cathedral. The center, which has exhibition
       space and a library, opened in 1980.

371 BRISAC, CATHERINE. "Le sacramentaire MS 63 de la Bibliothèque
     municipale de Clermont-Ferrand: Nouvelles données sur
     l'art figuré à Clermont autour de 1200." Bulletin histo-
     rique et scientifique de l'Auvergne (Clermont-Ferrand) 86,
     nos. 642-43 (1974):303-15.
         Christ in Majesty and a Crucifixion in the manuscript
     show Byzantine influence and are related to glass in the
     chapel of St. Anne.

372 CALLIAS BEY-DUFOURCQ, MARTINE. "Les vitraux de Notre-Dame de
     Saint-Lô." Art de Basse-Normandie 62 (1974):24-28.
         Catalog of the 15th and 16th century glass; describes
     its condition and restorations.

373 RAGUIN, VIRGINIA CHIEFFO. "The Genesis Workshop of the
     Cathedral of Auxerre and Its Parisian Inspiration." Gesta
     13 (1974):27-38.
         Affinities between a group of Auxerre windows of ca.
     1233-44 and Gercy glass (Seine-et-Oise) and Parisian
     styles.

374 _____. "Thirteenth-Century Choir Glass of Auxerre Cathedral."
     Ph.D. dissertation, Yale University, 1974.
         Iconographic program and stylistic groups; relations
     with Parisian and Burgundian sites. Revised for publica-
     tion by the Princeton University Press (see Fr. 426).

375 ZAKIN, HELEN JACKSON. "French Cistercian Grisaille Glass."
     Gesta 13 (1974):17-28.
         Examines extant 12th-13th century glass from La
     Bénisson-Dieu (Loire), Obazine (Corrèze), and Noirlac
     (Cher); and lost examples. Cites their relationship to
     motifs in sculpture and tiles and to the writings of St.
     Bernard. More fully published in her monograph (Fr. 407).
     Cf. Brisac, Fr. 391.

376 BECKSMANN, RÜDIGER. "Zum Werk des walburger Meister von
     1461." In Beiträge zur Kunst des Mittelalters: Fest-
     schrift für Hans Wentzel zum 60. Geburtstag. Edited by
     Rüdiger Becksman, Ulf-Dietrich Korn, and Johannes Zahlten.
     Berlin: Gebr. Mann Verlag, 1975, pp. 17-27.
         Works by a "Walburg Master," dated 1461 and ca. 1480, the
     latter in St.-Guillaume at Strasbourg. This artist is not
     identified with Peter Hemmel or the Master of the Karlsruhe
     Passion. Cf. other opinions in Fr. 245, Ger. 109.

Fr. 377

377 *BEUCHER, MONIQUE. "Les verrières hautes du choeur de la
   cathédrale d'Évreux antérieures à 1340." Thèse du 3e
   cycle, University of Paris IV, 1975.

378 GRODECKI, LOUIS. "Le 'Maître des vitraux de Jacques Coeur.'"
   In Études d'art français offertes à Charles Sterling.
   Edited by Albert Châtelet and Nicole Reyaud. Paris:
   Presses universitaire de France, 1975, pp. 105-25.
      Cites Flemish influence (van der Weyden, van Eyck) in
   the Annunciation window of the chapel of St. Ursin in
   Bourges Cathedral; and makes a stylistic comparison with
   the vault paintings of 1448-51 in the house of Jacques
   Coeur.

379 _____. "Le 'Maître du bon samaritain' de la Cathédrale de
   Bourges." In The Year 1200: A Symposium. Introduction
   by Jeffrey Hoffeld. New York: Metropolitan Museum of Art,
   1975, pp. 339-59.
      Takes up the question of the characteristic style and
   formation of the three ateliers working at Bourges between
   ca. 1205 and 1214 (cf. Gen. 40). English summary.

380 _____. "Les plus anciens vitraux de Saint-Remi de Reims." In
   Beiträge zur Kunst des Mittelalters: Festschrift für Hans
   Wentzel zum 60. Geburtstag. Edited by Rüdiger Becksmann,
   Ulf-Dietrich Korn, and Johannes Zahlten. Berlin: Begr.
   Mann Verlag, 1975, pp. 65-77.
      Glass divided into three groups: the apse clerestory
   of ca. 1180-1190, the Crucifixion in the tribune, and the
   earlier panels in the nave clerestory and apse tribune,
   some of which may date ca. 1150.

381 LAFOND, JEAN. "La verrière des sept dormants d'Éphèse et
   l'ancienne vitrerie de la cathédrale de Rouen." In The
   Year 1200: A Symposium. Introduction by Jeffrey Hoffeld.
   New York: Metropolitan Museum of Art, 1975, pp. 339-416.
      Twelve panels from this window are found in American
   collections and in storage at the Château of Champs; discusses the cult of the Seven Sleepers in the West. English
   summary.

382 LILLICH, MEREDITH PARSONS. "The Choir Clerestory Windows of
   La Trinité at Vendôme: Dating and Patronage." Journal of
   the Society of Architectural Historians 34 (1975):238-50.
      Critical reevaluation of the documentary and heraldic
   evidence which establishes a date of ca. 1290 instead of
   the traditional terminus post quem of 1308.

383   MORÉCHAND, V.   "Les vitraux du XIIIᵉ siècle de l'église Saint-
      Pierre de Dreux."   L'information d'histoire de l'art 20,
      no. 5 (1975):214-17.
         Discussion of the quality, iconography, and style of
      seventy-one panels related to the work of a Parisian
      atelier in the mid-13th century.

384   PERROT, FRANÇOISE.   "Note sur les arbres de Jessé de Gercy et
      de St.-Germain-lès-Corbeil."   In The Year 1200:   A Sym-
      posium.   Introduction by Jeffrey Hoffeld.   New York:
      Metropolitan Museum of Art, 1975, pp. 417-28.
         Parisian style of the first quarter of the 13th century.

385   ROLLET, JEAN.   "La Nativité vue à travers les vitraux du Moyen
      Âge français."   Connaissance des arts 286 (1975):102-13.
         Discussion of Nativity iconography that emphasizes exam-
      ples in 12th-16th century French stained glass.

386   GRODECKI, LOUIS.   Les vitraux de Saint-Denis: Étude sur le
      vitrail au XIIᵉ siècle.   Vol. 1.   Corpus Vitrearum Medii
      Aevi: France, Studies 1, Département de Seine-Saint-Denis.
      Paris: Arts et métiers graphiques, for C.N.R.S., 1976,
      251 pp., 15 color pls., 231 figs., plans in text.
         Detailed historical and archeological study of the 12th
      and 13th century glass in St.-Denis; documentation, resto-
      rations (with charts), suggested reconstructions.   Icono-
      graphic and stylistic study to follow.

387   HAYWARD, JANE.   "The Choir Windows of Saint-Serge and Their
      Glazing Atelier."   Gesta 15 (1976):255-64.
         Dates this work after ca. 1210 and associates it with
      Templar influences.   Cites work in the cathedral of Angers
      by the same atelier.

388   NETZER, NANCY D.   "A Stylistic Analysis of the Chartres
      Cathedral Nave Stained Glass Windows."   Master's thesis,
      Tufts University, 1976.
         Divides the glass in the nave clerestory windows between
      two masters, one of whom is identified with the Joseph-
      Lubin Master of the nave aisles; it is argued that the
      glazing followed closely on construction and that the
      painters were influenced by the transept sculpture of ca.
      1205-20.

France

Fr. 389

389 RAGUIN, VIRGINIA CHIEFFO. "Windows of Saint-Germain-lès-
     Corbeil: A Traveling Glazing Atelier." Gesta 15 (1976):
     265-72.
          Attributes windows in St.-Germain near Corbeil (Seine-
     et-Oise), dated ca. 1225, and at Semur-en-Auxois, Troyes,
     and Auxerre, ca. 1237, to the same atelier.

390 REINHARDT, HANS. "Le vitrail de la découverte des reliques de
     Saint Étienne à la cathédrale de Châlons-sur-Marne."
     Mémoires de la Société d'agriculture, commerce, science,
     et arts de la Marne 91 (1976):135-42.
          Suggests a date ca. 1000 for this glass on the basis of
     comparison with Carolingian works; compare the date of ca.
     1160 proposed by Grodecki (Fr. 200, 207, 235, 237).

391 BRISAC, CATHERINE. "Grisailles romanes des anciennes abba-
     tiales d'Obazine et de Bonlieu." Congrès national des
     sociétés savantes (Limoges) 102 (1977):129-43.
          Rigorous critique of the surviving, unpainted ornamental
     glass from these Cistercian sites; cites the relation of
     their motifs to fenestellae in stone (cf. Zakin, Fr. 375,
     407). For an English translation, see "Grisailles from the
     former Abbey Churches of Obazine and Bonlieu" in Zakin,
     Fr. 427, pp. 130-39.

392 _____. "Les vitraux de l'étage inférieur du choeur de Saint-
     Jean-de-Lyon." Thèse de 3e cycle, University of Paris IV,
     1977.
          Iconography, style, and date of this early 13th century
     glass.

393 LILLICH, MEREDITH PARSONS. "Les vitraux de Saint-Pierre de
     Chartres." Les monuments historiques de la France (1977):
     52-57.
          Summary of the chronology presented in her book (Fr.
     403).

394 _____. "Vitrail normand du XIIIe siècle aux armes de La
     Ferrière." Archivum heraldicum 3-4 (1977):34-37.
          Identification of shields of ca. 1250 in the parish
     church of Aunou-sur-Orne; their relation to Sées.

395 MAINES, CLARK. "The Charlemagne Window at Chartres Cathedral:
     New Considerations on Text and Image." Speculum 52 (1977):
     801-23.
          Detailed study of the textual sources; proposes a dif-
     ferent ordering of the scenes and their typological rela-
     tionships. Dates the window ca. 1225 (cf. Fr. 246).

396   *MUSSAT, ANDRÉ; GRUBER, JEAN-JACQUES; and BARRIÉ; ROGER. <u>Le</u>
       <u>vitrail breton</u>. Arts de l'ouest, 3. Rennes: Centre <u>de</u>
       recherches sur les arts anciens et modernes de l'ouest de
       la France, U.E.R. des arts, Université de Haute-Bretagne,
       1977.
           Summary by Brisac, <u>Bulletin monumental</u> 136 (1978):
       370-71.

397   PERROT, FRANÇOISE. "Les verrières du XIIe siècle de la façade
       occidentale [de la cathédrale de Chartres]: Étude archéo-
       logique." <u>Les monuments historiques de la France</u> (1977):
       37-51.
           Analysis of these three windows based on examination
       during recent conservation work; includes restoration
       charts and a discussion of medieval and modern replacements.

398   BRISAC, CATHERINE. "Iconographie pseudolégendaire des fonda-
       teurs de l'église de Lyon et reliques carolingiennes." In
       <u>Colloques internationaux du Centre national de la recherche</u>
       <u>scientifique</u>. No. 575, <u>Les martyrs de Lyon</u>. Paris:
       C.N.R.S., 1978, pp. 299-310.
           13th century window with the Life of St. Cyprianus of
       Carthage, restored in the 19th century as a cycle of the
       church's founders, Potinius and Irene.

399   COTHREN, MICHAEL WATT. "A Re-evaluation of the Iconography
       and Design of the Infancy Window from the Abbey of St.-
       Denis (Abstracts of Papers Delivered at the Thirteenth
       Conference on Medieval Studies, Kalamazoo)". <u>Gesta</u> 17
       (1978):74-75.
           Suggests that two panels, one with the Flight into Egypt
       now in the Pitcairn collection (Pa.) and another with
       Attendants at the Presentation formerly with Acézat, are
       from the Infancy window; the iconography, following Pseudo-
       Matthew, is plausible but the authenticity of the panels
       has been doubted. Cf. Exh. 52.

400   The following articles are printed in "Découvrir et sauver les
       vitraux," <u>Dossiers de l'Archéologie</u> 26 (Jan.-Feb. 1978).
       All have excellent illustrations in black and white and in
       color:

400a Beucher, Monique. "Les verrières du choeur d'Évreux."
       pp. 63-75.
           Examines the influence of Parisian manuscript illumina-
       tion, especially the style of Pucelle.

400b   Brisac, Catherine. "La peinture sur verre à Lyon."
        pp. 38-49.
            12th-13th century glass in the cathedral and the 12th
        century window at Le Champ-près-Froges; new observations
        on style.

400c   Foy, Danièle. "Le vitrail en France méridionale: Les
        verres trouvés dans les fouilles archéologiques."
        pp. 114-22.
            Scarcity of surviving glass in the south; excavated
        fragments of the 12th-14th centuries from Avignon,
        Marseille, Psalmodi, etc.

400d   Gatouillat, Françoise. "À Saint-Sulpice de Favières: Des
        vitraux témoins de l'art parisien au temps de Saint Louis."
        pp. 50-62.
            Postulates that some glass from ca. 1235-40 was reused
        in the new building ca. 1245-50.

400e   Hamy-Longuespé, Nicole. "Troyes, haut-lieu du vitrail."
        pp. 86-101.
            Richness of this site for the 15th-late 16th centuries;
        assigns St.-Pantaléon and some of the cathedral glazing to
        the first period (1490-1530). Notes the influence of
        Fontainebleau.

401   GRODECKI, LOUIS. "Les problèmes de l'origine de la peinture
        gothique et le 'Maître de Saint Chéron' de la cathédrale
        de Chartres." La revue de l'art 40-41 (1978):43-64.
            Stylistic developments in glass in relation to manu-
        scripts and sculpture; an atelier working in the ambulatory
        ca. 1230-35 influenced the glass of the Ste.-Chapelle in
        Paris.

402   GRODECKI, LOUIS; PERROT, FRANÇOISE; and TARALON, JEAN. Les
        vitraux de Paris, de la région parisienne, de la Picardie,
        et du Nord-Pas-de-Calais. Corpus Vitrearum Medii Aevi:
        France, série complémentaire: Recensement des vitraux
        anciens de la France, 1. Paris: C.N.R.S., 1978, 275 pp.,
        16 color pls., 141 figs., plans in text.
            Brief inventory of all the glass through the 16th cen-
        tury, selected illustrations; bibliography not complete.
        Useful for little-known glass of the late period.

403 LILLICH, MEREDITH PARSONS. The Stained Glass of Saint-Père de
      Chartres. Middletown, Conn.: Wesleyan University Press,
      1978, 212 pp., 12 color pls., 99 figs.
           Study of documents, archaeology, style, and iconography;
      argues that glass made ca. 1240-50 for the nave was in-
      stalled in the choir ca. 1270. New glass was provided for
      the hemicycle ca. 1295-1300 and for the nave ca. 1300-1315.

404 PERROT, FRANÇOISE. "Les vitraux de l'ancienne église Saint-
      Vincent remontés place du Vieux-Marche." Bulletin des amis
      des monuments rouennais (July 1978-May 1979):49-98.
           Surviving glass of 1515/20-1530 from this destroyed
      church was installed in another building; Christological
      and hagiographical windows were made by two ateliers, one
      local and the other the Le Prince workshop in Beauvais.
      Well illustrated in both color and black and white.

405 BOUCHON, CHANTAL; BRISAC, CATHERINE; LAUTIER, CLAUDINE; and
      ZALUSKA, YOLANTA. "La 'Belle-Verrière' de Chartres."
      Revue de l'art 46 (1979):16-24.
           Restoration chart for this famous window, based on an
      examination from a scaffold. Discusses iconography and
      style, including the additions of ca. 1215-20.

406 PAPANICOLAOU, LINDA MOREY. "Stained Glass Windows of the
      Choir of the Cathedral of Tours." Ph.D. dissertation,
      New York University, 1979.
           Analysis of iconographic and stylistic sources, with a
      new identification of one window with the Life of St.
      Julian of Le Mans; three glazing campaigns, ca. 1255, ca.
      1264, and ca. 1270, the first very closely dependent on
      the Sainte-Chapelle.

407 ZAKIN, HELEN JACKSON. French Cistercian Grisaille Glass.
      Outstanding Dissertations in the Fine Arts. New York and
      London: Garland, 1979, 439 pp., 192 figs.
           Analysis of the surviving glass establishes its charac-
      ter, design sources, and influence ca. 1175-1250.

408 RAGUIN, VIRGINIA CHIEFFO. "The Jesse Tree Prophet: In the
      Workshop Tradition of the Sainte-Chapelle." Worcester Art
      Museum Journal 3 (1979-80):28-35.
           Briefer version of Fr. 416. Well illustrated.

409   ANCIEN, JEAN. Vitraux de la cathédrale de Soissons. Reims:
      privately printed, [1980], 265 pp., 44 pls. (some color).
           History of the 13th century glass, restorations, etc.,
      with a critical review of literature. Discusses the
      iconography of the north rose and the ornament, including
      grisaille fragments in storage.
           Vitraux de la cathédrale de Soissons comme on les voyait
      entre 1817 et 1882, [1980], 46 pp., based largely on
      François de Guilhermy's notes (Paris, Bibliothèque natio-
      nale MS fr. 6109), is a supplement to the above.

410   COTHREN, MICHAEL WATT. "The Thirteenth and Fourteenth-Century
      Glazing of the Choir of the Cathedral of Beauvais." Ph.D.
      dissertation, Columbia University, 1980.
           Thorough examination of the iconography, styles, and
      dating of the lower and upper windows, with a critique of
      their authenticity.

411   DAGUENET, DOMINIQUE. "La chapelle du Château de Baye et ses
      vitraux." Congrès archéologique de France (Champagne,
      1977) 135 (1980):627-46.
           Places construction of this rare private chapel ca.
      1205-20; identifies seven windows, with a Tree of Jesse,
      Christ's Infancy and Passion, and the Lives of John the
      Evangelist, Mary Magdalene, and Lazarus; notes the stylis-
      tic proximity of the glass to Laon, Soissons, and St.-
      Quentin; dates the glazing ca. 1205-15/20.

412   LILLICH, MEREDITH PARSONS. "The Triforium Windows of Tours."
      Gesta 19 (1980):29-35.
           Identifies the arms of Guillaume de Binanville in the
      windows of the hemicycle; the glass was given by him ca.
      1255.

413   PERROT, FRANÇOISE, and PRESSOUYRE, LÉON. "L'église Saint-
      Alpin et ses vitraux." Congrès archéologique de France
      (Champagne, 1977) 135 (1980):307-59.
           Detailed description of the important early 16th century
      windows; Marianic and Christological subjects emphasize the
      Eucharist; donors are depicted. Publishes two 13th century
      panels not previously known.

414   *ROLLET, JEAN. Les maîtres de la lumière. Paris: Éditions
      Bordas, 1980. 301 pp., 180 color pls., 36 figs. and plans.
           Selected color photographs by the author, an amateur,
      accompany his text, which includes a checklist of sites
      with glass and a bibliography. [Annotation based on review
      by A. Granboulon, Bulletin monumental 139 (1981):202-3.]

France

Fr. 419

415 STAUDINGER, EVELYN RUTH. "Thirteenth Century Stained Glass in
Notre-Dame of Noyon." Master's thesis, Tufts University,
1980.
Reconstructs parts of the glazing program from documents
and studies the nine remaining panels from a Life of St.
Pantaleon attributed to a local atelier and dated ca.
1220-30.

416 CAVINESS, MADELINE H., and RAGUIN, VIRGINIA CHIEFFO. "Another
Dispersed Window from Soissons: A Tree of Jesse in the
Sainte-Chapelle Style." Gesta (Anniversary volume in honor
of H. Bober) 20 (1981):191-98.
Discovery of three prophets, in the Victoria and Albert
Museum, the Worcester Art Museum, and a private col-
lection, in the same style as other remnants of mid-13th
century glass in Soissons Cathedral (cf. Fr. 204, 247).

417 GRODECKI, LOUIS; PERROT, FRANÇOISE et al. Les vitraux du
Centre et des pays de la Loire. Corpus Vitrearum France,
série complémentaire: Recensement des vitraux anciens de
la France, 2. Paris: C.N.R.S., 1981, 336 pp., 16 color
pls., 287 figs., plans in text.
Presents a brief inventory of the glass in this very
rich area, including 19th century windows, as stipulated
in the new policy for the Corpus. Angers, Bourges,
Chartres, Evron, La Ferté-Bernard, Le Mans, Tours, and
Vendôme are among the sites reviewed. Selected illustrations include some little-known material. Sequel to
Fr. 402.

418 HAYWARD, JANE. "The Lost Noah Window from Poitiers." Gesta
20 (1981):129-39.
Early 13th century panel in the Metropolitan Museum,
New York, and four other now lost panels known from photographs made in 1882.

419 _____. "The Redemption Windows of the Loire Valley." In
Études d'art offertes à Louis Grodecki, by the International Center of Medieval Art and Association des Publications près les universités de Strasbourg. Paris:
Éditions Ophrys, 1981, pp. 129-44.
Iconographic study of a group of late 12th-early 13th
century east windows as they relate to the Easter liturgy.

191

420 LITTLE, CHARLES T. "Membra Disjecta: More Early Stained
Glass from Troyes Cathedral." Gesta 20 (1981):119-27.
Adds a lost Crucifixion to the known fragments of
twelfth century glass and reconstructs the Temptation, the
typological Crucifixion, and the Life of the Virgin windows. Makes a comparison with newly discovered fragments
from Vézelay. Cf. Fr. 362 and Tech. 111.

421 PAPANICOLAOU, LINDA MOREY. "The Iconography of the Genesis
Window of the Cathedral of Tours." Gesta 20 (1981):179-89.
Iconographic sources for the apocryphal cycles of the
Labors of Adam, Eve, Cain and Abel, and the Death of Cain,
represented in a choir window of ca. 1255.

422 _____. "Stained Glass from the Cathedral of Tours: The
Impact of the Sainte-Chapelle in the 1240s." Metropolitan
Museum Journal 15 (1981):53-65.
Four panels in the Cloisters are identified as Tours
glass; they include St. Louis carrying the crown of thorns
and Gauthier Cornut, Archbishop of Sens, displaying the
crown.

423 PRACHE, ANNE. "Le vitrail de la Crucifixion de Saint-Remi de
Reims." In Études d'art offertes à Louis Grodecki, by
the International Center of Medieval Art and Association
des publications près les universités de Strasbourg.
Paris: Éditions Ophrys, 1981, pp. 145-54.
The iconography of this late 12th century tribune window
discussed in the light of documents indicating its 19th
century restoration and its de-restoration by Jacques Simon
ca. 1950.

424 *GILMORE-HOUSE, GLORIA. "The Mid-Fifteenth Century Stained
Glass by André Robin in Saint-Maurice Cathedral, Angers."
Ph.D. dissertation, Columbia University, 1982.
Discusses the iconographic and stylistic sources of the
glass provided by Robin for the transepts after a fire in
1451, and their relation to the patronage of Duke René of
Angers.

425 KLINE, NAOMI REED. "The Stained Glass of the Abbey Church at
Orbais." Ph.D. dissertation, Boston University, 1982.
The extant glass in the church of St.-Pierre is consid-
ered in relation to the campaigns of building, the patronage of the Counts of Champagne, and glass at other sites.
Included are the typological crucifixion window, here dated
ca. 1200, ornamental windows and clerestory figures

resembling those of St.-Remi of Reims (ca. 1210-15), and a number of grisaille windows of ca. 1250-60.

426 RAGUIN, VIRGINIA CHIEFFO. <u>Stained Glass in Burgundy during the Thirteenth Century</u>. Princeton: University Press, 1982.

  Style and iconography of major sites, including Auxerre, St.-Julien-du-Sault, Semur-en-Auxois, and Dijon; their relation to Parisian ateliers.

427 ZAKIN, HELEN. "Cistercian Glass at La Chalade (Meuse)." In <u>Studies in Cistercian Art and Architecture</u>. Vol. 1, edited by Meredith P. Lillich. Cistercian Studies Series 66. Kalamazoo: Cistercian Publications, 1982, pp. 140-47.

  Early fourteenth-century grisaille designs with painted foliage and chimeras, compared with those of Altenberg bie Köln, and dated after 1301 on the basis of shields with the arms of Navarre, Bar and France.

Section VIII
Germany

The reader is also referred to the following entries in other sections: Gen. 31, 53, Fr. 166 (for glass in France associated with the Master E.S.), 307; It. 13, 19 (for glass in Italy that may be by German glass painters). Work by Hans Acker, Valentin Busch, Jacob Greisinger, Hans Baldung Grien, and Peter Hemmel von Andlau outside Germany may be found through the Index of Glass Painters and Designers.

1 MURR, CHRISTOPH GOTTLIEB von. "Von der Glasmalerey in Nürnberg." Journal zur Kunstgeschichte und zur allgemeinen Litteratur 15 (1787):51-59.
    Survey of technical treatises (Theophilus, etc.) and the modern literature; chronological listing of glass in Nuremberg, 13th-16th centuries, with notations of inscribed dates and, occasionally, of condition. Glass painters from the Hirsvogels to the 18th century.

2 *SCHREIBER, H. Geschichte und Beschreibung des Münsters zu Freiburg im Breisgau. Freiburg-im-Breisgau, 1820.
    Pp. 179-91 contain a description of the cathedral glass before its restoration.

3 WACKERNAGEL, WILHELM. Die deutsche Glasmalerei: Geschichtlicher Entwurf mit Belegen. Leipzig: S. Hirzel, 1855, 185 pp.
    Covers documentary evidence for pre-12th century glass programs and the texts of Suger, Theophilus, etc.; historical outline up to the 16th century.

4 *HERBERGER, THEODOR. Die ältesten Glasgemälde im Dome zu Augsburg mit der Geschichte des Dombaus in der romanischen Kunstperiode. Augsburg. Druck der J.P. Himmer'schen Buchdruckerei, 1860, 38 pp., 5 color pls.

5   MERLO, J.J. "Die Glasmalereien von 1508 und 1509 im kölner
    Dome und ihre Meister." Jahrbücher des Vereins von Alter-
    tumsfreunden im Rheinlande Bonner Jahrbücher 60 (1877):
    85-96.
        Cathedral accounts of 1504-10 mention Hermann Pentelinck,
    Jr., as glazier and also note that he was paid in 1506 for
    glass for the abbey church of the Maccabees. Relates the
    cathedral's north choir aisle glass to the style of the
    "Master of the Holy Kinship."

6   *SEPP, JOHANN NEPOMUK. "Ursprung der Glasmaler-Kunst im
    Kloster Tegernsee." In Festschrift bei Stiftung der
    Gedächtnisfenster am Erfindungsort der Glasmalerei zu
    Tegernsee. Munich: Kellerer, 1880-81. [Becksmann].

7   GROTEFEND, H. "Die Zunft der Glasmaler und Glaser in Frankfurt
    am Main." Mitteilungen des Vereins für Geschichte und
    Altertumskunde in Frankfurt a. M. 6 (1881):106-22.
        Guild records extending back to 1377 when the glass
    painters were grouped with other craftsmen (painters,
    harnessmakers, etc.); detailed accounts exist from the
    late 16th century.

8   SCHÄFER, C. "Die Glasmalerei des Mittelalters und der
    Renaissance." Zentralblatt der Bauverwaltung (1881):5 ff.
    Reprinted in Von deutscher Kunst: Gesammelte Aufsätze und
    nachgelassene Schriften (Berlin: Verlag von Wilhelm Ernst
    & Sohn, 1910), pp. 159-91.
        Outlines the history of glass painting, using Theophilus
    and examples of German glass. Includes ornament. Provides
    an index of sites with medieval glass in Germany.

9   SCHAEFER, CARL, and ROSSTEUSCHER, A. Ornamentale Glasmalereien
    des Mittelalters und der Renaissance nach Original-Aufnahmen
    in Farbendruck. Berlin: Wasmuth, 1888, 4 pp., 45 color
    pls.
        Scale drawings from rubbings of 12th-16th century orna-
    mental windows; chiefly German, but also includes Heiligen-
    kreuz and Strasbourg.

10 *RUPPERT, P. "Die Glasmalerei in Konstanz." In Konstanzer
    geschichtliche Beiträge. Vol. 2. Konstanz, 1890,
    pp. 1-8. [Becksmann].

11 DETZEL, [HEINRICH]. "Alte Glasmalereien am Bodensee und
    seiner Umgebung." Schriften des Vereins für Geschichte
    des Bodensees und seiner Ungebung 20 (1891):52-69.
        Identifies the subjects in Friedrichshafen: the
    Apostles, a prophet, and Christological and Marianic
    scenes belong to one group (ca. 1350); dates the other
    works later on the basis of observations of style and tech-
    nique. Cites glass in Eriskirch and Ravensburg. Not
    illustrated.

12 *DETZEL, HEINRICH. "Die alten Glasmalereien in der Frauen-
    kirche zu Ravensburg." Journal Archiv für christliche
    Kunst 9 (1891):74-79. [Becksmann].

13 *PRIESS, F. "Die Glasfenster der Cistercienser-Abteikirche
    Pforta." Zeitschrift für Bauwesen [Berlin] 43 (1893):
    585-88, unbound pls.

14 STIASSNY, ROBERT. "Baldung-Studien, III: Glasgemälde."
    Zeitschrift für bildenden Kunst (Kunstchronik), n.s. 6
    (1894-95):305-10, 325-27.
        Reviews those windows either documented or attributed to
    Baldung and discusses drawings related to those works. Not
    illustrated.

15 DERIX, HEINRICH. "Alte Glasmalereien des XV. Jahrhunderts im
    Dom zu Xanten." Zeitschrift für christliche Kunst 13
    (1900):173-78.
        15th century windows with donors and saints; contains
    observations made during restoration.

16 _____. "Spätgotisches Glasgemälde in der alten Sakristei des
    Domes zu Xanten." Zeitschrift für christliche Kunst 14
    (1901):289-94.
        Crucifixion window, probably dated ca. 1533-47; con-
    tains observations made during restoration.

17 *GEIGES, FRITZ. Der alte Fensterschmuck des freiburger
    Münsters. Part 1, 13. und 14. Jahrhunderts. Freiburg-im-
    Breisgau: Herder, 1901, 200 pp., 4 color pls.
        Only volume published. Cf. Ger. 58.

18 ROTH, F.W.E. "Zur Geschichte einiger Glasmalereisammlungen
    zu Köln im Anfang des 19. Jahrhunderts." Annalen des
    historischen Vereins für den Niederrhein 70 (1901):77-84.
        Collections of glass formed by Wilhelm Düssel, Christian
    Geerling, and Johann Baptist Hirn; notes regarding sale
    prices, inventories, and dispersal of the collections.

19 WOLFF, F. "Ein altes Glasfenster in der Klosterkirche zu
    Niedermünster, nach Hans Baldung's Zeichnung." Kunstge-
    werbe in Elsass-Lothringen (Strasbourg) 3 (1902-3):141-58.
        Panel with a Crucifixion related to a drawing by Baldung
    Grien.

20 *ENGEL, JULES. "Die Chorfenster der Elisabethkirche zu
    Marburg." Antiquitätenrundschau 2 (1904):86-88, 97; figs.
    on pp. 89, 99, 101 f.

21 LIELL, [Pater]. "Altromanische Glasmalerei in der Pfarrkirche
    zu Taben." Trierisches Archiv 7 (1904):29-33.
        Painstaking description of an enthroned figure which he
    dates 1056-76. No illustration found.

22 HOFMANN, FRIEDRICH H. "Das Markgrafenfenster in Sankt Sebald
    zu Nürnberg: Ein Beitrag zur Porträtkunde der fränkischen
    Hohenzollern." Hohenzollern Jahrbuch 9 (1906):67-77.
        Study of the portraiture in this window (1515); excel-
    lent photographs.

23 JOSEFSOHN, K. "Die alten Glasmalereien Soests." Zeitschrift
    Niedersachsen 12 (1906-7):277-82.
        Brief iconographic descriptions of glass in St. Mariä
    zur Wiese, St. Patrokli, and St. Pauli; illustrated with
    photographs made before restoration.

24 DERIX, HEINRICH. "Alte Glasgemälde im Dom zu Xanten."
    Zeitschrift für christliche Kunst 20 (1907):235-42.
        Observations made regarding this early 14th century
    glass in the course of its restoration.

25 HASELOFF, ARTHUR. Die Glasgemälde der Elizabethkirche in
    Marburg. Berlin: Max Spielmeyer, 1907, 21 pp., 22 pls.
    (3 color).
        Superb photographs of the 13th century glass, 1/4 and
    1/5 of its actual size. Introduction with notes on the
    reproductions (Rare).
        A summary and review of Haseloff, which questions the
    relation of the dedication of the church to St. Elizabeth
    of Thüringen (d. 1231) to the date of the choir glass
    (1250?), are contained in Stephen Beissel, "Die Glasge-
    mälde der Kirche der Hl. Elisabeth zu Marburg," Stimmen
    aus Maria-Laach: Katholische Blätter (Freiburg-im-
    Breisgau) 73 (1907):263-82.

26 *OIDTMANN, HEINRICH. Die Glasmalerei im alten Frankenlande.
    Leipzig, 1907. [Becksmann].

27 GEIGES, FRITZ. "Das St. Annen-Fenster im jetzigen Alexander-Chörlein." Freiburger Münsterblätter 4 (1908):41-81.
  Discusses the iconography, style, and authorship of a window with the Holy Family, dated 1515, in the Freiburg Minster.

28 *SCHINNERER, JOHANNES. Kirchliche Glasmalerei zur Zeit der Spätgotik und Frührenaissance in Nürnberg. 1908.
  Publication of a Ph.D. dissertation, University of Munich, 1907.

29 DIRR, PIUS. "Glasgemälde Hans Holbeins des Älteren." Münchner Jahrbuch der bildenden Kunst 4 (1909):33-45.
  The Adoration of the Magi window (ca. 1500) is compared with drawings by Holbein preserved in Basel; also discusses the condition of the window and its technique of execution.

30 OIDTMANN, HEINRICH. "Über die Glasgemälde im Kreuzgang der ehemaligen Prämonstratenserabtei Steinfeld." Trierisches Archiv 16 (1909):78-91.
  Description of the typological program (1527-56). Not illustrated.

31 _____. "Acht Scheiben kölner Kleinmalerei des XVI. Jahrhunderts." Zeitschrift für christliche Kunst 23 (1910):363-72.
  Examines a set of six roundels, dated 1532, with the story of the Prodigal Son and some other, later examples of Cologne glass painting.

32 _____. "Die romanischen Glasmalereien in der Pfarrkirche St.-Kunibert zu Köln." Zeitschrift für christliche Kunst 23 (1910):199-212.
  Examines mid-13th century glass in Cologne and documents concerning older glass. Gives a stylistic analysis of the saints' windows in St. Kunibert.

33 SCHINNERER, JOHANNES. "Das Konhofer-Fenster in der Sankt-Lorenz-Kirche zu Nürnberg." Repertorium für Kunstwissenschaft 33 (1910):155-58.
  Questions the date inscribed on the window (1452) and suggests that its style is closer to that of the Volkamer window of ca. 1487.

Ger. 34

34 FRANKL, PAUL. Beiträge zur Geschichte der süddeutschen Glas-
    malerei im 15. Jahrhundert. Strasbourg: Universitäts-
    Buchdruckerei (Heitz & Mündel), 1911, 100 pp. [References
    are made to plates but none are found in the text.]
        Based on a 1910 Munich dissertation published in an
    earlier form under the title, "Die Glasmalerei des 15.
    Jahrhunderts in Bayern und Schwaben." Parts were expanded
    for publication in 1912 (Ger. 37). Analyzes the develop-
    ment of glass painting in Swabia beginning with the late
    14th century medallion windows in the Frauenkirche,
    Munich.

35 FISCHER, JOSEF LUDWIG. "Die ältesten Glasmalereien in
    Augsburg." Zeitschrift für alte und neue Glasmalerei 1,
    no. 1 (1912):1-5.
        Dates the newly photographed prophets in the cathedral
    before 1065 based on the history of the building and com-
    parisons with Bamberg and Regensburg manuscripts. Recon-
    structs the lost window of the Virgin in SS. Ulrich and
    Afra and compares it with the Uta Codex.

36 _____. "Zur schwäbisch-tirolischen Glasmalerei in der ersten
    Hälfte des 16. Jahrhunderts." Zeitschrift für alte und
    neue Glasmalerei 1, no. 10 (1912):108-11.
        Roundels with Old Testament scenes painted by Hans
    Knoder after designs by Jörg Breu the Elder, ca. 1510.

37 FRANKL, PAUL. Die Glasmalerei des fünfzehnten Jahrhunderts in
    Bayern und Schwaben. Studien zur deutschen Kunstgeschichte,
    152. Strasbourg: Heitz & Mündel, 1912, 244 pp., 18 pls.
        Pioneering study of this "school," that includes glass
    in Ravensburg, Munich, and Ulm. Now outdated.

38 _____. "Der ulmer Glasmaler Hans Wild." Jahrbuch der könig-
    lich preussischen Kunstsammlungen 33 (1912):31-78.
        Traces the development of this glass painter's work from
    the dated windows of 1471 (Urach) and 1476 (Tübingen) and
    his "signed" work of 1479 in Ulm, through the 1480s [since
    1936 identified as Peter Hemmel von Andlau].

39 *WIENECKE, H. "Konstanzer Malereien des 14. Jahrhunderts."
    Ph.D. dissertation, Halle, 1912. [Becksmann].

40 OIDTMANN, HEINRICH. Die rheinischen Glasmalereien vom 12. bis
    zum 16. Jahrhundert. 2 vols. Preisschriften der
    Mevissen-Stiftung, 3. Vol. 1, Düsseldorf: L. Schwann,
    1912, 274 pp., 18 pls., 400 figs. Vol. 2, Düsseldorf:
    1929, 513 pp., 42 pls., 237 figs.

Still the best work on Rhenish glass. Excellent introduction on technique (based on Theophilus); sections on
Romanesque, early Gothic, etc. The first volume covers to
1400 (Boppard), the second volume the remaining two
centuries.

41 LEIDINGER, G. "Ein verschwindenes Glasgemälde vom Jahre
    1488." <u>Zeitschrift für alte und neue Glasmalerei</u> 2, no. 6
    (1913):65-66.
        Discusses a heraldic window in St. Martin's Church,
    Landshut, recorded in Viet Arnpeck's chronicle (d. 1495)
    and no longer extant.

42 PÖLLMAN, ANSGAR. "Beiträge zur Geschichte der schwäbischen
    Glasmalerei, I: Maler und Gläser." and "II: Aus den
    Nördlinger Rechnungsbüchern." <u>Zeitschrift für alte und
    neue Glasmalerei</u> 2, no. 1 (1913):1-3; 2, no. 3 (1913):
    32-34; 2, no. 4 (1913):44-47.
        Analyzes and edits a record of payments to several
    glaziers in Nördlingen, 1495-1548.

43 SCHINNERER, JOHANNES. "Wolfgang Katzenheimer von Bamberg."
    <u>Monatshefte für Kunstwissenschaft</u> 6 (1913):318-26.
        Woodblocks, panel paintings, and stained glass by this
    master, active ca. 1495-1508, include the Bamberg window at
    St. Sebald in Nuremberg and a related drawing.

44 FISCHER, JOSEF LUDWIG. <u>Handbuch der Glasmalerei</u>. Leipzig:
    K.W. Hiersemann, 1914, 318 pp., 135 pls.; 2d ed., 1937
    [identical].
        Excellent early survey of medieval and 19th century
    glass painting, no longer reliable for dates (e.g.,
    Augsburg, 11th century); the sections on technique and
    forgeries are still useful. The bibliography is good for
    19th century literature on this subject.

45 _____. "Zu den Beziehungen des Hans Baldung Grien zu der
    Glasmalerei." <u>Zeitschrift für alte und neue Glasmalerei</u>
    3, no. 5 (1914):65-66; 4, no. 6 (1915): illustration facing
    p. 66.
        Signed and dated St. Anne window (1515) in Freiburg-im-
    Breisgau, designed by Baldung Grien.

Ger. 46

46 SCHINNERER, JOHANNES. "Zur Datierung der Glasmalereien im regensburger Dom." Repertorium für Kunstwissenschaft 37 (n.s. 2) (1914):197-210.
Examines two groups of windows, comparing a cycle of three in the hemicycle of the choir with glass in the transept. Choir glass assigned a date of ca. 1320-30; the transept ca. 1360, on the basis of donors.

47 *GIESE, C. "Die Glasmalerei Mühlhausens: Ein Beitrag zur thüringisch-sächsischen Malerei der Hochgotik." Ph.D. dissertation, Halle, 1920.

48 HERTEL, BERNHARD. Die Glasgemälde des kölner Domes. Introduction by Paul Clemen. Berlin: Deutscher Kunstverlag, 1925, 9 pp., 17 pls. (3 color).
Superb photographs of some of the 13th-14th century glass.

49 ROTT, HANS. "Beiträge zur Geschichte der oberrheinisch-schwäbischen Glasmalerei: A) Konstanzer Glasmaler und Glasmalerei in der ersten Hälfte des 16. Jahrhunderts." Oberrheinische Kunst: Viertel jahresberichte der oberrheinischen Museen 1 (1925-26):21-32.
15th-16th century glass painting in Constance and its relation to Swiss centers and to Ulm, etc.; discusses the work of Christoph Bockstorfer, the monogramist C.B., Caspar Stillhart, etc.

50 BALCKE-WODARG, ELISABETH. "Die Glasgemälde der ehemaligen Kartause zu Freiburg im Breisgau vom Beginn des 16. Jahrhunderts." Oberrheinische Kunst: Viertel jahresberichte der oberrheinischen Museen 2 (1926-27):164-82.
Glass from the Carthusian church in Freiburg, sold in Cologne in 1897 and now scattered in collections, is attributed to the Ropstein atelier that also did work in the cathedral; some designs are by Hans Baldung Grien; the glass is dated ca. 1510-30.

51 ROTT, HANS. "Beiträge zur Geschichte der oberrheinisch-schwäbischen Glasmaleri: B) Konstanzer Glasmaler und Glasmalerei im 15. und 16. Jahrhundert." Oberrheinische Kunst: Vierteljahresberichte der oberrheinischen Museen 2 (1926-27):123-39.
Sequel to Ger. 49; provides a survey of 15th century works and an edition of the texts relating to 16th century painters.

52 BUCHNER, ERNST. "Studien zur mittelrheinischen Malerei und Graphik der Stätgotik und Renaissance." Münchner Jahrbuch der bildenden Kunst, n.s. 4 (1927):229-325.
Sections dealing with the Master W.B. and the Master of the Drachschen Offizin include glass paintings in their oeuvres (on the basis of comparisons with panel paintings and prints); late 15th century glass in Hanau is attributed to the Master W.B.

53 BRÜCKNER, MARGARETE, and HAETGE, ERNST. "Der Zyklus der far- bigen Glasfenster im Domchor." In Die Stadt Erfurt: Dom, Severikirche, Peterkloster, Zitadelle. Die Kunstdenkmale der Provinz Sachsen, vol. 1, edited by Karl Becker, M. Brückner, E. Haetge, and Lisa Schürenberg. Burg: August Hopfer, 1929, pp. 145-224.
Description of twelve windows, dated ca. 1370-1420, with a depiction of an Old Testament cycle on the south side and Christological and hagiographical subjects on the north. Some of the work by a shop from Cologne. Illustrated.

54 NEUNDÖRFER, L. Die Glasgemälde der Stadtkirche zu Friedberg, ein Beitrag zur Geschichte der Kunst am Mittelrhein im 14. und 15. Jahrhundert. Giessen, 1929, 18 pp., 1 fig. [Ab- stract of a Ph.D. dissertation, Giessen, 1923].
Discusses problems of restoration and reconstructs three windows in the hemicycle of the choir, dated ca. 1475-80, with saints under canopies. Cites stylistic affinities with windows in Hanau and with the work of Master Conrad and 'Hans Wild' [Peter Hemmel].

55 EICHLER, HANS. "Die Glasmalereien des altenberger Westfen- sters und ihr Kreis." Zeitschrift des bergischen Ge- schichtsvereins 59 (1930):5-29.
Late 14th century developments and comparisons with Soest, St. Pauli, etc. Illustrated with four photographs.

56 HAETGE, ERNST. "Die ältesten Glasfenster der Provinz Sachsen in der Barfüsserkirche zu Erfurt." Sachsen und Anhalt 6 (1930):207-26.
Reports the first detailed study of the remains of the three east windows and examines their condition, iconog- raphy, style, and dating (ca. 1240).

57 DREHMANN, L. "Die Glasmalereien im St. Patrokli-Dom." Heimatkalender des Kreises Soest 10 (1931):75-78.
History of the 13th century glass; excerpts from early writers; brief description.

58 GEIGES, FRITZ. Der mittelalterliche Fensterschmuck des frei-
    burger Münsters: Seine Geschichte, die Ursachen seines
    Zerfalles und die Massnahmen zu seiner Wiederherstellung,
    zugleich ein Beitrag zur Geschichte des Baues selbst.
    Freiburg-im-Breisgau: Breisgau Verein, [1931], 391 pp.,
    902 figs. [Also published in Schau-ins-Land 56-58
    (1931-33)].
        The standard work; lavishly illustrated with pre- and
    post-restoration photographs and studies of painting
    technique.

59 *KAUTZSCH, MARTIN. Anfänge der Glasmalerei in Nürnberg und
    Franken, 1240-1450. Ph.D. dissertation Halle-Wittenberg,
    Halle, 1931, 87 pp.

60 FRANKL, PAUL. Deutsche Glasmalerei: Der Meister des Specu-
    lumfensters von 1480 in der münchner Frauenkirche. Denk-
    mäler deutscher Kunst. Berlin: Deutscher Verein für
    Kunstwissenschaft, 1932, 73 pp., 97 pls., 2 color illus.
        Description of the surviving panels and a reconstruc-
    tion of the window.

61 *GALLINER, ARTHUR. Glasgemälde des Mittelalters aus Wimpfen.
    Denkmäler deutscher Kunst. Freiburg-im-Breisgau: Urban-
    verlag, 1932, 98 pp.

62 *OFFERMANN, RUDOLF. "Die Entwicklung des gotischen Fensters
    am Mittelrhein im 13. und 14. Jahrhundert." Ph.D. disser-
    tation, Wiesbaden, 1932.

63 FALKE, OTTO v. "Deutsche Rundscheiben." Pantheon 11 (1933):
    19-24.
        Roundels in the Deutsches Museum, Berlin, attributed to
    "Hans Wild" of Ulm (after 1480), and to the Master of St.
    Severin (ca. 1505), Anton Woensam (ca. 1540), and Bertel
    Bruyn (ca. 1530) of Cologne. Also includes Nuremberg works
    of ca. 1530. Well illustrated. Attributions outdated.

64 JUNGJOHANN, ADOLF. "Glasmalereien aus der ingelheimer Pfalz
    Barbarossas?" Zeitschrift des deutschen Vereins für Kunst-
    wissenschaft 1[=2] (1935):253-59.
        Magdalen at the Feet of Christ and Christ Clearing the
    Temple in the Berlin Museum [destroyed 1945] are compared
    with the Raising of Lazarus and the Betrayal in Wiesbaden;
    all are probably from Ingelheim [ca. 1170].

65 FISCHER, JOSEPH LUDWIG. "Der neuentdeckte Glasmaler Peter von
    Andlau, Strassburg, bisher Hans Wild von Ulm genannt, und
    sein Werk in der Tübinger Stiftskirche." Pantheon 17
    (1936):295-99.
        Discovery of a document recording payments to Peter
    Hemmel von Andlau, in the Oberehnheim archives. He re-
    places "Hans Wild" as author of a large group of windows;
    his shop was based in Strasbourg.

66 FRANKL, PAUL. Der Meister des Astalerfensters von 1392 in der
    münchner Frauenkirche. Deutscher Verein für Kunstwissen-
    schaft. Berlin: Walter de Gruyter, 1936, 64 pp., 59 figs.,
    20 unbound pls.
        Description and documentation of this important glass.

67 _____. "Die Herkunft der Helenascheiben im Genfer Museum."
    Genava 14 (1936):107-12.
        Two panels with St. Helena Carrying the Cross now in the
    Geneva Museum had been removed from a window (1420) in the
    church of Eriskirch and replaced by copies. This atelier
    also worked in Ravensburg.

68 HAUG, HANS. "Notes sur Pierre d'Andlau, peintre verrier à
    Strasbourg, et son atelier." Archives alsaciennes 15
    (1936):79-123.
        Biography and attributions of works to this 15th century
    Strasbourg glazier (formerly known as Hans Wild); discusses
    his influence on Grünewald.

69 ROTT, HANS. Quellen und Forschungen zur südwestdeutschen und
    schweizerischen Kunstgeschichte im XV. und XVI. Jahrhundert
    (Baden, Pfalz, Elsass). Stuttgart: Strecker & Schröder,
    1936, 366 pp.
        Excerpts from archival materials that concern glass
    painters and painters.

70 HEID, H. "Die Glasgemälde der Wallfahrtskirche zu Lauten-
    bach." Die Ortenau 24 (1937):89-107.
        Window of about 1482, outdated attribution to "Hans
    Wild."

71 KIPPENBERGER, ALBRECHT. "Grauteppichfenster der Elisabeth-
    kirche zu Marburg und des Zisterzienserklosters Haina."
    In Festschrift Richard Hamann. Burg: August Hopfer, 1939,
    pp. 40-45.
        Mid-13th century ornamental windows, now in the Univer-
    sity Museum, are compared with Cistercian designs.

Ger. 72

72 *ELSEN, ALOIS. <u>Der Dom zu Regensburg: Die Bildfenster</u>. Denkmäler deutscher Kunst. Berlin: Deutscher Verein für Kunstwissenschaft, 1940, 158 pp., 96 pls. (1 color).
Discusses the late 12th-15th century windows of the
cathedral and connections between stained glass and painting in general, notably in the 14th century.

73 LEHMANN, HANS. "Zur Geschichte der oberrheinischen Glasmalerei
im 16. Jahrhundert." <u>Zeitschrift für schweizerische
Archäologie und Kunstgeschichte</u> 2 (1940):30-52.
Attributes heraldic glass of 1532-33 in the town hall of
Rheinfelden to Balthasar Federlin of Constance; discusses
the work of Hans Gitschmann of Freiburg-im-Breisgau.

74 *KURTHEN, J. <u>Zur Kunst der steinfelder Kreuzgangfenster: Ein
Werkstattbesuch bei ihrem Meister Gerhard Remisch</u>. Eus-
kirchen: Volksblatt Verlag, 1941, 52 pp.
Premonstratensian cloister, glazed 1517-38.

75 RADEMACHER-CHORUS, HILDEGARD. "Zwei unbekannte Kabinetscheiben
aus dem Kreis des Hausbuchmeisters." <u>Pantheon</u> 27 (1941):
13-18.
Two secular medallions in the Landsmuseum, Bonn, since
1939 are identified as from Burg Bürresheim and dated by
heraldry to 1476-1500. They contain motifs borrowed from
the Housebook Master.

76 WINKLER, FRIEDRICH. "Nürnberger Vierpass-Scheiben und ihre
Entwerfer." <u>Pantheon</u> 28 (1941):243-49.
Examines panels of glass ca. 1500, in the form of
quatrefoils set in circles, and related drawings by Hans
von Kulmbach and Hans L. Schäufelein.

77 *SALMEN, GERTRUD. "Die spätromanische Glasmalerei Westfalens."
Ph.D. dissertation, Münster, 1942.

78 WENTZEL, HANS. "Die uracher Glasmalereien des Peter von
Andlau aus Strassburg." <u>Pantheon</u> 30 (1942):187-91.
A window with three lights, inscribed 1477, now in the
parish church but originally in the Bubenhofen Chapel of
the abbey church of St. Amandus, is a precious example of
the personal style of Peter Hemmel.

79 *SIMON, K. "Beiträge zur Geschichte der frankfurter Glasmalerei im 15. und 16. Jahrhundert." <u>Die graphischen
Künste</u>, n.s. 7 (1942-43):19-40. [Becksmann].

80   BOECKLER, ALBERT. "Die romanischen Fenster des augsburger
     Domes und die Stilwende vom 11. zum 12. Jahrhundert." Zeit-
     schrift des deutschen Vereins für Kunstwissenschaft 10
     (1943):153-82.
         Supports a 12th century date (ca. 1120-40) on the basis
     of comparisons with manuscripts, especially the Hirsau
     Passional in Stuttgart. Bibliography.

81   RACKHAM, BERNARD. "The Mariawald-Ashridge Glass." Burlington
     Magazine 85 (1944):266-73.
         Examples of stained glass from the Cistercian abbey of
     Mariawald in the chapel at Ashridge [and now preserved in
     the Victoria and Albert Museum, London] are identified as
     belonging to two early 16th century series and as differing
     in style from the panels of the abbey church of Steinfeld
     (1527-42).

82   *PREYSS, D. "Die Florentiuskirche zu Niederhaslach im
     Elsass." Ph.D. dissertation, Munich, 1945.

83   RACKHAM, BERNARD. "The Ashridge Stained Glass." Journal of
     the British Archaeological Association 10 (1945-47):1-22.
         Identification of 16th century glass originally executed
     for the abbey churches at Steinfeld and Mariawald and for a
     third unknown site; discusses the diversity of styles in
     the lower Rhineland. Cf. Ger. 81.

84   WENTZEL, HANS. "Die deutsche Glasmalerei von historischem
     Wert." Die Kunstpflege: Beiträge zur Geschichte und
     Pflege deutscher Architektur und Kunst (Festschrift Paul
     Clemen, edited by Georg Lill) 1 (1948):67-78.
         Notes on wartime destruction of 14th-15th century glass
     from the Marienkirche, Lübeck, and the Dominican church in
     Burg, and of churches whose glass had been safely stored.

85   WITZLEBEN, ELIZABETH SCHÜRER von. "Die augsburger Propheten."
     Kunstwerk 2, no. 10 (1948):11-14.
         Summarizes controversy over dating these works to ca.
     1065 or to the 12th century. Agrees with their association
     with the 12th century Hirsau manuscripts.

86   WENTZEL, HANS. "Das Bibelfenster der Zollern aus dem Kloster
     Stetten." Heilige Kunst (1949):18-30; and also *Jahrbuch
     des Kunstvereins der Diözese Rottenburg (Stuttgart) (1949):
     15 ff.
         Reconstruction of a typological Life of Christ origi-
     nally in three lights in the choir of the Dominican church
     in Stetten (ca. 1290) from panels in collections.

Ger. 87

87 _____. "Die westfälische Glasmalerei des Mittelalters:
Abriss der Forschungsaufgabe." Westfalen 27 (1949):215-20.
Major sites for and chronology of glass in Westfalia,
12th-16th centuries, including Legden, Soest, and Herford.
State of the question examined.

88 WITZLEBEN, ELISABETH SCHÜRER von. Die Glasfenster des kölner
Domes. Aschaffenburg. P. Pattlock, [1949], 49 pp.,
32 pls. (some color).
Brief guide to the 13th-16th century glass, with notes
on restoration, etc.

89 WENTZEL, HANS. "Die Katharinenscheibe aus Schwäbisch Hall auf
Schloss Lichtenstein." Jahrbuch Württembergisch-Franken
24-25 (1949-50):186-91.
The Martyrdom of St. Catherine (14th century) from her
church in Hall, now in a private collection.

90 BAUCH, KURT. "Ein oberrheinischer Glasmaler." In Form und
Inhalt: Kunstgeschichtliche Studien, Otto Schmitt zum
60. Gerburtstag. Stuttgart: W. Kohlhammer Verlag, 1950,
pp. 217-24.
Attribution of a panel in the Darmstadt Museum to
Valentin Busch through comparison with his (later) works
of ca. 1520 in Metz.

91 GERKE, FRIEDRICH. "Das lorscher Glasfenster." In Beiträge
zur Kunst des Mittelalters: Vorträge der ersten deutschen
Kunsthistorikertagung auf Schloss Brühl, 1948. Berlin:
Mann Verlag, 1950, pp. 186-92.
No archeological evidence is available for dating this
excavated head. Comparisons with early 12th century glass
(Augsburg, Neuweiler) and with the 11th century Wissembourg
head suggest it is Carolingian. Its style is based on
Hiberno-Saxon and Coptic prototypes.

92 WENTZEL, HANS. "Passionsfenster und Ornamentscheiben aus
Stetten." Heilige Kunst (1950):9-20.
Five panels from a Passion window in the Dominican
church at Stetten were taken to Burg Hohenzollern in 1823;
dated ca. 1290 and assigned to the same artist who did the
nave glass at Niederhaslach.

93 *ERFFA, HANS MARTIN von. "Die Verwendung des Glasfensters im
frühen deutschen Kirchenbau." Ph.D. dissertation, Munich,
1951.
Some sources give 1953.

94 PIEPER, PAUL. "Das Fenster von Legden." Westfalen 29 (1951):
       172-89.
           Description and iconographic analysis of this Tree of
       Jesse, which is supplemented with prophets; patriarchs,
       including Adam and Eve, Balaam, and the Queen of Sheba; and
       inscriptions. Compared with the Hildesheim ceiling and
       glass in St. Kunibert, Cologne and dated ca. 1230-40.

95 WENTZEL, HANS. "Das Ratsfenster von 1480 im Chor des ulmer
       Münsters und Meister Peter Hemmel von Andlau (mit Werk-
       katalog)." Ulm und Oberschwaben 32 (1951):9-46, pls. 1-24.
           Reevaluation of Frankl's documentary and stylistic evi-
       dence for attributions to this Master includes a separation
       of hands and the elimination of some works, notably Alt-
       Thann and Lautenbach, from his oeuvre.

96 _____. "Die Glasmalerei der Zisterzienser in Deutschland."
       Die Klosterbaukunst: Arbeitsbericht der deutsch-
       französischen Kunsthistoriker-Tagung, 1951. Mainz, 1951,
       [6 pp.] [Special issue of the Bulletin des relations
       artistiques France-Allemagne].
           Cistercian glass after the 1134 proscription of figural
       work; influence of grisaille designs outside the order.

97 _____. Meisterwerke der Glasmalerei. Denkmäler deutscher
       Kunst. Berlin: Deutscher Verein für Kunstwissenschaft,
       1951, 115 pp., 308 figs.; 2d enlarged ed., 1954, 121 pp.,
       208 figs.
           The best general treatment of German glass in the 12th-
       16th centuries, well illustrated and annotated.
           Review by Eva [Frodl-] Kraft, Kunstchronik 5 (1952):
       276-81 raises several problems regarding the relation of
       German to French glass.

98 SCHEUFFELEN, GERTRUD MARIA. "Die Glasfenster der Kirche St.
       Kunibert in Köln." Ph.D. dissertation, Munich, 1951.
       [Becksmann: "1952"].

99 [THELEN], LISELOTTE MOSCH. "Studien zu den Glasmalereien im
       erfurter Domchor." Ph.D. dissertation, Munich, 1952.

100 WILLE, C. "Die figürlichen Glasmalereien des 14. Jahrhunderts
       aus dem hessischen Raum." Nassauische Annalen 64 (1953):
       115-17.
           Résumé of an unpublished Ph.D. dissertation, Mainz,
       1952: three groups of windows found, one centered around
       St. Elizabeth in Marburg (ca. 1300), a second around

Ger. 101

Altenberg-an-der-Lahn (ca. 1320), and a third comprised of
several cycles dated 1350-70 (Limburg-an-der-Lahn,
Arnstein, etc.).

101   ECKERT, KARL. St. Bernard von Clairvaux: Glasmalereien aus
dem Kreuzgang von Altenberg bei Köln. Wuppertal:
Abendland-Verlag, 1953, 191 pp., 46 figs.
Series of 16th century panels from the cloister of
Altenberg (near Cologne) with the Life of St. Bernard, some
traced to collections, some lost. Discusses former attri-
butions. [Pieces thought to be in America are in the
Metropolitan Museum, New York].

102   *HERMANS, CLAUS. "Die Glasgemälde des freiburger Münsterchores
und ihr Meister Hans von Ropstein." Ph.D. dissertation,
Freiburg-im-Breisgau, 1953.

103   MOLLENHAUER, MAJA. "Die Glasewerter des St. Lukas-Büssenbuches
im Lüneburger Museum." Lüneburger Blätter 5 (1954):62-70.
Glass painters named in the guild records of St. Luke's,
1502-61.

104   SCHNEIDER, ARTHUR von. "Der Fensterschmuck des Rittersaales
auf Ebersteinschloss." Zeitschrift für die Geschichte des
Oberrheins 102 (1954):780-90; 103 (1955):282-90.
Late 15th century glass from Dühren and glass dated 1518
from Ottersweier, now in Eberstein. The former close to
Peter Hemmel's style, the latter based on Baldung Grien.

105   REINARTZ, NIKOLA. "Die alten Glasgemälde im Kreuzgang der
Prämonstratenserabtei"; and KURTHEN, J., and KURTHEN, W.
"Der Kreuzgang der Abtei Steinfeld und sein ehemaliger
Bildfensterschmuck." In Die Glasmalereien aus dem stein-
felder Kreuzgang. Kunstgabe des Vereins für christliche
Kunst im Erzbistum Köln und Bistum Aachen für das Jahr
1955, edited by Wilhelm Neuss. München-Gladbach:
B. Kühlen, 1955, 282 pp., 42 pls., figs. in text.
Glass sold in 1802 to an English collection (Ashridge
Park) and in 1906 to the Victoria and Albert Museum. Pro-
gram reconstructed from MSS. Identification of the donors
furnishes a date of ca. 1526-1550s for the cloister windows.
Includes a catalog.

106   *MATTHES, GISELA. "Die Farbenfenster von Havelberg--St. Marien:
Studien zur mittelalterlichen Glasmalerei." Thesis
(Diplomarbeit), Leipzig, 1955.

107 *RAGALLER, HEINRICH. "Die Glasgemälde des 15. und 16. Jahr-
     hundert in Mainfranken." Ph.D. dissertation, Würzburg,
     1955.
         Sometimes cited as Tübingen.

108 *FRANKL, PAUL. "Der Glasmaler Jakob Kistenfiger." Münchner
     Jahrbuch der bildenden Kunst, 3d ser. 7 (1956):111-19.
         South German glass painter; chronological list of his
     work, 1496-1524.

109 _____. Peter Hemmel, Glasmaler von Andlau. Denkmäler
     deutscher Kunst. Berlin: Deutsche Verein für Kunstwissen-
     schaft, 1956, 142 pp., 229 figs.
         Basic monograph on this glass painter from Strasbourg;
     examines documentation, attributions, style, and the prob-
     lem of collaborative work. (Cf. also Ger. 142).
         Review by Hans Wentzel, Kunstchronik 11 (1958):100-110,
     raises important questions about the stylistic "versatil-
     ity" of this painter: how much is due to others in the
     shop; did he do designs, or paint, or both?
         Paul Frankl, "Zu Paul Frankl: Peter Hemmel, Glasmaler
     von Andlau," Kunstchronik 14 (1961):281-86, responds in
     detail to several points in Wentzel's review.

110 *FRENZEL, GOTTFRIED. "Nürnberger Glasmalerei der Parlerzeit."
     Ph.D. dissertation, Erlangen, 1956.

111 *HOLM-HAMMER, EDITH. "Die Glasgemälde im Liebfrauenmünster zu
     Ingolstadt." Ph.D. dissertation, Mainz, 1956. Published
     in part in Sammelblatt der historischen Vereins Ingolstadt
     67 (1958):5-71.

112 LANDOLT, ELISABETH [née Wegener]. "Die Glasmalerei in Soest
     während der ersten Hälfte des 14. Jahrhunderts." Soester
     Zeitschrift: Zeitschrift des Vereins für die Geschichte
     von Soest und der Börde 69 (1956):29-54.
         Inventory of glass in the Paulikirche, Petrikirche, and
     Wiesenkirche. Based on a dissertation (Heidelberg, 1953).

113 KNAPPE, KARL-ADOLF. "Das Löffelholz-Fenster in St. Lorenz in
     Nürnberg und Hans Baldung." Zeitschrift für Kunstwissen-
     schaft 12 (1958):163-78.
         This window's design attributed to Baldung on the basis
     of comparison with panel paintings and drawings and dated
     ca. 1506.

Ger. 114

114   MERTEN, HEINZ. "Zu den alten Glasgemälden der münchner
      Frauenkirche." Das Münster 11 (1958):16.
      Installation of the old glass in the rebuilt church.

115   RENTSCH, DIETRICH. Glasmalerei des frühen vierzehnten Jahr-
      hunderts in Ost-Mitteldeutschland. Mitteldeutsche For-
      schungen, 10. Cologne and Graz: Böhlau, 1958, 176 pp.,
      147 figs.
      Inventory and critical analysis of windows in Arnstadt,
      Brandenburg, Erfurt, Magdeburg, etc. (Ph.D. dissertation,
      Freiburg, 1955). See also Ger. 124.

116   STRIEDER, PETER. "Eine Scheibe mit dem Bildnis Lorenz
      Tuchers." Zeitschrift für Kunstgeschichte 21 (1958):
      175-82.
      Portrait (dated 1487) of Lorenz Tucher, canon of St.
      Lorenz in Nuremberg, attributed to Dürer when he was in
      Wolgemut's workshop. Cf. Ger. 188.

117   WENTZEL, HANS. Die Glasmalereien in Schwaben von 1250-1350.
      Corpus Vitrearum Medii Aevi: Bundesrepublik Deutschland,
      vol. 1. Berlin: Deutscher Verein für Kunstwissenschaft,
      1958, 280 pp., 12 color pls., 646 figs.
      Complete inventory of glass before 1480 in Swabia, in-
      cluding the important 13th-14th century collections of
      Esslingen, Heiligkreuztal, Stetten, and Wimpfen-im-Tal.
      Bibliography, indexes of iconography and of artists.
      Lacks restoration charts.

118   _____. "Eine deutsche Glasmalerei-Zeichnung des 14. Jahr-
      hunderts." Zeitschrift für Kunstwissenschaft 12 (1958):
      131-40.
      Drawings on the reverse of a 1355 document from the
      abbey of Heiligenkreuz near Meissen: a window armature, a
      Christ Crucified, and two saints in quatrefoils. Compari-
      son with manuscripts from Meissen confirms that they are
      projects for glass, ca. 1355-60.

119   BEHLING, LOTTLISA. "Eine Hausbuchmeisterscheibe im kölner
      Schnütgen-Museum." In Festschrift Friedrich Winkler.
      Berlin: Verlag Gebr. Mann, 1959, pp. 141-48.
      Attribution of a late 15th century roundel with John the
      Baptist to the Housebook Master, whom she identifies as
      Erhard Rewich; the latter is documented as painting glass
      in Amorbach.

120 LANDOLDT-WEGENER, ELISABETH. Die Glasmalereien im Hauptchor der soester Wiesenkirche. Sonderheft der Zeitschrift "Westfalen," 13. Münster Westfalen: Aschendorffsche Verlagsbuchhandlung, 1959, 96 pp., 91 figs.
Cycle of prophets, apostles, and saints, with Christ and the Virgin, dated 1345-57 on the basis of the donors. Restorations, program, styles, and the church's relation to St. Peter and St. Paul in Soest and to St. Pancrator (Pankratiuskirche) in Mark (glass and wall paintings) discussed. Includes catalog and bibliography.
Review by Hans Wentzel, Westfalen 38 (1960):119-34, raises important questions about repainting, restorations, and copies.

121 RAGALLER, HEINRICH. "Die drei zerstörten Pilgerscheiben des Berliner Kunstgewerbe Museums." Berliner Museen, n.s. 9 (1959):33-41.
Three panels from a Life of St. Sebald, formerly in the Berlin collection but destroyed in the war, must have come from a window in Iphofen and are dated ca. 1425-30.

122 _____. "Würtzburg--ein Glasmalerei-Zentrum von ca. 1390-1440?" Mainfränkisches Jahrbuch für Geschichte und Kunst 11 (1959):92-109.
15th century glass in Iphofen and Münnerstädt from the same workshop; documentary evidence for glass painters and glaziers in Würzburg, with a list of names; connections with Nuremberg.

123 RENTSCH, DIETRICH. "Über Erhaltungszustand und Technik' der Sakristeifenster von St. Gereon in Köln." Jahrbuch der rheinischen Denkmalpflege 22 (1959):71-86.
Christological cycle, saints, and ornament in situ in a building of ca. 1315; notes on condition, etc. Very well illustrated, with some restoration charts.

124 _____. "Zur Rekonstruktion des 'Jungfrauenfensters' im Ostchor des naumburger Doms." Kunstchronik 12 (1959): 130-31.
Correction made to the schema presented in his book (Ger. 115).

125 WEGNER, WOLFGANG. "Die Scheibenrisse für die Familie Hoechstetter von Jörg Breu dem älteren und deren Nachfolge." Zeitschrift für Kunstgeschichte 22 (1959):17-36.
Drawings for stained glass roundels with the Labors of the Months (now in the Augsburg Museum) made by Jörg Breu the Elder ca. 1520-25; cites related paintings.

126   WENTZEL, HANS. "Zur Bestandsaufnahme der romanischen Chor-
      fenster von St. Patroklus in Soest." Westfalen 37 (1959):
      92-103.
            Three Christological windows of the choir very heavily
      restored in 1878; other fragments are in the chapter house.
      All should be dated before the wall paintings of 1166. Cf.
      Korn, Ger. 163.

127   _____. "Zur Diskussion um die Farbverglasung des Domes zu
      Speyer." Kunstchronik 12 (1959):331-35.
            1531 description by Theodor Reysmann of the lost glass
      of Speyer; speculates that it was at least as early as the
      12th century from the subjects represented (typological?),
      the use of inscriptions, and the colors described.

128   WITZLEBEN, ELISABETH SCHÜRER von. "Ein mittelrheinischer
      Glasmaler des 15. Jahrhunderts." Das Münster 12 (1959):
      415-18.
            Panels of ca. 1450-60 now in collections, identified as
      by a distinctive middle Rhenish master. English summary.

129   THIEM, GUNTHER, and BEUTLER, CHRISTIAN. Hans Holbein d. Ä.:
      Die spätgotische Altar- und Glasmalerei. Abhandlungen zur
      Geschichte der Stadt Augsburg, Schriftenreihe des Stadt-
      archivs Augsburg, 13. Augsburg: H. Rösler, 1960, 250 pp.,
      4 color pls., 54 figs.
            Second part, by Thiem, deals with the designs for glass
      and the workshop productions of ca. 1500 in Augsburg,
      Schwaz, Meran, Eichstätt, Straubing, and Landsberg-am-Lech.
      Based on "Holbein der Ältere und die augsburger Glasmalerei
      um 1500." Ph.D. dissertation, Freiburg-im-Breisgau, 1952.

130   FRENZEL, GOTTFRIED. "Veit Hirschvogel: Eine nürnberger
      Glasmalerwerkstatt der Dürerzeit." Zeitschrift für Kunst-
      geschichte 23 (1960):193-210.
            Distinction between styles practiced by the members of
      the Hirsvogel family, ca. 1460-1550. Attributions to Hans
      (1514), Veit (1517), and Augustin (1521-23). Relation of
      their work to designs by Hans von Kulmbach, Dürer, and
      H.S. Beham.

131   WENTZEL, HANS. "Fragmente aus den tübinger Farbfenstern im
      Museum zu Wiesbaden." Nachschrifttenblatt der Denkmal-
      pflege in Baden-Württemberg 3 (1960-61):10-15.
            Pieces eliminated by Friedrich Pfort in his restoration
      of 1847-49 and later scattered in collections include heads
      attributed to Peter Hemmel, 1476-80. These are in the
      Städtische Museum Nassauischer Altertümer in Wiesbaden.

132   BLEIBAUM, FRIEDRICH. "Klosterkirche von Haina, Raum, und
      Farbe." <u>Hessische Heimat</u> 11, no. 5 (1961):13-19.
         General description of 13th century ornamental windows
      in this Cistercian church. Well illustrated.

133   FRENZEL, GOTTFRIED. "Entwurf und Ausführung in der nürnberger
      Glasmalerei der Dürerzeit." <u>Zeitschrift für Kunstwissen-</u>
      <u>schaft</u> 15 (1961):31-59.
         Important study of the use of various kinds of drawings
      by glass painters around 1500, especially by the Hirsvogel
      atelier in their execution of designs by Dürer and von
      Kulmbach.

134   _____. "Zur Diskussion um die Farbverglasung des Domes zu
      Speyer." <u>Kunstchronik</u> 14 (1961):8-10.
         Fragments found at Speyer in 1960 confirm a 12th century
      date, probably after the fire of 1159, as proposed by
      Wentzel (Ger. 127).

135   GOERN, HERMANN. <u>Die gotischen Bildfenster im Dom zu Erfurt</u>.
      [Dresden]: Verlag der Kunst, 1961, 212 pp., 128 pls.
      (37 color).
         Cathedral glazed ca. 1370-1420; cites its relation to
      earlier windows in Erfurt; description, without notes, and
      scant bibliography. Now replaced by the Corpus (Ger. 214).

136   HEYE, EVA. "Werke der mittelalterlichen Glasmalerei in Hall."
      <u>Württembergisch Franken</u> 45 (1961):3-16.
         A Psychomachia and other subjects in 14th century glass
      in the church of St. Catherine.

137   KNAPPE, KARL ADOLF. <u>Albrecht Dürer und das bamberger Fenster</u>
      <u>in St. Sebald in Nürnberg</u>. Erlanger Beiträge zur Sprach
      und Kunstwissenschaft, 9. Nuremberg: Hans Carl, 1961,
      140 pp., 71 figs.
         Study of the surviving glass of ca. 1480-1510 in
      Nuremberg and of documented glass painters. The drawings
      for the Bamberg window are attributed to Dürer, while the
      execution may be that of the Hirsvogel atelier. Cf. Ger.
      43.

138   _____. "Baldung als Entwerfer der Glasgemälde in Grossgründ-
      lach." <u>Zeitschrift für Kunstwissenschaft</u> 15 (1961):60-80.
         Life of the Virgin and a Temptation of Christ illus-
      trated in five panels, one of which is dated 1505; these are
      compared with drawings of Baldung Grien, to whom the de-
      signs are attributed.

Ger. 139

139   MINOTT, CHARLES I. "A Group of Stained Glass Roundels at the
      Cloisters." <u>Art Bulletin</u> 43 (1961):237-39.
           Eight late 15th century roundels with Christological
      scenes, closely related to prints by the Master E.S., are
      perhaps from Strasbourg.

140   WENTZEL, HANS. "Die Farbfenster des 13. Jahrhunderts in der
      Stiftskirche zu Bücken an der Weser." <u>Niederdeutsche Bei-
      träge zur Kunstgeschichte</u> 1 (1961):57-72; 2 (1962):131-51;
      3 (1963):195-214.
           Examines the condition, iconography (the Passion, the
      Lives of St. Maternianus of Reims and St. Nicholas), style,
      and date (second third of the 13th century) of the three
      windows in the choir.

141   FRANKL, PAUL. "Die Italienreise des Glasmalers Hans Acker."
      <u>Wallraf-Richartz-Jahrbuch</u> 24 (1962):213-26.
           Attributes the glass in Besser Chapel in Ulm to Hans
      Acker, not Lukas Moser; dates it after 1429 on the basis
      of della Quercia's work in Bologna, which he claims is the
      source for the Explusion; also cites other Italian sources.

142   _____. "Nachträge zu den Glasmalereien von Peter Hemmel."
      <u>Zeitschrift für Kunstwissenschaft</u> 16 (1962):201-22.
           Corrects some of the dates and attributions he proposed
      in 1956 (Ger. 109); the Volkamer window in St. Lorenz,
      Nuremberg, is dated ca. 1480 on the basis of Lixheim, etc.

143   FRENZEL, GOTTFRIED. "Kaiserliche Fensterstiftungen des vier-
      zehnten Jahrhundert in Nürnberg." <u>Nürnberger Mitteilungen</u>
      51 (1962):1-17.
           Discusses fragments of glass from the second half of the
      14th century in the Churches of Our Lady, St. Lorenz, and
      St. Sebald; and drawings of lost glass of the same period.

144   KNAPPE, KARL-ADOLF. "Eine nürnberger Scheibe der Dürerzeit in
      London." <u>Pantheon</u> 20 (1962):355-62.
           Last supper, from a cartoon by Baldung Grien, made for
      the Augustinian church in Nuremberg ca. 1504.

145   SEIFERT, H. <u>Alte und neue Fenster im ulmer Münster</u>.
      Königstein-in-Taunus: Karl Robert Langewiesche, Nachfolger
      Hans Köster, 1962, 8 pp., 60 pls. (some color).
           Very slight but useful guide to medieval and modern
      glass.

146 JANSEN, ELMAR. <u>Kleine Geschichte der deutschen Glasmalerei,</u>
<u>von den Anfängen bis zum 17. Jahrhundert</u>. Dresden: Verlag
der Kunst, 1963, 111 pp., 38 figs. (7 color).
Introduction to the field; well-chosen illustrations;
brief guide to the bibliography.

147 MÜLLER, BRUNO. "Ein Scheibenzyklus Hans Schäufeleins." <u>Zeit-</u>
<u>schrift des deutschen vereins für Kunstwissenschaft</u> 17
(1963):89-98.
Discusses five quatrefoil panels (dated 1504-10) with
secular and religious themes, attributed to Hans Schäufelein, and related drawings.

148 *OETTINGER, K., and KNAPPE, KARL ADOLF. <u>Hans Baldung Grien</u>
<u>und Albrecht Dürer in Nürnberg</u>. Nuremberg, 1963.
[Becksmann].

149 ANZELEWSKY, FEDJA. "Peter Hemmel und der Meister der Ge-
wandstudien." <u>Zeitschrift des deutschen Vereins für Kunst-</u>
<u>wissenschaft</u> 18 (1964):43-53.
A group of drawings of ca. 1460-90 associated with the
circle of Peter Hemmel von Andlau; some are by the Master
of the Drapery Studies.

150 HEYE, EVA. "Alte Glasmalereien aus der Kilianskirche zu
Heilbronn." <u>Nachrichtenblatt der Denkmalpflege in Baden-</u>
<u>Württemberg</u> 7 (1964):7-52.
Saints, donors, shields, and other fragments, documented
to 1487 and reproduced for the first time.

151 [ANZELEWSKY, FEDJA.] <u>Dürer and his Time: An Exhibition from</u>
<u>the Collection of the Print Room, State Museum, Berlin</u>.
Washington, D.C.: Smithsonian Institution, 1965.
Drawings for stained glass by Hans von Kulmbach, Hans
Holbein the Elder, and Sebald Beham (p. 15, nos. 71, 72,
78, 110).

152 FRENZEL, GOTTFRIED, and FRENZEL, URSULA. "Die fünfzehn
Zeichen vor dem jüngsten Gericht in der S. Martha-Kirche zu
Nürnberg." In <u>Festschrift für Peter Metz</u>. Edited by
Ursula Schlegel and Claus Zoege von Manteuffel. Berlin:
Walter de Gruyter & Co., 1965, pp. 224-38.
Iconographic study of this 14th century window, the
earliest cycle of Signs of the End of the World.

Ger. 153

153 HEYE, EVA. "Die Rundscheiben aus Schloss Erbach in der
       Skulpturen-Abteilung." Berliner Museen 15 (1965):49-57.
            Medallions that entered the Berlin Museum in 1927 depict
       a Life of Christ. Dated about 1480 and related to glass in
       Alt-Thann and Ulm, especially examples from the Peter
       Hemmel workshop, and to the Housebook Master.

154 RAGALLER, HEINRICH. "Das Vituslegenden-Fenster im Chor der
       Pfarrkirche zu Iphofen." In Festschrift für Peter Metz.
       Edited by Ursula Schlegel and Claus Zoege von Manteuffel.
       Berlin: Walter de Gruyter & Co., 1965, pp. 239-48.
            Reconstruction of a window with the Life of St. Vitus,
       dated ca. 1430.

155 WENTZEL, HANS. "Gotische Glasmalereien für Amelungsborn."
       Pantheon 23 (1965):139-45.
            Discusses the few remaining fragments from the east
       window of the Cistercian church at Amelungsborn (ca.
       1330), destroyed in 1945, and glass from the north transept
       returned recently by a private collector. English summary.

156 _____. "Kabinettscheiben aus Neckar-Schwaben." Zeitschrift
       des deutschen Vereins für Kunstwissenschaft 19 (1965):
       117-33.
            15th century roundels and small panels from the region
       of Nuremberg and Ulm, dispersed in various collections.

157 WITZLEBEN, ELIZABETH SCHÜRER von. Farbwunder deutscher Glas-
       malerei aus dem Mittelalter. Augsburg: Josef Hannes-
       schläger, 1965; 2d ed., 1967, 264 pp., 47 color pls.,
       87 figs.
            Picture book of 12th-16th century glass, illustrated
       with semitransparent color plates. Brief introduction and
       notes on the illustrations; includes a bibliography. Use-
       ful supplement to Wentzel (Ger. 97).

158 WELLS, WILLIAM. "Stained Glass from Boppard-on-Rhine in the
       Burrell Collection." Scottish Art Review 10, no. 3 (1966):
       22-25.
            Reconstruction of windows made for the choir of the
       Carmelite convent during the second quarter of the 15th
       century, now dispersed in American collections and in
       Cologne.

159   BECKSMANN, RÜDIGER. "Bemerkungen zu einer gotischen Orna-
      mentsscheibe aus der colmarer Franziskanerkirche in der
      Sammlung Bremen." Bonner Jahrbücher: Jahrbücher des
      Vereins von Altertüms Freunden im Rheinlander 166 (1966):
      287-92.
          Recognizes two ornamental panels in the Bremen collec-
      tion as those from the Franciscan church in Colmar, on the
      basis of old photographs. The dates of the building and
      comparisons with Niederhaslach place them ca. 1280-90 (cf.
      W. Bremen catalog, Coll. 95).

160   KROOS, RENATE. "Zwei unveröffentlichte Glasmalereifragmente
      des 13. Jh. in Göttingen." Niederdeutsche Beiträge zur
      Kunstgeschichte 5 (1966):83-90.
          Two heads from Bücken identified in the Städtische
      Museum at Göttingen; a footnote to Wentzel's articles
      (Ger. 140).

161   WENTZEL, HANS. "Glasmalereien zu Wimpfen und verwandte spät-
      gotische Farbverglasungen in Hessen und Baden." Kunst in
      Hessen und am Mittelrhein 6 (1966):7-31.
          Late 15th century glass in Wimpfen and Langenberg and
      panels from Kleinbottwar now in collections are attributed
      to the same shop, perhaps that of Hans Konberger in
      Heidelberg.

162   _____. "Schwäbische Glasmalereien aus dem Umkreis des
      'Hausbuchmeisters.'" Pantheon 24 (1966):360-71.
          Six panels, including one with the arms of Abbot Blasius
      Schölltrus (1484-1503), are traced to the church of SS.
      Peter and Paul in Hirsau. These and another heraldic
      series are associated with the style of the Housebook
      Master. English summary.

163   KORN, ULF-DIETRICH. Die romanische Farbverglasung von St.
      Patrokli in Soest. Sonderheft der Zeitschrift "Westfalen,"
      17. Münster Westfalen: Aschendorffsche Verlagsbuchhand-
      lung, 1967, 114 pp., 3 color pls., 120 figs., figs in text.
          Painstaking study of the condition, authenticity, icon-
      ography, and style of two groups of windows from the choir
      and the Lady Chapel (with Christological and Marianic pro-
      grams), dated ca. 1166. Based on the author's disserta-
      tion.

Ger. 164

164 KRUMMER-SCHROTH, INGEBORG. <u>Glasmalereien aus dem freiburger</u>
<u>Münster</u>. Freiburg-im-Breisgau: Verlag Rombach, 1967,
208 pp., 21 color pls., 25 figs. [Unbound plates also
issued separately as a folio volume].
    Well-chosen plates of selected windows, ca. 1200-1530,
with a discussion of style, iconography, and dating.
Bibliography.

165 RENTSCH, DIETRICH. "Zu den Stilquellen der Glasgemälde von
St. Maria-Lyskirchen in Köln." In <u>Kunstgeschichtliche</u>
<u>Studien für Kurt Bauch zum 70. Gerburtstag</u>. Edited by
Margrit Lisner and Rüdiger Becksmann. Munich and Berlin:
Deutscher Kunstverlag, 1967, pp. 125-34.
    Windows of ca. 1525-30, made after the glazing of the
cathedral, reflect Flemish influence, especially that of
Joos van Cleve, who executed a painting for St. Maria im
Kapitol in 1523.

166 WENTZEL, HANS. "Die Farbfenster in Öhringen: Ein didak-
tisches Beispiel." <u>Zeitschrift des deutschen Vereins für</u>
<u>Kunstwissenschaft (Gedenkschrift Erich Meyer)</u> 21 (1967):
141-56.
    Examines the problem of reconstructing five windows from
the fragments now gathered in two; all are from one workshop, strongly influenced by Peter Hemmel, and date ca.
1457-75, but their style varies according to that of the
model used.

167 _____. "Glasmalereien zu Wimpfen am Berg und verwandte spätgotische Farbverglasungen in Hessen und Baden." <u>Kunst in</u>
<u>Hessen und am Mittelrhein</u> 6 (1967):7-31.
    Stresses the importance of this region in the 15th cen-
tury; cites its outstanding productions of ca. 1500, and
also those of Langenburg. Superseded by the Corpus volume
(Ger. 212).

168 BECKSMANN, RÜDIGER. "Das 'Hausbuchmeisterproblem' in der
mittelrheinischen Glasmalerei." <u>Pantheon</u> 26 (1968):
352-67.
    Reviews many attributions of glass to the Housebook
Master, adding a panel with a tournament now in Gross-
Karben Castle. This is attributed to the second of the
two artists who worked on the Housebook (Nikolaus
Nievergalt?). English summary.

169   _____. "Die ehemalige Farbverglasung der Mauritiusrotunde des konstanzer Münsters: Erkenntnisse aus einer historisierenden Restaurierung." Jahrbuch der Staatlichen Kunstsammlungen in Baden-Württemberg 5 (1968):57–82.
        Problems of reconstruction and style relating to glass of ca. 1315 and ca. 1450 from Constance, now in Freiburg.

170   FRENZEL, GOTTFRIED. Die Farbverglasung aus St. Lorenz, Nürnberg. Berühmte Glasmalereien in Europa. Augsburg: Josef Hannesschläger, 1968, 116 pp., figs.
        Picture book that uses semitransparent paper for the color plates. Brief introduction, without bibliography or notes.

171   _____. "Die Farbverglasung des Mortuariums im Dom zu Eichstätt." Anzeiger des Germanischen Nationalmuseums (Nürnberg) (1968):7–26.
        Reconstructs five windows, some of which are dated (1490 and 1502); assigns these to various hands and relates them to Holbein the Elder's vidimus and to a Martin Schaffner(?) print.

172   RODE, HERBERT. Glasmalereien in Deutschlands grösster Kathedrale: Der kölner Dom. Berühmte Glasmalereien in Europa. Augsburg: Josef Hannesschläger, 1968, 124 pp., 54 figs. (20 color), plan.
        Same format as Ger. 170.

173   SEIFERT, HANS, and WITZLEBEN, ELIZABETH SCHÜRER von. Glasmalereien einer bedeutenden Kirche: Das ulmer Münster. Berühmte Glasmalereien in Europa. Augsburg: Josef Hannesschläger, 1968, 132 pp., 47 figs. (24 color), plan.
        Same format as Ger. 170.

174   WENTZEL, HANS. "A Panel of Stained Glass from Erfurt Cathedral." Victoria and Albert Museum Bulletin 4 (1968):96–98.
        Recognition of the original Christ Entering Jerusalem of ca. 1375 from Erfurt, where it was replaced by a copy in 1899.

175   _____. "Sigmaringen-Saulgau-Ulm: Zur ulmer Glasmalerei, extra muros, um 1400." Jahrbuch der Berliner Museen 10 (1968):101–24.
        Reconstructs two windows of shortly after 1405 from the Ulm Minster; the glass was taken out ca. 1480 and is now in Altshausen and Sigmaringen; some had been installed in Saulgau. English summary.

176 _____. "Zwei nicht-schwäbische spätgotische Scheiben in Württemberg." <u>Kunst in Hessen und am Mittelrhein</u> 8 (1968): 33-40.
    Discusses two panels with St. George and a Palatine count depicted as donor, both dated ca. 1463; these are now in a Württemberg collection and were formerly in Hohenheim. They are compared with glass from Ulm and Schwäbisch Hall and with the work of Peter Hemmel and the Housebook Master.

177 BECKSMANN, RÜDIGER. "Das Jesse-Fenster aus dem spätromanischen Chor des freiburger Münsters: Ein Beitrag zur Kunst um 1200." <u>Zeitschrift des deutschen Vereins für Kunstwissenschaft</u> 23 (1969):8-48.
    Examines dating (ca. 1218), reconstruction, style (closer to Nicholas of Verdun than to Rhenish glass), and iconography. Cf. the shorter English version (Ger. 202).

178 CONRAD, M. "Zur Geschichte der alten Glasgemälde aus dem Kreuzgang von Kloster Mariawald." <u>Heimatkalender des Landkreises Schleiden</u> (Bonn) 19 (1969):95-102.
    Reconstructs the typological cycle of the first half of the 16th century recorded in the Mariawald Cloister in the 17th century; the glass was sold in 1802 and many panels are now in English collections.

179 HAYWARD, JANE. "Stained Glass Windows from the Carmelite Church at Boppard-am-Rhein: A Reconstruction of the Glazing Program of the North Nave." <u>Metropolitan Museum Journal</u> 2 (1969):75-114.
    Panels that passed through the Spitzer collection and are now dispersed in Europe and the U.S. (Burrell collection, Glasgow; Metropolitan Museum and Cloisters, New York, etc.); one is dated 1444. The subjects represented include a Throne of Solomon, a Marianic cycle, the Trinity, saints, etc.; these were executed by two ateliers.

180 KURRUS, KARL. "Die Wappenscheiben im Rathaus zu Endingen." <u>Schau-ins-Land</u> 87 (1969):5-24.
    Heraldic glass in the town hall (built 1527) is attributed to the shop of Hans Gitschmann 'von Ropstein' in Freiburg. Catalog of 15 panels, most dated 1528-29; complete set of illustrations.

181 RODE, HERBERT. "Die Namen der Meister der Hl. Sippe und von St. Severin: Eine Hypothese, zugleich ein Beitrag zu dem Glasmalereizyklus im nördlichen Seitenschiff des kölner Domes." <u>Wallraf-Richartz-Jahrbuch</u> 31 (1969):249-54.

Demonstrates a very close stylistic affinity between the
early 16th century glass of the Cologne Cathedral's north
aisle and the panel painting of the Masters of the Holy
Kinship and of St. Severin; the glass painter was probably
Hermann Pentelynk.

182 WENTZEL, HANS. "Eine Glasmalerei-Scheibe aus Boppard in
Glasgow." Pantheon 27 (1969):177-81.
Examines the style of the Christ on the Mount of Olives,
now in Glasgow, and other Boppard panels of ca. 1440-45 and
its relation to earlier glass in Settingen/Saar and to the
choir windows of Berne Cathedral (after 1447). English
summary.

183 ____. "Glasmalerei am Bodensee im 14. Jahrhundert." Unsere
Kunstdenkmäler 20 (1969):156-67.
Critical review of the literature on painting in the
region of Constance and Swabia ca. 1300.

184 ____. "Zu Hans von Ulm (Hans Acker)." Zeitschrift für
schweizerische Archäologie und Kunstgeschichte 25 (1969):
138-52.
Critique of Frankl (Sw. 29 and Ger. 141) and of documents concerning Hans von Ulm, Hans Acker, and other members of the family; reviews the problem of attributing
extant windows to this master or his atelier.

185 WITZLEBEN, ELIZABETH SCHÜRER von. Glasmalereien einer bedeutenden Kirche: Die Frauenkirche in München. Berühmte
Glasmalereien in Europa. Augsburg: Josef Hannesschläger,
1969, 128 pp., 44 figs. (19 color), plan.
Same format as Ger. 170, but with a short bibliography.

186 BECKSMANN, RÜDIGER. "Das schwarzacher Köpfchen, ein otto-
nischer Glasmalereifund." Kunstchronik 23 (1970):3-9.
A painted head, excavated in 1964-68 at Schwarzach
Cathedral, is convincingly dated to the late 10th century
through comparisons with Ottonian illumination (the Gospels
of Otto III).

187 ____. "Zur Werkstattgemeinschaft Peter Hemmels in den Jahren
1477-1481." Pantheon 28 (1970):183-97.
Associates two panels in the Karlsruhe Museum with the
Freiburg Minster. Dates them to 1480, when Peter Hemmel is
documented as having subcontracted to four Strasbourg glass
painters. English summary.

188 FRENZEL, URSULA. "Michael Wolgemuts Tätigkeit für die nürnberger Glasmalerei, dargestellt an der Bildnisscheibe des
Dr. Lorenz Tucher von 1485." Anzeiger des Germanischen
Nationalmuseums (Nuremberg) (1970):27-46.
The portrait of Tucher from St. Michael in Fürth is now
in the Nuremberg Museum. Formerly attributed to Dürer,
correct reading of the date and analysis of the style now
lead to an attribution to Wolgemut. Comparisons are made
with the panel paintings and glass in St. Lorenz, Nuremberg
(Kornhofer and Kaiserfenster). Cf. Ger. 116.

189 HOPP, GISELA. "Bayerisches Nationalmuseum, Munich: Stained
Glass from Ratisbon." Apollo 92 (1970):452-57.
Reconstructs three windows of ca. 1360-70 from the
Minorite church; these depicted Old Testament scenes, the
Passion of Christ, and the Life of St. Francis.

190 WERNER, NORBERT. "Zu den Glasgemälden der Besserer-Kapelle
des Münsters zu Ulm." Giessener Beiträge zur Kunstgeschichte (Festschrift Günther Fiensch zum 60. Geburtstag)
1 (1970):29-49.
Dates this glass ca. 1427-30 through comparisons with
panels from Lindau (1427) and Altötting (1426) and with
Lucas Moser's Tiefenbronner altar.

191 WORTMANN, REINHARD. "Neue Literatur zu den Glasfenstern der
ulmer Münsters." Ulm und Oberschwaben 39 (1970):238-41.
Review of the 1968 publications on Ulm Cathedral glass
which focuses on Lehmbruck's, Wentzel's and Pée's attribution to Hans von Ulm (Hans Acker).

192 HAAS, W. "Die alten Obergadenfenster des augsburger Domes:
Der ursprüngliche Ort der 'Prophentenfenster.'" Jahrbuch
der bayerischen Denkmalpflege 28 (1970-71):101-8.
Discusses the original form of the clerestory windows
that contained the prophets.

193 DINKEL, JOHN. "Stained Glass from Boppard: New Findings."
Scottish Art Revue 13, no. 2 (1971):22-27.
Reconstructs the Burrell collection cycle dedicated to
the Virgin and originally created for the north aisle of
the church at Boppard. His conclusions are based on photographs and drawings discovered in the collection of Robert
Goelet, Newport, R.I.

194   FRENZEL, GOTTFRIED. "Glasmalerei in Schwaben." In <u>Suevia</u>
<u>sacra: Frühe Kunst in Schwaben, Ausstellung im Rathaus</u>
<u>vom 3. Juni–16. Sept. 1973</u>. [Augsburg: Städt. Kunst-
sammlungen], 1973, pp. 53–56, 217–28.
    Thorough study of the 12th century Augsburg prophets,
with a reconstruction of the windows.

195   GORISSEN, FRIEDRICH. "Meister Matheus und die Flügel des
kalkarer Hochaltar: Ein Schlüsselproblem der niederrhein-
ländischen Malerei." <u>Wallraf-Richartz-Jahrbuch</u> 35 (1973):
149–206.
    Documentary and technical study of the Kalkar altar-
piece, commissioned from Master Matheus ca. 1495 and completed by Jan Joest. Cites the relation of the underdraw-
ing to that of glass panels from Cologne (Mariawald) now
in London. Bibliography.

196   *KNAPPE, U. "Die nürnberger Glasmalerfamilie Hirsvogel."
<u>Fränkische Lebensbilder</u> 5 (1973):64–96. [<u>Zeitschrift für</u>
<u>Kunstgeschichte</u> 39 (1976)].

197   KRUMMER-SCHROTH, INGEBORG. "Die Glasmalereien im freiburger
Münster und ihre Stifter aus dem Kreise Kaiser Maximilian."
<u>Mitteilungen der Gesellschaft für vergleichende Kunstfor-</u>
<u>schung in Wien</u> 25 (1973):20–21.
    Gifts of windows in the new choir, ca. 1506–27. No
bibliography or illustrations.

198   ROTH, HERMANN JOSEF. "Zu den altenberger Pflanzendarstell-
ungen." <u>Romerike Berge</u> 23 (1973):97–103.
    Discusses the historical and stylistic aspects of the
representation of real plant leaves (oak, mugwort, and
ivy) in this Cistercian glass of ca. 1400. Bibliography.

199   WORTMANN, REINHARD. "Eine verschollene Scheibe aus der
Neithartkapelle des ulmer Münsters: Ein Beitrag zur Bau-
und Ausstattungsgeschichte der Neithartkapelle sowie zur
Entwicklung der Glasmalerei im zweiten Viertel des 15.
Jahrhunderts in Ulm." <u>Ulm und Oberschwaben, Zeitschrift</u>
<u>für Geschichte und Kunst</u> 40–41 (1973):199–207.
    A lost panel with a canon of the Niethart family dated
ca. 1447–50 and its stylistic relation to Hans Acker's
shop.

Ger. 200

200 RODE, HERBERT. <u>Die mittelalterlichen Glasmalereien des kölner</u>
<u>Domes</u>. Corpus Vitrearum Medii Aevi: Bundesrepublik
Deutschland, vol. 4, pt. 1. Berlin: Deutscher Verlag für
Kunstwissenschaft, 1974, 227 pp., 16 color pls., 633 figs.,
text figs.
Complete description of this important 13th-16th century
glass including an analysis of its iconography, style, and
date.

201 _____. "Eine Ornamentscheibe aus der kölner Domgrabung und
Erwägungen zu den Glasfenstern des alten Doms." In <u>Albert</u>
<u>Verbeek zum 65. Geburtstag</u>. Die Kunstdenkmäler des Rhein-
landes, 20, edited by Günther Borchers. Düsseldorf:
Schwann Verlag, 1974, pp. 15-33.
A single fragment of excavated glass with a painted
acanthus rinceau is dated to the Carolingian era through
comparisons with ornament in other media.

202 BECKSMANN, RÜDIGER. "The Stylistic Problems of the Freiburg
Jesse Window." In <u>The Year 1200: A Symposium</u>. Introduction by Jeffrey Hoffeld. New York: Metropolitan Museum
of Art, 1975, pp. 361-72.
Finds that these panels of before 1218 are connected
with the styles of Nicholas of Verdun and Laon sculpture
rather than with Rhenish glass. Cf. Ger. 177.

203 BECKSMANN, RÜDIGER, and WAETZOLDT, STEPHAN. <u>Vitrea dedicata:</u>
<u>Das Stifterbild in der deutschen Glasmalerei des Mittel-</u>
<u>alters</u>. Berlin: Deutscher Verlag für Kunstwissenschaft,
1975, 63 pp., 12 color pls., 68 figs., drawings in text.
Chapters on the state of research in the field of German
glass, the donor windows in Lautenbach (ca. 1480-90), and
other German examples, 12th-15th centuries. Partially reprinted in the Corpus volume (Ger. 212).

204 KORN, ULF-DIETRICH. "Die romanischen Glasmalerei-Fragmente
aus Sieverstedt bei Flensburg." In <u>Beiträge zur Kunst des</u>
<u>Mittelalters: Festschrift für Hans Wentzel zum 60. Ge-</u>
<u>burtstag</u>. Berlin: Gebr. Mann Verlag, 1975, pp. 115-26.
Reconstructs the subject of glass fragments found in
this village church as an Annunciation; compares these
with glass in Gotland and Breitenfelde and provides a mid-
13th century date for the windows.

205 SCHMIDT, CHRISTA. <u>Die Glasfenster im naumburger Dom</u>. Vienna:
Edition Tusch, 1975, 86 pp., 32 color pls.
Good reproductions of 14th and 15th century glass in the
cathedral with notes on the glass.

206 WERNER, NORBERT. "Das 'Hornbeck-Fenster' der Benediktuskirche
     zu Freising." In Beiträge zur Kunst des Mittelalters:
     Festschrift für Hans Wentzel zum 60. Geburtstag. Berlin:
     Gebr. Mann Verlag, 1975, pp. 205-18.
          Remnants of a window given in 1412 by Eglolf von
     Hornbeck, now in the cathedral, and suggestions for its
     reconstruction. Attribution to the Master of the Astaler
     window in Munich, Frauenkirche, and dating of that window
     ca. 1400.

207 DRACHENBERG, ERHARD; MAERCKER, KARL-JOACHIM; and SCHMIDT,
     CHRISTA. Die mittelalterliche Glasmalerei in den Ordens-
     kirchen und im Angermuseum zu Erfurt. Corpus Vitrearum
     Medii Aevi: Deutsche Demokratische Republik, vol. 1,
     pt. 1. Berlin: Akademie-verlag, 1975, 286 pp., 224 pls.
          Standard catalog of the 13th-15th century glass in the
     churches of the Mendicant orders and the Augustinians.
     Includes restoration charts, bibliography, etc.

208 *LYMANT, BRIGITTE. Die mittelalterlichen Glasmalereien der
     Zisterzienserabteikirche Altenberg. Bergisch-Gladbach:
     Altenberger Dom-Verein, 1979, 273 pp., 2 pls., 144 figs.
     Ph.D. dissertation, Bonn, 1976.

209 SCHULZE, W.A. "Der Thron Salomos." Münster 29 (1976):160-61.
          Throne of Salomon as represented in glass in the area
     of Württemberg: in the Ritterstiftskirche and the
     Dominikanerkirche, Wimpfen; in the Frauenkirche, Esslingen;
     in the Berne Minster; and in St. Vitus, München-Gladbach.

210 SPAHR, GEBHARD. Spätmittelalterliche Glasmalerei: Liebfrau-
     enkirchen Ravensburg und Eriskirch. Constance: Poppe &
     Neumann, 1976, 347 pp., 114 figs. (some color).
          Iconographic description of this early and late 15th
     century glass. Plates of poor quality.

211 KORN, ULF-DIETRICH. "Glasmalereifunde in der ev. Pfarrkirche
     zu Weslarn." Westfalen 55 (1977):503 ff.
          Raises the possibility that the 12th century workshop of
     St. Patrokli of Soest also produced the Weslarn parish
     church windows.

212 BECKSMANN, RÜDIGER. Die mittelalterlichen Glasmalereien in
     Baden und der Pfalz ohne Freiburg i. Br. Corpus Vitrearum
     Medii Aevi: Bundesrepublik Deutschland, vol. 2, Baden
     und der Pfalz, pt. 1. Berlin: Deutscher Verlag für Kunst-
     wissenschaft, 1979, 340 pp., 14 color pls., 400 figs.,
     plans, figs. in text.

Ger. 212

Definitive publication of the glass in this region, chiefly 15th century in date; it also includes the 14th century windows at Constance and the Karlsruhe Museum collections.

213 *ULRICH, EVA. Studien zur nürnberger Glasmalerei des ausgehenden 15. Jahrhunderts. Erlanger Studien, 23. Erlangen, 1979, 361 pp., 13 pls., figs. in text.

214 DRACHENBERG, ERHARD. Die mittelalterliche Glasmalerei im Erfurter Dom. Corpus Vitrearum Medii Aevi, Deutsche Demokratische Republik, vol. 1, pt. 2: Textband. Berlin: Akademie-Verlag, 1980, 454 pp., 20 color pls., 24 figs., plans and restoration charts in text.
   Publication in standard Corpus format of this important glass of ca. 1370-1410, comprising Old and New Testament cycles in the choir. A second volume will contain black and white illustrations.

215 SCHROEDER, CARL. "Zum Schicksal der gotischen Glasfenster." In Der Trierer Dom. Rheinischer Verein für Denkmalpflege und Landschaftsschutz, Jahrbuch 1978-79. Neuss: Verlag Gesellschaft für Buchdruckerie, 1980, pp. 375-85.
   Glass of the 1470s, disposed of in the 19th century, has been rediscovered in St. Mary's Church, Shrewesbury, England, where it was attributed to Flanders. Panels installed in the aisles and transept have standing saints with donors and inscriptions.

Section IX
Iberian Peninsula:
Spain and Portugal

The reader is also referred to entry Gen. 29.

1   RICO y SINOBAS, MANUEL. Historia del trabajo, del vidrio, y
    sus artífices en España. Madrid: M. Rivadeneyra, 1873,
    58 pp.
        Traces the early history of glass making and the use of
    colored glass in windows. Notes Gothic sites and lists
    masters who worked in glass.

2   AINAUD de LASARTE, JUAN. Cerámica y vidrio. Ars hispaniae,
    10. Madrid: Editorial Plus-Ultra, 1952.
        Outline of stained glass in Spain (pp. 374-97).

3   GARCÍA CUESTA, TIMOTEO. "Las vidrieras pintadas de la cate-
    dral de Palencia (siglo XVI)." Boletin del Seminario de
    estudios de arte y arquéologia, Universidad de Valladolid
    25 (1959):69-88.
        Brief history of Spanish glass during the 15th and 16th
    centuries; documents concerning glass painters who worked
    in Palencia in the 16th century.

4   NIETO ALCAIDE, VÍCTOR MANUEL. "El maestro Enrique Alemán,
    vidriero de las catedrales de Sevilla y Toledo." Archivo
    español de arte 40 (1967):55-82.
        Documents this master's work in Seville (ca. 1478-84)
    and Toledo (1484-88) and attributes windows at those sites
    to him. Examines his stylistic development and his rela-
    tion to Peter Hemmel.

5   _____. "Sobre la formacion de Enrique Alemán: Un vidriero
    alsaciano en la España de los reyes católicos." Boletin de
    la Real academia de la historia (Madrid) 161 (1967):37-42.
        Identifies this German master, who worked in Seville and
    Toledo before 1493, with "Hans Wild" [Peter Hemmel], who
    may have painted the apse windows of Walbourg Church in
    1464.

Ib. 6

6 _____. Las vidrieras de la catedral de Sevilla. Corpus
   Vitrearum Medii Aevi: España, vol. 1. Madrid: Instituto
   de Diego Velásquez, 1969, 414 pp., 3 color pls., 131 figs.
   Complete description of the glazing program of 1477-
   1577, with an analysis of style and dating.

7 * _____. La vidriera del Renacimiento en España. Arte
   y artistas. Madrid: Instituto Diego de Velázquez, 1970,
   64 pp., 48 pls.

8 _____. "La vidriera del Renacimento en Segovia (inglesias
   románicas y Antigua catedral): Avance para su estudio."
   Archivo español de arte 43 (1970):219-29.
   Early 16th century glass in the churches of San Martín
   and la Trinidad and in the cathedral; the latter trans-
   ferred to the new building in 1558.

9 _____. "Función simbólica de la luz en la arquitectura
   española del siglo XVI." Revista de la Universidad com-
   plutense de Madrid 22 (1973):115-32.
   Rejection of the medieval use of colored light in favor
   of a greater clarity that is, however, still mystical.

Section X
Italy

The reader is also referred to Tech. 137.

1 MARQUAND, ALLAN. "Two Windows in the Cathedral of Florence."
   American Journal of Archeology 2d ser. 4 (1900):192-203.
   Discusses a Coronation of the Virgin, designed by
   Donatello after 1434; and a Resurrection scene made by
   Bernardo di Francesco in 1442, perhaps after a design by
   Ghiberti.

2 MANZONI, LUIGI. "Appunti e documenti per l'arte del pinger su
   vetro in Perugia nel secolo XV." Repertorium für Kunstwissenschaft 26 (1903):120-32.
   Documentary records of glass painted for various foundations in Perugia in the 15th century.

3 CRISTOFANI, GIUSTINO. "Le vetrate di Giovanni Bonino nella
   basilica di Assisi." Rassegna d'arte umbra 1, no. 1
   (1909):3-13.
   Attribution of windows (ca. 1340) by comparison with the
   master's work in Orvieto Cathedral.

4 POGGI, G. Il Duomo di Firenze. Italienische Forschungen.
   Kunsthistorisches Institut in Florenz, vol. 2. Berlin:
   Verlag von Bruno Cassirer, 1909.
   Documents pertaining to the 14th and 15th century win-
   dows in the cathedral (pp. 78-93).

5 CRISTOFANI, GIUSTINO. "Le vetrate del' 300 nella basilica
   inferiore di Assisi." Rassegna d'arte 11 (1911):153-68.
   Styles and attributions for the 13th-14th century glass
   at Assisi.

6 GIUSTO, P. EGIDIO M. Le vetrate di S. Francesco in Assisi:
   Studio storico, iconografico. Milan: Alfieri & Lacroix,
   1911, 375 pp., 41 pls. (some color).
   Scholarly description of the glazing programs, with
   selected passages from medieval and post-medieval documents

It. 6

concerning the glass. Now replaced by the Corpus volume
(It. 40).

7 CRISTOFANI, G. "L'iconographie des vitraux du XIIIᵉ siècle de
la basilique d'Assise." Revue de l'art chrétien 62 (1912):
111-16; 271-82.
Iconographic study of the 13th century glass in the
upper windows, believed to be the oldest glass in Italy;
attributed to a French or German glazier greatly influenced
by Italian art.

8 SHERRILL, CHARLES HITCHCOCK. A Stained Glass Tour in Italy.
London and New York: John Lane, 1913, 174 pp., 33 figs.
General introduction to the development of Italian glass
(14th-16th centuries), followed by a guide to specific
examples arranged topographically.

9 KLEINSCHMIDT, BEDA. Die Basilika San Francesco in Assisi.
3 vols. Berlin: Verlag für Kunstwissenschaft, 1915-28,
331 pp., 26 pls. (14 color), 375 figs.
Description of the 13th and 14th century glass (pp. 167-
245) illustrated with b&w photos and some poor color pls.
Superseded by It. 40.

10 ZUCCHINI, GUIDO. "Le vetrate di San Giovanni in Monte di
Bologna." Bollettino d'arte 11 (1917):82-90.
Questions the attribution, based on stylistic and documentary evidence, of the St. John the Evangelist window
(ca. 1482) to Francesco del Cossa; attributes it instead
to the school of Ferrara.

11 MONNERET de VILLARD, UGO. Le vetrate del Duomo di Milano:
Ricerche storiche. 3 vols. Milan: Editori Alfieri &
Lacroix, 1918-20. Vol. 1, 227 pp.; Vols. 2-3, 190 pls.,
3 figs.
Describes the early 15th-16th century glass and edits
documentary sources, including a register that burned in
1906. Index of artists. Very rare (Doucet).

12 TOESCA, P. "Vetrate dipinte fiorentine." Bollettino d'arte
14 (1920):3-6.
Three mid-15th century windows designed by great masters: one by Ghiberti in Sta. Maria del Fiore, one by G.
di Mario in Sta. Croce, and one by Andrea Bonnaiuti in Sta.
Maria Novella.

13   SUIDA, WILHELM. "Schwäbische Glasgemälde in S. Nazaro in
Mailand." Das schwäbische Museum (Augsburg) (1927):155-58.
Early 16th century window with a Life of St. Barbara in
S. Nazaro Maggiore in Milan is attributed to a Swabian
painter.

14   CECCHELLI, CARLO. "Vetri da finestra del S. Vitale di
Ravenna." Felix Ravenna 35 (1930):1-20.
Recent finds of glass at the east end of the church,
some colored with a mastic, some painted (a roundel with
Christ in Majesty). Dated in the 6th century, these exam-
ples were thus part of the original glazing. Illustrated.
(Cf. It. 18.)

15   CARLI, ENZO. Vetrata duccesca. Florence: Electa, 1946,
61 pp., 32 pls. (1 color).
Argues for a date of between 1287 and 1311 for the glass
in the Siena Cathedral oculus on the basis of documents and
attributes the work to Duccio on the basis of style and
probability.

16   POPE-HENNESSY, JOHN. "An Exhibition of Sienese Stained Glass."
Burlington Magazine 88 (1946):306.
Accepts Carli's proposed date for the oculus (It. 15),
but questions its stylistic relationship to early Duccio.

17   LANE, ARTHUR. "Florentine Painted Glass and the Practice of
Design." Burlington Magazine 91 (1949):43-48.
No medieval tradition of glass painting in Italy; the
art emphasized figural presentation by the end of the
Trecento; the Italian glazier was dependent on the artist
for his designs.

18   "I vetri nei monumenti ravennati." Felix Ravenna, 3d ser. 4
(1951):63-66.
Finds of glass fragments in 1905 in the Diakonikon and
in 1930 outside the apse wall of S. Vitale; reviews the 6th
century date proposed by Cecchelli and the alternative
types of glazing (It. 14). Not illustrated.

19   WENTZEL, HANS. "Die ältesten Farbenfenster in der Oberkirche
von S. Francesco zu Assisi und die deutsche Glasmalerei des
XIII. Jahrhunderts." Wallraff-Richartz-Jahrbuch 14 (1952):
45-72.
Emphasizes the non-Italian stylistic and iconographic
features of the three east windows of the upper church and
argues that they are mid-13th century products of a German
atelier.

20 RAGGHIANTI, CARLO L. "Il Foppa e le vetriere del Duomo di
    Milano." Critica d'arte 1 (1954):520–43.
        New conclusions concerning glaziers in the cathedral are
    based on a reassessment of the documents; refutes Monneret
    de Villard's arguments (It. 11); discusses attributions to
    Vincenzo Foppa (ca. 1458).

21 MARCHINI, GIUSEPPE. Le vetrate italiane. Milan: Banca
    nazionale del lavoro, 1955. 2d ed., Milan: Electra
    Editrice, 1956, 245 pp., 84 color pls., 34 figs. English
    editions. Italian Stained Glass Windows. London: Thames
    & Hudson, 1957, 264 pp., 133 pls. (some color); and
    Italian Stained Glass Windows. New York: H.M. Abrams,
    1957, 244 pp., figs. German edition. Italienische Glas-
    malerei. Munich: Hirmer, 1957, 86 pp., figs. French
    edition. Le vitrail italien. Paris: Arts et métiers
    graphiques, 1957, 250 pp., figs. Swedish edition.
    Italienskt glasmåleri. Malmö: Allhem, 1958, 248 pp.,
    4 pls., figs.
        Well-illustrated survey of the major sites, from the
    13th century (Assisi) to the 16th (Venice, Milan, Arezzo).
    Indexes include artists; short bibliography.

22 PANAZZA, GAETANO. "Vetrate pavesi." Critica d'arte 2, no. 9
    (1955):252–55.
        Three windows designed by Bernardino Lanzi and executed
    ca. 1509 for the church of S. Lanfranco.

23 RAGGHIANTI, CARLO. "Postilla Foppesca." Critica d'arte 2,
    no. 9 (1955):285–92.
        Refutes those attributions made by Constantino Baroni
    and Sergio Samek Ludovici concerning Milan Cathedral glass;
    in particular those made to Martino Spanzotti and Cristoforo
    de Mottis.

24 BOLOGNA, FERDINANDO. "Vetrate del Maestro di Figline."
    Bollettino d'arte 41 (1956):193–99.
        Attributes to this Forentine master the windows in the
    Bardi Chapel (early 14th century) formerly given to Giotto
    (cf. Marchini) as well as his contemporary works in Sta.
    Croce.

25 SALMI, MARIO. "Lorenzo Ghiberti e la pittura." Scritti
    storia dell'arte L. Venturi 1 (1956):223–37.
        Evolution of Ghiberti's style, 1405–45, as shown in his
    window designs for Florence Cathedral.

26 CASTELNUOVO, ENRICO. "Vetrate italiane." Paragone 8, no. 103
    (1958):3–24.

Summary of research on Italian stained glass; criticizes
Marchini views on Assisi, especially his emphasis on German
influence in the apse windows (ca. 1230-40), the left
transept and nave (ca. 1290), and the lower aisle glass
(first half of the 14th century).

27   VOLPE, CARLO. "Tre vetrate ferraresi e il rinascimento a
Bologna." Arte antica e moderna 1 (1958):23-37.
      Discusses a Madonna and Angel attributed to Cossa that
bears the date 1467 and a St. John in Patmos by Lorenzo
Costa dated ca. 1489, both from the church of S. Giovanni
in Monte; portraits by Ercole de' Roberti (1480-85); and
the relationship of this artist to others working in
Bologna.

28   COHN, WERNER. "Zur Ikonographie der Glasfenster von Orsanmichele." Mitteilungen des Kunsthistorischen Institutes in
Florenz 9 (1959):1-12.
      Twelve Florentine windows, late 14th-early 15th century,
with the Miracles of the Virgin, are based on a manuscript
account of the late 14th century by Duccio di Gano da Pisa.

29   *ALCE, V[ENTURINO]. "Il B. Giacomo da Ulma, maestro di
vetrate a Bologna dal 1463 al 1476." Memorie dominicane
78 (1961):129-51.

30   SALMI, MARIO. "Tre vetrate fiorentine del primo rinascimento."
In Festschrift Hans R. Hahnloser zum 60. Geburtstag. Edited by Ellen J. Beer, Paul Hofer, and Luc Mojon. Basel:
Birkhäuser, 1961, pp. 317-22.
      The late 15th century windows of Sta. Croce, Florence,
are compared with the paintings of Alesso Baldovinetti and
some panels are attributed to his circle and to several
contemporary hands.

31   ALCE, VENTURINO. "Der ulmer Glasmaler Jakob Greisinger in
Bologna." Ulm und Oberschwaben: Zeitschrift für Geschichte und Kunst 36 (1962):39-45.
      New documentary evidence for this German painter's work
in S. Domenico and S. Petronio in the 1460s-1470s and
examples of extant glass.

32   BETTOLI, G. "Andrea del Castagno." Arte cristiana 50 (1962):
9-13.
      The oeuvre of Castagno; cites an example of a 15th cen-
tury window representing the Deposition from Sta. Maria del
Fiore, Florence, attributed to him.

33   ÖSTERREICH, GEZA von. "Die Rundfenster des Lorenzo Ghiberti."
Ph.D. dissertation, University of Fribourg, 1965.

It. 34

34 GILLI PIRINA, CATERINA. "Precisazioni su Cristoforo de'
    Mottis." In Arte in Europa: Scritti di Storia dell'Arte
    in onore di Edoardo Arslan. 2 vols. Milan: Stampare
    della Tipogr. Artipo, 1965-66, 1:407-30, 2 pls.
        Study of the 15th century windows in Milan Cathedral
    executed by Cristoforo (called Master Gracile), based on
    documents published 1473-81.

35 _____. "Franceschino Zavattari, Stefano da Pandino, Maffiolo
    da Cremono "magistri a vitriatis" e la vetrata della "raza"
    nel Duomo milanese." Arte antica e moderna 33 (1966):
    25-44.
        Attributions of early 15th century glass in Milan and
    Monza Cathedrals.

36 MARCHINI, GIUSEPPI. "Le vetrate." In Primo rinascimento
    Santa Croce. Florence: Città di Vita, 1968, pp. 55-78.
        Attribution of designs for the 13th-16th century windows
    to Pacino di Bonaguida, Taddeo Gaddi, Jacopo del Casentino,
    Giovanni di Bonino, Maso di Banco, Agnolo Gaddi, Ghiberti,
    Alesso Baldovinetti, and Granacci.

37 GILLI PIRINA, CATERINA. "Michelino da Besozzo and the
    'Vecchioni' of the Stained-Glass Window of S. Giulitta."
    Burlington Magazine 111 (1969):64-70.
        Discusses six trefoils completed in the first years of
    the 15th century; the homogeneity of their style and docu-
    mented evidence proves that they were executed by Michelino
    da Besozzo (contrary to Monneret's conclusions, It. 11).

38 FRODL-KRAFT, EVA. "Das VII. Colloquium des Corpus Vitrearum
    Medii Aevi in Florenz, 1970." Österreichisches Zeitschrift
    für Kunst und Denkmalpflege 25 (1971):73-74.
        Summary of discussions of Umbrian glass.

39 MARCHINI, GIUSEPPE. "Le vetrate." In Civiltà delle arti
    minori in Toscana: Atti del Convegno, Arezzo, 11-15 Maggio
    1971. Florence: Edam, 1973, pp. 65-83.
        Brief history of glass painting in Italy, especially in
    relation to other media; attribution of designs for glass
    to Cimabue or Duccio, Jacopo del Casentino, Giotto, Maso di
    Banco, Taddeo Gaddi, etc.

40 _____. Le vetrate dell'Umbria. Corpus Vitrearum Medii Aevi:
    Italia, vol. 1. Rome: De Luca, 1973, 229 pp., 189 pls.
    (26 color), plans in text.
        Complete catalog of important 13th-15th century collec-
    tions of glass, including S. Francesco, Assisi; Orvieto;
    and Perugia.

41 _____. "Miracoli d'Orsanmichele." In <u>Mitteilungen des Kunst-</u>
<u>historischen Instituts in Florenz</u> (Festschrift Klara
Steinweg) 17 (1973):301-6.
The iconography of two windows from the Miracle of the
Virgin cycle in Or San Michele (end of the 15th century).

42 _____. "Un restauro." <u>Antichità viva</u> 12, no. 5 (1973):3-6.
The restoration of a 15th century window from Sta. Maria
Novella in Florence depicting the Virgin and Child above
SS. John and Philip; signed and executed by Filippino
Lippi.

43 SOLDANO, BIANCA TOSATTI. <u>Miniature e vetrate senesi del</u>
<u>secolo XIII</u>. Genoa: Università di Genova, 1978, 171 pp.,
40 pls.
"Le vetrate" (pp. 83-124) deals with the general history
of glass painting in Europe and with Italian glass of the
13th-14th centuries; includes documentation for Siena
Cathedral and examines the question of Duccio's involvement.

44 HAUSSHERR, REINER. "Der typologische Zyklus der Chorfenster
der Oberkirche von S. Francesco zu Assisi." In <u>Kunst als</u>
<u>Bedeutungsträger: Gedenkschrift für Günter Bandmann</u>.
Edited by Werner Busch, Reiner Haussherr, and Eduard Trier.
Berlin: Mann Verlag, [ca. 1978], pp. 95-128.
Systematically identifies typological subjects and com-
pares them with cycles in Austria, England, and Germany.

Section XI
Low Countries:
Belgium and Holland

The reader is also referred to Gen. 29 and Br. 203. For the work of Arnold of Nijmegen and Dirk Vellert outside the Low Countries see entries listed in the Index of Glass Painters and Designers.

1 GOOVAERTS, ALPHONSE. "Les ordonnances données en 1480, à Tournai, aux métiers des peintres et des verriers." Bulletin de la Commission royale d'histoire de Belgique, 5th ser. 6 (1896):97-182.
    Analyzes and edits the 1480 revision of the painters' and glass painters' guild regulations first issued in 1423. Includes terms of apprenticeship, etc.

2 *Casteele, Désiré Van de. Keuren: Livre d'admission et autres documents inédits concernant la Ghilde de Saint-Luc de Bruges, suivis des Keuren de la corporation des peintres, sculpteurs et verriers de Gand. Bruges, 1867.

3 ROMBOUTS, PHILLIPPE, and LERIUS, THÉODORE Van. Les liggeren et autres archives historiques de la gilde anversoise de Saint Luc, I: liggerie de 1453-1615. Antwerp: Félicien Baggerman, [1872], 792 pp.
    Annual lists of entrants to the guild, among whom are many glass painters.

4 GUICCIARDINI, LODOVICO. Descrittione . . . di tutti i Paesi Bassi, altrimenti detti Germania inferiore. Antwerp: Guglielmo Silvio, 1567, [379 pp.], maps. *[1588 edition more extensive.]
    Glass painting in the Low Countries in the early 16th century (pp. 100-101).

5 REIFFENBERG, F. de. "De la peinture sur verre aux Pays-Bas." Nouveaux mémoires de l'Académie royale des sciences et belles-lettres de Belgique (Séance du 19 novembre 1831) 7 (1832):1-79.
    Survey of the principal collections, many of which date after 1540; list of members' names for the guild of St. Luke in Antwerp; notes on lost glass.

L.C. 6

6   WEALE, J. <u>Divers works of early masters in christian decora-</u>
    <u>tion, with examples of ancient painted and stained glass</u>.
    2 vols. London: J. Weale, 1846, 52 pp., 75 pls.
        Large colored illustrations of 13th-16th century glass
    from several Belgian churches.

7   *DESCAMPS, ANDRÉ, and LEMAISTRE d'ANSTAING. <u>Les vitraux de la</u>
    <u>cathédrale de Tournay</u>. Brussels: Librairie scientifique
    et littéraire, 1848, 12 pp., 14 pls.
        Plates from drawings by Capronnier.

8   LÉVY, EDMOND. <u>Histoire de la peinture sur verre en Europe et</u>
    <u>particulièrement en Belgique</u>. Brussels: Tircher, 1860,
    476 pp., 37 pls.
        Part I is a general history and Part II provides de-
    scriptions of 13th-16th century glass at major sites.
    Illustrated by J.B. Capronnier, a glass painter.

9   WINSTON, CHARLES. "Remarks on the Painted Glass at Lichfield
    Cathedral." <u>Archaeological Journal</u> 21 (1864):193-208.
        Composition and style of the windows made for the abbey
    of Herckenrode 1532-39. See also Coll. 5, 58.

10 GÉNARD, P. <u>Notice des oeuvres d'art qui ornent l'église</u>
    <u>Notre-Dame à Anvers</u>. Antwerp: Buschmann, 1856, 16 pp.
    3d ed., 1877.
        Includes a Last Supper window executed by Nicolas
    Rombouts in 1503.

11 HELBIG, JULES. "Les vitraux de l'ancienne église abbatiale
    des dames nobles de Herckenrode." <u>Bulletin des Commissions</u>
    <u>royales d'art et d'archéologie</u> 16 (1877):366-82.
        Date (1532-39), style, and iconography of the glass from
    the choir of Herckenrode given to Lichfield Cathedral,
    England, in 1803; based chiefly on Winston (Br. 38; L.C. 9).

12 CAUWENBERGHS, CLÉMENT Van. <u>Notice historique sur les peintres</u>
    <u>verriers d'Anvers du xve au xviie siècle</u>. Antwerp: H. &
    L. Kennes, 1891, 82 pp.
        Detailed account of the history and development of the
    company of glaziers emphasizing information pertaining to
    individual glass painters and their activities.

13 GLÜCK, GUSTAV. "Beiträge zur Geschichte der Antwerpner
    Malerei." <u>Jahrbuch der kunsthistorischen Sammlungen des</u>
    <u>Allerhöchsten Kaiserhauses</u> 22 (1901):1-34.
        Identifies the monogrammist DV as the glass painter
    Dirk Vellert; and discusses attributions of glass, drawings,
    prints, and paintings to him.

14   BEETS, N. "Dirick Jacobsz Vellert, peintre d'Anvers." L'art
flamand et hollandais 6 (1906):133-48; 7 (1907):105-18;
10 (1908):89-110; 18 (1912):129-48; and Revue d'art
(Brussels) 25 (1925):116-45. [Also in Flemish, Onze Kunst,
1906, 1907, 1908, 1912, and 1922.]
     The 3d and 4th parts (1908, 1912) deal with designs,
many of which are for glass; the 5th part (1925) is on
extant glass paintings in the Low Countries and elsewhere,
dated chiefly to the 1520s.

15   VALLANCE, AYMER. "Some Flemish Painted Glass Panels."
Burlington Magazine 19 (1911):189-92.
     Eleven heraldic and figural panels of ca. 1477-93,
including portraits of Maximilian, Mary of Burgundy, etc.
Present whereabouts unknown.

16   PAUW, NAPOLÉON de. "La vie intime en Flandre au Moyen Âge
d'après des documents inédits." Académie royale de
Belgique: Bulletin de la Commission royale d'histoire 82
(1913):1-96.
     Mentions 1310 repairs to glass in the Abbey St.-Pierre
in Ghent.

17   CLEMEN, PAUL. "Die Glasmalereien in St. Gudula zu Brüssel."
In Belgische Kunstdenkmäler. Edited by Paul Clemen.
Vol. 2. Munich: F. Bruckmann, 1923, pp. 41-62.
     Large compositions, chiefly of the 1520s-1530s, and
related windows in Mons, Lüttich, etc.

18   BACON, P.C.H. "15th Century Jesse Window at St. Margaret's
Church, Margaretting." Journal of the British Society of
Master Glass-Painters 1, no. 3 (Oct. 1925):8-11.
     Flemish panels cut down to be installed in this Essex
church are compared with other Jesse windows in England
and abroad.

19   VELGE, HENRI. La collégiale des Sains Michel et Gudule à
Bruxelles. Brussels: A. Dewit, 1926, 390 pp., 100 pls.,
30 illus. in text.
     Describes fragments from the 13th-16th centuries and
15th and 16th century documents which refer to the glazing
and supply a list of glaziers.

20   POPHAM, A.E. "Notes on Flemish Domestic Glass Painting--I."
Apollo 7 (1928):175-79.
     Growth of this minor art in the 15th and 16th centuries
first connected with the school of van der Goes; discusses
the style of the Master of the Tobit Legend in his eponymous
15th century window.

L.C. 21

21 BYE, ARTHUR EDWIN. "Stained Glass Panels from the Workshop of
    Dirk Vellert in the Goldman Collection." <u>Art Bulletin</u> 11
    (1929):125-45.
        Evidence that Dirk Vellert, not Bernard van Orley, was
    the designer of many of these panels (ca. 1530) represent-
    ing the Life of Christ and medallions depicting prophet
    figures.

22 POPHAM, A.E. "Notes on Flemish Domestic Glass Painting--II."
    <u>Apollo</u> 9 (1929):152-57.
        Discusses 16th century roundels by the Master of the
    Acts of Mercy, Arnold of Nijmegen, and Dirk Vellert; the
    latter's style is rooted in 15th century painting.

23 *LAFOND, JEAN. <u>Arnoult de Nimègue et son oeuvre</u>. Rouen, 1930.
        16th century glass in Tournai, Malines, etc. attributed
    to this painter (Arnold of Nijmegen).

24 RACKHAM, BERNARD. "The Stained Glass in the Chapel of the
    Holy Blood at Bruges." In <u>Actes du XIIe Congrès inter-
    national d'histoire de l'art</u>. Vol. 2. Brussels: Musées
    royaux des beaux-arts de Belgique, 1930, pp. 424-31.
        Nine windows in museums representing members of the
    house of Burgundy and its successors, dated to the end of
    the 15th century, were perhaps executed by the same glazier
    who worked at Tournai.

25 HELBIG, JEAN. "A propos du déchiffrement de quelques 'signa-
    tures' sur nos anciens vitraux." <u>Art et vie</u> 3 (1936):
    359-66.
        Examines the problem of attribution through signatures
    and monograms as exemplified by the Tournai windows, cor-
    rectly attributed to Arnold of Nijmegen by Jean Lafond
    (L.C. 23, cf. Wayment, L.C. 52).

26 _____. "Les plus anciens vitraux conservés en Belgique."
    <u>Bulletin des Musées royaux d'art et d'histoire</u> (Brussels),
    3d ser. 1 (1937):2-11.
        Flemish glass from the 12th-14th centuries now in the
    Brussels museum and various churches in Belgium.

27 _____. "L'introduction du style Renaissance dans nos vitraux
    à l'époque austro-espagnole." <u>Bulletin des Musées royaux
    d'art et d'histoire</u> (Brussels), 3d ser. 3 (1937):50-60.
        Medallions dating 1482-1555 now in museum collections
    in Brussels.

28   _____. "La peinture sur verre dans les Pays-Bas, méridio-
naux." <u>Annales de la Société royale d'archéologie:
Bruxelles</u> 42 (1938):147-84.
        Brief outline of the sequence of styles.

29   BOOM, A. Van der. <u>Monumentale glasschilderkunst in Nederland</u>.
Vol. 1. Antwerp: Martinus, 1940, 224 pp., 57 figs. [No
other volumes published.]
        16th century glass painting in the north and south;
includes artists such as Bernard van Orley, Dirk Vellert,
Pieter Coecke the Elder, Arnold of Nijmegen, and Lucas van
Leyden, and discusses drawings for glass.

30   HELBIG, JEAN. "Verrières héraldiques de la famille de Charles
Quint." <u>Revue belge d'archéologie et d'histoire de l'art</u>
11 (1941):245-62.
        Comments on the increased production of stained glass
during the reigns of Marguerite of Austria (historiated
panels) and her nephew Charles V (heraldic glass), and, in
particular, on five windows attributed to Rombouts (Ste.
Waudru in Mons, 1511; St. Gommaire in Lierre, 1516-19; St.
Gudule in Brussels, ca. 1520).

31   _____. "'Dernières cènes' dans le vitrail belge." <u>Apollo:
Chronique des beaux arts</u> 12 (1942):17-20.
        Three windows (of 1535, 1538, and 1600) and their icono-
graphic relationship to Pieter Coecke's panel painting of
the Last Supper (1531) in the Musée de Bruxelles.

32   VROOM, N.R.A. "Een onbekende ontwerpteekening voor een
gebrandschilderd glas in de St. Lieve Monsterkerk te
Zierikzee." <u>Oud-Holland</u> 59 (1942):171-78.
        Drawing (<u>vidimus</u>) in the Public Record Office, Haarlem,
dated 1523 by its heraldry, was probably for a lost window
in the abbey church at Zierikzee.

33   HELBIG, JEAN. "La verrière de la nation espagnole à la
cathédrale d'Anvers." <u>Apollo: Chronique des beaux arts</u>
19 (1943):11-14.
        Reconstructs a window representing St. James and a Tree
of Jesse, executed 1481-82 by two artists from Louvain,
Nicolas Rombouts and Henri van Diependale. Archival documents support the reconstruction.

L.C. 34

34   _____. De glasschilderkunst in België: Repertorium en docu-
menten. 2 vols. Antwerp: De Sikkel, 1943-51. Vol. 1,
1943, 244 pp., 7 color pls., 262 figs. Vol. 2, with R.
van Steenberghe de Dourmont, 1951, 108 pp., 191 figs.
        Surveys technical developments up to the 18th century
and notes extant windows in Belgium. Provides iconographic
and typographical tables of extant and lost works and of
glass painters named in documents, including Flemish
artists working abroad. Bibliography.

35   BOGTMAN, W. Nederlandsche glasschilders. Amsterdam: De
Lange, 1944, 128 pp., 24 pls., figs. in text.
        Brief history, with a technical introduction. Empha-
sizes the major glass painters of the 16th century in the
Low Countries.

36   HELBIG, JEAN. "Le flux du style Renaissance dans les vitraux
liégeois." Revue belge d'archéologie et d'histoire de
l'art 14 (1944):69-80.
        Transformation of the Renaissance style in windows from
the first half of the 16th century attributed to Jean de
Cologne and Rombouts.

37   _____. "Deux inconnus dans les vitraux de la collégiale
Sainte-Gudule à Bruxelles." Pro arte: Internationale
Zeitschrift für alte und zeitgenössiche Kunst 5 (1946):
335-40.
        Five windows from the apse representing the family of
Charles V dated ca. 1520; the two donors may be portraits
of Don Juan d'Aragon and Marguerite of Austria.

38   BOOM, A. Van der. "Een Nederlands glasschilder in den
vreemde, Aerdt Ortkens van Nijmegen." Nederlandsch kunst-
historisch jaarboek (Bussum, Amsterdam) 2 (1948-49):75-103,
378.
        Attempts to connect drawings attributed to Arnold of
Nijmegen with windows in Tournai, Normandy, etc. identified
as his works by Lafond (L.C. 23). English summary.

39   HELBIG, JEAN. "La peinture sur verre en Belgique à l'époque
et à la suite de Rogier van der Weyden." In Fédération
d'archéologie, d'histoire de Belgique, 33e Congrès
(Tournai, 1949). Brussels: Éditions "Labor," 1951,
pp. 659-72.
        Concludes that Roger was not a glass painter or designer;
however, after his death his influence on these arts was
strong.

40 ____. "Les auteurs des verrières d'Hoogstraten." Revue
belge d'archéologie et d'histoire de l'art 18 (1949):35-51.
    Identifies ten painters who participated in the execution
of the glass and their characteristic styles.

41 *POUMON, ÉMILE. Le Hainaut--Les vitraux. Vilvorde: André
Mees, 1949, 33 pp., 18 pls.
    Documentation for lost and extant glass in Hainaut and
Tournai; presentation of surviving windows from these
ancient regions now in Belgium and France includes
Landelies, Mons, Tournai, and Hestrud. [Notes based on a
review by J. Helbig, Revue belge d'archéologie et d'histoire
de l'art, 19 (1950):227.]

42 *HELBIG, JEAN. "L'évolution du décor architectural dans le
vitrail belge pendant le premier quart du xvie siècle."
Bulletin de la Commission royale des monuments et des sites
(Brussels) 3 (1951-52):7-20. [Répertoire d'Art et
d'Archéologie].
    The assimilation of Renaissance architectural styles
more rapid in representations in glass than in other media
or than in architecture itself.

43 LAFOND, JEAN. "Le peintre-verrier Arnoult de Nimègue (Aert
van Oort) et les débuts de la Renaissance à Rouen et à
Anvers." In Actes du XVIIe Congès international d'histoire
de l'art (Amsterdam, 1952). La Haye: Imp. nationale des
Pays-Bas, 1955, pp. 333-44.
    Attributes three early 16th century windows to Arnold of
Nijmegen. Originally from Antwerp, these works represent
the Death of the Virgin, the Tree of Jesse, and the Foun-
tain of the Acts of Mercy. One window from Rouen (a St.
John the Baptist, dated 1507, now in Wells Cathedral)
demonstrates the artist's influence in Normandy.

44 DEVLIEGHER, LUC. "Enkele brugse glasramen uit het einde der
xve eeuw." Revue belge d'archéologie et d'histoire de
l'art 23 (1954):197-202.
    Development of glass around 1500--the influence of
Memling in the lost glass of Ste. Walburge (1496), known
from an 18th century drawing; and later trends in the
panels with St. George and St. Michael in the Gruuthuze-
museum, Bruges.

45 HELBIG, JEAN. "De glazeniers." In Flandria nostra. Edited
by J.L. Broeckx, C. de Clercq, J. Ohoudt, and M.A.
Nauwelaerts. Vol. 2. Antwerp: N.V. Standaard, 1957,
pp. 367-95.
    Brief survey of glass painters known to have worked in
the Netherlands and abroad and their extant works. Covers
the 13th-18th centuries. Indexes, short bibliography.

46 _____. "Vitraux XVIᵉ s. des églises liégeoises." In Actes du
1ᵉʳ Congrès des journées international du verre. Liège,
1958, pp. 131-32.
    Discusses a Coronation of the Virgin, dated 1530 and
attributed to Jean de Cologne; and windows from 1525-27 in
the churches of St.-Jacques and St.-Martin.

47 _____. Les vitraux médiévaux conservés en Belgique, 1200-1500.
Corpus Vitrearum Medii Aevi: Belgique, vol. 1. Brussels:
Weissenbruch, 1961, 296 pp., 171 figs. (10 color).
    Complete presentation of extant glass of the 13th-15th
centuries, including panels in museums not assigned to
specific sites or ateliers.

48 WINKLER, FRIEDRICH. "Eine flämische Folge von Rundscheiben
der Sakramente." Pantheon 19 (1961):284-88.
    One of the surviving roundels for the sacrament of
Marriage and a drawing for the sacrament of Baptism are
attributed to the same artist, active ca. 1475-85 in Ghent
or Bruges; his style is compared with that of Hugo van der
Goes, Sanders Bening (here identified with the Master of
Mary of Burgundy), and Gerard Horenbout. The other roundel
(Confession) is by a different hand but belongs to the same
series. English summary.

49 SCHAFFRAN, EMERICH. "Zwei Zeichnungen des Jan de Beer,
Neuerwerbungen der Albertina." Pantheon 20 (1962):48-50.
    Two full-size cartoons for a Tree of Jesse, ca. 1520.

50 BOON, K.G. "Two Designs for Windows by Dierick Vellert."
Master Drawings 2 (1964):153-56.
    A drawing for the window designs of the King's College
Chapel, Cambridge (ca. 1523), now in the Bowdoin College
Museum (Maine), and another for the cathedral of Antwerp
(ca. 1516), now in a private collection in Amsterdam, are
attributed to Dirk Vellert.

51 LEFÈVRE, P. "Textes d'archives relatifs aux vitraux disparus de la cathédrale Saint-Michel à Bruxelles." Cahiers bruxellois 11 (1966):149-67.
     List of 15th-17th century documents which refer to repairs made on the glass in the 13th-17th centuries.

52 WAYMENT, HILARY. "A Rediscovered Master: Adrian van den Houte (c. 1459-1521) and the Malines/Brussels School. I." Oud Holland 82 (1967):172-202.
     Distinguishes between Arnold of Nijmegen and Adrian van den Houte (cf. Lafond, L.C. 23); identifies the latter as the glazier for the Tournai windows and author of drawings formerly attributed to Arnold (Aert Ortkens, cf. Friedländer); appendix of surviving works by Arnold of Nijmegen.

53 HELBIG, JEAN. Les vitraux de la première moitié du xvie siècle conservés en Belgique: Province d'Anvers et Flandres. Corpus Vitrearum Medii Aevi, Addenda: Belgique, vol. 2. Brussels: F. Van Buggenhoudt, 1968, 317 pp., 226 figs. (11 color).
     Complete publication of glass in Antwerp, Bruges, Herentals, Hoogstraeten, Lierre, Rumberke, and Sint-Lenaarts.

54 WAYMENT, HILARY G. "A Rediscovered Master: Adrian van den Houte (c. 1459-1521) and the Malines/Brussels School. II: Adrian van den Houte as a Tapestry Designer." Oud Holland 83 (1968):71-94.
     Five tapestries attributed to him on the basis of style. Their process of design and execution similar to glass; compares them with work of the Tournai shop (which he dates ca. 1513). Follows L.C. 52.

55 VANDEN BEMDEN, YVETTE. "Vitraux brabançons du 16e s.: Anderlecht, Diest, Oisquercq, Steenhuffel." Revue d'archéologues et histoiriens d'art de Louvains 2 (1969): 104-5.
     Summary of a thesis (licence), University of Louvain, 1968. Windows of 1520-30 which represent a transition from the medieval to the Renaissance style.

56 WAYMENT, HILARY G. "An Early Work by Arnold of Nijmegen in the Rijksmuseum." In Miscellanea I.Q. van Retgeren Altena. Edited by H. Miedema, R.W. Scheller, and P.J.J. van Thiel. Amsterdam: Scheltema & Holkema, 1969, pp. 33-35, 257-59.
     Half-length figure of St. Catherine from St. Walburga, Zutphen attributed to Arnold of Nijmegen on the basis of style; review of the chronology of Arnold's works;

L.C. 56

suggested date of late in the 15th century since altered in
favor of ca. 1517 (communication from the author, 1981).

57 _____. "A Rediscovered Master: Adrian van den Houte of
Malines (c. 1459-1521) and the Malines/Brussels School
III: Adrian's Development and his Relation with Bernard
van Orley." Oud Holland 84 (1969):257-69.
Adrian identified as a stained glass painter influenced
by Nicholas Rombouts; eight drawings ascribed to Bernard
van Orley show a close relationship to Adrian's work (cf.
Lafond, L.C. 23).

58 GIBSON, WALTER S. "Two Painted Glass Panels from the Circle
of Lucas van Leyden." Bulletin of the Cleveland Museum of
Art 57 (1970):81-92.
Two panels representing the Judgment of Solomon and
Esther before Ahaseurus were executed as a pair ca. 1530;
discusses their iconography, technique, and style.

59 DEWAIDE, MYRIAM. "Les vitraux conservés à la chapelle
castrale d'Enghien." Revue d'archéologues et histoiriens
d'art de Louvains 4 (1971):276.
Summary of a thesis (licence), University of Louvain,
1970. Three 16th century windows from the church of Dion-
le-Val.

60 DEVLIEGHER, L. "Vondsten in de Sint-Jakobskerk te Ieper en in
de Sint-Walburgakerk te Veurne." Société d'emulation pour
l'étude de l'histoire et des antiquités de la Flandre 109
(1972):229-36.
Fragments found in the municipal works, dated early 13th
century by their technique. Largely grisaille.

61 MAES, PAUL VICTOR. "Oud Leuvens brandglas in Engeland." Arca
lovaniensis: Artes atque historiae reserans documenta
(Jaarboek vrienden Stedelijk Museum, Leuven) 1 (1972):
189-201.
Three groups of Flemish panels in English collections,
notably in the Victoria and Albert Museum. These include
early 16th and 17th century roundels for which there are
counterparts from the same cartoons in Louvain; and early
16th century colored panels. French summary.

62 BOON, K.G. "De vroegste glaskartons uit de Sint-Janskerk te
Gouda." Bulletin van het Rijksmuseum 21 (1973):151-75.
Cartoons for St. John's Church, Gouda, with the Sacraments are based on designs by Lucas van Leyden, perhaps
dated ca. 1508. English summary (pp. 201-3).

63   MAES, PAUL VICTOR. "Nicolaas Ruterius en de brandglassuite
     met de geschiedenis van Sint-Nicolaas." Arca lovaniensis:
     Artes atque historiae reserans documenta (Jaarboek vrienden
     Stedelijk Museum, Leuven) 2 (1973):181-208.
         Six panels with scenes from a Life of St. Nicholas, now
     dispersed in American and British collections, are identi-
     fied with the documented gift of a window to the chartreuse
     of Louvain by N. Ruterius (d. 1509). Henri Diependale was
     providing glass for that house up to 1509. French summary.

64   UYTVEN, RAYMOND van. "Leuvense glasschilders, Klaas Rombouts
     en Croy-Ramen te Aarschot en elders." Arca lovaniensis:
     Artes atque historiae reserans documenta (Jaarboek vrienden
     Stedelijk Museum, Leuven) 2 (1973):61-89.
         14th-17th century records of glass painters in Louvain
     associated with their extant works, e.g., parts of a window
     from Aarschot by Nicolas Rombouts, 1507-08, now in the
     Victoria and Albert Museum, London. English summary.

65   VANDEN BEMDEN, YVETTE. "Vitraux liégeois de la première
     moitiés du 16e siècle." Revue d'archéologues et histoiriens
     d'art de Louvains 6 (1973):224-29.
         Summary of a Ph.D. dissertation, University of Louvain,
     1972. Late medieval and Renaissance glass of ca. 1520-30.

66   HELBIG, JEAN, and VANDEN BEMDEN, YVETTE. Les vitraux de la
     première moitié du XVIe siècle conservés en Belgique:
     Brabant et Limbourg. Corpus Vitrearum Medii Aevi:
     Belgique, Addenda, vol. 3. Ledeberg/Ghent: Erasmus for
     the Ministère de l'éducation nationale et de la culture,
     1974, 296 pp., 205 figs. (11 color).
         Complete publication of glass from Brussels, Anderlecht,
     Diest, Louvain, Oisquercq, Steenhuffel, and s'Heren-Elderen.

67   VANDEN BEMDEN, YVETTE. Les vitraux de la première moitié du
     XVIe siècle conservés en Belgique: Provinces de Liège,
     Luxembourg, Namur. Corpus Vitrearum Medii Aevi: Belgique,
     vol. 4. Ledeberg/Ghent: Erasmus for the Ministère de
     l'éducation nationale et de la culture, 1981, 443 pp.,
     316 figs. (many in color).
         Complete publication of glass in Huy, Liège, St.-Hubert,
     and Namur.

Section XII
Scandinavia: Denmark, Norway, and Sweden

1   HASELOFF, ARTHUR. "Die Glasmalereien in der Kirche zu
    Breitenfelde und die deutsch-nordischen künstlerischen
    Beziehungen im 13. Jahrhundert." In Festgabe Anton
    Schifferer zum 60. Geburtstag. Veröff. d. Schleswig-
    Holsteinisch Universität-Gesellschaft, 37. Breslau:
    Hirth, 1931.
        A Christological cycle in the choir is dated, on the
    basis of style, mid-13th century and is related to the
    schools of Thuringia-Saxony and Gotland.

2   HABICHT, V. CURT. "Niedersächsische Glasmalereien in
    Skandinavien." Forschungen und Forschritte (Berlin) 9
    (1933):405-7.
        Summary of a dissertation (Technische Hochschule,
    Hanover). Provides a chronology for the stylistically
    related group of windows in Goslar (ca. 1200), Bücken (ca.
    1220), Breitenfelde (ca. 1235), and at the Swedish sites
    of Dalhem, Barlingbo, Lojsta, and Rone (ca. 1240).

3   *_____. Niedersächsische Glasmalerei des Mittelalters in
    Skandinavien. Osnabrück, 1943.
        Publication of a thesis (Sc. 2).

4   ROOSVAL, JOHNNY. "Medieval Schools of Stained Glass Painting
    in Gotland." Gazette des beaux-arts 28 (1945):193-204.
        Analyzes six schools of glass painters working from
    1220 to 1400; the early masters were of German origin; in
    the period 1270-1350 French, English, and Norwegian influ-
    ences are seen; 1360-1400 a period of diversity.

5   _____. Gotländsk vitriarius: De medeltida gotländska glas-
    målningarnas bestånd och historia [The glass painter in
    Gotland: Medieval stained glass in Gotland, its descrip-
    tion and history]. Stockholm: Esselte, 1945-46, 150 pp.,
    27 color pls., 150 figs. Basel: Holbein-Verlag, 1947,
    20 pp., 10 pls. (some color). Stockholm: Generalstabens

Sc. 5

Litografiska Anstalts Förlag, 1950, 236 pp., 54 pls. (27 color), 186 figs. [Only 1950 edition examined.]
   13th–15th century glass in Gotland with a catalog of sites. Discusses the stylistic relation to wall paintings, manuscripts, etc. and its iconography. Art historical analysis is lengthier than that of the Corpus volume (Sc. 6).
   In Swedish.

6   ANDERSSON, ARON; CHRISTIE, SIGRID; NORDMAN, CARL AXEL; and ROUSSELL, AAGE. Die Glasmalereien des Mittelalters in Skandinavien. Corpus Vitrearum Medii Aevi: Skandinavien. Stockholm: Almqvist & Wiskell, 1964, 321 pp., 203 pls. (30 color).
   Complete catalog, chiefly of 13th century glass, with an excellent introduction analyzing foreign influences. Lacks restoration charts.

Section XIII
Switzerland

The reader is also referred to Gen. 53.

1 LÜBKE, WILHELM. "Die Glasgemälde im Kreuzgange zu Kloster
   Wettingen." Mitteilungen der antiquarischen Gesellschaft
   in Zürich 14 (1863):113-28.
   Discusses the building's history and the glass, dating
   from the 14th century and ca. 1520-1623. Illustrations
   are from drawings.

2 _____. Über die alten Glasgemälde der Schweiz: Ein Versuch.
   Zürich: Verlag der schabelis'schen Buchhandlung (Cäsar
   Schmidt), 1866, 58 pp., no illustrations.
   General introductory history; examines the 13th century
   glass of Lausanne, etc.

3 *_____. Die Glasgemälde im Chor des Klosters Königsfelden.
   Zürich, 1867, 41 pls. [Becksmann].

4 *MÜLINEN, EGBERT FRIEDRICH von. Über die Glasmalerei in der
   Schweiz. Berne: Buchdrucker B.F. Haller, 1872, 16 pp.

5 RAHN, J. RUDOLF. "Die Glasgemälde in der Rosette der Kathedrale von Lausanne: Ein Bild der Welt aus dem XIII. Jahrhundert." Mitteilungen der antiquarischen Gesellschaft in
   Zürich 20, nos. 1-2 (1879):29-58. *French translation.
   Cart, W. "La rose de la cathédrale de Lausanne: Über-
   setzung des deutschen Textes von J.R. Rahn." Mémoires et
   documents publiés par la Société d'histoire de la Suisse
   romande (1879).
   Cosmological program of the 13th century rose is described and compared with Chartres sculpture, etc. Illustrations are from drawings.

6   HOWALD, K. "Der zehntausend Ritter-Tag und das zehntausend
      Ritter-Fenster im berner Münster." Berner Taschenbuch 34
      (1885):98-137.
         Examines the legend and cult of the 10,000 Martyrs and
      describes the 15th century window of that subject in Berne.
      Restorations noted.

7   BERLEPSCH, H.E. von. "Die Entwicklung der Glasmalerei in der
      Schweiz." Zeitschrift des Kunstgewerber-Vereins in
      München (1886):17-23.
         Survey of 15th-16th century sacred and secular glass,
      illustrated with the author's drawings, largely of details
      in Muri and of Kabinettscheiben in the Bürki collection,
      Berne, from the latter part of the 16th century.

8   BURCKHARDT, ALBERT. "Die Glasgemälde aus der Kirche zu
      Läufelfingen." Basler Jahrbuch (1888):260-67.
         Inventory of the 15th-16th century glass from this
      village church, some of which is now in collections. Not
      illustrated.

9   RAHN, J.R. "Das älteste Glasgemälde in der Schweiz."
      Anzeiger für schweizerische Altertumskunde 23 (1890):
      314-15.
         "Discovery" in 1884 of the Virgin and Child in Flums;
      dates it to the early 13th century or before. Illustrated
      with an engraving.

10   WACKERNAGEL, RUDOLF. "Die Glasgemälde der Basler Karthause."
      Anzeiger für schweizerische Altertumskunde 23 (1890):
      369-81; 24 (1891):432-35.
         Describes a lost window, dated 1487, made for the
      Carthusian church, donations of glass recorded for that
      church, description of surviving panels.

11   OIDTMANN, HEINRICH. "Die schweizer Glasmalerei vom Ausgange
      des XV. bis zum Beginn des XVIII. Jahrhunderts." Zeit-
      schrift für christliche Kunst 12 (1899):301-18; 14 (1901):
      129-40, 239-54, 261-76.
         Very general history, poorly illustrated.

12   LEHMANN, HANS. "Die Glasgemälde in aargauischen Kirchen and
      öffentlichen Gebäuden." Anzeiger für schweizerische
      Altertumskunde, n.s. 4 (1902-3):184-97.
         16th century panels in Uerkheim and Reitnau.

13 _____. "Zur Geschichte der Glasmalerei in der Schweiz, I:
Ihre Entwicklung bis zum Schlusse des 14. Jahrhunderts."
Mitteilungen der antiquarischen Gesellschaft in Zürich 26,
no. 4 (1906):157-316. Reprinted, with part II (Sw. 17),
as Zur Geschichte der Glasmalerei in der Schweiz. 2 vols.
(Zürich: Fäsi & Beer, 1925). Vol. 1, 162 pp., 43 pls.,
34 figs. in text. Vol. 2, 115 pp., 43 pls., 37 figs. in
text.
        General history, covering major Swiss monuments from
the 13th century on.

14 MANDACH, CONRAD de. "La peinture sur verre en Suisse [à
l'époque gothique]." In Histoire de l'art, by André
Michel. Vol. 2, pt. 1. Paris: A. Colin, 1906, pp. 397-
401.
        Survey of major sites of the 13th-14th centuries, in-
cluding Lausanne and Königsfelden.

15 _____. "La peinture en Suisse au XVᵉ siècle: Les vitraux
religieux." In Histoire de l'art depuis les premières
temps chrétiens jusqu'à nos jours, by André Michel.
Vol. 3, pt. 1. Paris: A. Colin, [1907], pp. 292-99.
        Discusses Berne, etc. Illustrated.

16 LEHMANN, HANS. "Die Glasmalerfamilie Wildermut zu Biel und
Neuenburg und die Glasgemälde in der Kirche zu Ligerz."
Anzeiger für schweizerische Altertumskunde, n.s. 12 (1910):
235-47.
        Documents concerning two glass painters named Jakob
Wildermut, active in Biel and elsewhere, 1467/68-1541, and
their surviving works.

17 _____. "Zur Geschichte der Glasmalerei in der Schweiz, II:
Die monumentale Glasmalerei im 15. Jahrhundert." Mitteilungen der antiquarischen Gesellschaft in Zürich 26, no. 10
(1910):420-34.
        For Part I and the 1925 reprint see Sw. 13.

18 _____. "Die Glasmalerei in Bern am Ende des 15. und Anfang
des 16. Jahrhunderts." Anzeiger für schweizerische Altertumskunde, n.s. 15 (1913):45-52, 100-116, 205-26, 321-46.
        Pp. 45-52 examines the documents about Peter Streiff's,
Hans Abegg's, and Hans Strumph's activity ca. 1480-1520,
and their surviving works. Pp. 100-116 discusses general
developments in heraldic glass, etc. ca. 1500 and the work
of Hans Hänle. Pp. 205-26 deals with the documented work
of Lukas Schwarz, ca. 1500-1520, which was chiefly

Sw. 18

heraldic. Pp. 321-46 continues the study of works attributed to Lukas Schwarz.

19   _____. "Die Glasmalerei in Bern am Ende des 15. und Anfang
des 16. Jahrhunderts." Anzeiger für schweizerische Alter-
tumskunde, n.s. 16 (1914):41-57, 124-50, 207-33, 304-24.
Continuation of Sw. 18; discusses the work of Lukas
Schwarz, Hans Sterr, Jakob Meier, Jakob Stächeli, Hans
Dachselhofer, Jakob Wyss, and Hans Funck (d. before 1545).

20   _____. "Die Glasmalerei in Bern am Ende des 15. und Anfang
des 16. Jahrunderts." Anzeiger für schweizerische Altertumskunde, n.s. 17 (1915):45-65, 136-59, 217-40, 305-29.
Continuation of Sw. 18 and 19; examines the work of Hans
Funck.

21   BURCKHARDT, RUDOLF F. Die gotischen Glasgemälde der ehemaligen
Karthäuserkirche, jetzigen Waisenhauskirche zu Basel.
Jahresbericht des Historischen Museums, 1915. Basel:
Basler Druck und Verlagsanstalt, 1916, 27 pp., 4 color pls.,
9 figs.
The central window of the choir was given in 1416; its
fragments and later panels were removed to the historical
museum in Basel.

22   LEHMANN, HANS. "Die Glasmalerei in Bern am Ende des 15. und
Anfang des 16. Jahrhunderts." Anzeiger für schweizerische
Altertumskunde, n.s. 18 (1916):54-74, 135-53, 225-43.
Continuation of Sw. 18, 19, and 20; study of drawings
attributed to Hans Funck and discussion of Niklaus (I.)
Schmalz. Includes notes, corrections, and an index.

23   SCHMARSOW, AUGUST. Das Franziskusfenster in Königsfelden und
der Freskenzyklus in Assisi. Bericht über die Verhandlungen
der sächsischen Akademie der Wissenschaften zu Leipzig,
Philologisch-historische Klasse, vol. 71, pt. 3. Leipzig:
B.G. Teubner, 1919, 38 pp.
Reviews dating (1320s-1330s) and the impact of Assisi
models on a northern Gothic atelier.

24   DEMOLE, H. "Note additionnelle." Genava 3 (1925):338-39.
Follows Sw. 25. Argues that the 15th century St.-Pierre
glass is not the work of one atelier from Paris (cf.
Deonna) and that some of the artisans were probably influenced by Flemish art.

25   DEONNA, W. "Les anciens vitraux de Saint-Pierre et leur
     restauration." Genava 3 (1925):319-38.
        Description and restoration of windows with various
     saints, from the end of the 15th century; all are from the
     same atelier but by different hands.

26   BROILLET, HENRI. "Les vitraux du choeur de l'abbaye
     d'Hauterive." Annales fribourgeoises (1926):30-42.
        Reconstruction of glass (1322-27) mentioned in two
     ancient documents and its restoration.

27   LEHMANN, HANS. Lukas Zeiner und die spätgotische Glasmalerei
     in Zürich. Mitteilungen der antiquarischen Gesellschaft,
     vol. 30, pt. 2. Zürich: Gebrude Leemann, 1926, 71 pp.,
     24 pls., 15 figs. in text.
        Definitive study of this painter's work (d. by 1519);
     mainly small heraldic panels.

28   _____. "Die schweizerische Kabinett-Glasmalerei." In XIVe
     Congrès international de l'histoire de l'art: Manuel.
     Basel: Holbein Verlag, 1936, pp. 92-98.
        Introductory essay provides definitions and outlines its
     secular character. Examples are of the late 15th-17th
     centuries.

29   FRANKL, PAUL. "Das Passionsfenster im berner Münster u. der
     Glasmaler Hans Acker von Ulm." Anzeiger für schweizerische
     Altertumskunde 40 (1938):217-42, 256-63.
        Examines documented and attributed works of Hans von
     Ulm and the problem of his identity as Hans Acker/Hans
     Deckinger.

30   COHN, WERNER. "Two Glass Panels after Designs by Hans
     Holbein." Burlington Magazine 75 (1939):115-21.
        Their style is characteristic of the non-classicizing
     phase in this artist's development, ca. 1517-18.

31   DIETSCHI, HUGO. "Statistik solothurnischer Glasgemälde."
     Jahrbuch für Solothurnische Geschichte 13 (1940):1-114;
     14 (1941):1-55.
        Inventory of glass in the district, some of which is
     dated before 1540. Bibliography and indexes of sites,
     donors, and glass painters. Not illustrated.

Sw. 32

32   LEHMANN, HANS. Geschichte der luzerner Glasmalerei von den
     Anfängen bis zu Beginn des 18. Jahrhunderts. Luzern Ge-
     schichte und Kultur, vol. 3, no. 5. Lucerne: Buch-
     druckerei Keller & Co., 1941, 283 pp., 288 pls.
         Chapter I deals with monumental glass and small panels
     up to the Reformation; includes artists, documents, and
     attributed works.

33   BACH, EUGÈNE. "Les vitraux." In La cathédrale de Lausanne,
     by E. Bach et al. Monuments d'art et d'histoire du canton
     de Vaud, 16. Bâle: Birkhäuser, 1944, pp. 245-65.
         Describes the rose window and the medallions represent-
     ing St. John the Baptist and the Passion (mid-13th cen-
     tury).

34   ZSCHOKKE, FRIDTJOF. Mittelalterliche Bildfenster der Schweiz.
     Basel: Holbein Verlag, 1946, 20 pp., 10 color pls. En-
     glish translation. *Mediaeval Stained Glass in Switzerland.
     Translated by Douglas Cooper. London: Falcon Press, 1947.
     French translation. Vitraux du Moyen Âge en Suisse.
     Basel: Holbein, 1947, 20 pp., 10 color pls.
         Excellent, large color reproductions of selected panels
     from the 12th (Flums) to late 15th centuries (Romont),
     including Königsfelden and Berne.

35   Königsfelden: Farbenfenster des XIV. Jahrhunderts. Intro-
     duction by Michael Stettler. Berne: Laupen bei Bern,
     Iris Verlag, 1949, 31 pp., 16 color pls. English transla-
     tion. Swiss Stained Glass of the 14th Century from the
     Church of Königsfelden. Iris colour books. London: B.T.
     Batsford, 1949, 31 pp., 16 pls., 6 illus. French transla-
     tion. Les vitraux de Königsfelden, XIVe siècle. Collec-
     tion "Iris," 13. Paris: Plon, 1949, 31 pp., 16 color
     pls., 6 figs.
         Windows were executed 1325-30, from east to west, and
     were conceived by a single master who was influenced by
     Viennese art as it was transmitted via Italy.

36   BLONDEL, LOUIS. "Liste des peintres verriers de la cathédrale
     Saint-Pierre, de la chapelle des Macchabées, et de Notre-
     Dame-la-Neuve." Genava 28 (1950):47-51.
         Lists windows from the beginning of the 15th century to
     the Reformation; all are now destroyed except for one in
     the Musée d'art et d'histoire in Geneva.

37   HAHNLOSER, HANS R. Chorfenster und Altäre des berner Münsters.
     Berner Schriften zur Kunst, 5. Berne: Benteli, 1950,
     57 pp., 8 color pls. (unbound), 23 figs.
        Fully annotated plates with details of the choir glass
     (1441 and 1450-51); discusses its relation to panel paint-
     ing. Bibliography. English and French summaries.

38   BAUM, JULIUS. "Ein Fenster des Markgrafen Christoph von
     Baden aus dem zürcher Augustinerkloster." Zeitschrift für
     schweizerische Archaeologie und Kunstgeschichte 12 (1951):
     216-17.
        Donor portrait of 1519 from the Augustinian convent in
     Zurich is recognized as that of Christoph von Baden (cf.
     Sw. 44).

39   DEONNA, W. "Cathédrale Saint-Pierre de Genève: Les vitraux."
     Genava 29 (1951):88-104.
        Reconstructs seven figural windows, partially destroyed
     in the 18th century on the basis of archeological docu-
     ments. These examples dating from the end of the 15th
     century are the last Swiss glasswork of the Gothic period.

40   BEER, ELLEN J. Die Rose der Kathedrale von Lausanne und der
     kosmologische Bilderkreis des Mittelalters. Berner
     Schriften zur Kunst, 6. Berne: Benteli Verlag, 1952,
     80 pp., 1 color pl., 65 figs. and pls.
        Pictorial and textual sources for the cosmological pro-
     gram of Lausanne's south rose, glazed by Peter of Arras
     before 1235. Additions and modifications in 1970 and 1975
     (Sw. 62, 66).

41   BOESCH, PAUL. "Quellen zur Kultur- und Kunstgeschichte:
     Die Glasgemäldesammlung von Johann Martin Usteri." Zeit-
     schrift für schweizerische Archaeologie und Kunstgeschichte
     14 (1953):107-10.
        Collection of 15th-17th century Swiss glass assembled by
     this painter early in the 19th century; inventories of 1829
     and 1894. Some of the collection is now in the Zurich
     Museum.

42   LAFOND, JEAN. "Les vitraux anciens de la cathédrale de
     Lausanne." Congrès archéologique de France (Suisse
     romande) 110 (1953):116-32.
        Examines the iconography and style of 13th century
     medallions from a Life of John the Baptist (cf. Sw. 40).

Sw. 43

43 STETTLER, MICHAEL. Alte Glasmalerei in der Schweiz. Zurich:
Schweizerische Zentrale für Verkehrsförderung, 1953,
48 pp., 20 color pls.
Poorly illustrated in a small format; informative captions. French and English editions.

44 BOESCH, PAUL, and SCHWARZ, DIETRICH W.H. "Markgraf Christoph I
von Baden als Scheibenstifter." Zeitschrift für schweizerische Archäologie und Kunstgeschichte 15 (1954):20-24.
Provenance of a donor portrait of Christoph I. von
Baden; the same donor appears in a Crucifixion panel,
dated 1519, in Zurich. The latter is attributed to the
same artist, who was from Lucerne or Zurich (cf. Sw. 38).

45 MAURER, EMIL. Das Kloster Königsfelden. Die Kunstdenkmäler
des Kantons Aargau, 3. Basel: Birkhäuser, 1954, 359 pp.,
1 color pl., 311 figs.
Thorough description and analysis of the 14th century
windows of the choir and nave: iconography, restorations,
etc. Chapter on stylistic origins and the variety of
styles within the Königsfelden workshop.

46 SCHNEIDER, JENNY. Die Standesscheiben von Lukas Zeiner im
Tagsatzungssaal zu Baden (Schweiz): Ein Beitrag zur Geschichte der schweizerischen Standesscheiben. Basler
Studien zur Kunstgeschichte, 12. Basel: Birkhäuser,
1954, 150 pp., 39 figs.
Detailed study of this series of town shields of 1501,
the work of Zeiner; their style, technique, and chronology
(a revision of Lehmann, Sw. 27).

47 BOESCH, PAUL. Die schweizer Glasmalerei. Schweizer Kunst,
6. Basel, Birkhäuser, 1955, 182 pp., 1 color pl., 98 figs.
Very brief treatment of 12th-15th century monumental
glass. The discussion of heraldic panels is more detailed
and includes lists of 16th century glass painters in Berne,
Zurich, etc., and their marks.

48 BEER, ELLEN J. Die Glasmalereien der Schweiz vom 12. bis zum
Beginn des 14. Jahrhunderts. Corpus Vitrearum Medii Aevi:
Schweiz, vol. 1. Basel: Birkhäuser, 1956, 140 pp.,
9 color pls., 98 figs.
Comprehensive treatment ranging from the Flums Madonna
(12th century) and Lausanne (before 1235) to Münchenbuchsee
and Sitten (ca. 1300).

49 MUCK, FRIEDRICH. "Mitteilungen zur Kärntner Heraldik und
     Genealogie: Zwei Votivfenster der Stiftskirche Viktring."
     Carinthia 1 (1957):620-22.
        Genealogy of the von Rottenstein family, donors of this
     15th century glass.

50 MAURER, EMIL. "Habsburgische und franziskanische Anteile am
     königsfelder Bildprogramm." Zeitschrift für schweizerische
     Archäologie und Kunstgeschichte 19 (1959):220-25.
        Identification of those members of the Habsburg family
     who appear as donors: Albrecht II of Austria, etc. Fran-
     ciscan elements in the program include motifs borrowed from
     Italian models.

51 FISCHEL, LILLI. "Die Chorfenster des berner Münsters: Zum
     Problem ihrer künstlerischen Herkunft." Kunstchronik 13
     (1960):297-98.
        Styles of the glass painters who provided the Three
     Kings, 10,000 Martyrs, and Old Testament cycles in the
     1440s are related to manuscripts, etc.

52 SCHNEIDER, JENNY; REINHARDT, HANS; and SCHEIDEGGER, ALFRED.
     "Sieben schweizer Glasgemälde." Verlag der eidgenöss-
     ischen Kommission der Gottfried Keller-Stiftung (1960-62):
     pp. 63-67.
        16th century panels; most are dated and contain armorial
     shields.

53 FISCHEL, LILLI. "Die berner Chorfenster: Ihre künstlerische
     Herkunft." Zeitschrift für Kunstwissenschaft 15 (1961):
     1-30.
        Four windows that follow the work of Hans Acker are
     identified as by a Swabian atelier, ca. 1447-55: the
     10,000 Martyrs, the Three Kings, a typological window, and
     the Eucharistic Mill. Their relation to works in other
     media is discussed.

54 ANDERES, BERNHARD. Die spätgotische Glasmalerei in Freiburg
     i. Ü. Freiburger Geschichtsblätter, 51. Fribourg
     (Switzerland): Paulusdruckerei, 1963, 240 pp., 1 color
     pl., 128 figs.
        Monumental glass painting and Kabinettscheiben in the
     region of Fribourg ca. 1400-1540. Based on a Ph.D. disser-
     tation, Fribourg, 1951.

Sw. 55

55   BEER, ELLEN J. "Mediaeval Swiss Stained Glass: An Artistic
      Interplay That Transcended Frontiers." Connoisseur 152
      (1963):94-101.
          Examples of extant 13th, 14th, and 15th century glass
      from various Swiss churches; cites widespread Swabian
      influence in the 14th century and Alsacian influence in
      the 15th.

56   _____. "Die bieler Glasmalerwerkstatt von 1457: Ihre Be-
      ziehung zu den berner Chorfenstern und zur gleichzeitigen
      Glasmalerei am Oberrhein und in Elsass-Lothringen." Unsere
      Kunstdenkmäler 15 (1964):129-37.
          Christological subjects and a Life of St. Benedict in
      the former abbey church of Biel; cites their stylistic
      relations with Berne, Thann, etc., and with works in other
      media (cf. Sw. 58).

57   _____. Die Glasmalereien der Schweiz aus dem 14. und 15.
      Jahrhundert, ohne Königsfelden und berner Münsterchor.
      Corpus Vitrearum Medii Aevi: Schweiz, vol. 3. Basel:
      Birkhäuser, 1965, 268 pp., 17 color pls., 216 pls., figs.
      in text.
          Comprehensive publication includes the important 14th
      century collections at Kappel-am-Albis, Frauenfeld-
      Oberkirch, Blumenstein, and Hauterive; the 15th century
      glass at Zofingen, Staufberg-bei-Lenzburg, Biel, etc.; and
      examples in Swiss and foreign museums.

58   GRÜTTER, MAX. "Ist der Meister des bieler Benediktfensters
      wirklich unbekannt?" Unsere Kunstdenkmäler 16 (1965):77-82.
          Suggests an attribution to Peter Glaser of Berne, the
      same artist who called himself Peter Maler in his signed
      wall paintings in Scherzligen.

59   _____. "Maler und Glasmaler Berns im 14. und 15. Jahrhun-
      dert." Zeitschrift für schweizerische Archäologie und
      Kunstgeschichte 24 (1965-66):211-38.
          Documents concerning painters and glass painters.
      Attributes wall painting in Scherzligen, signed Peter, to
      a glass painter who worked in Biel and Berne Minster (cf.
      Sw. 58).

60   ROUSSET, PAUL. "Un vitrail méconnu." Musées de Genève 84
      (1968):9-11.
          St. James Major from the cathedral of St.-Pierre, now
      in the Musée d'art et d'histoire, dates to the second half
      of the 15th century and was influenced by Burgundian art.

61   BÄCHTIGER, FRANZ. "Erörterungen zum 'Alten und jungen Eidge-
     nossen.'" Jahrbuch des bernischen historischen Museums in
     Bern 49-50 (1969-70):35-70.
         Historical context of a panel by Hans Funck (after 1532)
     showing the Battle of Novara and the confrontation between
     the old and new guard.

62   BEER, ELLEN J. "Nouvelles réflexions sur l'image du monde
     dans la cathédrale de Lausanne." Revue de l'art 10 (1970):
     57-62.
         The south transept rose, the work of Pierre d'Arras,
     1232-35, presents an imago mundi which goes back to
     antiquity. English and German summaries. (Cf. Sw. 40,
     66).

63   MAURER, EMIL. "Die Glasmalereien: Stiftung, Datierung,
     Technik." In Koenigsfelden: Geschichte, Bauten, Glasge-
     mälde, Kunstschätze, by Marcel Beck et al. Olten and
     Freiburg-im-Breisgau: Walter Verlag, 1970, pp. 53-114.
         Essay based on his more scholarly presentation of 1954
     (Sw. 45). Deluxe publication with numerous color plates.

64   SCHWARZ, DIETRICH W.H. "Ikonographie der Glasgemälde." In
     Koenigsfelden: Geschichte, Bauten, Glasgemälde, Kunst-
     schätze, by Marcel Beck et al. Olten and Freiburg-im-
     Breisgau: Walter Verlag, 1970, pp. 115-64.
         Synopsis of the figural subjects.

65   THÖNE, FRIEDRICH. "Zwei Risse zu schaffhauser Prädikanten-
     scheiben von Thomas Schmidt (?) und Hans Caspar Lang."
     Schaffhauser Beiträge zur vaterländischen Geschichte 49
     (1972):53-76.
         Discusses drawings for glass attributed to Schmidt and
     dated to the 1530s; relates these to panels executed by
     Lienhard Brun.

66   BEER, ELLEN J. "Les vitraux du Moyen Âge de la cathédrale."
     In La cathédrale de Lausanne. Berne: Société d'histoire
     de l'art en Suisse, 1975, pp. 221-56.
         Examines the iconography and style of the 13th century
     rose window and its attribution to Pierre of Arras (ca.
     1230); concludes that fragments of the Life of St. John
     the Baptist and the Passion of Christ were executed by a
     different hand, ca. 1219 (cf. Sw. 40, 48, 62).

Sw. 67

67 *WALT, BARBARA SAMMET. "Der Glasmalereizyklus in der Pfarr-
       kirche zu Lauperwil, Kanton Bern." Ph.D. dissertation,
       University of Zürich, 1976.

Section XIV
Other Countries:
Czechoslovakia, Hungary,
Poland, and Turkey

1 *ESSENWEIN, A. Die mittelalterlichen Kunstdenkmale der Stadt
   Krakau. Leipzig, 1869, illustrated. [Duncan, 3854].

2 *DANKÓ, JÓZSEF. Geschichtliches, beschreibendes, und urkund-
   liches aus dem graner Domschatz. Gran: [Druck von A.
   Holzhauen in Wien], 1880, [168 color pls, 2 b&w pls.?]

3 KOPERA, FÉLIX. "Alte polnische Glasmalereien." Zeitschrift
   für alte und neue Glasmalerei 2, no. 9 (1913):97-99.
        Glass painting in Cracow in the 14th-15th centuries.

4 F[ISCHER], J[OSEF] L[UDWIG]. "Altungarische Glasmalereien."
   Zeitschrift für alte und neue Glasmalerei 3, nos. 9-10
   (1914):115-17.
        14th and 15th century glass in Aranyosmaroth and records
   of glazing in Hungary.

5 ANDERSSON, A. "Til det böhmiska glasmåleriets historia pa
   Karl IV:s tid" [On the history of Bohemian glass painting
   in Charles IV's time]. Konsthistorisk tidskrift [Journal
   of art history] 16 (1947):27-39.
        Importance of Bohemia, especially Prague, in the 14th
   century. Only five panels are preserved in Kolin and
   Karlstein; at the latter site Italian influence is seen in
   the painting of a Crucifixion and traditional stained glass
   is used in conjunction with precious gems.
        In Swedish.

6 PIENKOWSKA, HANNA. "Konserwacja witrazy Dominikanskich w
   Krakowie" [Conservation of the stained glass of the
   Dominican church in Cracow]. Ochrona Zabytków [Preserva-
   tion of ancient monuments] (Warsaw) (1949):182-89, 216.
        14th-15th century glass from the Dominican church in
   Cracow removed for conservation and installed in the
   museum; general problems and policies of glass conservation; history of glass painting in Poland, with bibliography.
        In Polish.

Oth. 7

7   LJUBINKOVIĆ, RADIVOJE. "Sur un exemplaire de vitraux du
monastère de Studenica." Archaeologia jugolsavica
(Belgrade) 3 (1959):137-41.
       First publication of a window in Studenica (ca. 1200?)
where the designs of animals, etc., are cut out in lead
instead of being painted. Associated with Byzantine
decorative traditions (cf. Oth. 8).

8   RADOJKOVIĆ, BOJANA. "Olovni prozor iz Bogorodicine crkve u
Studenici" [A leaded window in the Church of the Virgin
in Studenica]. Musej primenjene Umetnosti: Zbornik
[Journal of the Museum of Applied Arts] (Belgrade) 6-7
(1960-61):19-26.
       The leaded window in Studenica, associated with Byzan-
tine traditions, has parallels in 12th century western
painting, especially Mosan. French summary (cf. Oth. 7).
In Serbo-Croatian.

9   KWIATKOWSKI, EDWARD. "Witraze gotyckie z Torunia i Chelmna w
zbiorach Muzeum w Toruniu" [Gothic stained glass from
Toruń and Chelmno in the Museum of Toruń]. Rocznik Muzeum
w Toruniu [Annual bulletin of the Museum of Toruń] (Toruń)
1, no. 3 (1962):98-133.
       14th century panels from Chelmno and Toruń now in the
museum in Toruń, with a catalog. Poorly illustrated.
In Polish.

10   MEGAW, ARTHUR. "Notes on Recent Work of the Byzantine Institute in Istanbul." Dumbarton Oaks Papers 17 (1963):333-71.
       Excavated fragments of life-size figures from Zeyrek
Camii, Istanbul, executed ca. 1126 by a local atelier;
evidence that a strong tradition of glass painting existed
in the east and may have been influential in the west;
similar glass found in Kariye Camii is dated ten-twenty
years later.

11   MAKOUŠ, FRANTIŠEK. "Sklomalby ze Žebnice: Několik poznámek k
jejich slohu" [Die Glasmalereien aus Žebnice: Einige Bemerkungen zu ihrem Stil]. Sbornik národniho Musea v Praze:
Historia (Prague) 21 (1967):233-38.
       Glass from the Cistercian church at Žebnice, now in
museums, is dated ca. 1325-50 on the basis of style and
dates of building and is related to French and Austrian
trends. German summary.

12   LAFOND, JEAN. "Découverte de vitraux historiés du Moyen Âge à
      Constantinople." <u>Cahiers archéologiques</u> 18 (1968):230-38.
          Fragments [now in the Archeological Museum of Istanbul]
      from the church of Kariye Camii show strong affinity with
      German glass. These are not oriental in origin (cf. Megaw,
      Oth. 10) and may postdate the Crusaders' conquest (1204).

13   CIEPIELA, STAWOMIRA. "Le verre en Pologne à la fin du Moyen
      Âge." In <u>Annales du 5e Congrès de l'histoire du verre
      (Prague, 1970)</u>. Liège, 1972, pp. 125-36.
          Technique of stained glass and its production in the
      14th and 15th centuries; some fragments discussed.

14   MATOUŠ, FRANTIŠEK. <u>Mittelalterliche Glasmalerei in der
      Tschechoslowakei</u>. Corpus Vitrearum Medii Aevi:
      Tschechoslowakei. Prague und Vienna: Herman Böhlau,
      1975, 99 pp., 9 color pls., 83 figs.
          The most complete publication of this important Bohemian
      glass from ca. 1350-1500; includes glass in museums.

Author Index

Kleinschmidt, Beda, It. 9
Kline, Naomi Reed, Fr. 425
Knappe, Karl-Adolf, Ger. 113,
137-38, 144, 148
Knappe, U., Ger. 196
Knowles, John Alder, Gen. 30;
Tech. 26, 30-31, 34, 38,
43-44, 46, 49, 60; Br. 70,
88, 89, 98, 103-4, 111-13,
117-19, 124-26, 133-36,
145-46, 149-50, 152-53,
159-61, 169, 196-97, 215,
218, 224-25, 233; Fr. 119
Koch, Walter, Aus. 39
Kolb, Hans, Gen. 17
Kopera, Félix, Oth. 3
Korger, Franz, Aus. 21
Korn, Ulf-Dietrich, Gen. 73f;
Tech. 102, 134e, 153,
Exh. 46; Fr. 376, 380;
Ger. 163, 204, 211
Kraft, Eva. See Frodl-Kraft, Eva
Kraus, Henry, Fr. 300, 308, 315,
319
Kroos, Renate, Ger. 160
Krummer-Schroth, Ingeborg,
Exh. 35; Ger. 164, 197
Kühn, Margarete, Fr. 288
Kühnel, H., Exh. 24
Kühne, Klaus, Tech. 77
Kunze, Hans, Fr. 100
Kurrus, Karl, Ger. 180
Kurthen, J., Ger. 74, 105
Kurthen, W., Ger. 105
Kwiatkowski, Edward, Oth. 9

Lafond, Jean, Gen. 45, 60;
Tech. 53, 64, 78, 82, 96;
Coll. 89-90, 109; Br. 191,
229; Fr. 141, 156, 170, 173-
74, 188, 205, 209-11, 214-15,
223-24, 232, 237, 240, 242,
248, 256-60, 263, 266-67,
274-75, 320-21, 333-35, 363,
381; L.C. 23, 43; Sw. 42;
Oth. 12
Lahanier, Charles, Tech. 99, 106c
Lamborn, E.A. Greening, Br. 200
Lammer, Alfred, Br. 226
Landolt, Elizabeth Wegener,
Ger. 112, 120

Lane, Arthur, It. 17
Langlois, E.-H., Gen. 4; Fr. 4
Lassus, J.B., Fr. 10
Lasteyrie, F. Ferdinand de,
Fr. 22
Laugardière, [M.] de, Fr. 150
Lautier, Claudine, Gen. 74;
Tech. 140c; Fr. 405
Leber, C., Gen. 2
Lecoq, Georges, Fr. 45
Ledeur, Lucien, Fr. 328
Ledit, Charles Jean, Fr. 357
Lee, Lawrence, Gen. 72
Lees, Thomas, Br. 44
Lefèvre, P., L.C. 51
Lefèvre-Pontalis, D. Eugène,
Fr. 108-9
Lefrançois-Pillion, Louise,
Fr. 92, 211
Legge, Thomas, Coll. 43
Lehmann, Hans, Ger. 73; Sw. 12-
13, 16-20, 22, 27-28, 32
Lehmbruck, Wilhelm, Exh. 34
Leidinger, G., Ger. 41
Leiste, Christian, Tech. 3
Lemaistre d'Anstaing, L.C. 7
Lenoir, Alexandre, Gen. 3; Fr. 26
Lenoir, Marie Alexandre, Coll. 2
Lepke, R., Coll. 72
Lerius, Théodore van, L.C. 3
L'Escalopier, Charles de, Tech. 3
Lessing, G.F., Tech. 3
Lethaby, William Richard, Br. 82,
99, 105
Levèque, Janine, Fr. 185
Le Vieil, Pierre, Fr. 2-3
Lévy, Edmond, L.C. 8
Leyris-Beaury, [Mme], Gen. 32
Liell, [Pater], Ger. 21
Lifsches Harth, Erna, Aus. 39
Lill, Georg, Coll. 32; Ger. 84
Lillich, Meredith Parsons,
Exh. 42; Fr. 322, 336-37,
358, 364, 382, 391, 393-94,
403, 412, 427
Lind, Karl, Aus. 4-5, 7, 10
Lisini, Alessandro, Tech. 7
Lisner, Margrit, Ger. 165
Little, Charles T., Exh. 56;
Fr. 420
Ljubinković, Radivoje, Oth. 7
Lötsch, K., Tech. 92

Rademacher-Chorus, Hildegard,
Ger. 75
Radojković, Bojana, Oth. 8
Ragaller, Heinrich, Ger. 107,
121-22, 154
Ragghianti, Carlo L., It. 20, 23
Raguin, Virginia Chieffo,
Fr. 373-74, 389, 408, 416,
426
Rahn, Johann Rudolf, Coll. 17,
19; Exh. 2; Sw. 5, 9
Ranquet, Henry du, Fr. 134, 151
Ransome, David R., Br. 228
Raspe, R.E., Tech. 3
Raukamp, P. Petrus, Aus. 21
Rayon, E., Fr. 89, 93, 115-17,
127, 142, 153
Read, Herbert, Br. 93, 107, 226
Regnier, Louis, Fr. 69
Reiffenberg, F. de, L.C. 5
Reinartz, Nicola, Ger. 105
Reinhardt, Hans, Fr. 277, 390;
Sw. 52
Rennie, D.W., Br. 3
Renouvier, Jules, Fr. 6
Rentsch, Dietrich, Tech. 73;
Ger. 115, 123-24, 165
Reyaud, Nicole, Fr. 378
Rico y Sinobas, Manuel, Ib. 1
Ridgeway, Maurice H., Br. 193,
195
Riou, Yves-Jean, Fr. 295
Ritter, Georges, Fr. 126
Robinson, J. Armitage, Tech. 46;
Coll. 61; Br. 147
Rode, Herbert, Coll. 102;
Exh. 40; Ger. 172, 181,
200-201
Roffignac, Bertrand de, Fr. 186
Rollet, Jean, Fr. 385, 414
Rombouts, Ph., L.C. 3
Rondot, Natalis, Fr. 62
Roosval, Johnny, Sc. 4-5
Roques, [Mlle], Fr. 278
Rossteuscher, A., Ger. 9
Roth, F.W.E., Coll. 22; Ger. 18
Roth, Hermann Josef, Ger. 198
Rothier, F., Fr. 71
Rott, Hans, Ger. 49, 51, 69
Roussel, Jules, Fr. 111

Roussell, Aage, Sc. 6
Rousset, Paul, Sw. 60
Rugerus. See Theophilus
Rukschcio, Beate, Aus. 40
Ruppert, P., Ger. 10
Rushforth, Gordon McNeil, Br. 83,
85, 91, 94, 115, 127-28,
139-40, 170, 172, 199

Sabin, Arthur, Br. 221
Sablayrolles, J., Fr. 190
Saint, Lawrence B., Gen. 21, 39
Salmen, Gertrud, Ger. 77
Salmi, Mario, It. 25, 30
Salvini, Joseph, Fr. 238, 324
Salzman, L.F., Br. 108, 121-22,
129, 214
Sauvel, Tony, Fr. 193
Sayre, Edward V., Tech. 108, 121
Schaaf, A., Fr. 325
Schäfer, Carl, Gen. 14; Ger. 8-9
Schaffran, Emerich, L.C. 49
Scharf, George, Br. 31
Schauenbourg, P.R. de, Fr. 35, 52
Scheffler, K., Gen. 22
Scheidegger, Alfred, Exh. 7;
Sw. 52
Scheller, R.W., L.C. 56
Scher, Stephen K., Fr. 366
Scheuffelen, Gertrud Maria,
Ger. 98
Scheyer, Ernst, Coll. 84
Schimansky, Dobrilla-Donya,
Exh. 38
Schinnerer, Johannes, Coll. 26;
Ger. 28, 33, 43, 46
Schlegel, Ursula, Ger. 152, 154
Schlosser, Ignaz, Exh. 13
Schmarsow, August, Gen. 23, 25;
Sw. 23
Schmidt, Christa, Tech. 128;
Ger. 205, 207
Schmitz, Hermann, Gen. 28;
Coll. 33
Schmitz, Josef, Tech. 28-29
Schneegans, L., Fr. 21
Schneider, Arthur von, Coll. 62,
83; Ger. 104
Schneider, Jenny, Coll. 107;
Sw. 46, 52
Schönberger, Arno, Exh. 41

Vassas, C.D., Tech. 106d-e
Vasselle, F., Fr. 187
Velge, Henri, L.C. 19
Verdier, Philippe, Coll. 91;
    Fr. 233, 268
Verhaegen, N., Fr. 60
Veritá, M., Tech. 145
Verrier, Jean, Tech. 69; Fr. 177,
    191, 237, 240
Villette, Jean, Fr. 279
Villinger, Carl J.H., Coll. 115
Viollet-le-Duc, Eugène Emmanuel,
    Gen. 15
Volpe, Carlo, It. 27
Vroom, N.R.A., L.C. 32

Wackernagel, Rudolf, Sw. 10
Wackernagel, Wilhelm, Ger. 3
Waetzoldt, Stephan, Ger. 203
Wagner, Hugo, Exh. 52
Walford, Weston Styleman, Br. 33
Waller, John Green, Br. 18c, 27
Walt, Barbara Sammet, Sw. 67
Walter, J., Exh. 12
Walter, Jacques, Fr. 135
Warrington, William, Gen. 10
Way, Albert, Tech. 2
Wayment, Hilary G., Tech. 148;
    Br. 222, 239, 252, 254,
    256-57; L.C. 52, 54, 56-57
Weale, J., L.C. 6
Wegener, Elizabeth. See Landolt
Wegner, Wolfgang, Ger. 125
Wehdorn, Manfred, Aus. 39
Weiss, Peg., Exh. 42
Wells, William, Coll. 88;
    Exh. 21, 28, 45; Ger. 158
Wentzell, Hans, Gen. 43, 44i;
    Tech. 84, 100; Coll. 85, 93,
    96; Fr. 179, 206; Ger. 78,
    84, 86-87, 89, 92, 95-97,
    109, 117-18, 120, 126-27,
    131, 140, 155-56, 161-62,
    166-67, 174-76, 182-84;
    It. 19
Werck, Alfred, Gen. 26
Werner, Ferdinand, Gen. 73
Werner, Norbert, Aus. 30;
    Ger. 190, 206

Westlake, Nat Hubert John,
    Gen. 16
Weyman, Henry Thomas, Br. 63
Whall, Christopher, W., Tech. 20
Wienecke, H., Ger. 39
Wild-Block, Christiane, Exh. 50;
    Fr. 293, 329, 350, 369
Will, Robert, Fr. 262
Wille, C., Ger. 100
Willement, Thomas, Gen. 5
Williams, Emily, Br. 56
Winkler, Friedrich, Ger. 76;
    L.C. 48
Winston, Charles, Br. 19-20,
    22-23, 25-26, 28, 32-35, 38;
    L.C. 9
Witzleben, Elisabeth Schüer von,
    Gen. 38, 42, 75; Coll. 82,
    110; Fr. 310; Ger. 85, 88,
    128, 157, 173, 185
Wolff, A., Tech. 122f, 133
Wolff, F., Ger. 19
Woodforde, Christopher, Coll. 63,
    75; Br. 155-56, 162-63, 171,
    174, 177, 180-81, 188, 192,
    205, 208, 217
Woodhouse, (Dean), Coll. 5
Wortmann, Reinhard, Ger. 191, 199

Zahlten, Johannes, Fr. 376, 380
Zakin, Helen Jackson, Fr. 375,
    391, 407, 427
Zaluska, Yolanta, Fr. 405
Zappert, F.H.G., Aus. 1
Zoege von Manteuffel, Claus,
    Ger. 152, 154
Zschokke, Fridtjof, Exh. 7, 14;
    Fr. 178-79; Sw. 34
Zucchini, Guido, It. 10

Index of Glass
Painters and Designers

Entries that mention a large number of artists have not been indexed; these include some listed here under the heading <u>guilds</u>, and the following items: Gen. 18, 26, 33, 47, 70; Aus. 2, 23; Br. 118-19, 121-22, 129, 162, 205; Fr. 31, 62, 65, 185; Ger. 1, 69, 97, 103, 117, 127, 137; Ib. 1; It. 21, 36; L.C. 19, 34, 40, 45, 53, 65; Sw. 31, 36, 47.

Abegg, Hans, Sw. 18a
Acker, Hans (von Ulm), Gen. 43, 44f, 44i; Exh. 34; Fr. 37, 265, 350; Ger. 141, 173, 184, 190-91; It. 29; Sw. 29, 37
Acker, Jakob, Ger. 173, 184
Acker, Peter, Gen. 43; Ger. 184
Aeps, Jean, L.C. 27
Aerdt van Nijmegen. See Arnold of Nijmegen
Aldegrever, H., Fr. 63, 234
Alemán, Cristóbal, Ib. 6
Alemán, Enrique, Ib. 4-6
Almayn, John, Br. 227
Andlau, Peter Hemmel von. See Hemmel
Andrea del Castagno, It. 32
Angui de Normandia, Zaninus, It. 20
Antonio da Pisa, Tech. 5
Arnao de Flandes, Ib. 6
Arnold of Nijmegen, Fr. 173, 223, 259, 263, 363; L.C. 4, 22-23, 25, 27-29, 33, 35, 38, 42-43, 52, 56, 59
Arnoult de Nimègue. See Arnold of Nijmegen
Athelard, John, Br. 108

Baldovinetti, Alesso, It. 30
Baldung, Hans, called Grien, Gen. 75; Coll. 52, 62, 101; Exh. 19; Fr. 212, 327; Ger. 14, 19, 45, 50, 68, 104, 113, 138, 144, 148, 164
Baudichon, Jean, Fr. 278
Baumeister, Simprecht ("der Glaser"), Sw. 22
Beauneveu, André, Fr. 366
Beer, Jan de, L.C. 49
Beham, Hans Sebald, Exh. 19; Ger. 130, 151
Bernardo di Francesco, It. 1
Bessele, Guillaume van, L.C. 28
Blaise de Lyon, Fr. 278
Bléville, Mathieu, Fr. 258
Bockstorfer, Christoph, Ger. 49, 51; Sw. 32
Boghem (or Beughem), Louis van, Fr. 278
Bonaiuti, Andrea, It. 12
Bond, Richard, Br. 210, 222
Bonino, Giovanni, It. 3, 5
Bounde, Richard. See Bond
Bousch, Valentin. See Busch
Brachon, Jean, Fr. 278
Breu, Jörg d. Ä., Coll. 101; Ger. 36, 125

Topographical Index

Aachen, private collection, Coll. 92

Aargau (canton), Sw. 12

Aarschot, Church of Our Lady, L.C. 64

Airaines (Sommes), Church of St.-Denis, Fr. 91

Alby, Ste.-Cécile, Fr. 6

Alençon, Notre-Dame, Fr. 8, 65

Alsace, Gen. 73a-b; Tech. 11; Fr. 34-35, 75, 148, 206, 226, 328; Ger. 69

Alston Court (Suffolk), Br. 188

Altenberg-an-der-Lahn, Abbey Church, Ger. 100

Altenberg-bei-Köln, Cistercian Abbey, Gen. 36, 69, 71; Coll. 22; Ger. 55, 96, 101, 198, 208

Altenryf. See Hauterive

Altötting, Parish Church, Ger. 190

Altshausen, Castle, Ger. 175

Amelungsborn (Lower Saxony), Cistercian Church, Ger. 155

Amiens, Cathedral of Notre-Dame, Tech. 48, 106a, 135; Exh. 39; Fr. 74, 118

Amorbach, Heimatmuseum, Ger. 119

Amsterdam, Musée néerlandais d'art et d'histoire, L.C. 14

-Rijksmuseum, Exh. 39; L.C. 56

Anderlecht (Brabant), L.C. 55

Angers, Tech. 69; Fr. 417

-Abbey Church of St.-Serge, Fr. 12, 387

-Cathedral of St.-Maurice, Fr. 12, 90, 95, 167, 299, 307, 387, 424

-Musée St.-Jean (formerly Hôpital), Fr. 105, 164, 419

Anjou, Fr. 236

Annaberg, Aus. 35

Antwerp (city), L.C. 3-5, 12-13

-Cathedral of Notre-Dame, Tech. 124; L.C. 10, 31, 33, 50

-St. Jacques, L.C. 31

Antwerp (province), L.C. 53

Anvers. See Antwerp

Aranyosmaroth, Oth. 4

Ardagger, St. Margaret's Church (Stiftskirche), Gen. 44d; Aus. 12, 33

Ardennes, Tech. 19

Argentan (Orne), St.-Germain, Fr. 215

-St.-Martin, Fr. 215

Argoules (Sommes), Church, Fr. 187(19)

Arnstadt, Liebfaukirche, Ger. 115

Arnstein-an-der-Lahn, Premonstratensian Church, Ger. 100

Ashridge Park (Hertfordshire) Chapel, Coll. 49-50; Ger. 81, 83, 105, 178

Ashton (Devon), Church, Br. 64

Ashton-under-Lyne (Lancashire), Church of St. Michael, Br. 62, 77

Frémont (Somme), Church,
    Fr. 187(14)
Fresnoy, La (Somme), Church,
    Fr. 187(4)
Fribourg. See Freiburg-im-Ü.
Friedberg. See also Gross-Karben
-Stadtkirche, Ger. 54
Friedrichshafen (Summer residence
    of the kings of Württemburg),
    Coll. 14; Ger. 11; Sw. 44
Fürth, Parish Church of St.
    Michael, Ger. 188
Füssen, Schlossmuseum, Ger. 147
Furnes (=Veurne), St. Walburge,
    L.C. 60

Gaisberg (near Salzburg), Parish
    Church, Aus. 31
Ganagobie, Priory Church,
    Fr. 400c
Garcy. See Gercy
Gargilesse (Indre), Notre-Dame,
    Fr. 295
Gars, Gertrudskirche, Tech. 65
Geisenheim, Freiherrlich von
    Zwierlein collection,
    Coll. 11, 18, 22
Geneva, Cathedral of St.-Pierre,
    Sw. 24-25, 36, 39, 60
-Musée de l'Ariana, Tech. 150;
    Fr. 188
-Musée d'art et d'histoire,
    Sw. 36, 39, 60
-Museum, Ger. 67
-Notre-Dame-la-Neuve, Sw. 36
Gercy (Seine-et-Oise), Abbey
    Church of St.-Martin,
    Fr. 61, 373, 383-84, 426
Ghent, L.C. 2
-Abbey Church of St.-Pierre,
    L.C. 16
Gipping (Suffolk), Church,
    Br. 251
Gisors, Tech. 16
Glasgow, Burrell collection,
    Tech. 115, 152; Coll. 69, 88,
    93, 110, 116; Exh. 21, 28,
    45; Ger. 158, 179, 182, 193;
    L.C. 63

Gloucester, Cathedral, Br. 28,
    34, 81, 89, 91
Gloucestershire, Br. 101
Göttingen, Städtisches Museum,
    Ger. 160
Goslar, Marktkirche, Exh. 47,
    Sc. 2, 3
Gotland, Sc. 4-5
Gouda, Church of St. John,
    L.C. 62
Granada, Cathedral, Ib. 9
Gran, Cathedral, Oth. 2
Grately (Hampshire), Church,
    Br. 105
Graz, Aus. 42
-Alte Galerie am Landesmuseum
    Joanneum, Exh. 44; Aus. 22
-Leechkirche, Tech. 109-10
-Stift St. Lambrecht, Exh. 51
Great Bookham (Surrey), Church,
    Coll. 110
Great Malvern, Priory Church,
    Tech. 34; Br. 53, 83, 127,
    170, 225, 234, 240
Grossgründlach, Parish Church,
    Ger. 138
Gross-Karben Castle (Friedberg),
    Ger. 168

Haarlem, Public Record Office,
    L.C. 32
Haddon Hall (Derbyshire), Chapel
    of St. Nicholas, Br. 60
Hagenau, Museum, Fr. 318
Haina, Cistercian Abbey Church,
    Gen. 58, 71; Ger. 71, 96,
    100, 132
Hainaut, L.C. 41
Hal, Church of St.-Martin,
    L.C. 26
Hall (Tirol), Parish Church,
    Aus. 20
Hamburg, Museum für Kunst und
    Gewerbe, Exh. 30
-Stein collection, Exh. 30
Hampstead, Sidney collection,
    Coll. 53, 76
Hampton Court (Herefordshire),
    Chapel, Coll. 116; Br. 235

Läufelfingen, Village Church,
Sw. 8
Lanchester (Durham), Parish
Church, Br. 80
Landsberg-am-Lech, Parish Church,
Ger. 129
Landshut, St. Martin, Ger. 41
Langenburg, Stadtkirche, Ger. 161
Langenstein, Douglas collection,
Coll. 23
Laon, Cathedral of Notre-Dame,
Gen. 44a; Fr. 53, 219, 247,
288, 306, 339
Laperswil, Church, Sw. 18d
Lauperwil (Berne), Parish Church,
Sw. 67
Lausanne, Cathedral, Sw. 5, 33,
40, 42, 48, 62, 66
-Rathaus, Sw. 20
Lautenbach, Wallfahrtskirche,
Ger. 70, 203
Lavantthale. See Saint Leonhard
im Lavantthale
Laxenburg, Tech. 65
Legden, Village Church,
Tech. 102; Exh. 46; Ger. 94
Leicester, Museum, Br. 48, 85
Leipzig, Felix collection,
Coll. 13
Lenzburg, Schloss, Exh. 27
Leoben, Waasenkirche, Tech. 109;
Aus. 37-38
Lesnovo (Macedonia), Monastery,
Oth. 7
Lichfield, Cathedral, Coll. 5,
46, 58; Br. 203; Fr. 173;
L.C. 9, 11, 38, 43
Lichtenstein, Schloss, Ger. 86
Liège, L.C. 25, 67
-Abbey Church of St.-Jacques,
L.C. 36, 46, 65
-Cathedral of St.-Paul, L.C. 36,
46, 65
-St.-Martin, L.C. 36, 46, 65
Liercourt (Somme), Church,
Fr. 187(2)
Lierre, Collegiate Church of
St.-Gommaire, Tech. 124;
L.C. 30, 57
Ligerz, Church, Sw. 16
Limbourg (province), L.C. 66

Limburg-an-der-Lahn, St.-Anna-
Kirche, Tech. 21; Ger. 100
Limoges, St.-Michel-des-Lions,
Fr. 283
Limousin, Fr. 13
Lincoln, Cathedral, Gen. 73h;
Br. 13, 25, 30, 32, 55, 156,
191
Lincolnshire, Br. 9
Lindau, Barfüsser Kloster,
Ger. 190
Lindena, Church, Tech. 122e
Linsell (Essex), St. Mary the
Virgin, Br. 138
Linz, Aus. 15
Llandyrnog (Denbighshire),
Church, Br. 127
Llanrhaiadr-yn-Cinmerch
(Denbighshire), Br. 186, 223
Locksley Hall (Lincolnshire),
Coll. 63; Br. 188
Löwenburg-bei-Kassel, Chapel,
Ger. 100
Lohne-bei-Soest, Parish Church,
Gen. 73f
Loir-et-Cher, Fr. 142
London, Br. 86, 96, 111, 179, 228
-Arts Council of Great Britain,
Exh. 45
-Christie, Manson and Woods
auction house, Coll. 4, 57,
76, 116, 118
-St. George's, Hanover Square,
Fr. 173; L.C. 38, 43
-Essex House, Coll. 1
-Fine Art Society, Exh. 4
-Gray's Inn, Br. 168
-Grosvenor Thomas collection,
Coll. 34, 41
-Lambeth Palace, Coll. 10
-Manton collection, Coll. 57
-Pall Mall, Coll. 3-4, 6
-Sotheby and Co., Coll. 49-50,
116, 118
-Victoria and Albert Museum,
Tech. 78; Coll. 31, 46, 56,
73; Br. 93, 238; Fr. 230,
252-53, 273, 312, 416;
Ger. 81, 105, 174, 178, 195;
L.C. 24, 61, 63, 64; Sw. 57
Long Melford (Suffolk), Church,
Br. 114, 205

Long Sutton (Lincolnshire),
Br. 155
Lorraine, Fr. 328
Lorsch, Tech. 59, 62
-Abbey, Ger. 91
Los Angeles County Museum,
Coll. 81
Lothringen, Fr. 265
Louvain (Leuven), Gen. 33;
L.C. 64
-Chartreuse, L.C. 63
-Hospices, L.C. 61
Lowick (Northumberland), Br. 174
Lucerne, Coll. 30; Sw. 32, 44
-Thomas Fischer saleroom,
Coll. 66
Ludlow (Shropshire), Parish
Church of St. Lawrence,
Br. 63, 174, 223, 229
Lübeck, Marienkirche, Ger. 84;
L.C. 14
Lüneburg, Ger. 103
Lyon, Cathedral Church of St.-
Jean, Tech. 106a, 150;
Fr. 49, 252, 392, 398, 400b
Lyonnais, Fr. 94

Madley (Herfordshire), Church,
Br. 120, 174
Magdeburg, Johanniskirche,
Ger. 115
Mailleraye-sur-Seine, La, Chapel,
Fr. 248
Malvern. See Great Malvern
Mancetter (Warwickshire), Church,
Br. 141, 174
Mans, Le, Cathedral of St.-
Julien, Tech. 16, 69, 135;
Fr. 40-41, 125, 163, 250,
322, 417
Marburg, Franciscan Church of
St. Elisabeth, Ger. 20, 25,
71, 100
-Universitätsmuseum, Ger. 71
Mareuil (Somme), Church,
Fr. 187(1)
Margaretting (Essex), Church of
St. Margaret, Ger. 223;
L.C. 18

Maria Strassengel, Wallfahrts-
kirche, Tech. 92
Mariawald, Cistercian Abbey,
Ger. 81, 83, 178, 195
Marienburg, Marienkirche, Ger. 84
Marienstatt, Cistercian Church,
Gen. 58
Mark-bei-Hamm (Kreis Unna),
Pankratiuskirche (Dorfkirche),
Ger. 120
Marseille, St.-Victor, Fr. 400c
Martigny, Church, Fr. 218
Martin-ès-Vignes (Aube), Fr. 5
Meissen, Magdalenenkapelle,
Ger. 115
Melbury Bubb (Dorset), Parish
Church, Br. 127
Meran, Parish Church of the Holy
Spirit, Ger. 129
Merevale (Warwickshire), Church
of St. Mary the Virgin,
Br. 141, 174
Mersham (Kent), Church, Br. 167
Mesnil-Villeman, Le (Manche),
Church, Tech. 64
Metz, Tech. 69
-Cathedral of St.-Étienne,
Fr. 139, 162, 227, 296, 365
-St.-Martin, Fr. 297
Midlands (England), Br. 230
Migennes, Fr. 23
Milan, Cathedral, It. 11, 20, 23,
34-35, 37
-S. Nazaro Maggiore, It. 13
Moncontour (Côtes-du-Nord),
Church of St.-Mathurin,
Fr. 192
Mons, Ste.-Waudru, L.C. 30, 57
Montmorency, Collegiate Church
of St.-Martin, Fr. 57, 213,
216
Montoire, St.-Gervais, Fr. 47
Montréal (Yonne), Fr. 23
Montreal (Quebec, Canada), Museum
of Art, Fr. 230
Montreuil-sur-Loire, Parish
Church, Fr. 231, 419
Mont-St.-Michel, Abbey Church,
Tech. 99, 106a, 106c
Monza, It. 35

Topographical Index

-Germanisches Nationalmuseum,
  Coll. 15, 95; Exh. 17, 19,
  37, 41, 47; Ger. 149, 188
-St. Jakob, Ger. 137
-St. Johannis, Ger. 137
-St. Lorenz, Tech. 51, 97, 113;
  Ger. 33, 38, 109, 113, 116,
  133, 137, 142-43, 170, 188,
  213
-St. Martha, Fr. 307; Ger. 152
-St. Sebald, Tech. 28, 70, 76;
  Exh. 17, 37; Ger. 22, 43,
  130, 137, 143
-zu Unserer Lieber Frau, Ger. 143

Obazine (Corrèze), Cistercian
  Abbey Church, Gen. 58;
  Fr. 44, 196, 375, 391, 407
Oberehnheim i. e. See Obernai
  (Bas-Rhin)
Oberlin College, Allen Memorial
  Museum, Coll. 108
Obernai (Bas-Rhin), Ger. 65
-Hôtel de Ville, Fr. 212
-Musée historique, Coll. 52
-Sts.-Pierre-et-Paul, Coll. 52;
  Fr. 227
Öhringen, Stiftskirche, Ger. 166
Offenhausen (glass now in Urach),
  Ger. 92
Oise, Fr. 127
Oisquercq (Brabant), L.C. 55
Oppenheim, Katharinenkirche,
  Tech. 76
Orbais (Marne), Abbey Church,
  Br. 244; Fr. 425
Orne, Fr. 116
Orvieto, Cathedral, It. 3, 40
Ottersweier-an-der-Ortenau,
  Parish Church, Ger. 104
Oxford (city), Br. 9, 13, 51, 84
-All Souls College, Br. 198
-Merton College Chapel, Br. 21,
  143
-New College, Tech. 60; Br. 208
-Oriel College Chapel, Br. 139
Oxford (diocese), Br. 199
Oxfordshire, Br. 250

Paillart (Oise), Church,
  Fr. 187(20)
Paris, Fr. 402
-Abbey Church of St.-Germain-des-
  Prés, Fr. 221, 230, 233, 268
-Acézat collection, Coll. 105
-Cathedral of Notre-Dame, Br. 41;
  Fr. 2, 226, 240, 290, 300,
  308, 319
-Engel-Gros collection, Coll. 39
-Galerie Georges Petit, auction
  house, Coll. 25, 38
-Grand Palais, Exh. 55
-Heilbronner collection, Coll. 38
-Homberg collection, Coll. 25
-Hôtel de Cluny. See Musée de
  Cluny
-Hotel Drouot, auction house,
  Coll. 39, 105
-Musée des arts décoratifs,
  Exh. 16
-Musée de Cluny, Tech. 140b;
  Coll. 100, 111; Fr. 61, 205,
  341, 364, 373, 384, 426
-Musée du Louvre, Exh. 23, 33;
  Fr. 146
-Musée Marmottan, Fr. 247
-Musée des monuments français,
  Fr. 26
-private collection, Fr. 273
-Ste.-Chapelle, Tech. 111;
  Coll. 89; Fr. 12, 24, 42,
  154, 191, 240, 303, 312, 331
  340, 347, 374, 401, 406, 408,
  422, 426
-St.-Germain l'Auxerrois,
  Fr. 120, 333
-Sts.-Gervais-et-Protais, Tech. 12
-Spitzer collection, Coll. 20-21
-Trétaigne collection, Coll. 24
-Union centrale des arts
  décoratifs, Exh. 1
Pas-de-Calais, Fr. 402
Passau, Coll. 96
Pavesi, S. Lanfranco, It. 22
-Sta. Maria del Carmine, It. 22
Penrith (Cumberland), Church,
  Br. 207

Copyediting supervised by Ara Salibian.
Text formatted and produced by Fred Welden.
Camera-ready copy typed by Geraldine Kline
on an IBM Selectric.
Printed and bound by Braun-Brumfield, Inc.,
of Ann Arbor, Michigan.